HISTORY OF WORLD ARCHITECTURE

Pier Luigi Nervi, General Editor

ISLAMIC ARCHITECTURE

John D. Hoag

Harry N. Abrams, Inc., Publishers, New York

Project coordinator: Giuseppe Positano de Vincentiis

*Produced under the supervision of Carlo Pirovano,
editorial director of Electa Editrice*

Design: Diego Birelli, art director of Electa Editrice

Photographs: Bruno Balestrini

Drawings: Studio of Enzo Di Grazia

Library of Congress Catalogue Card Number: 76-41805

Library of Congress Cataloging in Publication Data

Hoag, John D.
  Islamic architecture.

  (History of world architecture)
  Bibliography: p.
  Includes index.
  1. Architecture, Islamic. I. Title.
NA380.H58   720'.917'671   76-41805
ISBN 0-8109-1010-1

PREFACE

Architectural criticism has nearly always been concerned with the visible aspect of individual buildings, taking this to be the decisive factor in the formulation of value judgments and in the classification of those "styles" which appear in textbooks, and which have thus become common knowledge. But once it is recognized that every building is, by definition, a work subject to the limitations imposed by the materials and building techniques at hand, and that every building must prove its stability, as well as its capacity to endure and serve the needs it was built for, it becomes clear that the aesthetic aspect alone is inadequate when we come to appraise a creative activity, difficult enough to judge in the past, rapidly becoming more complex in our own day, and destined to become more so in the foreseeable future.

Nevertheless, what has struck me most, on studying the architecture of the past and present, is the fact that the works which are generally regarded by the critics and the general public as examples of pure beauty are also the fruit of exemplary building techniques, once one has taken into account the quality of the materials and the technical knowledge available. And it is natural to suspect that such a coincidence is not entirely casual.

Building in the past was wholly a matter of following static intuitions, which were, in turn, the result of meditation, experience, and above all of an understanding of the capacity of certain structures and materials to resist external forces. Meditation upon structural patterns and the characteristics of various materials, together with the appraisal of one's own experiences and those of others, is an act of love toward the process of construction for its own sake, both on the part of the architect and his collaborators and assistants. Indeed, we may wonder whether this is not the hidden bond which unites the appearance and substance of the finest buildings of the past, distant though that past may be, into a single "thing of beauty."

One might even think that the quality of the materials available not only determined architectural patterns but also the decorative detail with which the first simple construction was gradually enriched.

One might find a justification for the difference in refinement and elegance between Greek architecture, with its basic use of marble—a highly resistant material, upon which the most delicate carvings can be carried out—and the majestic concrete structures of Roman architecture, built out of a mixture of lime and pozzolana, and supported by massive walls, to compensate for their intrinsic weaknesses.

Would it be too rash to connect these objective architectural characteristics with the different artistic sensibilities of the two peoples?

One must recognize, therefore, the importance of completing the description of the examples illustrated with an interpretation of their constructional and aesthetic characteristics, so that the connection between the twin aspects of building emerges as a natural, logical consequence.

This consequence, if understood and accepted in good faith by certain avant-garde circles, could put an end to the disastrous haste with which our architecture is rushing toward an empty, costly, and at times impractical formalism. It might also recall architects and men of culture to a more serene appraisal of the objective elements of building and to the respect that is due to a morality of architecture. For this is just as important for the future of our cities as is morality, understood as a rule of life, for an orderly civil existence.

PIER LUIGI NERVI

TABLE OF CONTENTS

	Page
PREFACE by Pier Luigi Nervi	5
INTRODUCTION	9
CHAPTER I The Beginnings of Islamic Architecture	13
CHAPTER II Umayyad Architecture	15
CHAPTER III Abbasid Architecture	34
CHAPTER IV The Early Islamic Architecture of North Africa	60
CHAPTER V The Early Islamic Architecture of Spain	77
CHAPTER VI The Classic Islamic Architecture of North Africa and Spain	94
CHAPTER VII The Later Classic Islamic Architecture of North Africa and Spain	116
CHAPTER VIII The Classic Islamic Architecture of Egypt: The Fatimids	136
CHAPTER IX The Later Classic Islamic Architecture of Egypt: Ayyubids and Mamluks	152
CHAPTER X The Early Islamic Architecture of Persia: Samanids and Ghaznavids	184

Page

CHAPTER XI
The Classic Islamic Architecture of Persia:
    The Seljuks   192

CHAPTER XII
The Classic Islamic Architecture of Syria
    and Iraq   210

CHAPTER XIII
The Classic Islamic Architecture of Anatolia   222

CHAPTER XIV
The Later Classic Islamic Architecture of Persia:
    Ilkhanids and Timurids   250

CHAPTER XV
The Classic Islamic Architecture of India   280

CHAPTER XVI
The Architecture of the Ottoman Empire   308

CHAPTER XVII
The Architecture of the Safavid Empire   345

CHAPTER XVIII
The Architecture of the Moghul Empire   364

SYNOPTIC TABLES   391

GLOSSARY   405

SELECTED BIBLIOGRAPHY   407

INDEX   409

LIST OF PLATES   418

PHOTOGRAPHIC CREDITS   424

If we define the architecture of Islam as that building produced by the followers of the Prophet Muhammad between the seventh and the eighteenth or nineteenth century of our era (in a few cases even later) wherever the religion he founded—variously called Islamic or Muslim or Muhammadan—flourished, we sense a remarkable diversity at first. Materials vary from stone through baked and unbaked brick to wood, and construction techniques are legion, from solid ashlar through numerous forms of veneered masonry over concrete-like cores and from solid masses of burnt brick to veneers of burnt brick over cores of adobe, unburnt brick, or *terre pisée*. Again at first sight design seems to follow as many forms as there were peoples who embraced Islam in this period of twelve hundred years or so. Yet after an analysis of all these seemingly diverse factors, we detect the emergence of certain unifying principles worth noting here.

The first of these may be explained as the survival of antique architectural principles in a far more fundamental way than survived in the West, at least after the Carolingian Empire. Until the eleventh century there seem to have been two major regions from which antique forms (including plans as well as building techniques) were adapted into Islamic architecture. The first of these regions comprised southwestern Anatolia in the neighborhood of Antioch; northern Syria, including the areas around Damascus and Rusafa; Palestine, centering around Jerusalem; and the ruins at Amman (known to the Greeks as Philadelphia) and Gerasa in present-day Jordan. Moving southwestward, this region extended through Egypt—at least that area north of Hermopolis Magna—and still further west to North Africa, including the shores of Libya and much of Tunisia, particularly Kairouan. In the Maghrib a few surviving ancient centers such as Thamugadi (modern Timgad, in Algeria) and Volubilis (in North Africa) may have influenced early Islamic builders, but so much has been lost that this is rather uncertain; however, Spain's Visigothic architecture, as crude as it was, certainly seems to have exerted some influence. And since all of this region had been under Roman and later Byzantine control, in most cases it remained economically viable enough to supply the new Islamic rulers with skilled masons, mosaicists, and other craftsmen.

The second region from which much of Islamic architecture's early ideas were derived was Mesopotamia, that ancient land of the Twin Rivers (the Tigris and Euphrates). Here and in adjacent Persia, despite successive waves of Hellenistic and later Roman influence, many traditional techniques and forms had survived, at least from the time of the Neo-Babylonians. The Muslims inherited these from the conquered Sassanian Empire, which had remained independent from and antagonistic to both Rome and her Byzantine successors. We might conceivably carry this search for Islamic architectural origins even further east into what is now Afghanistan, Pakistan, and India—but Persian ideas diffused by the Sassanians and their predecessors had so permeated these regions that early Islamic builders would have found little else to inspire them. (Later Indo-Islamic architecture need not concern us here, as it falls into the period after the eleventh century.)

From both regions specific examples of borrowing or survivals are cited in the appropriate chapters. It suffices here to make a few generalizations to define the process. A striking example is provided by the so-called paradise garden, a square irrigated tract divided into four equal parts by intersecting elevated paths, often associated with radially symmetrical water tanks that were also raised above the planting areas. Two such gardens, whose plans have not yet been published, were laid out about A.D. 950 below the palace complex at Medina al-Zahra in Spain during the Cordoban Caliphate. Nearly all their elements, though arranged somewhat more freely, can be found in the ancient Roman gardens of Pompeii and particularly of Herculaneum—where the so-called Palaestra (if indeed it was one) has a raised cruciform pool with transverse pools at the ends of the arms of the cross. However, since these examples were destroyed in the earthquake of A.D. 79 one must look elsewhere for direct antecedents to the Islamic version. These are not hard to find in the gardens of Volubilis, which we know was occupied for a time by the founder of eighth-century Fez. However, it seems more likely that late antique or Byzantine villas near Damascus or on the coast of Palestine provided models for the Umayyads, who in turn would then have brought these influences with them to Spain; the idea of the *chahr bagh* or four-part garden as a symbol of Paradise has generally been accepted as Persian and as an outgrowth of Sassanian palace gardens, though no Sassanian example is known so far. Yet even if such a garden should be found, it must be remembered that the palaces of the Hellenistic rulers in Antioch and Alexandria were themselves equated with Paradise, an idea clearly transmitted to the Romans, who designated the Triclinium of Domitian's palace on the Palatine as the Seat of Jove. The later wide proliferation of such gardens throughout the world of Islam, their continued association with Paradise, and even their application to tombs such as Humayun's in Delhi and the Taj Mahal at Agra can thus be seen as the survival of a form and a meaning going back at least as far as the third century B.C. No such continuity can be observed in any aspect of architecture in Western Europe.

It is somewhat more difficult to demonstrate the survival in Islamic architecture of ancient Mesopotamian and Persian forms.

9

The hypostyle congregational mosque comes to mind, its prayer hall continuing perhaps the tradition of the Achaemenid Persian *apadana*, in itself the survival of Hittite and later Urartian halls of assembly. However, such mosques, though founded at Kufa and Wasit in the central Mesopotamian region, may owe more to the Roman transformation of the Greek agora into a colonnaded square with an adjoining basilica (for example, the Caesareum at Cyrene or part of the later Forum of Trajan at Rome). Certainly the function of early Islamic mosques as places of assembly, schools, commercial hubs, and law courts, as well as places of prayer follows an antique precedent more Western than Oriental.

If the congregational mosque is of mixed origins, a technique as old in Mesopotamia at least as the Assyrians was to have an exclusively Islamic future. This was the method of encrusting walls with glazed brick or tile to form patterns covering all or part of the surface. The Ishtar Gate of Babylon with its parade of animals and monsters and the great tile panel from Nebuchadnezzar's throne room, both now in the Staatliche Museen in East Berlin, are notable examples. Either the technique lay dormant for centuries or we have yet to find examples of such decoration to bridge the gap, because after the fall of the Achaemenid Empire it disappears (save for a few possibly tenth-century tiles from Ghazna) until its revival in twelfth-century Persia at Maragha. From that time forward polychrome tile ornament gradually became a major factor in Islamic architectural design. This was so even for masonry buildings, though in such cases it was usually confined to interior ornament. However, in all countries where building in baked or crude brick or in *terre pisée* (all Mesopotamian techniques) survived, glazed tile ornament flourished: from India to the Atlantic Coast, such masterpieces as the Masjid-i-Shah at Isfahan, the Mosque of Wazir Khan at Lahore, and the intricate *zellij* or tile mosaic of so many Moroccan and Spanish monuments of the fourteenth century and later may be cited.

Having suggested that the survival in form and perhaps in meaning of very ancient elements of design is far more likely in Islamic than in Western European architecture may provide a fruitful method of understanding the former, yet it remains for us to devise an approach which will articulate this vast subject in some meaningful way. Though hardly original, it seems useful to apply to Islamic architecture certain terms employed in the study of the high cultures of the New World. The first is Pre-Classic or Formative, equivalent to Oleg Grabar's designation of Early Islamic as defined in his recent work, *The Formation of Islamic Art*. This would include the architecture of the Umayyad Caliphate and that of its Abbasid successor until about A.D. 1100. In North Africa and Egypt the architecture of the

Aghlabids and the early Fatimids until about 1085 would fall under this term, as would in Spain that of the Cordoban Caliphate and its Taifas successors until the Almoravid conquest of 1086. In Persia and further east the Formative period would include the architecture of the Samanids and Ghaznavids, ending only with the maturity of Seljuk architecture in the last quarter of the eleventh century. This period is characterized by the active and rapid utilization of diverse forms and techniques from the pre-Islamic past. Assimilation, however, never quite seems to take place and although major monuments were created their parts retain evidences of borrowed motifs. For example, arches in a single structure may range from semicircular or slightly horseshoe-shaped through pointed with no attempt at uniformity. Throughout this period there develops an increasing tendency for a more immediate sharing of ideas from one end of the Islamic world to the other.

Classic and Late Classic Islamic architecture coincides roughly with the spread of the *muqarnas* (stalactite or honeycomb vault) throughout Islam. The phenomenon is discussed elsewhere; it suffices here to say that although it was probably invented in Pre-Classic Persia its rapid spread took place toward the end of the eleventh century and was accompanied by the universal use of the pointed arch—either horseshoe-shaped as in Spain and North Africa or simple. The rise of the Classic phase coincides with Almoravid rule in North Africa and Spain, that of the later Fatimids in Egypt, and of the Zengids and their Ayyubid successors in Syria and Egypt. In Persia the Seljuks perfected the Classic style, and their relatives in Anatolia brought it there through their Byzantine conquests. The Ghurids of Afghanistan brought Classic Seljuk forms to India, but special conditions in that country were to give it a somewhat altered form.

Throughout the Classic and the Late Classic periods techniques and formal ideas flowed freely from one area of Islam to the other despite doctrinal and dynastic disputes. Syrian stone marquetry became highly developed in Egypt and Anatolia, while techniques of mosaic tile encrustation and later of painted tile traveled throughout Islam. Translations of an ornamental scheme from one material to another and sometimes back again were frequent—for example, the borrowing of Persian carved stucco forms for stone ornament in Seljuk Anatolia or the interchange between stucco and carved wood in Morocco. In India stonemasons derived inspiration not only from stucco and brick motifs but also from Hindu wooden architecture.

Late Classic Islamic architecture continues the forms as well as the fluid interchange of ideas of the Classic period. However, beginning in about the late thirteenth or early fourteenth century there is a reduction everywhere in the scale of ornament with relation to the surfaces it ornaments or to the size of the structure as a whole. This is apparent in the architecture of the Nasrids of Granada and that of their Marinid contemporaries in North Africa. The Mamluks of Egypt and Syria treated the forms inherited from their Ayyubid predecessors in much the same way. In Persia after the Mongol devastation the Ilkhanids, again without changing the basic forms, reduced the scale of Seljuk ornament. This is quite apparent in the colossal architecture of their Timurid successors, with its small scale of exquisite ornament in tile stucco and even in marble. Similar developments appear in the stone architecture of India from the Khalji Dynasty through that of the Lodis (until 1526).

The Post-Classic period as interpreted by Americanists covers the rise, if not of nations, at least of military hegemonies, sometimes of vast extent. Between these militant entities there seems to have been little communication of ideas. In conjunction with Islam the term will be used here with reference to the last great innovators in Islamic architectural development. These were the Ottoman Empire after the conquest of Constantinople in 1453, the Safavid regime in Persia after about 1550, and Moghul India after the return of Humayun in 1555. These three empires differed from all previous Islamic regimes in that each had developed a certain self-consciousness, a kind of national self-awareness similar to the contemporary evolution which from the culturally rather homogeneous lands of the Middle Ages created the varied European nations we know today. Each of the three adapted the architectural forms, ornament, and materials locally available and made of them a unique and wholly individual style while devising highly original solutions for the age-old problems of the mosque, the residential dwelling, and the tomb. All three empires, set apart by doctrinal differences, nevertheless shared contiguous borders. This geographical proximity did not, however, result in actual cross-cultural exchange. Ideas and craftsmen were exported to the provinces of each empire but almost never across their borders. It might be argued that Moghul India did indeed feel the inspiration of Safavid Persia, yet on closer examination the apparent similarity in their art is more easily explained by the fact that both India and Persia inherited Timurid forms which each then transformed quite independently.

One might also ask about the evolution of architecture throughout those areas of Islam omitted from this book. This would comprise Hafsid Tunisia and part of Algeria after 1228, and Morocco after 1511. In neither did there occur any very interesting architectural innovations. Past styles were repeated with increasingly mechanical and banal results, as in late Mamluk Cairo, until either the imitation of European forms or a wave of Ottoman imitation after the Turkish conquests along the coast wiped out whatever remained of the earlier styles. The present work, competent or otherwise, being done in the restoration of old monuments or even in the creation of new ones in earlier styles throughout these areas, and indeed throughout Islam as a whole, lies beyond the scope of this book.

Chapter I THE BEGINNINGS OF ISLAMIC
ARCHITECTURE

Ibn Sa'd (d. A.D. 845), in his biography of Muhammad, relates a story first told by Abd Allah ibn Yazd who visited Medina in 707, when the Prophet's residence was still intact. There Abd Allah met and talked to a grandson of one of Muhammad's widows, Umm Salama. She had told her grandson that when Muhammad was away on the expedition to Duma in the year 626 she had built an addition to her apartment with a wall of burnt bricks. On his return Muhammad rebuked her, saying, "Oh, Umm Salama! Verily the most unprofitable thing that eateth up the wealth of a believer is building." This opinion seems to have prevailed among the Arabs throughout the period of the Orthodox Caliphate. K. A. C. Creswell has gone so far as to say that Arabia at this time presented "an almost perfect architectural vacuum and the term 'Arab' should never be used to designate the architecture of Islam."

At his death in 632 Muhammad was succeeded by four elected caliphs, or leaders of the faithful, who combined as Muhammad had done both religious and secular functions. They were Abu Bakr (632–34), Umar (634–44), Uthman (644–56), and Ali (656–61). All were related to the family of the Prophet and of his tribe, the Khuraysh. Under these men, called the Orthodox Caliphs, whose names appear prominently displayed in most mosques to this day, occurred the first great conquests of Islam. By the end of Umar's reign Damascus and Jerusalem had fallen, and the entire Tigris and Euphrates basin as well as the Nile Valley and the south coast of the Mediterranean as far as Carthage were within the *Dar al-Islam*, or "abode of peace." By the time of Uthman's death the conquest of eastern Persia as far as Merv had sealed the fate of the Sassanian Empire, already robbed by Umar (in 637) of its western capital, Ctesiphon. The Byzantine Empire, though truncated, survived; for another seven hundred years its fluctuating borders, often violated in both directions, signaled the division between the *Dar al-Harb* ("abode of war") and the *Dar al-Islam*.

The Congregational Mosque and Its Elements
Despite the complete lack of surviving monuments from the first two generations of Islam, there is abundant literary evidence that certain building practices evolved first in Medina itself and then in the foundation of new settlements (*amsars*, or military camps) such as Basra, Kufa, or al-Fustat which were to give Islamic architecture some of its most characteristic and enduring forms. The first of these was the congregational mosque, sometimes also known as a Friday mosque. This was a *masjid*, or place of prayer, in the center of the camp large enough to hold the entire male population during the Friday prayer. Elsewhere in the camp tribal units marked out other, smaller, *masjids* for daily prayer—but about these very little is known. Ever since 624, when Muhammad himself had decreed that the *qibla*, or direction of prayer, be oriented toward the Kaaba in Mecca, all mosques followed this plan regardless of the placement of the buildings and roads around it. (The Kaaba was the pre-Muslim holy place and pilgrimage center whose idols the Prophet was to order destroyed upon his triumphant return to Mecca, the city to which he decreed a pilgrimage be made at least once in the lifetime of every believer.)

In 628 the crowds who came to hear Muhammad in the courtyard of his house at Medina became so large that a pulpit was devised for him, raised on two or more steps. From this *minbar* he led his followers in prayer, dispensed justice, and promulgated his new law as did all his successors. Ascent of the *minbar* in the congregational mosque to conduct the Friday prayer became the prerogative of the caliphs and of their local governors, thus making the act political as well as religious. The fact that the *adhan*, or call to prayer, was delivered vocally by the *muezzin*—in contrast to the East Christian practice of using a wooden clapper, or the Hebrews' use of the *shofar*, or ram's horn—prepared the way for the eventual introduction of the *minaret* into the architectural scheme of the mosque, though the roof of the mosque itself was to serve its purpose for many years.

In 638–39 Sa'd ibn al-Waqqas, the first governor and founder of the town of Kufa, built a congregational mosque there. The structure was a square about 340 feet on each side (*Plate 1*). Though subjected to numerous rebuildings, the present Great Mosque on the same site or very near it measures internally 328 by 354 feet, quite close to the original dimensions. We are told that the space was originally defined only by a ditch. Toward the *qibla* there was an unwalled portico of reused marble columns covered perhaps by a trussed and gabled wooden roof after the manner of Syrian churches. The original congregational mosque at Basra, constructed three years earlier, had been marked only by a fence of reeds.

As simple as these first mosques were, they yet contained the image of their vast successors. They were essentially rectilinear forum-like enclosures oriented in the direction of Mecca, with a roofed columnar hall like a Greek stoa or better yet an Achaemenid *apadana*. Indeed, at Istakhr (near ancient Persepolis) a mosque with bull capitals is known to have existed, and one column actually survives. We must not imagine that the use of such spaces was exclusively religious. Like the Greek agora or the Roman forum, the great court of the Islamic mosque was also a place of public assembly. It served as a law court and debating hall and, most important for later architectural history, it was the place where the Caliph or his appointed governor was acclaimed and accepted by the community.

13

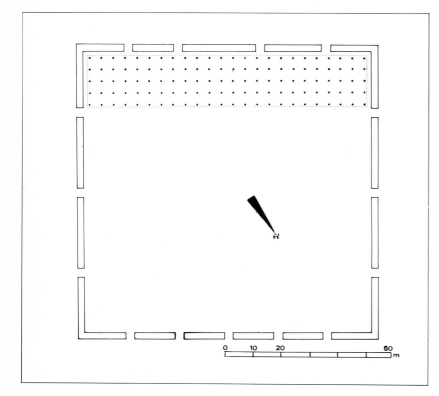

The Dar al-Imara

To the northeast of the mosque at Basra there was built in the year 635 a Dar al-Imara, or place of government, which included a *diwan-i-am* (public audience hall) and a prison. At Kufa in 638–39 a Dar al-Imara which included a *bayt al-Mal* (public treasury) was built on the *qibla* side of the mosque but separated from it by a narrow street. After thieves broke into the treasury the Caliph Umar ordered the Dar al-Imara rebuilt adjacent to the *qibla* of the mosque though somewhat east of it. The building (shortly before 644) was in reused baked brick and the architect was a Persian. After 644 and before 656 Mu'awiyah I, Governor of Damascus and the future Caliph, built a Dar al-Imara on the south or *qibla* side of the great temenos (sacred precinct) of that city's Temple of Bel, then being used jointly as a place of worship by both Christians and Muslims. The structure, of baked brick, was called the Qubbat al-Khadra and therefore as the name implies had a dome, perhaps covered in green tiles; the Dar al-Imara communicated directly with the mosque. Mu'awiyah's residence had no architectural pretensions and was described by a Greek envoy in these words: "The upper part will do for birds and the lower for rats." Despite such sarcasm the dome, almost certainly over the *diwan*, suggests that some of the symbols of Roman as well as Sassanian sovereignty were already being adopted by those men who had quite literally inherited the rule of a large part of the known world. However, such few works as were built in this period, even had they survived, would probably offer no more than the general outline of what architecture was to follow.

Mu'awiyah I (661–80), governor of Damascus from 641, had never accepted the authority of Ali, the last Orthodox Caliph, and after the latter's murder in 661 persuaded Ali's son, al-Hasan, to relinquish his rights to succession. Thus was founded the Umayyad Caliphate, which takes its name from Mu'awiyah's Meccan clan. Expansion of the *Dar al-Islam* continued but with decreased momentum. In the first two decades of the eighth century there were raids eastward into Transoxiana and Sind on the west coast of India; to the west Visigothic Spain fell to Islam in 711 (after the decisive defeat of Poitiers in 723, however, Western Europe remained forever the *Dar al-Harb*). Failure by the Muslims to take Constantinople after sieges in 673–78 and in 716–17 may, as will be shown, have inclined the later Umayyads toward the use of Sassanian royal trappings and symbols, to whose empire they were the indisputable heirs.

Creswell believes that the art of architecture, as opposed to simple building, was first introduced into Islam by Ziyadh ibn Abihi, who had served Ali but was induced to transfer his allegiance to Mu'awiyah. He had first served as governor of Istakhr, and then was appointed to the politically turbulent and faction-ridden post at Basra in 665. There his first act was to deliver a purely political speech in the mosque, a speech famous ever since as a model of decision and brevity. In the same year Ziyadh ordered the congregational mosque rebuilt in baked brick with columns of stone and a roof of teak. Against its *qibla* wall he had the Dar al-Imara rebuilt. Within the prayer hall he installed a *maqsura*, as Mu'awiyah had done the year before at Damascus. The *maqsura* is a screened enclosure, generally of wood, in the center of the *qibla* wall. Within it was the *minbar* and the *mihrab*, the latter a niche whose sole function was to indicate the direction of Mecca. It was first introduced in 706 by the Caliph al-Walid when he rebuilt the mosque which had been Muhammad's house at Medina. His Coptic workmen followed an Egyptian Christian model which drew some criticism from the more conservative Muslims. At Basra Ziyadh also ordered a door made giving direct access from the Dar al-Imara to the *maqsura*. He said at the time that "it was not fitting that the *imam* [meaning himself] should pass through the people." Clearly the appurtenances and symbols of power had already begun to accumulate around the early leaders of Islam.

The Great Mosque and Dar al-Imara at Kufa

Soon after his appointment to Basra, Ziyadh was made Governor of Kufa as well. There in 670 he rebuilt the congregational mosque on stone columns 51 feet tall and supporting a flat roof of teak (*Plate 2*). The prayer hall had five rows of columns and, probably for the first time, the other three walls were provided with porticoes or *riwaqs* of

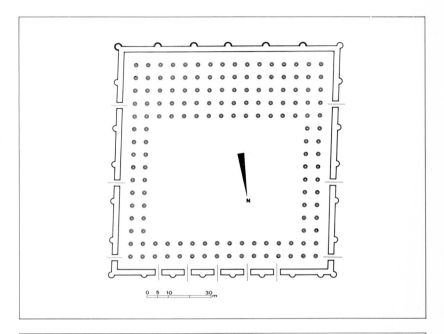

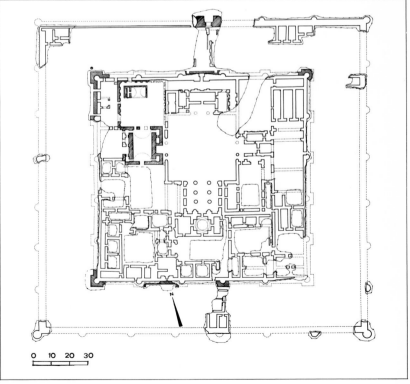

2. *Kufa, Great Mosque as rebuilt by Ziyadh ibn Abihi in 670, plan*

3. *Kufa, Dar al-Imara, plan*

4. *Jerusalem, Haram al-Sharif, plan*
5. *Jerusalem, Qubbat al-Sakhra (Dome of the Rock), 685/86 or 687/88–692, axonometric section*

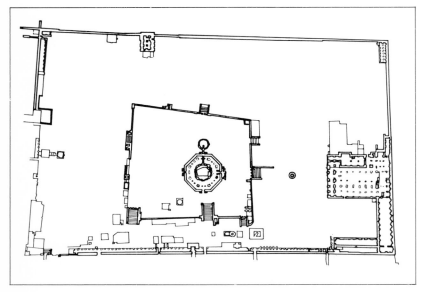

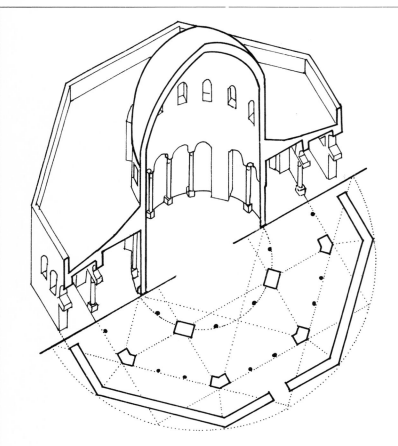

two rows each around the *sahn*, the interior central court. The outer walls were of baked brick buttressed by semicylindrical towers. The architects of the rebuilt work were Persians who had worked for the Sassanians.

Ziyadh also rebuilt the Dar al-Imara at Kufa (*Plate 3*). The present elaborate building, brought to light in a series of excavations not yet completed, belongs to at least three periods and only its position, somewhat east of the *qibla* wall of the mosque, suggests that it occupies the site of the structure built in 635 and rebuilt in 644 under Sa'd ibn al-Waqqas. In fact the strict axial plan of the second period with its elaborate basilical throne hall can only be matched by that at Mshatta, built toward the end of the Umayyad Dynasty, or at Ukhaidir, from the early Abbasid period. Therefore even with Ziyadh's Persian experience, his political intent, and his use of experienced architects it seems doubtful that any more than the foundations of the inner enclosure and perhaps some parts of the outer enclosure remain from his time.

The Dome of the Rock in Jerusalem
The Caliph Yazid (680–83), son of Mu'awiyah, who had with great difficulty established the principle of inheritance instead of election, had the misfortune to be blamed for the death at Kerbela of Husein, brother of Hasan. This led Ibn al-Zubayr, a partisan of Ali, to set himself up as a rival Caliph at Mecca, where he reigned until defeated by the Caliph Abd al-Malik (685–705) in 693. The occupation of Mecca by a rival may have inspired Abd al-Malik when in 685/86 or 687/88 he began the construction of the Qubbat al-Sakhra, the famous Dome of the Rock in Jerusalem, completed (according to its inscription) in 692. The rock, sheltered today by the Haram al-Sharif or Noble Sanctuary—the great centrally planned building that acts as a kind of ciborium—has many associations for all three major faiths (*Plate 8*). On it or near it the Prophet Muhammad is said to have begun his famous Night-Journey to Heaven. The rock may have stood, as the cave beneath it suggests, below the altar of burnt offerings of the Jewish temple; there is a persistent belief that, as the summit of Mount Moriah, it was the site of Abraham's sacrifice of Isaac, from whom the Arabs believe they are descended. The design, with an inner and an outer ambulatory, suggests that it could have been intended as a rival to Mecca's Kaaba, where ambulation is also a major part of the ritual. Whether or not this aim was uppermost in the mind of Abd al-Malik, the overall design embodies many more interesting features.

The exterior of the octagon is sheathed (*Plate 6*) in quartered marbles up to the window line. Above, where there are new Turkish

6. *Jerusalem, Qubbat al-Sakhra (Dome of the Rock), exterior*

tiles dating from 1554, there were once glass mosaics which covered the drum of the dome as well. The subjects of these mosaics are known to have included trees, flowering plants, and buildings. They were probably intended as symbols of Paradise, as are those which still remain in the *riwaqs* of the Great Mosque at Damascus. The wooden dome, with a painted inner shell and an outer one slightly convex in outline and gilded, was rebuilt in the early eleventh century but in much the same form (*Plate 10*). Four portals, each originally with a two-columned vaulted porch, face the cardinal points and give access to the outer ambulatory whose emphasis is horizontal, accented by the very Roman entablature linking the twenty-four arches and eight piers of which its inner boundary is composed (*Plate 9*). Above these arches on both the inner and outer face runs the first monumental inscription in all Islamic architecture; we shall return to it later. The inner ambulatory is screened from the central chamber by the sixteen arches and four piers supporting the drum of the dome: here only the beams impede the view which rapidly expands into the soaring luminous space under the dome proper (*Plate 8*).

The plan (*Plate 5*) is based on the 45-degree turning of one square upon another. The eight points of the rather blunt star thus created locate the four piers and the four center columns of the sets of three which support the drum of the dome. Extensions of the sides of the two original squares into another eight-pointed star locate the piers of the other ambulatory as well as another larger pair of interlaced squares around whose points can be drawn a circle within which the outer dimensions of the octagon are constructed. That such geometric refinements were not new in Syria can be proven by the similarly complex plans of the fourth-century Church of the Ascension on the Mount of Olives and the fifth-century tomb of the Virgin, to say nothing of the Anastasis over the tomb of Christ—where not only the dimensions of the inner circle of piers and columns are almost identical, but the same alternation of twelve columns and four piers is used (paired, however, in the Anastasis). We see then that the plan of the Dome of the Rock alludes specifically to well-known local Christian shrines, as do the interior mosaics and inscriptions. The plan generated countless numbers of those endlessly intricate nets of ornament which Islamic art in its maturity displayed over walls, ceilings, metalwork, and textiles.

The wonderful mosaics below the inscription on both sides of the inner octagon and in the spandrels of the outer side of the drum as well as on the inner side of the drum itself all the way up to the spring of the dome remain substantially as Abd al-Malik's designer intended, despite the repairs of the eleventh century and later. Vegetable motifs in the form of whole trees and vine scrolls issuing from

◁ *10. Jerusalem, Qubbat al-Sakhra (Dome of the Rock), interior view of the cupola with mosaics showing jewels*

11. Jerusalem, Mosque of al-Aqsa as completed by al-Mahdi c. 780, reconstruction of plan

12. Jerusalem, Mosque of al-Aqsa, interior

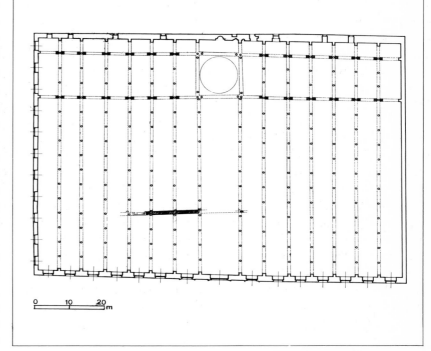

vases or clumps of acanthus are spread over the surface in rich profusion. Though Oriental (Sassanian) motifs occur, Greco-Roman sources predominate, as they will subsequently at Damascus. Geometric ornament, however, and the interlace, so characteristic of all later Islamic ornament, are totally absent. On the inner face of the octagon and, though less profusely, on the inner face of the drum representations of rich jewels (crowns, elaborate necklaces, pendants, etc.) are frequent (*Plate 9*). Some of the crowns are combined with crescents or with the winged motif associated with Sassanian royalty. Oleg Grabar has suggested that the crowns have a function analogous to similar representations in a Christian context, that is, as votive crowns dedicated in a shrine. Here they symbolize Islam's victory over the Persian Empire and the anticipated victories over Byzantium and other Christian powers. Grabar's interpretation, which has not gone unchallenged, seems to be supported by the monumental inscription, the first in Islam and about 787 feet long. Its Koranic quotations are directed to "the people of the book," that is, Jews, and more particularly Christians, emphasizing that Islam, now the only true faith, accepts the prophets and Christ as a prophet though denying His divinity. For the Muslims the inscription and the building itself were an answer to the frequently feared attraction that Christianity and its ritual had for the simple Bedouin. They were a triumphal assertion of the superiority of Islam morally and, in this case, in artistic richness as well.

The Mosque of al-Aqsa

Although the present structure—much changed and reduced—owes more to the Abbasid Caliphate than to the Umayyad (*Plate 12*), it is appropriate to discuss its entire history here rather than to return to it later. All we know of the first al-Aqsa of the Caliph Umar was that he ordered a group of ancient ruins, probably those of Herod's great stoa along the south retaining wall of the temple area, roofed over. The structure seems never to have been more than a temporary one of no architectural pretensions. Recently the Aphrodito papyri from Egypt have shown that al-Walid I (705–15), the successor of Abd al-Malik, was being sent craftsmen from Egypt between the years 709 and 715 for work on "the mosque of Jerusalem" and the palace (Dar al-Imara) of the Emir al-Muiminin, the remains of which have recently been discovered below the south wall of the Haram al-Sharif. A reference to al-Walid's use of mosaics at Jerusalem can now be interpreted as regarding the Mosque of al-Aqsa. Recent research by Robert W. Hamilton indicates that at least one of the arcades just east of the present dome is the work of al-Walid. If so this is the earliest mosque in Islam to deploy its arcades at right angles rather than paral-

lel to the *qibla* wall. The intent must have been to orient the *mihrab* aisle upon the south entrance of the Dome of the Rock, as is that of the present mosque. Al-Walid thus reinforced the sanctity of the site by equating the mosque not only with Constantine's basilica (which had a similar relation to the Anastasis) but with the Church of the Nativity at Bethlehem, which has the same orientation toward Christ's birthplace.

Al-Walid's mosque, except near the *mihrab*, was severely damaged in the earthquake of 747/48 and ordered repaired by the Abbasid Caliph al-Mansur, probably in 758/59. Al-Mansur's successor, al-Mahdi (775–85), almost entirely rebuilt and vastly enlarged al-Aqsa, adding a wooden dome over the *mihrab* and extending the building some 59 to 65 feet north. His work, probably completed for a visit to Jerusalem he made in 780, had seven aisles east and seven west of the much wider *mihrab* aisle, all perpendicular to the *qibla* wall (*Plate 11*). This building was in turn almost entirely destroyed in an earthquake of 1033 and was rebuilt by the Fatimid Caliph of Egypt, al-Zahir (1021–36), in 1035. Al-Zahir's mosque probably had no more than the three aisles east and west of the *mihrab* aisle in the present structure, which incorporates substantial parts of it (*Plate 12*).

The Great Mosque of Damascus

Al-Walid's Great Mosque at Damascus soon became the most influential building of its time in Islam and remains today, even in a heavily damaged and much rebuilt state, one of the major monuments of the Islamic world. At the time of the conquest of Damascus (635), as we have seen, the inner colonnaded temenos of what had been the early first-century Temple of Jupiter Damascenus surrounded the Theodosian church of St. John on or near the site of the original temple. The eastern half of the temenos was then taken over as a mosque whose *mihrab*, not then a niche, was the one now called that of the Companions of the Prophet. Both Christians and Muslims used the west portal at the time. Al-Mu'awiyah's *maqsura* of 664 must have surrounded the *mihrab* of the Companions of the Prophet, and his palace—the Qubbat al-Khadra—would have stood due south of this part of the temenos wall. Late in 706 al-Walid obtained the church from the Christians, destroyed it as well as everything else within the temenos except the four corner towers, and began the new Great Mosque, which was completed in 714/15 (*Plate 14*).

Long walls to east and west negated the inner projection of the towers. The *sahn* was then surrounded on all four sides by a two-story arcade not corresponding to any inner horizontal division. The lower arcade alternated two columns and a pier like the atrium of Hagia Sophia and perhaps of Constantinopolitan palaces as well. The

14. *Damascus, Great Mosque, plan in the time of al-Walid*

16. *Damascus, Great Mosque, prayer hall*

15. *Damascus, Great Mosque, prayer hall*

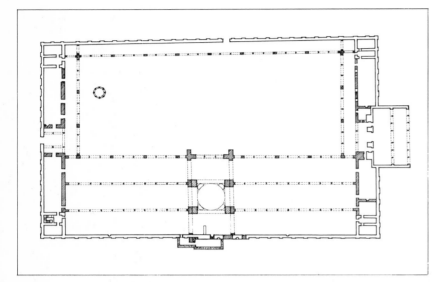

17. *Damascus, Great Mosque*, sahn, *detail of portico with mosaic revetment*
18. *Ravenna, San Apollinare Nuovo, mosaic showing the Palace of Theodoric before 525*

upper "story" consisted of biforia on colonnettes, roughly one to each arch of the lower "story" (*Plate 13*). The prayer hall was divided into three broad aisles with gabled roofs parallel to the south wall of the old temenos, the *qibla*. This arrangement may well have evolved from the frequent habit of converting Syrian basilicas to mosques: because Mecca was due south, the Muslim had only to pray across the aisles of a structure that normally pointed east. The theory, however, that the present prayer hall is actually the old church of St. John has long been discarded.

The most striking feature of the Great Mosque's prayer hall is the great central transept, which had a wooden double-shelled dome over the middle bay. This burned down in 1069 and was replaced in stone by the Seljuk Sultan, Malik Shah. His dome too was destroyed, and the present structure was itself rebuilt after the fire of 1893. The north facade of the transept with its triple portal (*Plate 17*) has been compared to the Chalki Gate in the palace at Constantinople. No illustration of that structure survives, but the striking similarity of the prayer hall facade to that of Theodoric's palace at Ravenna, as shown in the mosaics of 490–520 at San Apollinare Nuovo (*Plate 18*), has often been noted. The Caliph was thus provided here with a fastigium like that of Diocletian at Split (285–300), which also leads to a domed chamber.

Again like Theodoric's palace, the facade of al-Walid's Great Mosque was encrusted with mosaics and, it is said, was originally separated from the *sahn* by rich curtains as at Ravenna. These parallels cannot have been fortuitous: there seems to be no question that certain forms traditionally associated with sovereignty were here reworked in a new setting for a new world ruler. Given the religious and political significance to Islam of the Great Mosque in its capital, as Damascus then was, this should not be surprising.

A revetment of quartered marble up to the spring of the arches completely lined the three sides of the *sahn* and very probably the walls of the prayer hall as well. Nearly all of this vanished in the fires of 1069, 1401, and 1893. Behind the east and west *riwaqs* of the *sahn*, the long rooms between the towers were lighted by round-arched windows let into the revetment. These had marble grilles, six of which survive, the oldest examples in Islam of the use of the geometric interlace (*Plate 19*). Creswell has shown that some of these were created by the use of equilateral triangles forming hexagons and others by the use of the octagon in various combinations, both patterns being well known in the Greco-Roman world.

Above the marble revetment, covering walls and arches inside and out, were mosaics; Creswell estimates more than an acre of them. Their beauty as much as anything else made the Great Mosque at

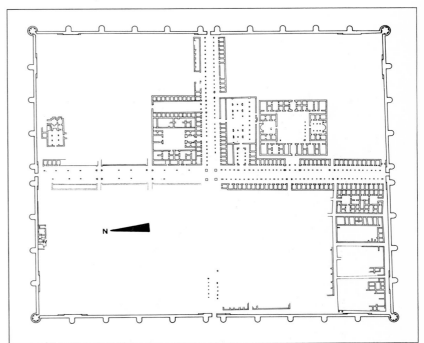

Damascus a legend throughout the world of Islam. Little is left of this vast scheme and even that is much restored, but from what remains it seems that the naturalistically portrayed palms, fruit trees, and vine scrolls of Jerusalem's Dome of the Rock were repeated here (without crowns or jewels, however). Around the *sahn* there survive fragments of a fanciful frieze depicting villages, towns, and palaces, often shown situated above running water (*Plate 20*). The Koranic Paradise is probably the subject, but it is one without human inhabitants. Later, written inscriptions taken from those *surahs* of the Koran describing Paradise will replace visual representations of it. Except for the windows, the shape of the arches is not consistently semicircular as it was in the Dome of the Rock, ranging instead from slightly pointed to stilted or moderately horseshoe-shaped. Pointed arches were occasionally used in sixth-century Byzantium, while pre-Muslim horseshoe arches are fairly common in Syria, Anatolia, and Spain. One feels here in the Great Mosque, as in all Umayyad work, that the shape of the arch had yet to be definitively established.

UMAYYAD SECULAR ARCHITECTURE

The ruins of several palaces (or perhaps more accurately manor houses), bath-audience halls, *caravanserais* (*hans*), and of at least two planned towns have been published, thus providing us with an idea of the nature of Umayyad secular architecture. The earlier and somewhat overly romantic explanation for the isolated manor houses and baths was attributed to the reluctant conversion of the Umayyad elite from a nomadic to a sedentary urban life. It was postulated that these aristocratic Arabs yearned for open, solitary, desert places free of the older crowded commercial centers like Damascus or even the new centers of Basra and Kufa, whose populations were rapidly increasing. Though this theory should not be entirely discarded, recent research suggests that most if not all of these installations may have been in or near elaborately irrigated agricultural domains capable of producing more than was consumed by their inhabitants. At least one site, Kasr al-Khayr al-Sharki in southern Syria, according to Oleg Grabar's recent excavations, may well have been planned as a self-sufficient military colony intended to provide provisions and pasturage for an army camped temporarily nearby. Space permits only a few representative structures to be treated here, but information on all is readily available in Creswell's monumental works on early Muslim architecture.

Anjar

Though authorities are not all in agreement, there would appear to be little doubt that the site of Anjar (in the Beqa Valley of Lebanon, not far from Baalbek) was under construction during the reign of al-

Walid I. Inscriptions in a nearby quarry, where stone was obtained for the finished outer surfaces of the walls, refer to al-Walid and name the site as well as the date 714–15; moreover, the dispatch of laborers from Egypt is mentioned in the Aphrodito papyri. The plan of Anjar is remarkably like that of a Roman camp with an arcaded *cardo* and *decumanus* intersecting at a tetrapylon (*Plate 22*) and a grid of rectangular *insulae*. However, the "palace" in the southeast quadrant displays typical Umayyad *bayts* found also at Khirbat Minyah and several other Umayyad sites, and is situated due south of the *qibla* wall of the mosque, which follows a rather atypical plan. The palace originally had two apsidal audience halls or *majlis* (a *diwan-i-am* and a *diwan-i-khas*), at least one of them two stories high (*Plate 23*). Khirbat Minyah had one, perhaps also two stories high, and at Kasr al-Khayr al-Gharbi and Khirbat al-Mafjar one or two probably occupied the now vanished upper stories. In Anjar's southwest quadrant two houses (placed back to back) have square courts and one *bayt*, each very like the more expansive but also standardized structure we know existed at Kasr al-Khayr al-Sharki (*Plate 29*). Near the north gate is a typical bath-audience hall very like that at Qusayr Amra. It has a tripartite throne chamber with a square niche and once contained a rich mosaic floor. Another building with a square court and *bayts*, at the corner of the northeast quadrant opposite the mosque and occupied on three sides by rows of shops at ground level, may well have been a Dar al-Imara like that at Kasr al-Khayr al-Sharki and not another palace as Creswell believes.

In the absence of firm evidence to the contrary, Anjar would seem to be an Umayyad foundation which—in an area well within the former Roman orbit—took as its model Rusafa, the Sergiopolis of Justinian times. The resemblance to Diocletian's palace at Split or even to Trajan's Thamugadi (Timgad) is startling. The functions of the smaller enclosure at Split or the much larger one at Thamugadi are quite clear but that of Anjar less so. The two axial streets, with arcades in groups usually of three arches on two columns flanked by piers (as at Damascus), seem clearly to have been *suqs* or markets flanked by continuous rows of stalls like Roman *tabernae*. To judge by the two rather spacious houses uncovered in the southwest quadrant, this space might have held a total of twenty-four such houses of similar dimensions. Assuming one head of a household for each—there is less space in the other three quarters—not many more than eighty households could have been quartered here, a very small entourage for a caliph. Perhaps, then, Anjar was a craftsmen's settlement intended only for occasional state visits or another camp for military provisioning as Kasr al-Khayr al-Sharki may have been, or even a rather sumptuous retail market for the entire region.

Khirbat al-Mafjar

After al-Walid I three short and turbulent reigns brought near disaster to Islam, including the failure of the second siege of Constantinople. With the advent of Hisham (724–43), fourth son of Abd al-Malik, the empire regained much of its power. Lost territories in Transoxiana and the Maghrib were restored and revenues increased. Hisham was a great builder, founding among much else a palace and *caravanserai* outside the walls of Rusafa, his favorite residence, another palace at Kasr al-Khayr al-Gharbi, and the eastern site of Kasr al-Khayr al-Sharki.

The Khirbat al-Mafjar complex (*Plate 24*) stands within a large agricultural estate, once elaborately irrigated. All the buildings were found violently overturned, probably by the earthquake of 747/48. None at that time had been finished save for the bath-audience hall, which showed signs of use. Graffiti in a foundation trench of the palace referred to Hisham, but Hamilton in his monograph of 1959 believed the patron to have been Hisham's dissolute nephew al-Walid ibn Yazid who succeeded as al-Walid II in February 743 and was assassinated in April of the next year. Creswell in the second edition of his *Early Muslim Architecture* (1969) disagrees, suggesting that the work, begun as late as 739, was indeed made for Hisham and interrupted by his death. Richard Ettinghausen's remarkable interpretation (1972) of the iconography of the bath-audience hall tends to accept the attribution to al-Walid II. Whichever of the two was in fact the patron of Khirbat al-Mafjar, the decorative emphasis relied quite strongly on symbols of sovereignty.

The bath complex, mosque, and square Kasr were given unity—perhaps as an afterthought—by a rectangular arcaded court about 177 by 443 feet, some of it hardly begun by the time of the earthquake. In the center was a pavilion with a fountain, whose plan was inspired by the same scheme used for the Dome of the Rock. The bath-audience hall had a monumental entrance (*Plate 25*) clearly adapted from a Roman triumphal arch, perhaps a tetrapylon. Even so the crenellations, the style of the stucco ornament, the style of the niche, and the iconography of the subsidiary sculpture are all firmly based on Sassanian symbols of kingship. Within the portal was a dome richly ornamented with three-dimensional images of ibexes (the *hvarnath* of Sassanian kingship), athletes, armored warriors, and dancing girls. The throne hall had a vaulted roof culminating in a central dome supported by sixteen great compound piers (*Plate 26*). The central quincunx was surrounded by a lower ambulatory billowing out into eleven great exedrae. The most richly ornamented of these, on an axis with the portal, was dense with Sassanian royal symbols—including a stone image of a *tawila* or caliphal headdress suspended

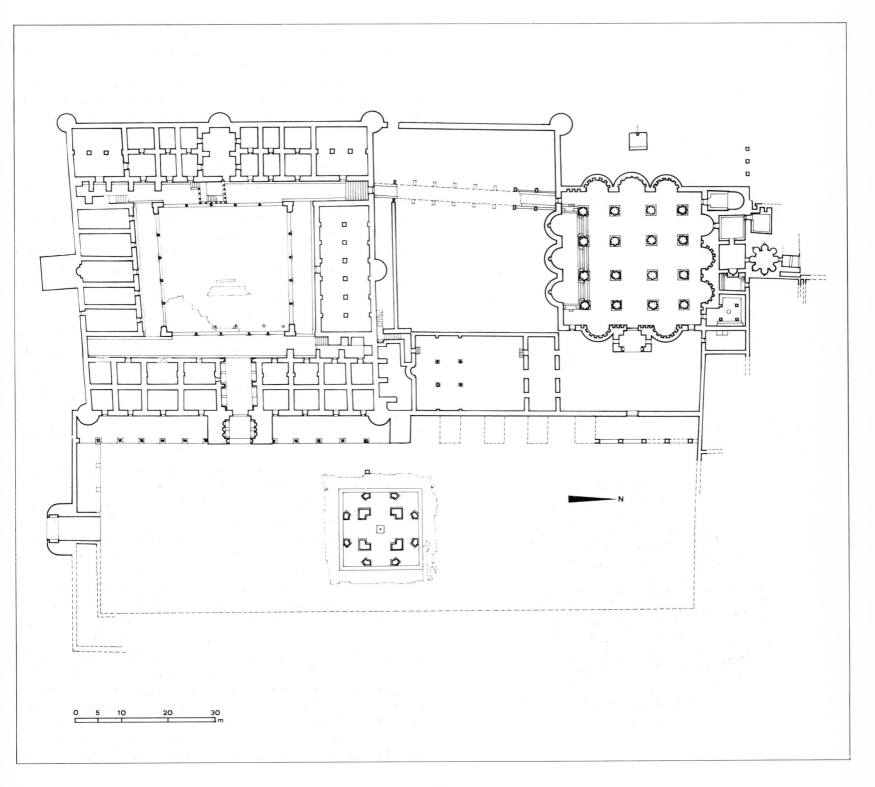

from the vault as the crown of the Sassanian monarch Chosroes had been at Ctesiphon. Ettinghausen relates the niches to the imperial *triclinia* or banqueting halls of late antiquity but speculates that the whole may be a symbolic re-creation of the great throne *iwan* of Ctesiphon. Oleg Grabar in 1973 suggested that audience halls like these may have been *majlis al-lahwah* (places for entertainment) as opposed to the more formal *majlis* (throne or reception halls) in the Kasr itself, if there was one, nearby. There seems to be no reason why they could not have served both functions.

North of the throne hall was a small *diwan* lavishly ornamented in stucco and mosaic and lighted by a dome on pendentives with a windowed drum. On the pendentives appeared winged horses, again a Sassanian royal symbol, and within the dome human heads in high relief projecting from a great rosette of acanthus may have symbolized Paradise. The only figural mosaic in the entire Khirbat al-Mafjar complex (*Plate 27*), found within a semicircular niche, imitates an embroidered textile. Clearly of local Palestinian workmanship, it shows a tree to the right of which (hence at the left hand of the ruler) a lion is attacking gazelles while to his right two gazelles browse peacefully. Could these, as Ettinghausen suggests, symbolize the *Dar al-Harb* and the *Dar al-Islam*? Like the two throne halls of the Kasr at Anjar, here again we may have the *diwan-i-am* and the *diwan-i-khas* of a Moghul palace. East of the *diwan* is a small bath complex, richly decorated with marble and mosaics. The last room to the east is a latrine of truly awesome proportions, suggesting the considerable size of the assemblies which must have gathered in the throne hall.

The mosque at Khirbat al-Mafjar had a triple public entrance from the forecourt of the throne hall and a private entrance into the *maqsura* from the second story of the Kasr. A sheltered walk also permitted the patron private entry into the throne hall. The Kasr itself probably had *bayts* and two tripartite clerestoried throne halls to west and east on its second floor. From the eastern throne hall the great court could be surveyed through an elaborate window.

Khirbat al-Mafjar represents the mingling of Roman, Byzantine, and Sassanian elements into a harmonious assemblage—but not their fusion into a new style. Architectural forms and structural procedures seem almost entirely of Western origin, even those used with an iconographic intent—for example, the exedrae of the throne hall, the dome and niche of the *iwan*, and the basilical halls of the Kasr. The ornament, however, with respect to materials, technique (except for the mosaics), and iconography, is predominantly Sassanian or Eastern. Such Oriental incursions are very marked in late Umayyad times as though increasingly the caliphs, unable to capture Constantinople, turned to the trappings of the Sassanian Empire whose heirs they were.

Curiously enough, the patron of Kasr al-Khayr al-Gharbi—almost surely Hisham—may have been quite consciously aware of the multiple nature of the Islamic heritage and even symbolized it there. In the two well-known frescoed floors in the stairwells, that to the south in the general direction of Iraq and Persia is of marked Sassanian inspiration while that to the north in the direction of the old Roman lands represents the earth goddess Gaea surrounded by hypocamps of Greco-Roman style and iconography.

Mshatta

The vast unfinished enclosure at Mshatta (*Plate 28*), about twenty miles south of Amman in Jordan, has been attributed since its discovery in the early nineteenth century to every Near Eastern civilization since the Parthians, but there is now general agreement that it is of late Umayyad origin—built probably either by al-Walid II (743–44) and left unfinished at his death or by a later ruler and interrupted by the fall of the dynasty. The enclosure, 1,593 square feet, is exceeded in size only by Anjar (121 by 101 feet) and is much larger than the planned town of Kasr al-Khayr al-Sharki (861 square feet). The existing interior divisions consist of an elaborate entrance complex leading to an interior court upon which opens the triple portal of a basilical throne hall terminating in a triconch, perhaps once domed, around which are four typically Umayyad *bayts*. Flanking the center division in the outer walls are double columns, which suggest that rows of living quarters were intended to front two more long and narrow courts.

The triconch was probably adopted here because it had, at least by the fourth century, become closely associated with imperial symbolism in the West. The palace at Piazza Armerina in Sicily, probably built around 300 by the Tetrarch Maximianus, has a triconch, as has the palace at Ravenna, built between the time of the Western emperor Honorius and that of Theodoric. Closer still is the probable triconch at Kasr ibn Wardan, completed by a Byzantine architect in 564 for the Ghassanid Prince, Harith ibn Jabala. The tripartite opening into the court suggests a Sassanian *iwan*, though there are Western examples such as the early sixth-century Governor's Palace at Apollonia.

A significant aspect of Mshatta is the evidence it provides of the increasing formality of the caliphal court. The function of space is now connected with the *adventus* and other ceremonies centering around the entranceway, which has grown much more elaborate. Even though some of the settings for this increased formality may have been Western in inspiration, the development probably first occurred in Iraq. The Dar al-Imara at Kufa (*Plate 3*), even if rebuilt later, shows a gate complex, a square court, and a basilical hall leading to a cruciform chamber, probably predating Mshatta. At Kasr al-Khayr al-

Sharki (*Plate 29*) it is the *medina* founded by Hisham in 728/29 and not the palace that again may be of Iraqi inspiration. Here four gates lead to a central court about 452 square feet. Around this are arranged six commodious residences—each with adjacent commercial premises, a Dar al-Imara, and a mosque. The whole seems to foreshadow al-Mansur's round city of Baghdad.

The facade of the palace at Mshatta as originally planned (*Plate 30*) was to have consisted of a frieze of porous limestone resting on and framed by a rich molding and divided by a zigzag acanthus cornice into fifty-six triangles, each with an enormous rosette alternately eight-lobed and octagonal in the center. Around these the ground is, or was to be, filled with a densely carved pattern of rinceaux inhabited (except for the host of birds on the right-hand portion outside the mosque) by animals and fantastic creatures. Here, unlike most of the wall surfaces at Kasr al-Khayr al-Gharbi and Khirbat al-Mafjar, the patterns are not infinitely repetitious since they are cut off by the frames. Instead, as in Greco-Roman and even earlier Sassanian ornament, each plant grows from one or more stems, sometimes from an urn, and always from the bottom up. Ultimately the Mediterranean idea of an ornament complete within its individual frame will be discarded by Islam, only to reappear centuries later in the decorative arts of the Ottomans and the Moghuls.

Conclusion

With the Umayyads the Islamic Empire began to acquire the secular as well as the religious trappings of a great power. This was not an easy process, for the Koran, much less flexible than the Christian Bible, opposed secularism and all ostentation. Indeed, in a sense, all art was suspect: if not actually the work of Satan, visual adornments were considered to distract the thoughts of the faithful from moral contemplation. As we have seen, the already well-established late antique and Byzantine forms of the fastigium and the martyrium were re-employed by Islamic artists, their old meanings being accommodated to the new faith. Sometimes, as in the Great Mosque at Damascus, secular Byzantine forms were used in an Islamic religious context—probably because that building was so intimately related to the Caliph himself, but also perhaps because the institution of the Friday mosque still had the political connotations of a forum as well as a place of prayer.

The princely country residences, so numerous under the Umayyads, will soon disappear under Abbasid rule and with them much of the early synthesis of Western and Oriental architectural expression they initiated. These residences show more clearly than do the great urban mosques the selective adoption by early Islam of local and im-

28. *Mshatta, c. 744–50, plan of the palace*

29. *Kasr al-Khayr al-Sharki, founded 728/29, plan of the greater enclosure*

30. *Mshatta, detail of the south facade of the palace. East Berlin, Staatliche Museen*

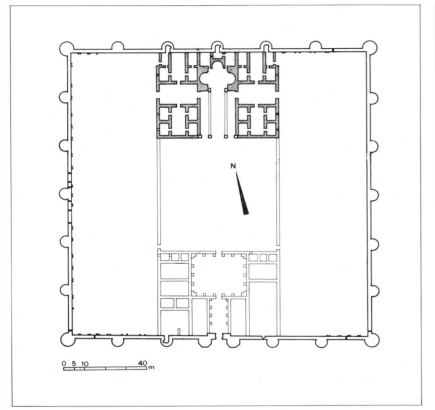

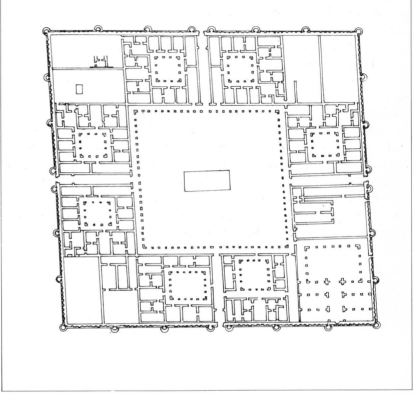

ported pre-Islamic customs. Grabar has called them in many ways illusionistic: they are turreted and crenellated like forts, but the towers are either filled with rubble or serve as latrines. Their stone or rubble walls are often concealed behind panels of endless stucco ornament or even painted imitations of Sassanian textiles, and the rich mosaic floors frequently imitate embroidered or woven textiles. The contribution of this aristocratic and princely style to what in the eleventh, twelfth, and thirteenth centuries was to emerge as Classic Islamic architecture lies primarily in the relation of their decoration to their architectural forms. Panels with geometric, floral, or mixed forms create infinite networks of patterns across surfaces often rather arbitrarily chosen. The patterns seem to continue uninterruptedly beyond their confining frames and at the same time to transform and veil the surfaces they cling to. Beginning with the Umayyads this tendency, developed by the Abbasids, will spread from one end of Islam to the other.

The City of Baghdad

The Abbasids, descendants of the Prophet's uncle, al-Abbas, felt they had a more legitimate claim to the caliphal office than the Umayyads and from the beginning stressed the theological aspect of their rulership. Persian ideas of divine kingship may also have been introduced by the followers of Abu Muslim, whose revolt in Khorassan in 747 did so much to place the Abbasids in power. The first Abbasid Caliph, Abu al-Abbas—known as al-Saffah (750–54)—assumed power in Kufa and soon acquired as his secretary the famous *mawla* (converted Muslim) Khalid ibn Barmak, son of the powerful hereditary abbot of the famous Buddhist monastery in Balkh. Al-Saffah was succeeded by his brother, Abu Jafar al-Mansur (754–75), whose first act was to lure the powerful Abu Muslim to his court in 755, where he had him murdered. Before his death Abu Muslim had built a Dar al-Imara at Merv; according to a description, it consisted of a domed chamber 82 1/2 feet tall with four doors leading into as many *iwans* (each 90 by 45 feet), which in turn led into four square *sahns*. Such radial symmetry is mirrored in several later Abbasid palaces at Samarra.

Nothing remains of al-Mansur's famous circular city of Baghdad —begun in 762 and called the City of Peace—but many contemporary descriptions allow us to make a hypothetical reconstruction (*Plate 31*). The double-walled moated enclosure was about 2,515 yards in diameter. The four gates, halfway between the cardinal points and surmounted by four golden-domed audience chambers, looked out on the major directions of the empire: the Khorassan gate toward the northeast, the Kufa gate toward Mecca and the southwest, the Shami gate toward Byzantium and the northwest, and the Basra gate toward India and the southeast. Within a circular inner city surrounded by administrative buildings and residences for al-Mansur's relatives stood the 900-square-foot Dar al-Khilafah (residential palace) at the *qibla* wall of the great mosque—also a square, of 450 feet. The palace had a so-called Golden Gate, an *iwan* 45 feet deep and 30 wide, and two 45-square-foot domed chambers one above the other. The uppermost was called the Qubbat al-Khadra, like Mu'awiyah's in Damascus and Hisham's at Rusafa. Creswell's suggestion that the palace, like that of Abu Muslim in Merv, was radially symmetrical is not justified by the written accounts. However, Oleg Grabar's recent speculation on the meaning of Baghdad probably also applies to Abu Muslim's work. He believes that Baghdad was a conscious attempt to symbolize the universal rule of the Muslim prince. Not without reason, later geographers placed Baghdad at the hub of the universe and Iraq in the central and most favored climatic zone of the world.

As in so many other instances, the means by which this symbolism was achieved were not new. Assyrian military camps were round, as were Darabgird, a Parthian foundation, and Firuzabad, founded by the Sassanian Ardashir I. The last two also had circular inner enclosures and four equidistant gates. Circular enclosures appear very early in Transoxiana as well, and Charles Wendell has recently suggested that Khalid ibn Barmak may have had a hand in designs there. As a recent convert from Buddhism, Khalid would have been aware of the tradition of the Chakravartin, the ruler among whose insignia was a spoked wheel—a symbol of the sun, but also of his rule over the four quarters of the universe. At Baghdad the "spokes" were shifted from the relatively meaningless cardinal points and directed instead toward the essential regions of the Islamic domain.

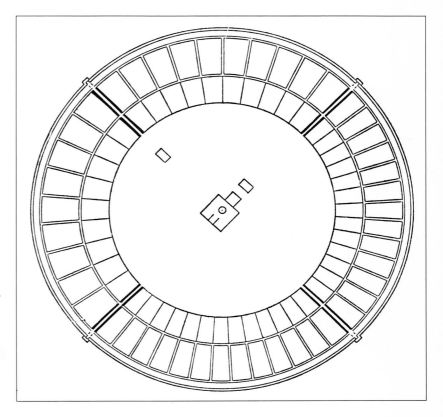

Ukhaidir

As successor to his brother al-Mansur, al-Saffah had named Isa ibn Musa, his nephew. Isa was made Governor of Kufa and occupied a great palace in the new Baghdad, but beginning in 764/65 a number of attempts were made to depose him in favor of al-Mansur's son, al-Mahdi. When treachery and poison failed, a threat to the life of Isa's son compelled the father to give up his rights on payment of ten million *dirhams*, while retaining the right to succeed al-Mahdi. Finally, in 778, when Isa refused again to give up his right of accession in favor of al-Mahdi's son, Harun al-Rashid, he was deprived of the governorship of Kufa and retired to his estate, visiting Kufa only for Friday prayers. Creswell has ingeniously suggested that Ukhaidir, the only desert palace known from the Abbasid period, was this estate and that it was built sometime after 764/65 or in 778 amid an extensive, once irrigated, agricultural domain about fifty miles west of Kufa.

Ukhaidir (*Plate 32*) consists of an inner enclosure about 367 by 269 feet entered from the north through a portal flanked by quarter-circle towers. After construction had reached about 10 feet above ground level the outer four-gated enclosure (*Plate 33*) of about 574 by 554 feet was begun—perhaps in 778, when Ibn Musa might have felt he needed added protection. Where the north wall of the outer enclosure enveloped that of the inner one, three stories of assymetrically arranged rooms rose against it; all other parts of the palace were of one story, like Mshatta. Immediately within the outer enclosure is a transverse corridor with a fluted dome at the portal which once must have given access to courtyard A and the mosque, both now somewhat curtailed. Today it leads right and left to the outer court (*Plate 36*). Proceeding south, one enters the Great Hall with its pointed brick barrel vault two stories high (*Plate 35*). Next comes another transverse corridor which isolates the Court of Honor and the throne

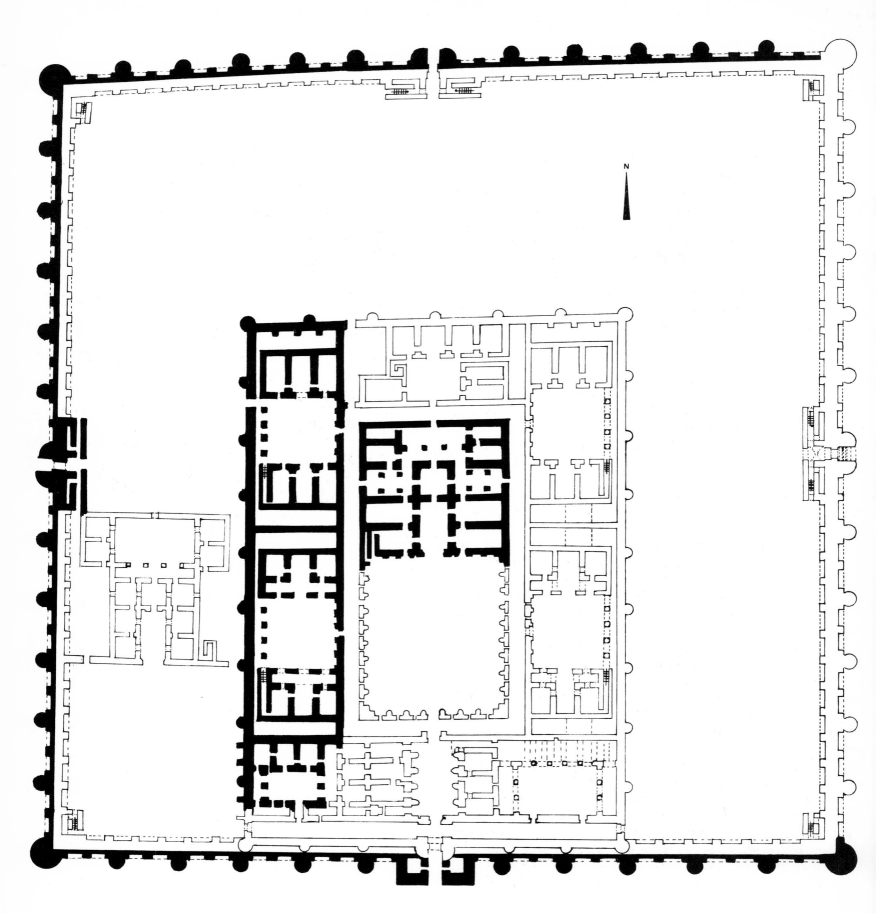

complex while providing the only access to three of the four *bayts* (the fourth was totally isolated from the rest of the complex). The Court of Honor, a rectangle about 99 by 111 feet (*Plates 37, 39*), is surrounded by hooded arcading which employs bare brick ornamentally for the first time in Islamic architecture. The south facade of the court, now restored, presents a triple portal (*Plate 38*) whose wider central opening is crowned by a *pishtaq* or false front. Behind it is an *iwan* leading to a square chamber (once domed) opening onto three columned halls.

The four *bayts* are quite unlike the Umayyad *bayts* of Mshatta and earlier. Each has two suites north and south of a court with a central *iwan* flanked by matching chambers of a more private character. The north pair in addition have a transverse antechamber or foyer. It is this complex, introduced into Egypt probably by Ibn Tulun in the late ninth century, which will ultimately become the *qa'a* or reception room characteristic of Egyptian domestic architecture into the nineteenth century. The historian al-Mas'udi, who died in 956, tells us that the Caliph al-Mutawakkil (847–61) adopted a system invented by the Lakhmid kings of Hira—whose architecture symbolized a battle order. Thus the *iwan* became the *sadr* or breast, where the royal council met, while two flanking *kumans* or sleeves stood for the right and left wings of the army. Almost identical *bayts* are found in a similar position in relation to the throne room in the so-called Imarat i-Khusraw of 590–628 at Qasr i-Shirin on the Baghdad-Kirmansha road. The Lakhmids may well have adopted this scheme too but al-Mas'udi is, of course, wrong in attributing their introduction into Islamic architecture to al-Mutawakkil.

The inner enclosure at Ukhaidir is obviously a much elaborated version of Mshatta. Even more than the latter, it emphasizes the ceremony surrounding the isolated patron. The great corridor has an almost exact parallel in the Imarat i-Khusraw. As in many details of its style and in its rubble masonry construction, so also in its planning Ukhaidir borrows heavily from Sassanian Iran. If we can use Ukhaidir —as we probably can—to show what al-Mansur's palace at Baghdad must have looked like (albeit on a much grander scale), then it is clear that the Abbasids far more than the Umayyads had turned to Sassanian models for the ceremonies and symbols of power by which they surrounded themselves. There is no evidence of imitation of the grand processions and acclamations of the Byzantine court, still menacingly alive beyond Islam's frontiers. Instead Ukhaidir follows the hieratic immobility of the enshrined Persian king and the grandees, tribute bearers, and entertainers of his court—a court by now safely receding into legend and ultimately totally supplanted by the power of Islam.

36. *Ukhaidir, detail of the corridor*
37. *Ukhaidir, Court of Honor looking north, reconstruction*
38. *Ukhaidir, Court of Honor, south facade*
39. *Ukhaidir, Court of Honor, north facade* ▷

40. *Damghan, Tarik Khana, c. 750–89, plan of the mosque*
41. *Damghan, Tarik Khana, the mosque seen from the* sahn

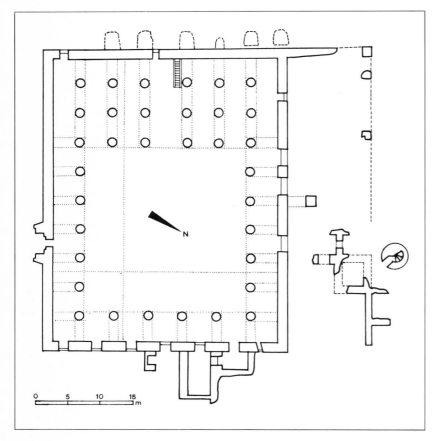

The Tarik Khana of Damghan

Monuments of the early Abbasid period are rare in Persia but at Damghan, due south of the easternmost tip of the Caspian Sea, there is a hypostyle mosque of Arabic plan (*Plate 40*) but Sassanian structure (*Plates 41, 42*). Heavy cylindrical piers of baked brick support arcades perpendicular to the *qibla* wall with its elliptical arches, some almost pointed. Wooden tie beams are used, as at Ukhaidir, and the *mihrab* aisle is notably wider than that at al-Aqsa in Jerusalem. The arcades originally supported barrel vaults of unbaked brick, and the *riwaqs* were also barrel-vaulted perpendicularly to their outer walls (*Plate 43*). A date sometime between 750 (when the *minbar* was first permitted in all Friday mosques) and 789 (when the Abbasids first began to use the pointed arch consistently) has been suggested for the Tarik Khana. The building is simple, massive, and utterly without ornament, relying—much as do parts of the palace at Ukhaidir—on the heavy, rhythmic succession of pier and arch for its great force and dignity.

The Samarra of al-Mu'tasim

Harun al-Rashid died suddenly in Tus in 809; he had designated as his successor a younger son, al-Amin, to be succeeded thereafter by an older but more capable son, al-Ma'mun, half Persian, whom he named Governor of Khorassan. Enmity soon arose between the brothers: al-Amin, after declaring his own son his successor in 810, was murdered when al-Ma'mun's forces took Baghdad in 813. Al-Ma'mun, who remained in Merv, designated as his heir the Alid Prince Ali al-Rida, who was poisoned at Tus in 818. The next year al-Ma'mun himself entered Baghdad, where he attempted to impose the reform doctrine of Mu'tazilism upon the community. This was the doctrine of the created Koran, a kind of Islamic fundamentalism which at the same time emphasized the preeminence of the Caliph. The doctrine pleased neither the Sunni nor the Shi'ite sects, and Baghdad remained turbulent. To make matters worse, al-Ma'mun's brother and heir al-Mu'tasim (833–42) had amassed a Turkish slave army of over 4,000—which rose to 70,000 after his succession. These young *ghulams*, bought for the most part at Samarkand, had no local loyalties and made excellent soldiers, often being promoted to high military or civil rank. They were, however, so unpopular in Baghdad that in 836 al-Mu'tasim set out to find a new site for his palace administration and barracks. Before it was abandoned in 892, Samarra, his new city, about sixty miles north of Baghdad, came to occupy a narrow strip no less than 22 miles long, principally on the east bank of the Tigris. There were caliphal palaces, barracks, markets, two Friday mosques, and numerous gardens and private mansions unevenly distributed like those parts of Baghdad outside al-Mansur's

44. *Samarra, Kasr al-Jiss (Gypsum Palace), c. 836–37, plan*
45. *Samarra, Jausaq al-Kharqani, c. 836–37, Bab al-Amma Gate*

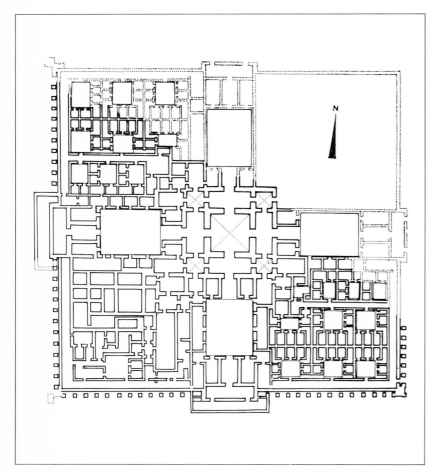

round city. Samarra—which must have had, Oleg Grabar believes, a roughly similar relationship to Baghdad as Versailles had to Paris—was never walled and indeed, with few exceptions, the palaces within it lacked even symbolic fortification.

Al-Mu'tasim, before settling upon Samarra proper, first chose a site nearer Baghdad but soon rejected it for another at a place called al-Qatul. Here construction continued until the soil was found unsuitable. There is at the southern end of Samarra a site called Qadisiyya where an octagonal fortified enclosure with habitation areas around the walls encloses what looks like an inner square. Nearby across a canal is an unfortified palace enclosure some 711 by 924 yards with the remains of a square ornamental lake on axis. If this site is indeed al-Qatul it seems that al-Mu'tasim repeated the arrangement of al-Mansur's secure circular city but built near it a more open palace—as al-Mansur himself had done about 773 at al-Khuld, a Baghdad suburb.

The Kasr al-Jiss

Excavations by the Iraqi government from 1936 to 1939 at Huwaissalat, on the west bank of the Tigris near the Ishaqi canal, uncovered what may be al-Mu'tasim's Gypsum Palace or Kasr al-Jiss, mentioned by Ibn Serapion around 945. The building (of baked brick and a kind of *terre pisée* found later in North Africa) is 167 square yards (*Plate 44*) and stood within an outer enclosure of mud brick 442 square yards, presumably with four portals corresponding to those of the inner enclosure. Here Abu Muslim's famous palace at Merv is resurrected complete with a central, almost certainly domed, chamber and four *iwans* leading to as many open courts. The outer enclosure may have accommodated courtiers, guards, and servants, as it did in al-Mansur's round city, though on a more modest scale here. The rows of buttresses close to the walls of the inner enclosure were probably linked to them and to each other with arches suggesting the blind arcading of the outer walls of Ukhaidir. They would have supported a fairly ample passage behind a parapet and suggest that there were fortifications as well—a feature absent in al-Mu'tasim's far grander establishment across the Tigris.

The Jausaq al-Kharqani

Although set some distance south of the Kasr al-Jiss, this vast structure of al-Mu'tasim's may have had the same relation to the former that his unfinished palace at al-Qadisiyya had to the octagonal enclosure there or al-Khuld to the circular city at Baghdad. In other words, it may have functioned as a *plaisance*, open and unfortified, with convenient access to a fortified keep in which considerable magnificence was available, though on a reduced scale.

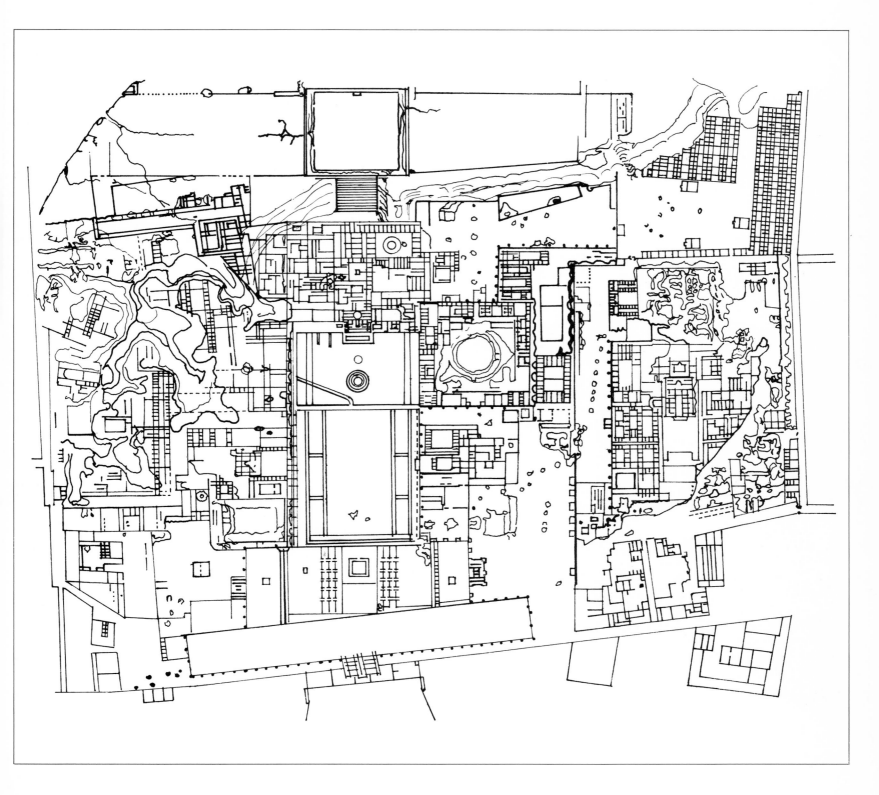

47. *Balkh, Masjid-i-Tarikh, reconstruction plan*
48. *Balkh, Masjid-i-Tarikh, detail of the stucco decoration*

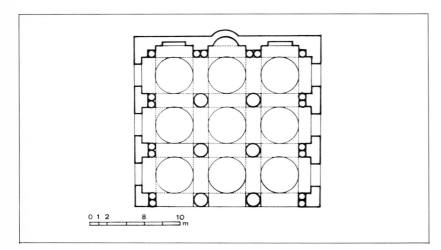

The area encompassed by the Jausaq, also called the Bayt al-Khalifa, is immense (*Plate 46*). From the pavilion on the Tigris opposite the Bab al-Amma, the gate of public audience, to the easternmost pavilion overlooking the racecourse in the game preserve the distance is no less than 1,531 yards. In area the building covers some 432 acres, of which 172 were gardens. Although it has been questioned, there seems little doubt that the Bab al-Amma (*Plate 45*), or gate of the people (*ummah*), served both as palace entrance and public audience hall where the canopied throne (*sidilla*) was placed in the central *iwan*. Behind it a complex series of courts led to the cruciform throne complex. There in a domed chamber at the junction of four basilical halls the Caliph held private audience as in a *diwan-i-khas*, and there he also may have slept surrounded by his guards. All these chambers were richly paneled in marble, carved stucco, and painted and gilded teakwood. Nothing could better express the god-like seclusion of the person of the Caliph just at that point in time when his real power was beginning to decline.

Ernst Herzfeld has reconstructed a carved stucco dado from the Bab al-Amma in a form which closely follows the scheme of the Mshatta facade, but the detail is quite different. Here the vine scrolls, with no animals at all, are so stylized as to be almost abstract and yet they retain enough reference to reality to allow recognition of the grape leaves. Either coeval with this or somewhat later appears the famous "bevelled" style of Samarra (*Plate 51*), which also appears in the throne room at the Jausaq, perhaps redecorated when al-Muntasir took up residence there after 847.

ABBASID ARCHITECTURE IN TRANSOXIANA

The Masjid-i-Tarikh at Balkh

By comparing its stuccoes with Samarra-type work found on the Bab al-Amma Lisa Golombek, who first recognized its importance, dates the Masjid-i-Tarikh in the first half of the ninth century (*Plates 48, 49*). She believes both its decoration and plan (*Plate 47*) to have been imported from the West into Central Asia. The structure was once a pavilion, formed on a quincunx plan of nine domed squares open on all but the *qibla* side, with a two-columned portico to the northeast. It must at one time have stood in an enclosure that protected its users from the bustling city nearby. Such small oratories sometimes were associated with family burial enclosures, like that of the Sharif Tabatabai in Cairo of about 950, but closer in plan to this building are the Tleta Biban or three-doored mosque at Kairouan of 866 and the famous Bib Mardun Mosque in Toledo of 999. Their original purpose remains unknown. Ettinghausen has recently suggested that the central quincunx of the throne hall at Khirbat al-Mafjar may have been the model for this series.

49. *Balkh, Masjid-i-Tarikh, view of the ruins*

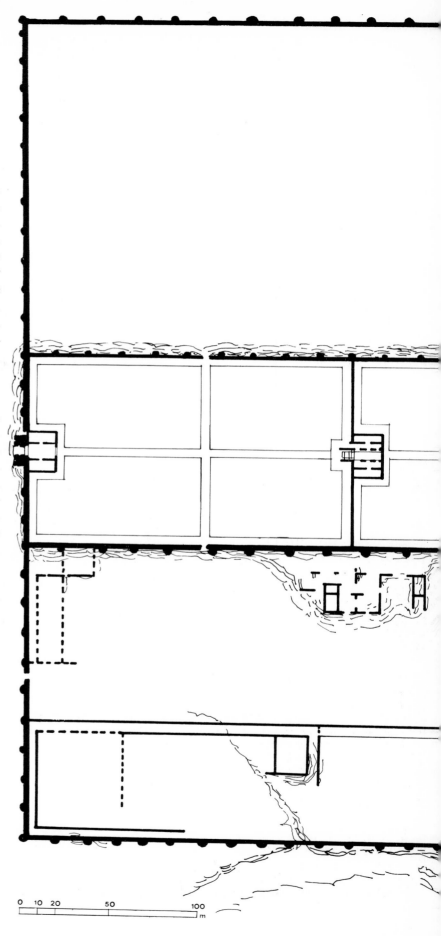

The Samarra of the Later Caliphs

Al-Mutawakkil (847–61) took up residence at the palace of Haruni, constructed by his predecessor. He installed one son, al-Muntasir, in the Jausaq al-Kharqani, another in a palace called al-Matira, and the third, al-Mutazz, in the Bulkawara Palace. In 859–60 he ordered an entirely new quarter, the Jafariya, built to the north, complete with a Friday mosque (that of Abu Dulaf), a vast palace, and all other necessary administrative, commercial, and residential buildings. The work was complete by March of 861, when al-Mutawakkil moved in, saying: "Now I know that I am a King for I have built myself a town and live in it." His joy was brief, as he was murdered the following December. His successors then returned to Samarra proper, remaining there until the seat of power was returned to Baghdad.

The Bulkawara Palace

This complex, in which the name of al-Mutazz appears on a beam of the throne room, cannot have been begun much before 849 when he first used this name, nor after 859 when construction of the Jafariya district was begun. The palace has better defined boundaries than the Jausaq al-Kharqani and is entered from the northeast rather than from the Tigris bank (*Plate 50*). A prominent central axis is punctuated by a series of monumental gates and courts arranged like Persian *chahr baghs* or four-part gardens. The third and fourth gates take the form of triple *iwans* with porticoes. Then follows the cruciform throne complex, another large triple *iwan* facing the Tigris and another *chahr bagh*, and finally the river, at a distance of some 820 yards. The southeasternmost *iwan* was encrusted in glass and mother-of-pearl mosaic forming vine tendrils against a gold ground. The Paradise symbolism of this and the four-part garden was certainly intentional.

The stucco ornament throughout was in what Creswell designates as Style C, sometimes also called the "bevelled" style or (Herzfeld) *schrägschnit*. This consists of the endless repetition of intricate curvilinear—but not interlaced—ornament totally abstract in nature (*Plate 51*). It was usually cast, but ornament of identical style appears all the way from Egypt to Transoxiana carved in wood and marble as well. Creswell believes this style began to coexist with the earlier styles about 847, but it is also possible it had originated before then, only becoming more popular as construction accelerated under al-Mutawakkil. A Central Asian, possibly even a very early Turkish origin, has been suggested, perhaps transmitted by metalwork.

The Great Mosque of al-Mutawakkil

Work began in 848/49 on Samarra's Great Mosque, the replacement of an earlier Friday mosque, and the dedication took place in 852.

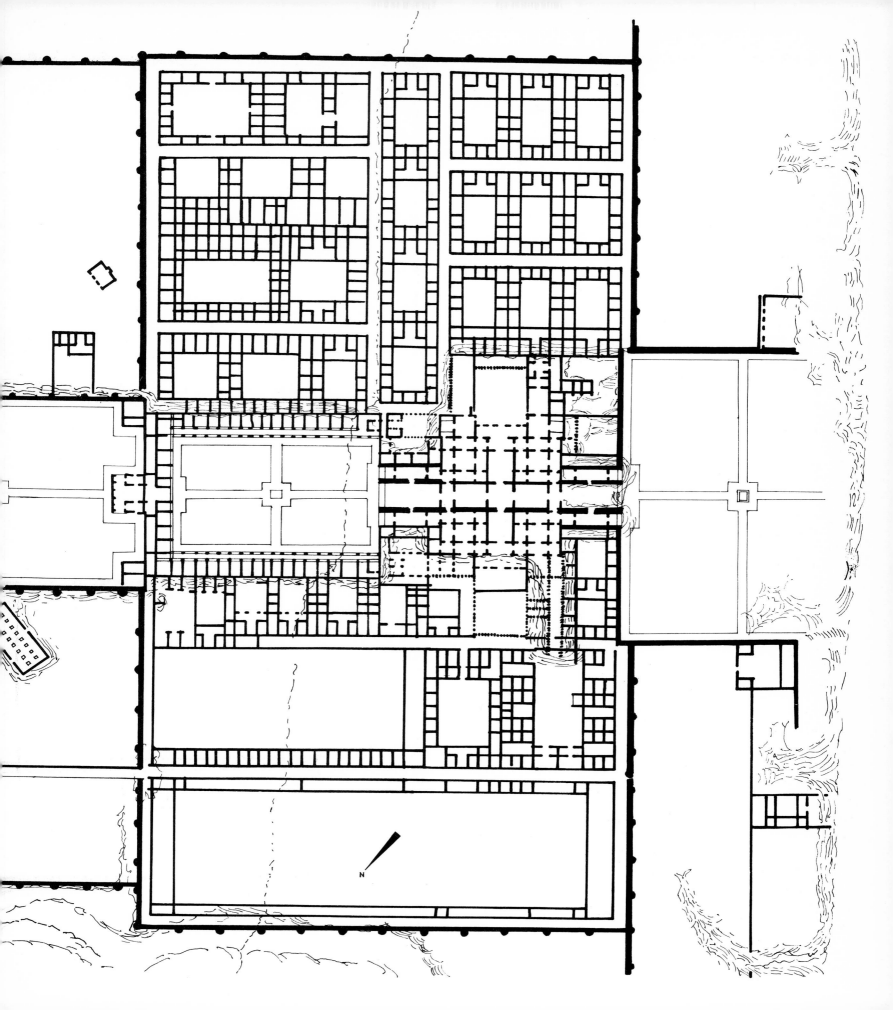

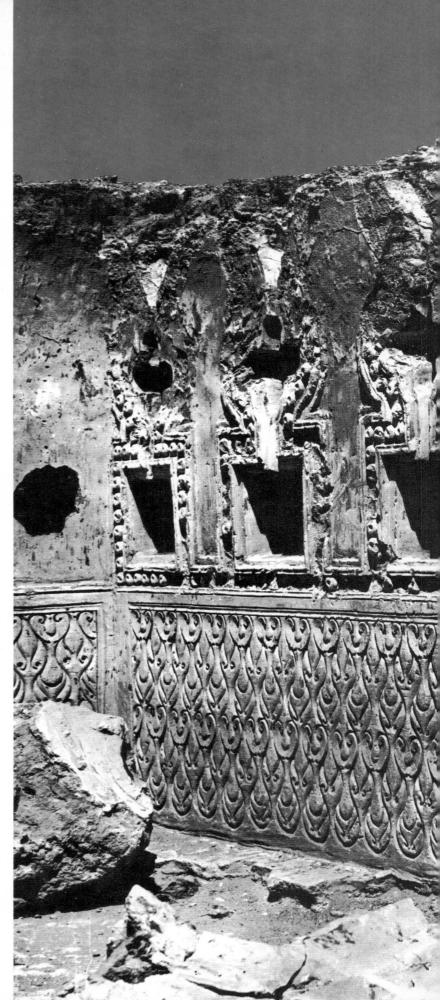

Today only the towered enclosure walls of burnt brick survive (*Plates 53, 54*), once surmounted by stepped crenellations above a row of circular medallions exactly like those at Ctesiphon. They enclose a vast space 787 by 512 feet, still the largest in the Islamic world (*Plate 52*). The interior supports, all fallen, were compound piers composed of octagonal brick cores disguised as marble and surrounded by four salvaged column shafts. Similar piers occurred at Khirbat al-Mafjar but in coursed masonry. The flat roof of teak rested directly on the piers; hence, the prayer hall was multidirectional like those of nearly all the other so-called hypostyle mosques of Iraq. The remains of fallen glass mosaics and slots for wooden paneling around the *mihrab* attest to the richness of the original ornament. Thirteen portals, probably with wooden lintels under segmental relieving arches, opened onto an inner *ziyadah* (addition or extension) enclosing all but the *qibla* wall. This in turn was enclosed by a vast outer *ziyadah* adjoining a shop-lined street. The famous Malwiya, the "snail shell" minaret to the north and exactly on axis (*Plate 55*), conforms to an ancient local tradition going back to the ziggurats of Khorsabad and Babylon, the latter still recognizable as a spirally ramped tower, though square, as late as the twelfth century. A certain type of spiral tower of uncertain purpose in Sassanian Persia may have served as an intermediary, however.

The Qubbat al-Sulaybiyah

A survey of the literature made by Herzfeld informs us that the first caliph whose burial place was generally known was al-Muntasir (d. 862), because his Greek mother had obtained permission to build him a tomb. This structure, the Qubbat al-Sulaybiyah, is built of the curious artificial stone of later Samarran buildings, and lies on the west bank of the Tigris. In all, three tombs have been found at this site: we know that two later caliphs were buried here, making it almost certain that the third one (al-Muntasir's) is the oldest monumental tomb in the history of Islamic architecture (*Plate 56*).

Since the inner and outer octagons are open on all four sides and never had doors, the Koranic injunction that the tomb of a believer should be open to the sky was not entirely violated. The source of the design is certainly the Dome of the Rock in Jerusalem, with an intermediary model being the fountain at Khirbat al-Mafjar. Creswell calls this type a canopy tomb, which may be square or octagonal provided it has portals on at least three or more sides. The only octagonal canopy tombs with ambulatories similar to this Samarran example appear in fourteenth-century India (see Chapter XV), but it has been impossible as yet to trace the connection, if any, between them.

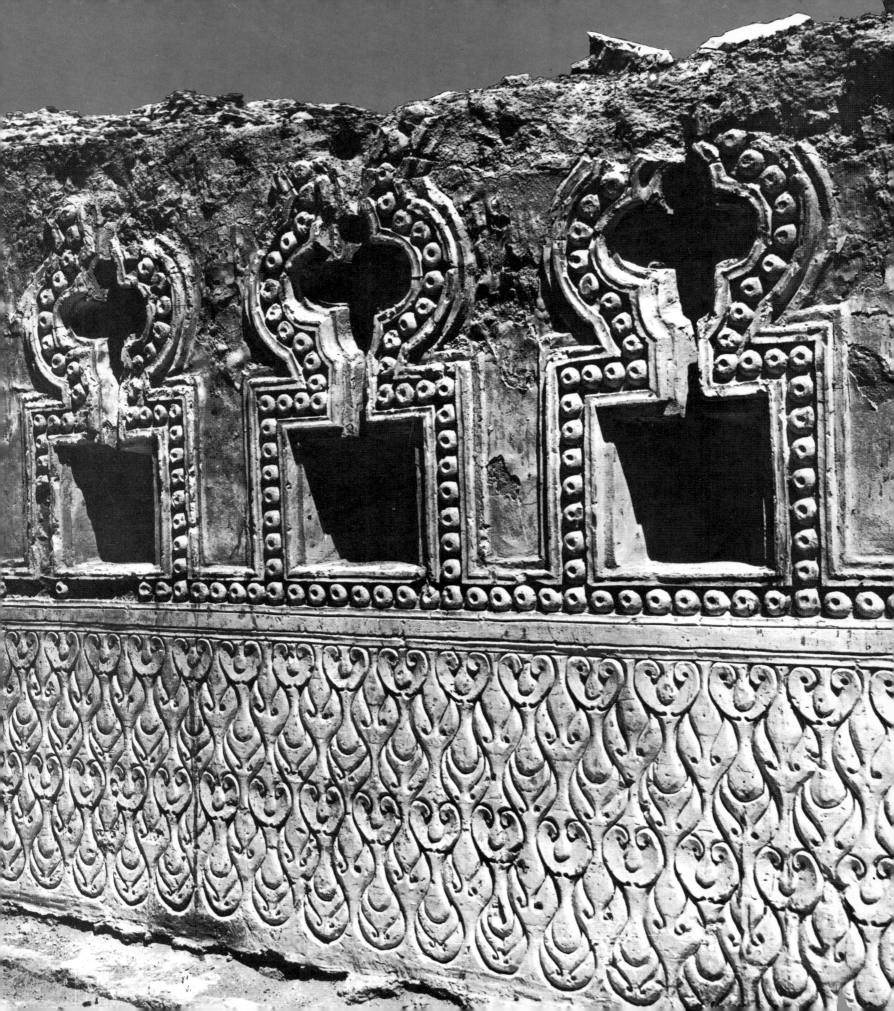

52. *Samarra, Great Mosque of al-Mutawakkil, 848/49–852, plan*

53. *Samarra, Great Mosque of al-Mutawakkil, aerial view*
54. *Samarra, Great Mosque of al-Mutawakkil, the Malwiya (minaret)*
55. *Samarra, Mosque of Abu Dulaf, minaret* ▷

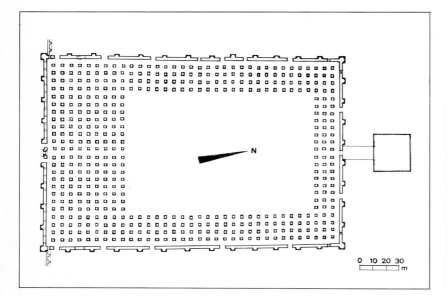

56. *Samarra, Qubbat al-Sulaybiyah, begun 862, plan*
57. *Cairo, Mosque of Ibn Tulun, 876/77–879, plan*

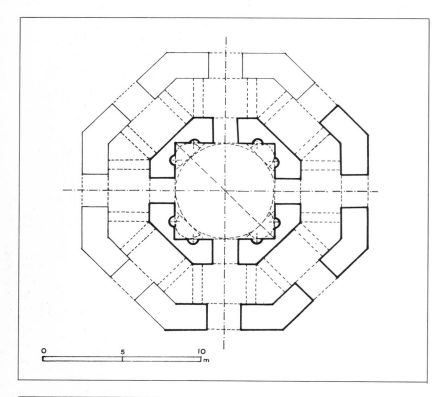

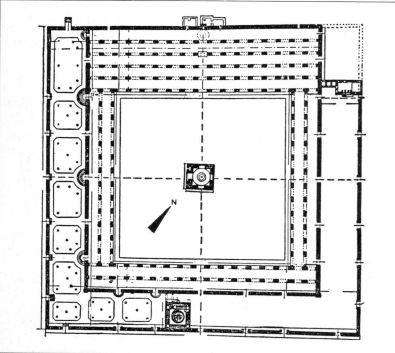

ABBASID ARCHITECTURE IN CAIRO

The Mosque of Ibn Tulun

Ahmad Ibn Tulun, born in 835, was the son of a Turkish slave received as tribute from Bukhara by the Caliph al-Ma'mun. Ahmad, who was given an excellent education considering his lowly birth, soon distinguished himself in the caliphal service and was appointed deputy to the viceroy of Egypt—who, as was the custom, received revenues from Egypt but resided in Samarra. In 868 Ahmad set out with an army for his new post in Cairo, where he soon succeeded to the governorship of both Egypt and Syria, founding a dynasty which survived until 905. In 870 Ahmad founded al-Qatai, a separate quarter bounded on the north by the hill on which stood the citadel (at whose foot he also built a palace and a hippodrome) and on the south by his congregational mosque. A Dar al-Imara was added on the mosque's *qibla* side (876/77–879) after the old mosque of Amr had become too small to accommodate the congregation.

The mosque, entirely of well-fired red brick faced in stucco, follows the tradition of Samarra in its use of *ziyadahs* and of Abu Dulaf in its arcades on piers. At the corners of each pier an attached column is imitated in brick, recalling the real columns used by al-Mutawakkil in Samarra. In its plan (*Plate 57*) Ibn Tulun's structure recalls the earlier Iraqi tradition of Kufa and Wasit, although without the semicircular buttresses found there and in Samarra. The *sahn* is about 990 square feet and, although the walls of the mosque proper form a rectangle about 400 by 459 feet, the three *ziyadahs* bring the outer dimensions back to an almost perfect square of 1,744 feet (*Plate 58*). The outer wall of the northwest *ziyadah*, once the principal facade, has a *pishtaq* about 3 feet high corresponding to the width of the mosque proper, which rises some 16 feet higher than the outer walls. The view must once have been very striking, with five regularly spaced central portals. The symmetry may originally have been further accented by a spiral minaret on axis. The present stone minaret (*Plate 59*) is, as Creswell has shown, a reconstruction made by Lajin in 1296. It is off-center and has no organic relation to the earlier building. Tulunid literary sources and others of the tenth century affirm that Ibn Tulun's original minaret was of spiral form and of stone; hence it was probably on axis, as at the two Samarra mosques.

It would be difficult anywhere to match the solemn peace of the interior, where a dignified procession of heavy piers and broad arches channels movement down the spacious aisles (*Plate 61*) and muffles all sounds. Indeed, the building can never have been very successful as a preaching mosque—which may explain why Lajin's refounding included functions more appropriate to its use as a *madrasa*. The

59. *Cairo, Mosque of Ibn Tulun, sahn (in background, minaret of 1296)*
60. *Cairo, Mosque of Ibn Tulun, interior, view of the* mihrab *and* minbar
61. *Cairo, Mosque of Ibn Tulun, interior* ▷

broad and robust stucco moldings of the central *mihrab* (*Plate 60*) as well as its marble columns with their Byzantine capitals are what remain from the period of Ibn Tulun, but the paneling of the niche itself and the mosaic inscriptions above it must date, as does the *minbar* and the wooden dome, from the time of Lajin.

The carved (not cast) stucco ornament of the soffits of the arches, their surroundings, the exquisite stucco window grilles, and what is left of the wooden lintels of the numerous portals indicate that all Samarran styles were here mixed, although the "bevelled" manner survives only in the woodwork. The geometric nets which frame the typical vine leaves and palmettes in the soffits of the arches and which form the window grilles are based on the same constructions found in the marble window grilles at Damascus and Khirbat al-Mafjar. The long foundation inscription, repeated at least four times, was inscribed on a wooden frieze above the inner arcades in a position comparable to the inscription in the Dome of the Rock. That organic unity between architecture and epigraphy so essential to the character of mature Islamic architecture seems not yet to have developed here in Ibn Tulun's work of the late ninth century.

Conclusion

With the triumph of the Abbasids, the Umayyad architecture of the ancient cities of Kufa, Basra, and Wasit began to prevail. Unfortunately, we know rather little about it, but these were the regions in which the flat-roofed hypostyle mosque on wooden (later stone) columns was first evolved, probably based on the idea—though not the fact—of Muhammad's house at Medina. Here too one often hears the architects identified as Persian. It was they who brought to Islamic palace architecture the Sassanian four-part court and probably the *iwan* leading to a domed chamber. Their influence must have been much augmented by the influx of Khorassanians from eastern Persia under the caliphs of the late eighth century and by the introduction of Sassanian ceremonial rites into the Islamic court.

With the "bevelled" style at Samarra and even with the more conservative arch soffits at Ibn Tulun's mosque in Cairo, certain types of ornament appear which, though simpler than they will be later, have already acquired a dynamic and limitless movement; thus a kind of infinite growth becomes possible which is no longer contained within the frame that bears the decoration. Such will be the development of ornament, so essential a part of all later Islamic architecture.

The first Muslim city in North Africa was Kairouan, founded in 663/64 by Uqba ibn Nafi, who fell in a battle with the Berbers twenty years later. Arab history in the region remains obscure even through the conquest of Spain in 711. Fanned by the Kharjite movement brought from Iraq, Berber unrest was continuous and erupted into major rebellions in 740 and 750. Sidi Uqba built a mosque and a Dar al-Imara at Kairouan, but they must have been very modest affairs. After he had established at least temporary peace with the Berbers, Yazid ibn Hatim (Abbasid governor of Ifriqiya) rebuilt the mosque at Kairouan in 772–74. Alexandre Lézine has recently shown that Yazid's well-cut stone *mihrab* survives as a doorway within the *maqsura* of the present building. This is the oldest Islamic monument in North Africa and proof that the horseshoe arch was already in use at this early date. Yazid's mosque occupied the southwest corner of the present structure (*Plate 62*), which was enlarged by Ziyadat Allah I in 836. Yazid's prayer hall was about 164 feet wide and as deep as that of 836. A surviving cistern, already called the "old" cistern in al-Bakri's day and almost directly on axis with the *mihrab*, probably occupied the center of Yazid's *sahn*. These discoveries make it impossible to claim that the minaret was, as previously thought, the work of the Caliph Hisham, since it would have been well outside the *sahns* of either of the earlier structures.

The Ribat of Sussa

Recent work on this monument suggests that only the southeast tower was erected in 821 by Ziyadat Allah I, as its inscription affirms (*Plate 65*). The rest of the building, like the similar but less well preserved structure at Monastir, dates from the late eighth century, at least before 796. A *ribat*, following Creswell's definition, was a small fortified barracks built on the frontiers of Islam and garrisoned with volunteers who, in the intervals between skirmishes, gave themselves up to religious devotions and learning.

The Ribat of Sussa, much of which has been preserved, consists of a fortified enclosure about 371 square feet, internally defended by circular and semicircular turrets on square or rectangular bases and by a monumental projecting south portal (*Plate 63*). The forms throughout, though in ashlar, recall the rubble masonry of Ukhaidir or the brickwork of Samarra. Inside, two stories of barrel-vaulted cells surround a court with a single-storied cloister supporting a terrace. A mosque two bays deep occupies the south side of the second floor. Its eleven barrel-vaulted aisles are perpendicular to the *qibla* wall; four portals open onto the terrace (*Plate 64*). The *mihrab* is marked by a small cupola which crowns the monumental entrance but has no actual connection with the prayer hall below (*Plates 66, 67*). All the

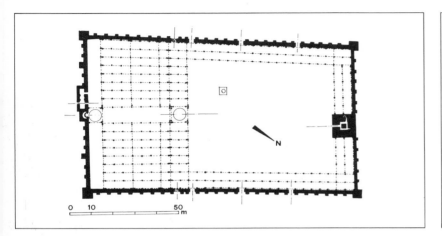

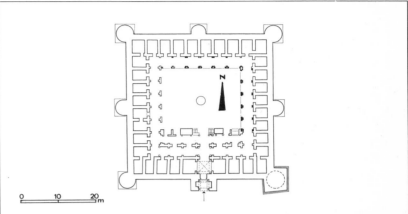

◁ 65. *Sussa, Ribat, wall and portal*
66. *Sussa, Ribat, interior of the portal*
67. *Sussa, Ribat, portal*

arches, unless rebuilt, are round and either slightly stilted or slightly horseshoe-shaped. Ziyadat Allah's tall cylindrical tower, rising from a square base which he also rebuilt, may have been a signal tower allowing communication with neighboring *ribats* (Monastir's, for example), but its primary use was probably that it has today, as a minaret for the mosque within the Ribat itself and for the nearby Friday mosque in the city. The monument probably belongs to the period when, under Aghlabid prosperity, the province of Ifriqiya for a time ceased to be an outpost on the frontier and when the *ribats*, while retaining their religious function, ceased to have a military purpose. The Ribat at Sussa is one of the extremely rare examples (if not the only one intact) of a type of structure of great importance to Islam whenever its borders with the *Dar al-Harb* became relatively stabilized.

The Great Mosque of Kairouan

In 800 Harun al-Rashid granted Ibrahim ibn al-Aghlab, son of a Khorassanian officer, Ifriqiya in return for an annual tribute. After Ibrahim had suppressed the last of the Kharjite Berber rebellions, his office was made hereditary. Under Ziyadat Allah I (817–38), the province's third ruler, the conquest of Sicily was begun. With expansion Kairouan prospered and the size of its congregation outgrew the mosque of Yazid. According to recent studies by the late Alexandre Lézine, Ziyadat Allah's new mosque, finished in 836, consisted of a prayer hall (*Plate 71*) about 236 feet wide, with sixteen aisles of seven bays each flanking a much wider *mihrab* aisle (*Plate 72*) leading to a dome over the *mihrab*. The support for the latter here generated the typical T-shaped plan of so many later North African mosques and goes back, if not to al-Walid's mosque at Medina, certainly to al-Mahdi's al-Aqsa of 780. It is most unlikely that there were *riwaqs*. Of the two doors that are today blocked off, that to the west by Ziyadat must have led directly into the now much larger *sahn*, whose northwest boundary is marked by Ziyadat's minaret (*Plate 70*). The latter is built off axis, perhaps as a miscalculation (the whole plan is irregular), but also perhaps deliberately to leave room for a portal on the *mihrab* axis. Since the entire northeast wall was rebuilt after 1300, only excavation would provide the answer. Throughout Ziyadat Allah's structure the arches, whether of brick—as are most of the outer walls—or of stone, were predominantly round or very slightly horseshoe-shaped; those supporting the gored dome were slightly pointed. According to al-Bakri, at the time of the destruction of Yazid's mosque in 774 the people strongly protested the dismantling of the "*mihrab* of Sidi Uqba." Since the first *mihrab* in all Islam had been introduced into al-Walid's rebuilding of the mosque at Medina in 706,

69. *Kairouan, Great Mosque, aerial view*

70. *Kairouan, Great Mosque,* sahn *and minaret* ▷
71. *Kairouan, Great Mosque, prayer hall* ▷

72. *Kairouan, Great Mosque,* mihrab *aisle*

73. *Kairouan, Great Mosque, "narthex" of Abu Ibrahim Ahmad, 862–63* ▷

74. *Mahdiya, restored plan (c. 921) of the peninsula. 1) mosque 2) palace 3) harbor*

75. *Mahdiya, Great Mosque, central portal*

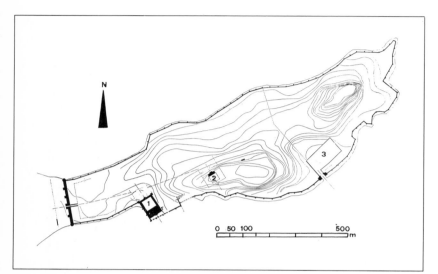

it is unlikely that Sidi Uqba would also have built one. It is apparent that by the ninth century popular belief had identified Yazid's mosque with that of Ziyadat Allah, which as we have seen left the earlier mosque largely intact. Ziyadat Allah's own *mihrab* was completely rebuilt by Abu Ibrahim Ahmad (856–63), Ifriqiya's fifth Amir, who added luster tiles and richly carved openwork marble panels brought from Samarra or possibly Syria. He also commissioned the magnificent *minbar* of teakwood. During the same period (862–63) Abu Ibrahim added the *riwaqs* as well as a "narthex" which deepened the prayer hall by two bays and which featured another dome, now much rebuilt, at the entrance of the *mihrab* aisle (*Plates 69, 73*).

The last significant addition to the building was a wooden *maqsura* in an unusual position. It did not enclose the principal *mihrab* or the *minbar*, but only the *imam's* door and the old *mihrab*, then probably believed to be Sidi Uqba's. The work executed before 1042 bears the name of al-Muizz (1016–62), the Zirid governor of Kairouan who in 1041 had renounced his Shi'ite overlords, the Fatimids of Cairo. In revenge the Fatimids encouraged bands of unassimilated Bedouin nomads to move into Ifriqiya and the Maghrib. This movement, the Hillalian invasion, forced the Zirids to evacuate Kairouan in 1042; thus began a period of decline for the Great Mosque, arrested only by the Hafsids in the thirteenth century. It is now believed that it was they who doubled the arcades of the *mihrab* aisle and extensively rebuilt all the facades overlooking the *sahn*.

The marble panels of Abu Ibrahim Ahmad's *mihrab* and the contemporaneous teak *minbar* show a distinct similarity to a marble *mihrab* now in the Baghdad Museum which may have belonged to the mosque of al-Mansur. They are also very similar to certain carved wood panels of about 780 in the Mosque of al-Aqsa at Jerusalem, showing the same balanced but not yet assimilated mixture of Eastern and Western motifs characteristic of all early Islamic art through the tenth century, before a new style had been fully defined. The same ambiguity is apparent in the shapes of the arches: Ifriqiya had not and would not for some years to come adapt a consistently pointed arch, although this had already occurred (789) in the cistern at Ramlah and in the buildings at Samarra. It is probable that the pointed arch was introduced into Ifriqiya only in Almoravid times during the late eleventh century, perhaps in the same wave of renewed Eastern influence which brought with it the *muqarnas* vault as well.

The Great Mosque of Mahdiya

Certain Alid descendants of the Prophet, including the Idrissids at Fez, had already carved out princedoms for themselves in the Maghrib by the late eighth century, but they did so as individuals with the

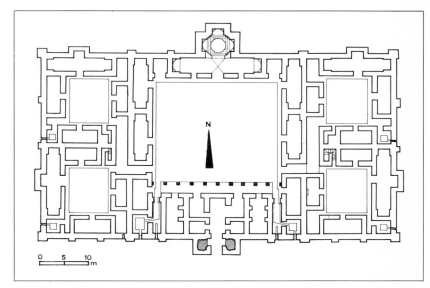

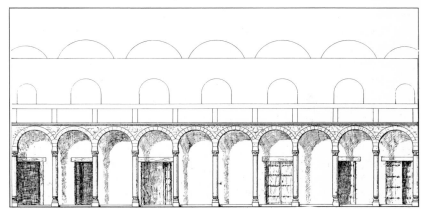

minimum support of personal followers. In the case of the Fatimids the procedure was very different. From the East they sent forth a propagandist, Abu Abd Allah al-Shi'i, in the late ninth century to rouse the Kutama Berbers to revolt. Abu conquered the Aghlabids and took Kairouan in 909. Ubayd Allah, the Fatimid claimant, then had to be rescued under mysterious circumstances from Sijilmasa, south of Marrakesh, for his triumphal entry into Kairouan the next year. After the failure of an attack on Egypt in 913–14, Ubayd Allah (909–34), realizing more preparation would be needed to succeed in its capture, founded a new capital at Mahdiya in a well-defended position. There his regime withstood a serious Berber revolt that was only finally put down in 947.

Very little remains of Ubayd Allah's capital (*Plate 74*). It was heavily fortified across the narrow neck of the peninsula, had a Dar al-Imara, two palaces for the Caliph and his heir, an enclosed harbor, an arsenal, and a Great Mosque. Like al-Mansur's round city of Baghdad, it was not so much a city as an administrative center with a commercial and residential quarter outside the walls. Work began in 916; Ubayd Allah moved his residence there from Kairouan in 921, in which year (or a little later) the Great Mosque was begun. Except for the north facade the building had already been destroyed and rebuilt several times. In 1965–66 a total restoration was effected, and beyond the monumental entrance the structure is entirely new. However, excavation carried out by Lézine in preparation for the rebuilding revealed the original tenth-century plan almost completely. This proves to have been based largely upon Kairouan, but with certain important modifications. A monumental projecting portal (*Plate 75*), borrowed from palace architecture and here applied to a mosque for the first time in Islam, is flanked by two lesser portals and leads to a squarish *sahn* of about 138 by 164 feet. Single-aisled *riwaqs* surround the *sahn* on four sides, linked by square chambers at the corners. The south facade of the *sahn*, supported by doubled columns, resembles the "narthex" of 862–63 at Kairouan. The prayer hall, nine-aisled and three bays deep, shows the familiar T-shaped plan of Kairouan but emphasizes the *mihrab* aisle more strongly with its clusters of four-column shafts. Finally, the *mihrab* dome was supported by extraordinary compound piers in coursed masonry that imitated eight clustered shafts. Since the original *qibla* wall fell into the sea in the late tenth or early eleventh century, only its position is certain in the reconstruction.

The modifications made in the adaptation of Kairouan's plan all had a single purpose—to emphasize the semidivine status of the Shi'ite Caliph. Mahdiya's center portal in its monumental recall of a Roman triumphal arch is like the bath-audience hall portal at

Khirbat al-Mafjar and the multiple portals of the processional way at the Bulkawara Palace in Samarra. Through it, on axis with the *mihrab*, Ubayd Allah would have proceeded between files of his retainers to the strongly emphasized *mihrab* aisle, doubtless reserved for him in its entirety as a *maqsura*. The north facade with its side portals recalls the triple facades of so many of Samarran palaces—even to the projecting corner towers which here seem never to have supported minarets. It is likely that the *muezzin* made the call to prayer from the roof of the center portal.

The Palace of Ziri at Ashir

The badly ruined north facade of a palace west of the Great Mosque at Mahdiya probably belonged to Ubayd Allah. A projecting portal led to a vestibule from which one had to turn east or west to enter the central court. Though a far larger building, its plan is strikingly similar to a palace recently uncovered at Ashir in Algeria. The Sanhaja Berber, Ziri, a supporter of the Fatimid Caliph al-Qaim (934–46), founded Ashir in 935/36. It is said that an architect and materials were sent from Mahdiya. It was Ziri's son, Yusuf Buluggin, appointed Governor of Ifriqiya after the departure of the Caliph al-Muizz (953–75) for Cairo in 972, who founded the Zirid Dynasty.

The palace at Ashir is in plan (*Plate 76*) notably unlike either Umayyad or Abbasid palaces. A monumental portal along the south side very like that of the Great Mosque at Mahdiya led into a vestibule with guard rooms and then by two doors off-center to a round-arched portico (*Plate 77*). Opposite, across a square central court, was a three-doored transverse antechamber; behind this a cruciform *diwan*, very probably domed, must have sheltered a throne. Flanking the central block are four separate but entirely equal apartments, each with its own court and transverse audience hall with a central niche. A third form, the Zirid *bayt*, is thus added to those of the Umayyads and Abbasids already described. It seems probable they were occupied by Ziri's four legitimate wives. Like the Abbasid *bayt* as transformed into the Egyptian *qa'a*, the Zirid *bayt* became the basic form for the houses of most if not all the later dynasties of the Maghrib down to the nineteenth century.

The Qala of the Bani Hammad

Under the great-grandson of Ziri the Zirid domain, grown too large to be governed from Kairouan alone, was divided in 1015. The western portion was granted to Hammad ibn Buluggin ibn Ziri, whose residence was the Qala of the Bani Hammad in what is present-day Algeria. The ruins of the Qala were first investigated by L. de Beylié in 1908 and sporadically by others ever since. They are very difficult

to date securely, since the Hammadids were forced to withdraw from the Qala to Bougie on the coast during the Hillalian invasions; they frequently returned, however, and work could have continued on it as late as its final destruction by the Almohads in 1152.

The Qala is an irregular walled enclosure extending up to the fortress of Takerbous (*Plate 78*). The central residential complex, probably the oldest part (*Plate 80*), was bounded on the south by a mosque (*Plate 79*) which may belong to the early eleventh century. The latter, a rectangle of 184 by 200 feet, had a wooden roof supported on antique columns. The *maqsura*, entered by a door to the left of the *mihrab*, was provided with a niche into which the *minbar* could recede—a tenth-century innovation characteristic of North Africa and Spain. A wall, probably once pierced by thirteen doors (as many as there were aisles), separated the prayer hall from the rectangular *sahn* with its *riwaqs* on all four sides; this followed the model of Mahdiya but even more the mosque at Medina al-Zahra in Spain. The square stone minaret projects into the *sahn* on axis with the *mihrab* as at Kairouan and Spain. Its southern facade (*Plate 81*) is richly decorated with lobate, mixtilinear, and round arches, and with pointed biforia; there are also round-headed blind niches with ceramic encrustation. The whole recalls the twelfth-century Norman palaces of Sicily, which may owe more of their inspiration to the Zirids and Hammadids than to the Fatimids of Egypt.

The central residential complex (*Plate 80*) has at its southernmost end the vast Dar al-Bahr or Sea Palace, which is approached from the east through a monumental portal, once domed, set in a niched facade. This leads through an elaborate series of long transverse halls to a shallow rectangular lake, formerly encircled by a cloister, of about 226 by 160 feet. Along this axis and flanked by reception halls a very large room or courtyard, now in ruins, leads to a western court. The whole suggests the central portion of the palace at Ashir, albeit on a much grander scale. Further to the north a complex identified by de Beylié as the private quarters of the Emirs consists of an outer court into which protrudes a throne complex, probably domed, behind a transverse antechamber. North of this through a monumental portal is a square court with another audience chamber, similar to one of the four *bayts* at Ashir. Excavations in 1952 revealed that the Qasr al-Salam or Palace of Peace, southwest of the main complex, also has an exterior throne hall with private apartments to the right, while a very similar set of structures has appeared near the Qasr al-Manar or Lighthouse Palace, directly east of the main complex. These inner and outer reception halls again suggest a *diwan-i-am* and a *diwan-i-khas*. Unfortunately, the exact chronology of all these structures is very uncertain—doubly so

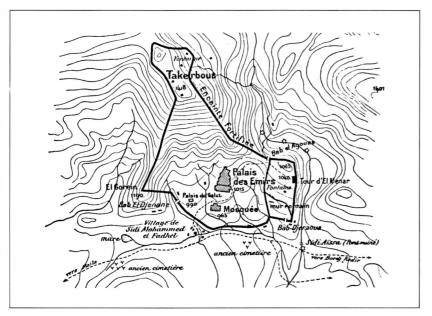

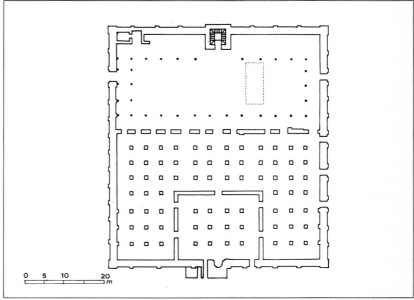

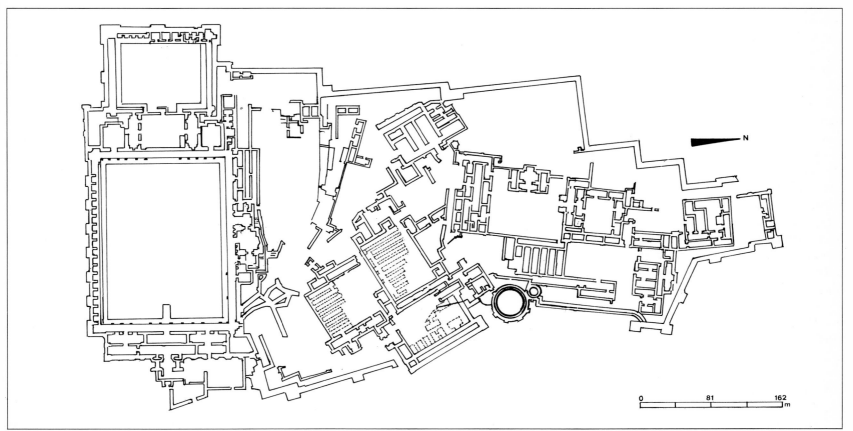

78. *Algeria, Qala of the Bani Hammad, 1015–1152, site plan*

79. *Algeria, Qala of the Bani Hammad, plan of the mosque*

80. *Algeria, Qala of the Bani Hammad, plan of the central residential complex*

because in the Qasr al-Salam and at the portal of the Qasr near the al-Manar unmistakable remains of *muqarnas* or honeycomb vaulting in plaster were found in 1956. All that can now be said is that these probably were installed well after 1015, since they belong to structures situated well away from the central core. Most likely they date from the late eleventh century and thus are the second oldest in North Africa (after the Egyptian examples of 1085–87). A full discussion of the *muqarnas* vault will be found in Chapter VIII.

Conclusion

Prior to the establishment of the Almoravid and Almohad empires, the Islamic architecture of North Africa belongs to its developmental or archaic period. Nevertheless, certain long-lived types become fixed at this time. The hypostyle mosque with a T-plan and aisles perpendicular to the *qibla*, based on al-Mahdi's al-Aqsa of 780, is established as the standard pattern for North Africa. The introduction of the Zirid *bayt* and the cruciform throne room behind a transverse reception hall will affect all future palace design down to the fourteenth-century Alhambra in Spain, and consequently sumptuous houses in general from Tunisia west through Algeria and Morocco. Finally, a major decorative element—the *muqarnas*—appears probably in the late eleventh century. It seems strange that this should first be seen in as remote and provincial a site as the Qala in Algeria, but until more is known of the palaces near Kairouan or at Bougie this is all the knowledge we have about the honeycomb vault.

Although conditions were too chaotic to have permitted the construction of artistic monuments in Spain between its conquest by Arabs and Berbers in 711 and the establishment of the Umayyad Emirate in 756, a society was in the process of formation there that was in many ways unique in Islam. The Muslims, being a military force, lacked women and so nearly all married Spanish wives. Furthermore, this was the period when many Christians converted to Islam and they, along with the Mozarabic Christians, retained their Romance language, giving Islamic culture in Spain a unique flavor soon reflected also in architecture. Such was the land Abd er-Rahman I ibn Mu'awiyah (756–88), grandson of Hisham and the last Umayyad, found when he arrived at Seville in 755. A year later in Cordoba he was recognized as Amir of all Spain. Rebellions among the Arabs and Berbers as well as intrigues among his own followers in Cordoba probably delayed his architectural projects until nearly the end of his reign.

The Great Mosque of Cordoba: First Stages

Abd er-Rahman's stone-walled Friday mosque of 786/87 took only a year to build. It had a prayer hall with eleven aisles of twelve bays each, perpendicular to the *qibla* wall (*Plate 82*)—in the manner of al-Mahdi's mosque in Jerusalem and probably of its Umayyad predecessor, but without a dome over the *mihrab*. The *sahn* had no *riwaqs* and communicated with the prayer hall through doors set between heavy T-shaped piers to counter the thrusts of the unique double arcades of horseshoe arches below and round ones above (*Plate 84*). These, modeled after a Roman aqueduct at Merida, copy late Roman masonry even in their alternation of red brick courses and white stone voussoirs. They supported the flat wooden roofs of the aisles, which were indicated on the exterior by parallel gables. This last innovation was soon exported to Morocco, where it became standard. The exterior walls, at least those of the prayer hall, had rectangular buttresses like those of the Kairouan mosque of 774; both buttresses and walls were capped by stepped merlons. The Portal of St. Stephen (*Plate 83*), although partially rebuilt in 855, retains its original tripartite form and some of its rather coarse vegetal decoration. The interior facade, very likely dating from 786/87, shows a horseshoe-shaped arch within an *alfiz* or rectilinear frame crowned by miniature stepped merlons in relief. It is strikingly like Kairouan's *mihrab* of only a decade earlier. The horseshoe arch was frequent in Visigothic Spain before the Arab conquest, and it often also appeared in decorative contexts in Iraq and Syria and seems to have been in fairly regular use in Ifriqiya. It was, however, under Abd er-Rahman's successors at Cordoba through the ninth and tenth centuries that the form was to be most widely exploited for both its structural and its decorative possibilities.

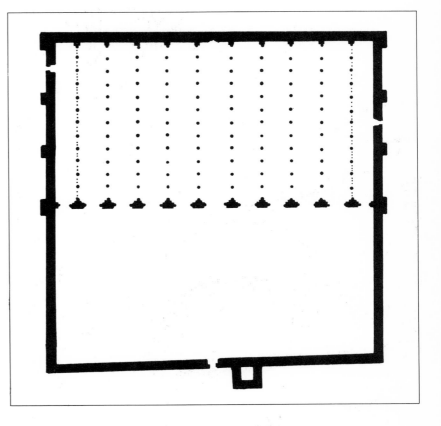

82. *Cordoba, Great Mosque of Abd er-Rahman I, 786/87, plan*

83. *Cordoba, Great Mosque, Portal of St. Stephen, 786/87, partially rebuilt 855*
84. *Cordoba, Great Mosque, arcades of Abd er–Rahman I* ▷

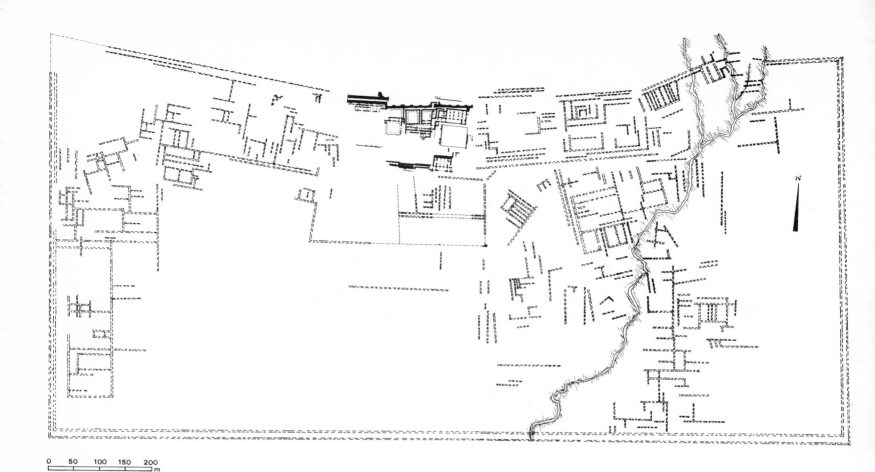

0 50 100 150 200
m

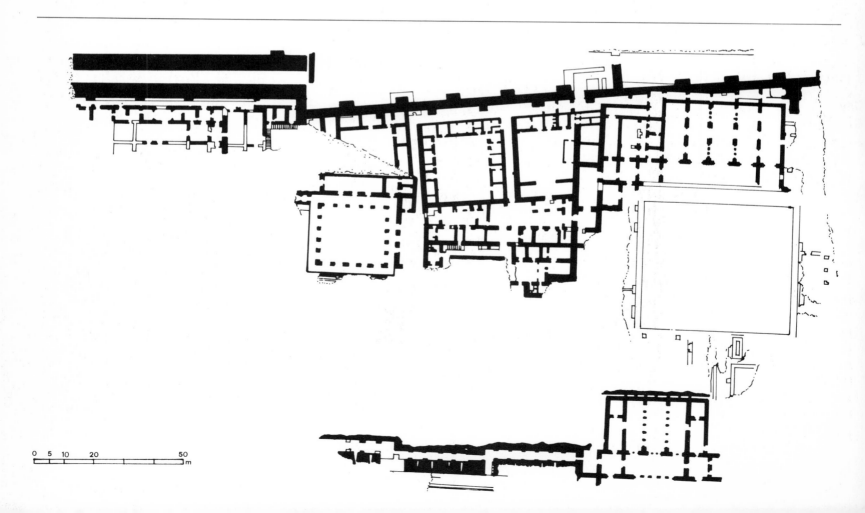

0 5 10 20 50
m

◁ 85.   *Medina al-Zahra, 936–81, general plan*
◁ 86.   *Medina al-Zahra, palace complex, plan*

87.   *Medina al-Zahra, Salon Rico, 953–57, exterior*
88.   *Medina al-Zahra, Salon Rico, inner facade*

Under Abd er-Rahman II (821–52) Spain enjoyed a period of relative peace and security, experiencing a strong influence from Baghdad and Samarra, the new centers of Islamic culture that no longer posed a threat to the Cordoban Amirate. Between 832 and 848 the prayer hall of the Great Mosque received eight more bays in the direction of the *qibla*. These matched those of the older section, except that while Abd er-Rahman I had used only Visigothic, Roman, and salvaged capitals, his successor had new ones carved following classic Roman models even down to the plasticity of the acanthus leaves—in striking contrast to the rather rigid Byzantine models the Aghlabid sculptors were then using at Kairouan.

Medina al-Zahra

Again after a period of chaos a new age began for the Amirate of Cordoba with the accession of Abd er-Rahman III (912–61). He took the title of Caliph in 929 under the name of al-Nasir li din Allah, "Defender of the Religion of Allah," in opposition to the recent founding of the Shi'ite Caliphate of the Fatimids at Mahdiya. Between 933 and 980 the Cordoban Caliphate controlled the destiny of Fez, whose architecture during this period shows a strong influence from Spain.

Abd er-Rahman's principal foundation was the residential and administrative center of Medina al-Zahra, begun in 936 and to which the court moved in 945. Abd er-Rahman's son, later Hakam II (961–76), was overseer of the works and made substantial additions from 971 to 975. (All work must have ceased in 978–79 when the vizier al-Mansur founded another capital, Medina al-Zahira, to which the court was transferred in 981.) At Medina al-Zahra double masonry walls enclose an immense rectangle of about 875 by 1, 230 yards (*Plate 85*). The north side, on the slope of the hill and on several levels, unites the loosely grouped structures of the palace (*Plate 86*). The westernmost, only partially preserved, is that of Hakam II; all the rest were built for his father. Informally grouped courtyards with or without cloisters are notable in that they exhibit neither the Umayyad nor the Abbasid *bayt*, being carefully isolated instead by communicating passages, presumably for servants. The two basilical halls may have served for public and private audiences. The larger northern hall—probably the older of the two—has retained little of its ornament, but the southern hall (953–57), called the Salon Rico by its discoverers, has retained so much that a complete restoration is now underway (*Plates 87–89*). Both halls consist of a tripartite basilica opening upon a transverse portico flanked by square chambers facing a large square court. In the case of the southern structure, the court contained a deep pool. The form seems to have evolved from a blend of the Umayyad

throne hall as found at Anjar and the Abbasid *bayt* in its most evolved form—the throne complex of the Jausaq al-Kharqani at Samarra.

Everywhere at Medina al-Zahra innumerable fragments of carved limestone and marble revetments were found; now they are being reassembled like immense jigsaw puzzles. In the Salon Rico it seems that the promise of the skilled marble workers of Abd er-Rahman II is revived for his successor but in a drier, more linear manner. For capitals, bases, and pilaster capitals the basic pattern of the Roman composite order is retained by the carvers, who often signed them (by which we know that four carvers working here later signed their names to the new *mihrab* at Cordoba in 964). The antique plasticity, revived in the ninth century, is gone and the acanthus has become as rigid as Byzantine work of the sixth century. It also stands out from the background with a sharp black-and-white clarity probably once enhanced by gilding. Above a low dado, interior walls were embellished with rectangular panels about 6 1/2 feet tall, framed in bands of interlace or rinceaux. In each panel a central stem branches out symmetrically to frame abstract fruit and flower forms. Although the overall pattern is as hard to follow as at Mshatta, nowhere does there appear the same endless repetition of such panels. As at Mshatta too—but with no birds or beasts—each panel is a self-contained unit, a remote descendant of such classical vegetal panels as those of the Ara Pacis.

MOSQUES: 941–87
The Mosque of Medina al-Zahra
Abd er-Rahman III built a mosque at Medina al-Zahra, south of the Salon Rico. Dedicated in 941, its much denuded foundations were excavated shortly before 1965 and from them a partial plan can be reconstructed (*Plate 90*). The building had five aisles perpendicular to the *qibla* (the center one somewhat wider than the others), a *sahn* with *riwaqs* on three sides, and three symmetrically spaced portals. This meant that the minaret projecting into the *sahn* was displaced to permit an axial approach to the *mihrab*. The center arches of the three *riwaqs* were also wider, defining cross axes. Sometime after the completion of the mosque a second—false—*qibla* wall was added, with a passage behind the true *qibla* (probably a recess into which the *minbar* could be withdrawn) and perhaps with a private entrance into the *maqsura* as well for the use of the Imam-Caliph.

The Great Mosque of Cordoba: Later Stages
In 951 Abd er-Rahman III extended the *sahn* to the south and built a new minaret for the Great Mosque at Cordoba. The minaret, projecting into the *sahn* and avoiding the *mihrab* axis as at Medina al-Zahra, was about 91 square feet and 111 feet tall, with three tiers of paired win-

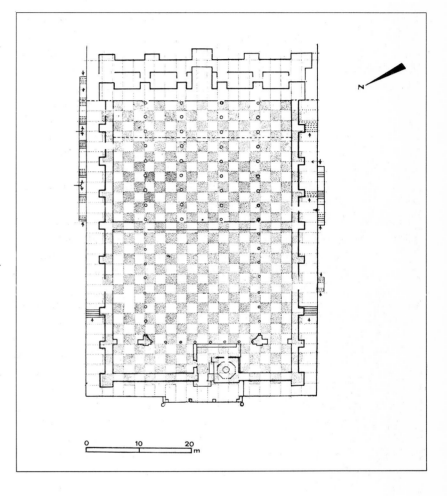

91. *Cordoba, Great Mosque as enlarged by Hakam II, 962–66, plan*
92. *Cordoba, Great Mosque, lantern of Hakam II, supporting arches* ▷
93. *Cordoba, Great Mosque, lantern of Hakam II* ▷
94. *Cordoba, Great Mosque, vault of the* maqsura ▷

dows and two access ramps. Part of it, encased in seventeenth-century masonry, survives. The Caliph was probably also responsible for the three *riwaqs* of the *sahn*. These, rebuilt in the sixteenth century but using the old materials, alternate two columns with a pier after the manner of the Great Mosque at Damascus.

In 962, a year after he came to the throne, Hakam II began the final southward extension of the Great Mosque. He added twelve bays and a double *qibla* wall, following the example of Medina al-Zahra (*Plate 91*). His most splendid achievements are the four superb stone vaults, one (in the Capilla de Villaviciosa) on the *mihrab* aisle at the beginning of his extension (*Plate 93*) and three in a T-shaped pattern over the *maqsura*. His inspiration must have been the Great Mosque of Kairouan in its final form, as is attested here by the frequent use of gored domelets between the interlacing arches of all four vaults. The origin of the latter is probably Persian, though it cannot at present be traced. As at Kairouan clusters of columns, no longer salvaged but made especially for the building, bear the added thrusts. Cross bracing is provided by intricately interlaced lobate arches with carved voussoirs (*Plate 92*) rising from additional columns—a perfect complement to the three-dimensional interlaces of the vaults (*Plate 97*).

As Grabar has recently said, the fact that the *mihrab* functions as an indicator of the direction of Mecca cannot be the only reason for its existence. At Medina the first *mihrab* (the word had royal connotations in pre-Islamic Arabic) marked the site from which the Prophet had led his people in prayer. Here at Cordoba the niche has become an octagonal chamber (*Plate 95*), perhaps suggesting that through the arch divine grace comes to the faithful. At any rate, nearly all later Spanish and North African *mihrabs* assume this form. The decoration of the entire mosque at Cordoba reaches its apex with the center bay of the *maqsura* that terminates Hakam's richly ornamented *mihrab* aisle. Here mosaics executed by a Byzantine craftsman who came with his glass tesserae from Constantinople cover the facade of the *mihrab* (*Plate 96*) and encrust the vault above (*Plate 97*). Except for the inscriptions (which give the date of 965), plant forms—somewhat more naturalistic than usual in Cordoba—account for most of the decoration and may correspond to a lost Byzantine secular style that has been preserved nowhere else. Within the *mihrab* itself, although the motifs are closer to those of Medina al-Zahra, the material is stucco, a technique perhaps imported from Iraq about this time.

In 987 al-Mansur, vizier to the ineffectual Caliph Hisham II (976–1009), again enlarged Cordoba's mosque, but this time to the west since the river prevented a further southern extension. He added eight new aisles and correspondingly enlarged the *sahn* (*Plate 98*),

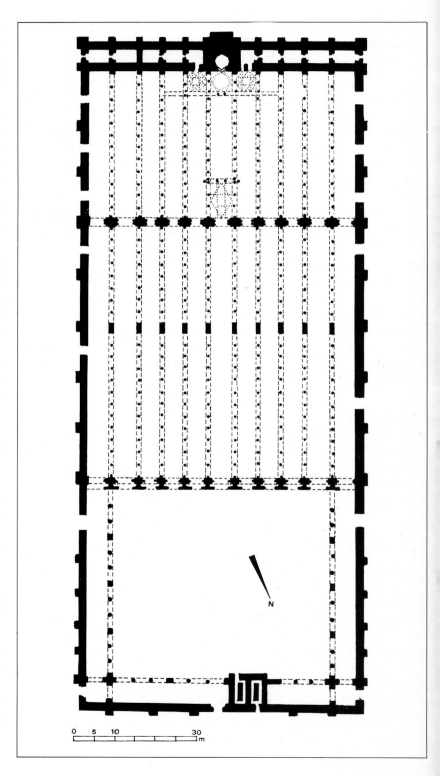

95. *Cordoba, Great Mosque, vault of the* mihrab
96. *Cordoba, Great Mosque, outer facade of the* mihrab
97. *Cordoba, Great Mosque, vault above the* mihrab *bay* ▷

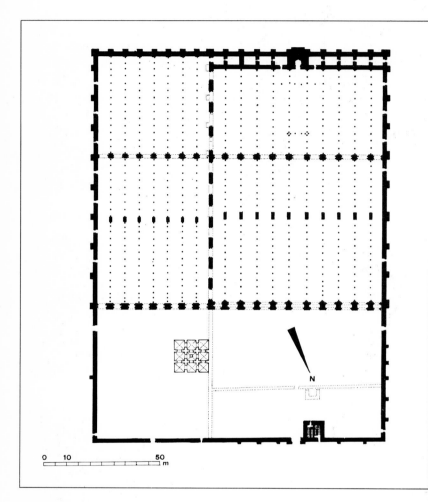

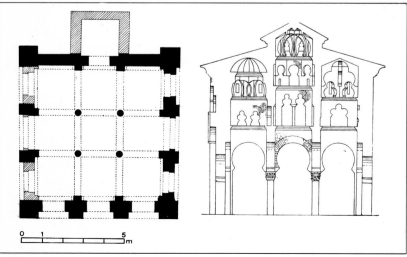

copying most of the details of the earlier structure even down to the wall remnants marking the successive enlargements of the older section.

The Mosque of Bib Mardun in Toledo

This mysterious building, completed in 999, must have been a *musalla* —a small place for private devotion, perhaps connected with a palace and near one of the city gates as its name suggests. Only 26.4 feet square, it was originally a pavilion open on all sides except that toward the *qibla* (*Plate 99*). Only the north facade employs masonry piers (*Plate 100*). The rest is brick, an indication perhaps, like the use of stucco at Cordoba, of the increasing orientalization of the Caliphate. Inside (*Plates 102–109*), eight tiny ribbed vaults, each one different, are illuminated by a ninth one (*Plate 101*) rising like a clerestory above the rest. There is no other surviving ornament in the mosque, and the reused Visigothic capitals suggest that a decline in stone carving had already set in. The design recalls the type of the Masjid-i-Tarikh at Balkh, and must have originated in the eighth century somewhere in the heartland of Islam.

The Aljaferiya Palace in Zaragoza

Under the vizier al-Mansur the policies of Abd er-Rahman III and Hakam II were continued, but a rapid decline set in after his reign. Medina al-Zahra, already abandoned, was sacked in a Berber revolt of 1010 and in 1031 the Caliphate itself came to an end. Numerous independent principalities, both Berber and Arab, as well as the Taifas Kingdoms, then sprang up whose rivalries paved the way for the eventual Christian reconquest. Two such dynasties ruled Zaragoza before its fall to the Christians in 1118: the Tojibids (1019–39) and the Hudids (1039–1118), of pure Arab stock. Perhaps for this reason the art of Cordoba, infused with new Eastern elements, was preserved and further developed at Zaragoza.

The Aljaferiya Palace was added to the rectangular Torre del Homenaje (probably a tenth-century structure) during the reign of Abu Jafar al-Muqtadir (1046–81), from whom its name is derived. Investigations in 1962 made the plan (*Plate 110*) clearer, but we must still rely on the (fortunately accurate) drawings of 1757 to reconstruct the original appearance of the outer walls. These, enclosing a roughly rectangular area 279 by 238 feet, have semicircular exterior towers recalling the Ribat of Sussa and emphasizing the closeness of Zaragoza to the Christian frontier. The rich interior has, however, none of the austerity of a typical *ribat*. The palace proper consisted of a north-south complex dividing the interior roughly into thirds as at Mshatta. To the north, between two projecting pavilions, there was a rec-

100. *Toledo, Mosque of Bib Mardun, exterior*
101. *Toledo, Mosque of Bib Mardun, central vault*

102–109. *Toledo, Mosque of Bib Mardun, the eight ribbed vaults*

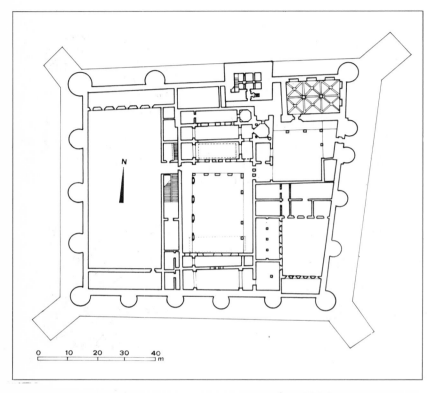

tangular pool and behind it a portico (*Plate 111*). Behind this a transverse hall had at its east end a small octagonal oratory (*Plates 112, 113*). Still further north behind a screen of arches was another transverse hall flanked by square chambers. At the south end of the court which today has a cloister (a thirteenth-century addition), another rectangular pool was followed by two transverse halls separated by more screens of columns.

The arches of the northern complex, all of stucco, are interlaced and lobate like those of Cordoba (some are *in situ* and others are in the archaeological museums of Zaragoza and Madrid). However, their detail is smaller in scale and their outline taller; their form approaches, though always by means of interlacing circular segments, the pointed horseshoe arch to be introduced later by the Almoravids. The stone capitals recovered from the ruins and still *in situ*—at least one of which bears Jafar's name—follow the composite order of their Cordoban prototypes, but the tiers of acanthus leaves are taller and their ornament suggests that their original function has been lost. The small oratory has the remains, now very much restored, of a richly carved stucco interior with mixtilinear arcades interlaced below and arcading of interlaced lobate arches above. Recent investigation has shown that, although the *mihrab* has a gored shell form in stucco, the ceiling, destroyed by the addition of a floor in the fifteenth century, was of that intricately intertwined polychrome woodwork called *artesonado* in Spain, perhaps the earliest known example of such work. It is difficult to explain why the recent restorers chose to duplicate the vault of the *mihrab* bay at Cordoba. Although only negative evidence exists, it is worth noting that no example of *muqarnas* (stalactite) ornament has yet been found at this site.

Conclusion

The architecture of the Cordoban Caliphate from beginning to end would appear to have been primarily a continuation of that of Umayyad Syria, modified only by such local innovations as the exclusive use of the rounded horseshoe arch and the double-tiered aisle arcades of the Great Mosque. The many Sassanian decorative devices of Khirbat al-Mafjar seem never to have been introduced into Cordoba (and were perhaps never so important in Damascus either). In the tenth century when probable Oriental ideas were adapted, including ribbed vaults and stucco work, this was balanced by an even greater reliance on traditional Roman decorative forms. It is possible that this interest in the antique was encouraged by Cordoba's close and often cordial contacts with Byzantium, then under the Macedonian dynasty which was undergoing its own revival of antiquity.

This heritage, through the intermittent caliphal presence in Fez,

112. *Zaragoza, Aljaferiya Palace, oratory, vault*
113. *Zaragoza, Aljaferiya Palace, oratory, mihrab wall*

was to be passed on to the Almoravids and the Almohads. Ultimately it was also this style which, toward the end of the Muslim presence in Spain, gave birth to the exquisite architecture of the Marinids and the Nasrids.

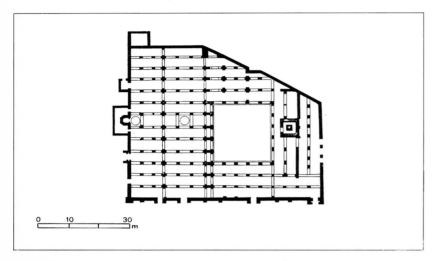

114. *Tlemcen, Great Mosque soon after 1082, plan*
115. *Tlemcen, Great Mosque, prayer hall*

THE ALMORAVID DYNASTY

In the early eleventh century a Sanhaja Berber chief, Yahya ibn Ibrahim, returned from the pilgrimage to Mecca full of spiritual enthusiasm. His followers came to be known as Murabitun from a *ribat* they had established at the mouth of the Senegal River. In midcentury, under Yusuf ibn Tashufin (1061–1106), they moved north, founding Marrakesh in 1062, Tlemcen in 1082, and finally reaching Algiers. A year after the fall of Toledo to the Christians in 1085, the Almoravids entered Spain as deliverers and remained as rulers. The rise of a new power, the Almohads, in the early twelfth century so weakened the Almoravids that they were unable to prevent the fall of Zaragoza to the Christians in 1118 and lost Marrakesh in 1147 (although a branch of the dynasty lingered into the thirteenth century in the Balearic Islands).

The Great Mosque at Tlemcen

Probably soon after he founded Tagrart (present-day Tlemcen) in 1082, Yusuf ibn Tashufin began a Friday mosque there of stucco and brick which survives as the nucleus of a much enlarged structure (*Plate 114*). Georges Marçais believes the original building was a structure of thirteen aisles perpendicular to the *qibla*. The prayer hall was three bays deep, while the next three bays framed a rectangular *sahn* seven aisles wide. The aisle arcades are formed of round horseshoe arches, while the transverse arcade at the third bay of the old prayer hall has lobate arches (*Plate 115*). The vault over the *mihrab* bay, the *mihrab* itself, and the arches near it are works of 1136 and will be treated later. The minaret, dated 1236, probably originates from the time the old *sahn* was filled in and the new square one added.

The Great Mosque at Algiers

The congregational mosque at Algiers must have been completed not long before the *minbar* (dated 1096) was installed. Eleven aisles of five bays form the prayer hall, which is about 72 feet deep. The *sahn* accounts for another three bays and is five aisles wide (*Plate 117*). Such rectangular *sahns*, perhaps inspired by the final shape of the *sahn* at Cordoba, will become standard in nearly all later Moroccan mosques. The aisle arcades are formed of moderately pointed horseshoe arches springing from square or cruciform piers of brick. As at Tlemcen, the transverse arches are nearly all lobate (*Plate 116*); one interlaced lobate arch appears in the *mihrab* aisle (*Plate 119*).

The Qubbat Barudiyin at Marrakesh

The Qubbat Barudiyin (*Plate 120*), recently cleared by Jacques Meunié and Henri Terrasse, sheltered a fountain for ablutions in an

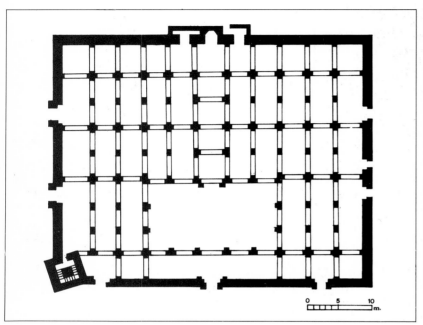

117. *Algiers, Great Mosque shortly before 1096, plan*
118. *Algiers, Great Mosque,* mihrab *aisle*
119. *Algiers, Great Mosque,* mihrab *dome* ▷

120. *Marrakesh, Qubbat Barudiyin, c. 1120, exterior*
121. *Marrakesh, Qubbat Barudiyin, projection and plan of the dome*

120. *Marrakesh, Qubbat Barudiyin, c. 1120, exterior*
121. *Marrakesh, Qubbat Barudiyin, projection and plan of the dome*

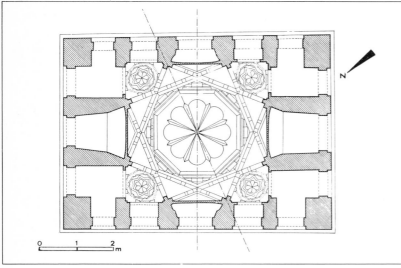

annex of the Friday mosque of Ali ben Yusuf (1106–42), completed in 1120 but now entirely rebuilt. It is a rectangular pavilion with five lobed arches at the ends and pairs of pointed horseshoe arches at the side supports; above is a tier of windows and a row of crenellations, a stuccoed brick dome decorated in relief with interlaced arches, and a seven-pointed star in a herringbone pattern. Inside and quite independent of the exterior is a very complex and completely decorative vault originally lighted by twelve inner windows of colored glass set in stuccoed grilles. Eight interlacing arches support an eight-gored bulbous domelet (*Plates 121, 122*) as in the vault over the *mihrab* bay at Cordoba. However, the mixtilinear shape of the arches, which support eight more of similar shape just under the dome, is—along with the rich stucco ornament—reminiscent of the oratory of the Aljaferiya at Zaragoza. In the eight upper arches and in the four seven-pointed star-shaped vaults in the corners of the octagon appears the *muqarnas*, still in a rather flat and experimental form. The interior structure is, then, a late Cordoban vault to which the *muqarnas* has been sparingly added, fitted under a brick dome reminiscent of Ifriqiya and quite unlike the pyramidal tiled roofs supported by wooden frameworks of Spain and Morocco.

The Lantern of the Great Mosque at Tlemcen
An inscription in the *mihrab* bay indicates that the lantern was completed in 1136, but the name of the donor was obliterated by the Almohads. There can be little doubt, however, that it was Ali ben Yusuf. Preceded by a richly figured lobate arch (*Plate 123*), the vault rises from twelve mixtilinear arches like those at Marrakesh (*Plate 124*). These support twelve interlacing arches of a rounded horseshoe shape. From the dodecagon formed at their intersection there rises a *muqarnas* domelet of considerably greater sophistication than the *muqarnas* at Marrakesh. The *muqarnas* appears again in the four corners of the vault. Between the ribs is spread a web of openwork stucco tracery which originally might have contained colored glass. The whole fantastic structure, supported by fragile arches of thin tiles, is protected by a windowed wooden pavilion with a tiled roof. Here, though the precedents of Cordoba and the Aljaferiya are recognizable, is evidence of an extraordinarily inventive architect who has blended the traditional window grilles with the vault itself to produce a splendid veil of light over the most holy place of the mosque.

The Qarawiyin Mosque at Fez
This mosque was begun in 857 as a private foundation by the daughter of a wealthy Arab immigrant from Kairouan. Its prayer hall (*Plate 125*) originally comprised the four aisles, parallel to the *qibla*,

123. *Tlemcen, Great Mosque,* mihrab
124. *Tlemcen, Great Mosque, vault above the* mihrab *bay, finished 1136* ▷

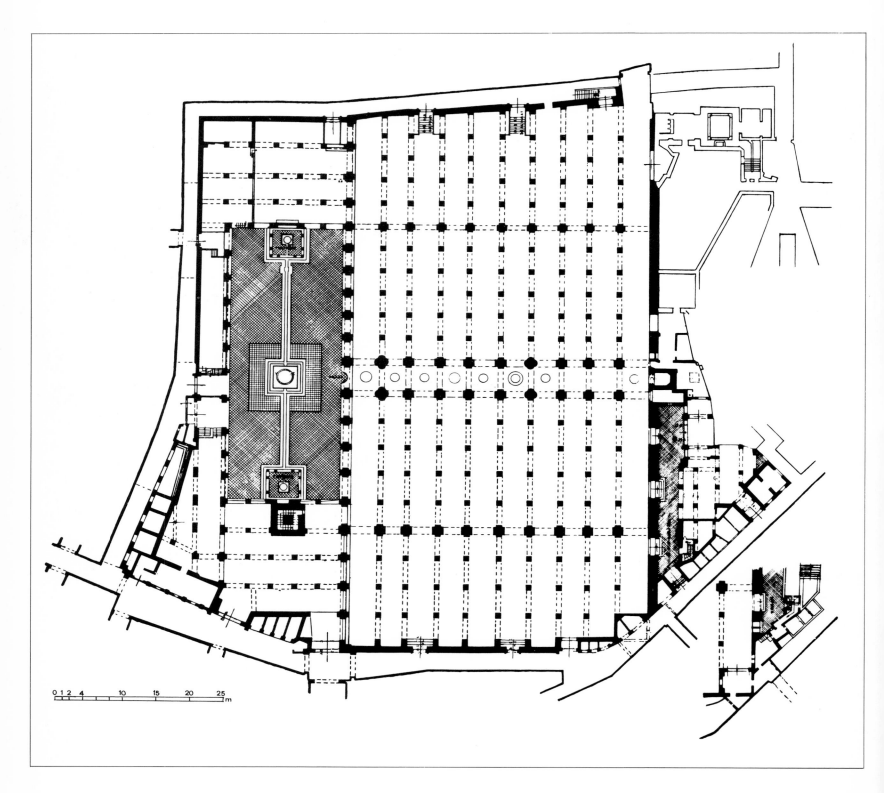

which in the present hall are those between the fourth and seventh aisles counting from the *sahn*; it was twelve bays wide, the bays left of the *mihrab* aisle being slightly compressed for symmetry. Arcades perpendicular to the *qibla* mark the former exterior walls and also the *mihrab* aisle. Nothing is known of the nature of the supports and the shape of the original arches, but a minaret stood opposite the *mihrab* aisle as it did at Kairouan. Either in 919 or 933, under Fatimid domination, the building became a Friday mosque. When Fez returned to Sunni hands under the Zenata Berber Emirs, who were clients of the Spanish Umayyads, increased trade and peace encouraged population growth and an expansion of the mosque was approved and funded by Abd er-Rahman III. The present minaret (*Plate 126*)—of Cordoban style except for its parapet and dome, which recall the Ribat of Sussa—was completed in 956, according to a now-lost inscription. The other additions probably date from that time as well. Without moving the *qibla*, the prayer hall was enlarged east and west to its present dimensions and to the north by three bays occupying the old *sahn*. A new *sahn* was added which must have centered on the minaret to the west, but its appearance is unknown because this section was subjected to much later rebuilding. All the additions used brick for piers and arches, a form of cement for the outer walls, and stone for the now stuccoed minaret. The arches were rounded horseshoes typical of Cordoba, as the ninth–century arches may also have been.

In 1069 Fez became part of the Almoravid Empire and, although not the capital, a city of great importance. Its two quarters, the Andalusian and the Kairouani, were joined behind a single wall and a citadel was built for the Governor. In 1134 Sultan Ali ben Yusuf began the final expansion of the city's mosque by adding three aisles the full width of the earlier building south of the old *qibla* and endowing the *mihrab* aisle with its present magnificent *muqarnas* vault. The vault within his new *mihrab* and the rectangular vault covering the first two bays of the Almoravid extension are dated 1136 (*Plate 127*). Structural work was complete by 1143 and the new *minbar* is dated in the following year. Soon after the city fell to the Almohads (in 1146) the rich sculptured and painted ornament of the vaults was covered in plaster and whitewash to conform to the puritanism of the conquerors. (This has recently been partially removed under the direction of Henri Terrasse.) The last major additions to the mosque were the two pavilions projecting into the *sahn* built by the Saadien Sultan Abdallah ibn al-Shaikh (1613–24). They contain fountains and, obviously copied after those in the Court of Lions at the Alhambra in Granada, seem out of place in a mosque.

Now that more of their original ornament is visible, it is clear

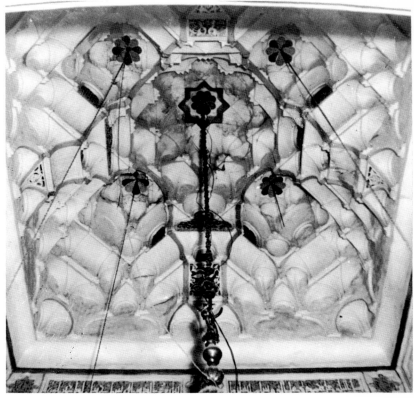

128. *Fez, Qarawiyin Mosque, prayer hall, view from the third bay of the* mihrab *aisle*

that the designer of the vaults of the *mihrab* aisle intended that the ornament should reach a climax of elaboration and color as the *mihrab* was approached. Counting from the *sahn*, the fifth vault is a typical example of the almost playful elaboration throughout. Its lateral supporting arches were replaced by five lobed arches with carved voussoirs as at Cordoba. It was then provided with a *muqarnas* dome on squinches, based not on an octagon as are most such vaults but a pentagon, in harmony with the position of the vault and the number of lobes in the arches. The sixth bay is vaulted by eight interlaced arches with an eight-gored domelet in the center like the vaults which flank the *mihrab* bay at Cordoba. Bays eight and nine, the first two of the Almoravid addition, are unified by a single very high rectangular vault. Along the *mihrab* aisle both the lateral and transverse arches of the Almoravid extension are either eleven-lobed (*Plate 128*) or an early and robust form of what is called the lambrequin arch. Here pendants begin to hang vertically from the soffit, perhaps inspired by the pendant profile of the *muqarnas* itself. Finally, the *mihrab* itself is a disappointment, its facade having been reworked in the eighteenth century. However, the vault within the octagonal chamber is original and richly adorned with acanthus leaves.

Terrasse believes that the *minbar* of 1144, like Ali ben Yusuf's earlier one (of 1120) for his mosque in Marrakesh, was made in Cordoba. This merely adds to the overwhelming evidence that the art of Cordoba as continued by the Taifas Kingdoms, particularly Zaragoza, played a dominant role in the formation of Almoravid architecture. Probably many craftsmen came from Spain, and work done in Spain itself for Almoravid patrons presumably reflected local styles even more strongly; very little evidence of this survives, however.

The Castillejo of Monteagudo in Murcia
Among the few remaining monuments of this type, this ruined house is unique in that it gives us some idea of a princely country residence of the first third of the twelfth century (*Plate 129*). A rectangular garden about 59 by 108 feet is surrounded by a rigidly symmetrical complex of chambers and corridors difficult to interpret; six may contain square niches like those at Ashir. The enclosed garden is a typical *riadh* (the Moroccan and Spanish version of a Persian *chahr bagh*), with four sunken parterres divided by intersecting paths, probably a fountain in the middle, and perhaps two projecting pavilions at the short ends. A much smaller *riadh*, only about 33 feet long, but of almost identical pattern, was found in the very scanty ruins of Ali ben Yusuf's palace of 1131/32 at Marrakesh under the now likewise destroyed first Almohad Kutubiyya Mosque. Perhaps the court of

129. *Murcia, Castillejo of Monteagudo, early twelfth century, plan*

130. *Tinmal, Friday Mosque, finished 1153–54, plan*
131. *Tinmal, Friday Mosque,* qibla *aisle* ▷
132. *Tinmal, Friday Mosque,* mihrab ▷

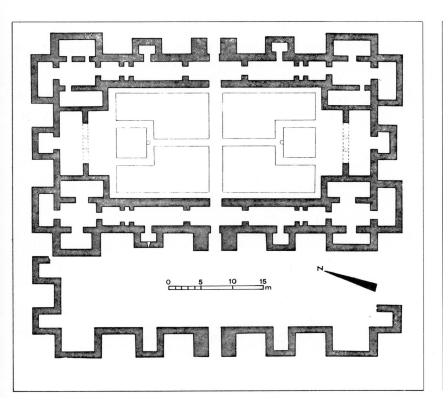

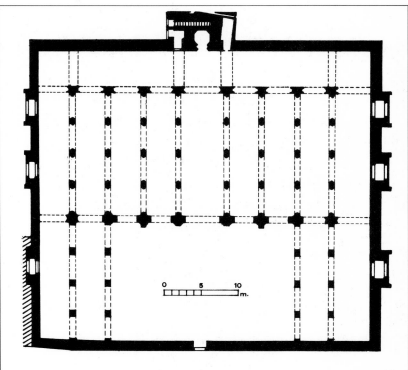

the Aljaferiya once had a similar form, despite the fact that the intersecting paths linking the north and south pools and bisecting the center are missing. If they existed, then the *riadh*—like so much else in Morocco—may have been imported from Spain, though the four-part courts of the ninth-century Bulkawara Palace at Samarra probably inspired both.

THE DYNASTY OF THE ALMOHADS

The Almohads, or al-Muwahhidun, those who affirm the unity of God, represented a protest against legalistic Malikism and the moral laxity of the later Almoravids. Their founder, Muhammad ibn Tumart (d. 1130), called himself the Mahdi, and Abd al-Mumin (1130–63) proclaimed himself Caliph. The Almohads took Marrakesh in 1141 and made it their capital, thus restoring order to Spain which had again split into factions with the decline of the Almoravids. In

Spain itself they established a powerful kingdom at Seville. With the Christian victory of Las Navas de Tolosa in 1212 the Almohad regime in Spain ended, and revolts in Tlemcen and Tunis lost them most of what is now Algeria and Tunisia. Finally, when Marrakesh fell to the Marinids in 1269, the Almohad Dynasty ended.

The Friday Mosque at Tinmal

Tinmal, where Ibn Tumart began his teaching and where he is buried, has a Friday mosque completed in 1153–54. The outer walls, as is usual in Morocco, are of a kind of concrete or a lime-impregnated *terre pisée*, but the piers and arches are of stuccoed brick (*Plate 130*). Within a rectangle of about 157 by 144 feet, nine aisles of four bays, perpendicular to the *qibla* (the two outer aisles and the *mihrab* aisle notably wider), spring from a transverse *qibla* aisle in characteristic T-form. On each side two aisles are prolonged to form the *sahn,*

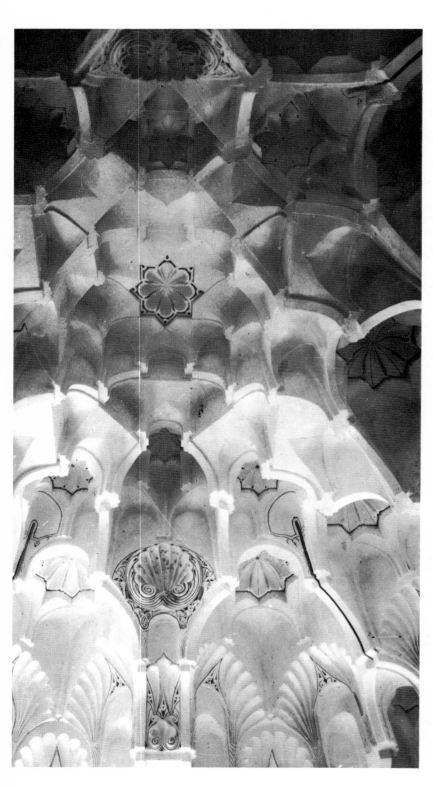

five aisles wide and four bays deep, whose north wall lacks a *riwaq*. The *mihrab* and *qibla* aisles (*Plates 131, 132*) are further set off by lambrequin arches much more complex than the earlier ones at Fez. *Muqarnas* vaults cover the *mihrab* bay and the two corner bays where in a Fatimid mosque there might have been domes. All the other transverse arches have fifteen lobes, but the surviving lateral arches are all pointed horseshoes of a peculiarly graceful and vigorous shape. The chambered *mihrab* is encased in a rectangular tower which served as a minaret. To the left is a door for the *imam* and to the right a deep slot for the storage of the *minbar* (*Plate 132*). The stucco ornament—bold, predominantly geometric and abstract, in contrast to the earlier Almoravid intricacy—was doubtless once pure white. The geometric interlace framing the *mihrab* is a Seljuk Persian motif, used in a similar way to frame the portal of the Rabat-i-Malik of 1078, but has a very long history and will reappear in the marble borders of the Taj Mahal gardens.

The Kutubiyya Mosque in Marrakesh

In Marrakesh in 1147 a mosque was begun whose north wall was either part of or stood on the foundations of a stone citadel built by the Almoravid Yusuf ben Tashufin. Vastly larger than Tinmal's, this mosque had a prayer hall of seventeen aisles perpendicular to the *qibla* aisle and seven bays deep. Four aisles to east and west were extended another four bays to define a rectangular *sahn* with only a wall arcade on T-shaped piers to the north. The recent excavations have brought to light trenches surrounding the *mihrab* bay and two more flanking it, into which a wooden *maqsura* could be lowered. This curious arrangement seems never to have been repeated.

Shortly before 1162 the original mosque was duplicated to the south on a nearly identical plan, but some 13 feet larger (*Plate 134*). Eleven portals cut through the *qibla* wall of the first mosque prove that the two buildings coexisted for a certain time before the earlier was destroyed. Since an attempt was made to correct the direction of the *qibla*, the later mosque is trapezoidal. As at Tinmal, the *qibla* aisle here has only lambrequin arches and no less than five square *muqarnas* vaults (*Plate 133*) expressed outside by pyramidal roofs. Elsewhere nearly all the transverse arches are lobate (*Plate 135*), while those perpendicular to the *qibla* are pointed horseshoes. Notable here and at Tinmal are the colonnettes attached to the piers wherever arches spring from: their derivation is, of course, the real columns which so often occupy such positions in Cordoban examples but which constitute a refinement apparently absent in the Almoravid style.

The stone minaret must have been begun at the same time as

134. *Marrakesh, second Kutubiyya Mosque, plan*
136. *Marrakesh, second Kutubiyya Mosque, minaret*
135. *Marrakesh, second Kutubiyya Mosque, prayer hall*

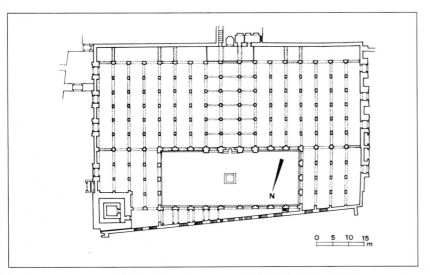

◁ *137. Seville, Great Mosque, 1172–82, sahn*

138. Seville, Great Mosque, reconstruction of plan
139. Seville, Great Mosque, minaret of 1184–95 (called the Giralda Tower)

the second mosque, but was not finished until the time of Yaqub al-Mansur (1184–99)—who, however, probably provided only the lantern (*Plate 136*). The ornament surrounding the windows differs in design and placement according to the position of the inner ramp, a curious asymmetry corrected in later towers. Lambrequin, lobate, and interlaced arches frame the windows and blind niches. Finally, a band of large blue-green glazed tiles (probably of the late twelfth century) runs above the blind arcading of the last story.

The Great Mosque of Seville

The Great Mosque of Seville was begun in 1172 by Abu Yaqub Yusuf I (1163–84), who had lived in Cordoba before his accession to the throne. The structure was finished early in 1182. Since, except for the minaret and a portion of the *sahn*, the whole was replaced by the present cathedral in the fifteenth century only a hypothetical reconstruction is possible (*Plate 138*). As in the Kutubiyya Mosque in Marrakesh, there were seventeen aisles perpendicular to the *qibla*, yet the prayer hall—perhaps referring back to Cordoba—was very deep in relation to its width. Two extensions of the aisles flanked the *sahn* east and west, but a single-aisled *riwaq* screened the north wall (*Plate 137*), again as at Cordoba. The east portal of the *sahn* preserves its *muqarnas* vault, the oldest surviving one in Spain.

The famous minaret (*Plate 139*), known as the Giralda Tower, was of concrete and brick like the mosque. It was begun in 1184 by the architect Ahmad ibn Baso, who had also built the mosque, but the death in the same year of Abu Yaqub Yusuf I delayed further construction until 1188–89 when Yaqub al-Mansur ordered the work continued. This was carried out under Ali de Gomara until its completion in 1195. The minaret's original appearance can be reconstructed from early episcopal seals and from a model made before the Renaissance additions. What seemed tentative and rather coarse at Marrakesh is here given better articulation through the tall panels of interlaced arches and the greater similarity between the four sides.

The Mosque of Hassan at Rabat

The Sultan Yaqub al-Mansur refounded Rabat as Ribat al-Fath in 1191. It was probably at the same time that he began his enormous Friday mosque, left unfinished at his death in 1199. The building, had it been completed, would have been second in size only to al-Mutawakkil's in Samarra. Excavations in 1943 and 1948 have permitted a reconstruction as it would have appeared if completed (*Plate 140*). A vast almost square prayer hall 446 by 449 feet interrupted by two courts for both lighting and ventilation was to have been supported on stone columns built up in drums. The arches would certainly have

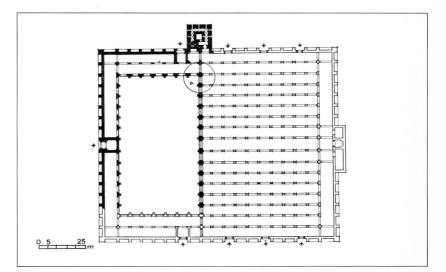

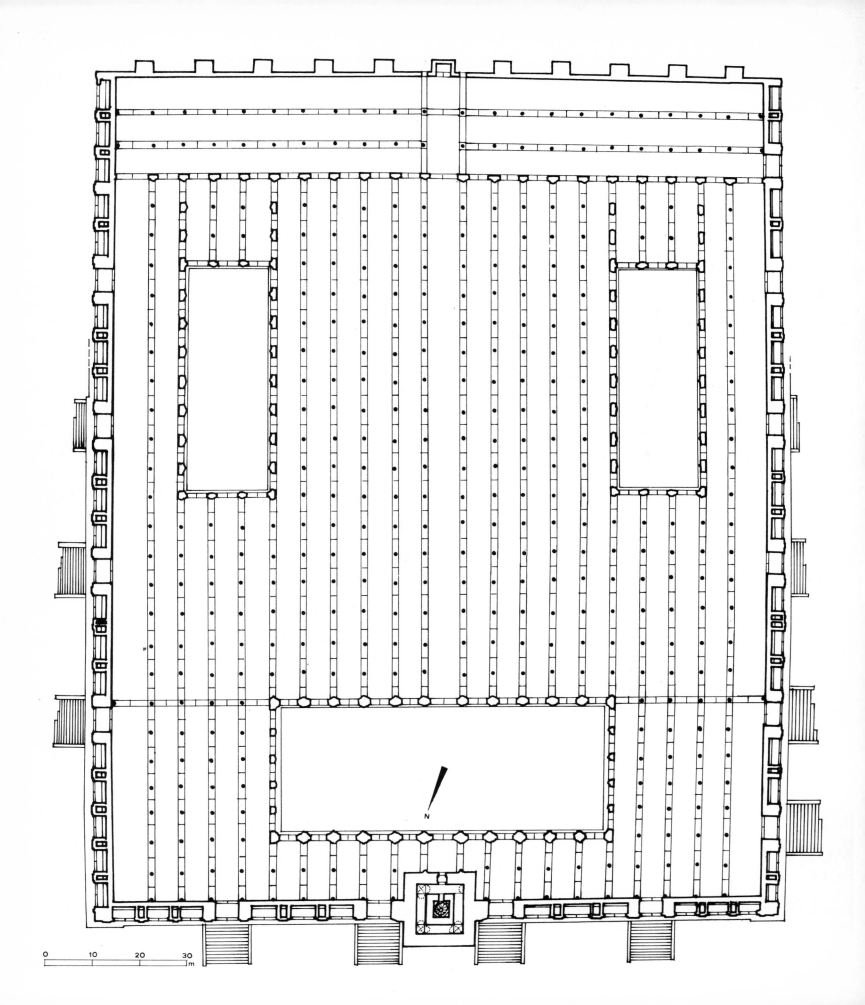

0 10 20 30
m

N

been brick and the outer walls of the usual semiconcrete. The rectangular *sahn* and its *riwaqs* bring the total length to 594 feet.

The stone minaret (*Plate 141*) is ascended by a ramp which winds around a square inner core composed of a series of vaulted chambers. At the base the north facade differs from the other three, but all four sides become uniform above due to the use of a triple interlaced arch motif which was to have extended almost the full height of the first stage. This motif alone would soon be used for all successive Almohad minarets and continued under the Marinids.

The Gate of the Ouadiah Kasba in Rabat

Several Almohad gates and fortifications survive in fair condition in Marrakesh and Rabat, but the most important is surely the imposing entrance complex Yaqub al-Mansur added after 1191 to the Ouadiah Kasba, which had been rebuilt after 1146 by Abd al-Mumin as a fortified palace. Since Yaqub intended Rabat as his capital and his palace was in the Kasba, it is not surprising that a Muslim contemporary called this gate the "palace's majestic gallery." A richly carved arch in fine ochre masonry (*Plate 143*) leads to a succession of spacious vaulted chambers (*Plate 142*) whose function seems more concerned with pomp than with defense. The second chamber has a vault on pendentives, suggesting that the masons had some acquaintance with work then going on in southern France. The third chamber is barrel-vaulted and communicates with the interior of the Kasba, indicating its possible use as a court of justice. The inner portal is as richly carved as the external one and both must once have had elaborate projecting cornices of wood (called *aleros* in Spain) supported on stone brackets at the corners. Later examples of these are numerous.

Conclusion

Terrasse has suggested that the scanty remains of Yusuf ben Tashufin's stone citadel at Marrakesh have affinities with the fortifications and with various portals of the Qala of the Bani Hammad. As we have seen, after 1086 the principal influence upon Almoravid architecture was Spanish save for one important element, the *muqarnas*, which may also have been introduced from the Qala in the late eleventh century. The motif first appears around 1120 as a minor element in ribbed vaults at Cordoba and Zaragoza. Then, suddenly, one finds fully developed *muqarnas* vaults of great intricacy, in stucco, datable at the earliest to 1134. It is altogether possible that the wonderful wooden *muqarnas* vault of the Cappella Palatina at Palermo is of about the same date (even in Sicily architecture has closer affinities with the Zirid and Hammadid traditions of Ashir and the Qala than they do with Fatimid Egypt). The pointed horseshoe arch replaced the rounded version sometime in the late eleventh century, it too introduced from the East. The Almohad conquerors, though they began as reformers, lost no time in acquiring all the refinements of their predecessors. By and large their mosques employed the style of those of the Almoravids, but the proportions were taller and slenderer and the articulation of plan and elevation more precise and systematic. The *sahn* was always rectangular with the length parallel to the *qibla*. The T-shaped plan was dominant and the solution of seventeen aisles perpendicular to the *qibla* first used at Aghlabid Kairouan in 836 was revived at Marrakesh in 1147 and at Seville in 1172.

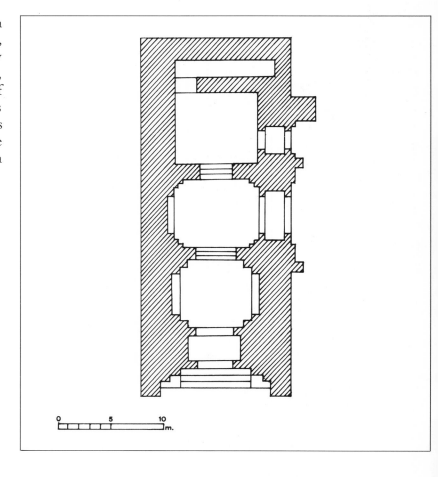

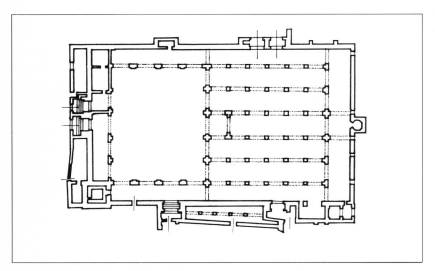

144. *Fez al-Jedid, Friday Mosque, begun 1276, plan*
145. *Taza, Great Mosque, 1291–94, vault over the* mihrab *bay*

THE MARINID DYNASTY

This dynasty was founded by a tribe of Zenata Berbers, few in number and without the driving religious force of the Almoravids or the Almohads. They first invaded Morocco from the Sahara in 1216. By 1250 they had conquered Fez, which became their capital; Marrakesh fell only in 1269. In 1275 the Marinids invaded Spain, winning the battle of Ecija, but they never succeeded in extending their rule there or turning back the tide of the Christian reconquest (Cordoba had fallen in 1236 and Seville in 1248). After a disastrous defeat at the Rio Salado in 1340, the Marinids never again intervened in Spain though they maintained close relations with the court at Granada. In North Africa, although they took Tlemcen in 1336, they never defeated the Hafsids in Tunisia. A period of decline began in the late fourteenth century. The dynasty's direct line became extinct in 1465, and the Wattasid line was succeeded by the Sa'di Sharifs in 1549.

The Friday Mosque at Fez al-Jedid

The flourishing of Islamic architecture nearly always required the patronage of enlightened princes with money to spend from new conquests (not always of Christians). Such conditions ceased to exist for the Almohads after the death of al-Mansur in 1199 and did not begin for the Marinids until the founding of Fez al-Jedid, New Fez, in 1276, a year after the battle of Ecija, under Abu Yusuf Yaqub (1258–86). Nothing remains of the city's palaces, and the walls have been much repaired. The spacious Friday mosque, on the other hand, though redecorated in 1395, retains its original plan (*Plate 144*). The building occupies a rectangle of about 177 by 111 feet with a prayer hall of the traditional T-plan and seven aisles perpendicular to the *qibla*, two of which are extended to form the *riwaqs* of the quadrangular *sahn*. The latter was perhaps influenced by the square *sahn* added in 1236 in the rebuilding of the mosque at Tlemcen, which also spans five aisles. The minaret here occupies the northwest corner of the *sahn* —a feature that became standard in fourteenth-century Marinid mosques, along with the five regularly spaced portals, two of them doubled. An elaborate cupola covers the *mihrab* bay and the same aisle begins with a rib vault rather like the later one at Taza.

The Mihrab Vault at Taza

Under Abu Ya'qub Yusuf (1286–1307) the Great Mosque at Taza, founded by the Almohads, was provided with a vault over the *mihrab* bay between 1291 and 1294 (*Plate 145*). The square bay becomes an octagon through *muqarnas* squinches, which in turn (by means of sculptured pendentives on miniature colonnettes) is converted into a

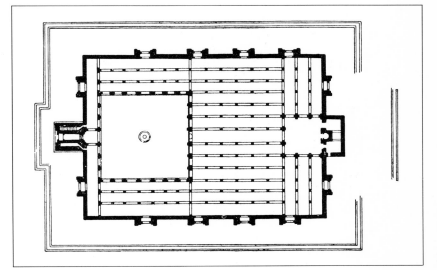

dodecagon from whose corners spring twelve slender interlaced arches. These rise to a central *muqarnas* domelet as at Tlemcen, but instead of crossing to the opposite corner each falls back to the fifth angle of the dodecagon. Whatever structural function the arches at Tlemcen preserved is here denied; also in contrast with Tlemcen, the ornament is more intricate and two-dimensional and the light still more diffuse. As in so many other late manifestations of a given Islamic style, the ornament is reduced in scale in relation to the architecture to which it is applied.

The Great Mosque of Mansura at Tlemcen

In 1303, after the first Marinid conquest of Tlemcen by Abu Ya'qub Yusuf, the Great Mosque of Mansura was begun in the new town he founded outside the old; but, since the portal inscription mentions him as deceased, the building must have been completed after the reconquest of the town in 1336 under Abu-l-Hasan Ali (1331–48). Like the Mosque of Hassan at Rabat upon which it is modeled, the structure was planned for the use of an army of occupation; nor was either ever finished. The Mansura mosque occupies a rectangle of about 197 by 279 feet (*Plate 146*). As at Rabat, stone columns supported the nearly square prayer hall, three of whose aisles paralleled the *qibla*. Unlike Rabat, however, is the 151-square-foot *maqsura* which was probably covered by a pyramidal wooden roof. This recalls the Mosque of Sultan Baybars at Cairo or even some of its Seljuk predecessors. Like most other Marinid mosques, the *sahn* here is square but the thirteen regularly spaced portals again recall Rabat, as does the position of the stone minaret—though its use as a portal is unique. Like its Almohad models, the minaret (whose southern half has crumbled) had an access ramp circling a square central core (*Plates 147, 148*). The decorative scheme also belongs to the great series of Almohad works, but the portal reduces the scale of the ornament in relation to the size of the structure.

The Gate of the Chella at Rabat

Abu Ya'qub Yusuf was killed in battle at Algeciras. According to his instructions, his body was reburied later in the Chella outside the walls of Rabat, where a *zawiya* or monastic institution was established with endowed Koran readers. The complex was also called a *ribat*, and its associations with the Holy War were stressed; nearly every member of the Marinid dynasty was buried there through Abu-l-Hasan Ali. In 1338–39 the latter had the tombs and *zawiya* surrounded with a wall, a mock fortification referred to in its inscription as a *ribat*. The gate (*Plate 149*) has flanking towers whose projecting corners are supported by corbels of *muqarnas*, one of the rare instances in

North Africa or Spain when this motif was translated into stone, perhaps under Egyptian influence.

The Attarine Madrasa at Fez

Sufism was very strong in Morocco, where it encouraged the worship of local "saints" (often called *marabouts*) whose tombs with adjoining *zawiyas* abound and were frequently patronized by Marinid sultans. Perhaps to counterbalance the often over-emotional if not downright heretical aura of such foundations and to obliterate what they considered the Almohad heresy, all the fourteenth-century caliphs were zealous in the founding of *madrasas* (*mederses*) to teach the fundamentals of Sunni doctrine and to provide trained bureaucrats for the *makhzen* or palace administration.

One of the most perfect of these is the Attarine Madrasa or *madrasa* of the perfume sellers just north of the Qarawiyin Mosque at Fez. Built by the Sultan Abu Said Uthman (1310–31) in 1323–25, its essential elements (Plate 150), like those of all *madrasas*, consist of a court with an ablution basin and arcades entered by a narrow passage from the street, a *midha* surrounded by latrines, tiers of students' cells and passageways (not shown in the plan), and a nearly square prayer hall surmounted by a pyramidal wooden roof. The court (Plate 151) is a marvel of intricate ornament almost miniature in scale. Tile mosaic, tile sgraffito (wherein the glaze is cut from the finished tile in patterns), carved stone (for the shafts and capitals of the columns), carved stucco (originally polychrome and carved), and carved gilded wood all play their part. The capitals (Plate 152) descend from the Cordoban version of the Roman composite order, through the Almohad simplification of the acanthus to the point where the capital becomes a cylinder supporting a half cube with incised relief ornament. A similar simplification is applied to the shapes of the arches: the round horseshoe arch is revived, but its return at the base is often almost imperceptible. Pointed arches are usually extremely obtuse, and the lobate arch loses its force due to the excessive multiplication of its lobes.

The Bou Inaniya Madrasa at Fez

This is the most monumental *madrasa* ever erected by the Marinids. Its founder, Abu Inan (1348–59), who built it between 1350 and 1355, intended it for the Friday prayer as well as for the lodging and instruction of students. It seems also to have had another important function. The tall minaret in the northwest corner overlooked all the others in Fez. Accessible to the minaret across a corridor running high up over the domed porch of the north portal was an elaborate water clock, now ruined, from which the time for prayer could be quickly communicated to this and all the other mosques of Fez. At the north

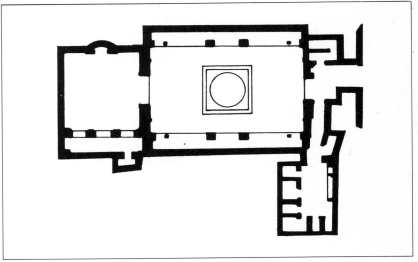

151. *Fez, Attarine Madrasa, court looking west from the prayer hall*
152. *Fez, Attarine Madrasa, court, detail of a capital*

153. *Fez, Bou Inaniya Madrasa, 1350–55, plan*

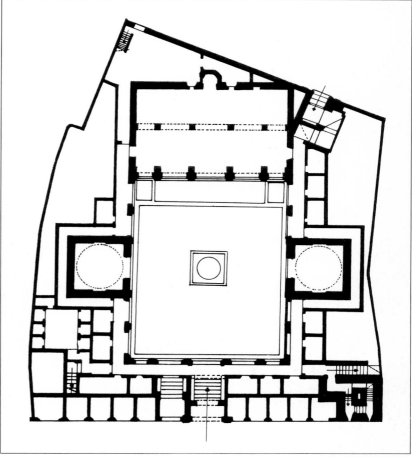

121

facade shops lined both sides of the street and included, opposite the portal, an enormous and luxurious public latrine supplementary to a smaller one within the *madrasa*.

Multiple functions dictated a complex plan (*Plates 153, 154*). A marble-paved court about 194 square feet is surrounded on three sides by a cloister on heavy piers screened by *mushrabiyya* panels. It supports a windowed second story and at both levels is lined with students' cells. To east and west lambrequin arches open onto lecture halls (*Plate 156*) 54 square feet and two stories high, with *muqarnas* vaults alongside the cloister corridors. Such halls are like Persian and Egyptian *iwans*, but are uncommon in Fez because most students attended classes either in the Qarawiyin or Andalusian mosques.

The prayer hall facade of five unequal arches on piers, rather like the Syrian *madrasas* of Aleppo, is separated from the court by the channel of the Oued Fez which, crossed by two bridges, serves, like the central basin, for ablutions. The hall has two aisles parallel to the *qibla*, supported upon heavy onyx columns with rather gross capitals (*Plate 155*); it is roofed by the parallel vaults of magnificent wooden *artesonado* paneling. Despite the fact that the pointed horseshoe arches of the prayer hall regain some of the vigor of the Almohad style and that the court has a monumental grandeur, the ornament, when examined in detail, shows a loss of delicacy. The precision of the Attarine Madrasa is gone, and it is apparent that Marinid art will soon enter a period of decline.

THE NASRIDS OF SPAIN AND THE ALHAMBRA

In 1238 Muhammad I al-Ghalib, called Ibn al-Ahmar (1230–72), an Arab descendant of Ahmad III al-Mustansir (1119–42), the last Hudid king (in exile) of Zaragoza, established the Kingdom of Granada and erected the citadel called the Alhambra, the "red fortress," which became his capital. There he founded the Nasrid Dynasty, allies and tributaries of Ferdinand I and Alfonso X of Castile until their final expulsion in 1492.

The Palace of Yusuf I and the Earlier Structure

The Alhambra is the only major surviving Nasrid structure in Spain and its miraculous preservation is doubly fortunate in that no Marinid palace survives. Literary evidence suggests, however, that, although larger, the Marinid palaces were very like the Alhambra. Recent research by Frederick P. Bargebuhr suggests that a substantial residence had already been built here about 1060 by Yehoseph ibn Naghralla, Jewish vizier to the Berber Taifas king, Ibn Habbus. Masonry typical of Habbus' period exists at the base of the outer walls, but within the palace only the lion fountain (which may still stand in its

157. *Granada, Alhambra, thirteenth and fourteenth century, plan*
1. *Entrance* 2. *First court* 3. *Ruins of the mosque* 4. *Road* 5. *Court of Machuca*
6. *Tower of Machuca* 7. *Mexuar* 8. *Court of the Cuarto Dorado* 9. *Cuarto
Dorado* 10. *Court of Myrtles* 11. *Salon de la Barca* 12. *Tower of Comarès and
Hall of the Ambassadors* 13. *Baths* 14. *Court of the Screen* 15. *Apartments of
Charles V* 16. *Tower of the Queen's Boudoir* 17. *Garden of Daraxa* 18. *Mirador
of Daraxa* 19. *Hall of the Two Sisters* 20. *Court of Lions* 21. *Hall of the
Muqarnas* 22. *Hall of Justice* 23. *Hall of the Abencerajes* 24. *Cistern* 25. *Ditch*
26. *Rauda (necropolis)* 27. *Chapel of the Palace of Charles V* 28. *Palace of
Charles V*

158. *Granada, Alhambra, view of the palace from the north*
159. *Granada, Alhambra, Cuarto Dorado, south facade* ▷

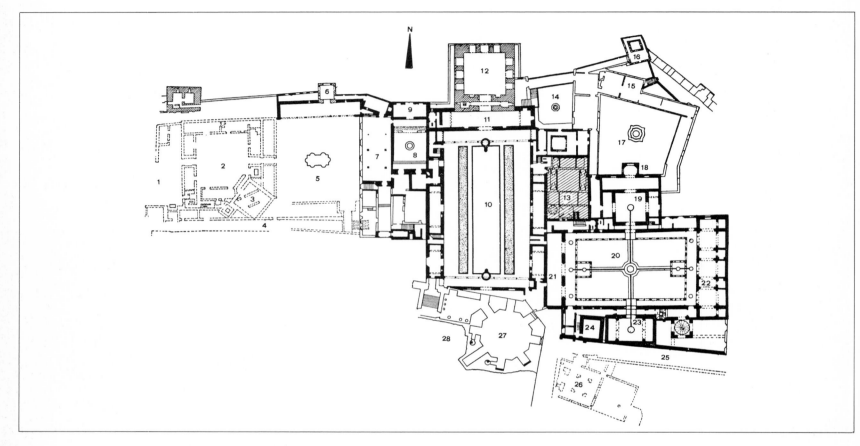

original position) survives. The oldest surviving Nasrid remains in the Alhambra (*Plate 157*) are the foundations of courts (1, 2, 5) through which the palace was approached from the heavily fortified western tip of the plateau (*Plate 158*). From court 5 (called the Court of Machuca) the Mexuar (7) was entered, perhaps an outer reception hall with a small oratory to its north. After this one entered a square porticoed court (8) with a narrow room, the Cuarto Dorado (9), overlooking the plain to its north (*Plate 159*). This part of the palace was probably erected before the accession of Yusuf I in 1333, though later redecorated. Through a narrow entrance the Court of Myrtles (10), also called the Patio de los Arrayánes or de la Alberca, is next entered (*Plate 160*). A pool with fountains and porticoes to north and south nearly fills the space. To the north stands the Tower of Comarès (12) containing a room 121 1/2 square feet with an antechamber, the Salon de la Barca (11). The square chamber, called the Hall of the Ambassadors (*Plate 161*), was undoubtedly a throne hall, as these inscriptions in Arabic over the three windows of the north wall proclaim:

"Long may you live!" Thus when you enter in
mornings and evenings, the mouths of boon,
bliss, felicity, and charm greet you in
my name,

She is the high-domed hall and we are her daughters;
however, mine is the pre-eminence and the
honor in rank,

We are members among which I am the heart,
unchallenged; for the power of spirit
and soul originates in the heart.

And if my symbols represent the constellations
of her heaven, then in me, and not among them,
is the grandeur of the sun.

My master Yusuf has decked me (may God support him!)
in garments of pride and flawless artistry.

He made me the seat of the kingdom, and thus she
[the hall] has strengthened his rank

*Translated by Frederick P. Bargebuhr, *The Alhambra*, Berlin 1968, pp. 190–191, from Emilio Lafuente y Alcántara, *Inscripciones árabes de Granada*, Madrid 1859.

with the true light, with the seat and the
throne.*

This identification is confirmed by the presence of Surah LXVII, the Surah of the Kingdom, inscribed in the wooden cornice of the superb *artesonado* vault (*Plate 162*), whose seven tiers of eight- and sixteen-pointed stellar interlaces allude to the seven heavens mentioned in the Surah. This part of the palace, doubtless a *diwan-i-am*, and the adjoining baths to the east are all the work of Yusuf I (1333–54), though the fabric of the Tower of Comarès is probably earlier.

The Court of Lions

This is by far the most famous complex in the palace (*Plate 163*), consisting of the court itself (20) and four principal surrounding chambers, the Hall of the Muqarnas (21), the Hall of Justice (22; *Plate 164*), the Hall of the Abencerajes to the south (23), and the Hall of the Two Sisters (19) with its Mirador of Daraxa or House of Aisha (18) to the north. All were built around the earlier fountain with its twelve stone lions by Muhammad V (1354–59; 1362–91). Marble, carved and painted stucco (often pierced straight through), tile mosaic, carved and once gilded wood, and above all water—there are no less than eleven fountains—combine to form a perfect metaphor for the Koranic Paradise, described as "pavilions beneath which water flows." The longer east-west axis is defined by projecting pavilions sheltering fountains whose overflow, draining through channels to the center, forms two of the rivers of Paradise. Behind the pavilions richly ornamented transverse halls were surely used for court functions. They are linked publicly by the exquisite cloisters, but passages behind the north and south walls of the court allowed hidden access for servants as at Medina al-Zahra. Fountains in the centers of the Hall of the Abencerajes (*Plate 165*) and of the Two Sisters drain again into the center, symbolizing the other two rivers of Paradise.

The Hall of the Two Sisters, which probably served as a *diwan-i-khas*, is inscribed with a poem of twenty-four verses written by Muhammad's court poet, Ibn al-Zamrak, on the occasion of the circumcision of one of the princes (no mention is made of the young man, however). The chamber itself and the court opening from it are compared to the constellations, while the *muqarnas* vault is said to be "brilliant," to have beauties both apparent and hidden. The stars, the verses claim, would prefer to remain here rather than in the heavens. The arches of the court "vault over columns, adorned with light like the celestial spheres which are over the glowing pool of the dawn." All this light and water symbolism is summed up in the verses around the rim of the new basin added to the lion fountain by Muhammad

162. *Granada, Alhambra, Hall of the Ambassadors, wooden vault*
163. *Granada, Alhambra, Court of Lions, 1354–59; 1362–91* ▷
164. *Granada, Alhambra, Hall of Justice* ▷

V, who removed the old dodecagonal basin to the Hall of the Abencerajes. Among other verses we read here:

> I am thinking of a carved monument whose veil
>   of splendor consists of pearl
>   and which adorns the environs with the
>   diffusion of gems.
> [One sees] silver melting which flows between
>   jewels, one like the other in beauty,
>   white in purity.
> A running stream evokes the illusion of being
>   a solid substance for the eyes,
>   so that we wonder which one is in
>   truth fluid.
> But of course, it is the water that is running
>   over the rim of the fountain—
>   the monument offering long channels
>   for the water—*

Legions of sentimental visitors have reiterated the opinion that the Alhambra is a magical place, an insubstantial dream, too exquisite to have been made by human hands. It is interesting to find that the inscriptions show this was exactly the effect intended by its builders.

It remains for us to examine the physical means by which this magic was carried out. The slender, once highly polished marble columns of the court in their complex alternation of 1, 2, 3, and even 4 clusters at the pavilions set the whole composition in motion. They support a wooden frame from which all their arches and spandrels are suspended. This being so, each of these plaster webs may be pierced to admit light. Thus what we expect to be solid is as insubstantial as a cloud. The wonderful *muqarnas* vaults, likewise suspended from wooden frames, dematerialize the ceilings in a similar manner, suggesting infinite space. Most are lit from below by rows of small windows (*Plate 165*) originally closed by pierced shutters or grilles of colored glass. Since even the *muqarnas* was polychromed and gilded, the effect must have been magical indeed.

If vertical space tends to seem infinite, horizontal space does not. Here, rather than unified or flowing space in the Baroque European sense, we are presented with a succession of independent cells each complete in itself and separated from its neighbors by a screen of

*Translated and amended by Frederick P. Bargebuhr, *The Alhambra*, Berlin 1968, p. 171, from Emilio Lafuente y Alcántara, *Inscripciones árabes de Granada*, Madrid 1859.

165. *Granada, Alhambra, Hall of the Abencerajes, vault*

columns or an arch. At only one point, in the Mirador of Daraxa, is there an opening to the outside world at eye level—and that probably had shutters originally. It should also be remembered that the building was designed for people who normally sat on or near the floor. This explains why, with the exception of the central one, all the other fountain basins, some quite large, are flush with the marble floors. They overflow into narrow depressions around their edges and each has a single slender jet which agitates but does not destroy the reflections in the water. These reflections, best observed while seated beside them, literally set all the rich ornament in motion; hence the verses around the central fountain basin. It is quite probable that the four quarters of the court, now covered with ochre sand flush with the pavements, were originally some three or four feet lower, after the manner of the Moroccan *riadh*. Flowers and flowering bushes or even small trees would then have been nearer the eye level of persons seated in the porticoes, but they would not have obscured their view of the court. The present bareness is not consistent with the reiteration of the Paradise metaphor emphasized everywhere. We are here in the presence of a masterpiece equaled only in the Moghul gardens of India. Its very perfection hovers on the brink of decadence—one last supreme expression of a culture about to be banished forever from the Iberian peninsula.

Conclusion

Marinid and Nasrid architecture, like the Almoravid and the Almohad creations of Spain and the Maghrib, form a stylistic unit. It seems likely that, as in the days of the early Almoravids when craftsmen might have fled to Morocco after the fall of the Cordoban Caliphate, so too there was an exodus from Andalusia after the Christian conquest in the thirteenth century. When the Marinids and the Nasrids again had the means to build, they could avail themselves of such craftsmen or of their sons, who had lost little of their skill. Indeed, these artisans were also available to Christian and Jewish patrons in Burgos, Toledo, Zaragoza, and Seville, where they produced the splendid works of thirteenth- and fourteenth-century Mudejar architecture which fall outside the range of this book. By the fifteenth century, however, despite the finesse of the craftsmanship, there is apparent a decrease in vigor and an over-richness of ornament applied without much understanding or discretion. This becomes painfully evident in Morocco, where the successors of the Marinids contributed little or nothing to the development of Islamic architecture and thus are omitted from our discussion. In Spain the same happened to the Mudejar style, which increasingly incorporated first Gothic and then Renaissance details.

Reign of the Caliph al-Muizz (953–75)

The origins and early history of the Fatimids have already been treated. It remains here to chronicle the apogee of their glory as rulers of Egypt and their swift decline. Like all Shi'ite Muslims, the Fatimids were strongly inclined to mysticism, which often led to a deep dependence on astrology. When al-Muizz began his preparations in 967 for the conquest of Egypt he was probably inspired by the propitious conjunction of Saturn and Jupiter in the sign of the Ram that took place that year. In 969 his Sicilian-Byzantine general Jawhar, having defeated the Ikshidids and taken al-Fustat, camped on unoccupied land to the north and immediately began an enclosure of very large unbaked bricks about 1,435 square yards (*Plate 166*) to house a palace, barracks, and administrative buildings. Apparently its original name was to have been al-Mansuriya, "the Victorious," after the suburb outside Kairouan founded for the same purpose in 945–49. A propitious moment chosen for the filling of the foundation trenches was to have been signaled by a string of bells, but a crow landed prematurely inside the enclosure before work began. This happened in the ascendency of the planet Mars (Qahir al-Falak). When four years later al-Muizz arrived from Kairouan he deemed this horoscope propitious and the site was renamed al-Qahira, "the Triumphant." This story of the founding of present-day Cairo, as Creswell points out, may well be legendary since twenty-six years before a similar account had been given of the foundation of Alexandria, but it is worth recounting for what it reveals of the very real non-practical basis of some Islamic city foundings. Essentially the first enclosure was not intended as a true city any more than the circular city of Baghdad had been. Rather it was a palatial residence and administrative quarter like Mahdiya or even the Forbidden City of Peking; the walled compounds of the city palaces of the present Moroccan dynasty in Marrakesh, Meknes, and Fez are its direct descendants.

A major north-south street linked the old Bab al-Futuh gate with the old Bab Zuwayla, both named for gates at al-Mansuriya. Part of this street survives in the modern Sharia al-Muizz li-din-Illah. On either side of this, north of the Mosque of al-Azhar, stood the eastern palace laid out by Jawhar and the western palace first built by al-Aziz (975–96). Between them was a very large open square, the Bayn al-Kasrayn ("between the two palaces"). No trace remains of the eastern palace, but literary sources summarized by Creswell inform us that it consisted of a walled enclosure with nine gates of stone and burnt brick. At least one of these, probably the Bab al-Dahab or Golden Gate, had a window from which on occasion the Caliph appeared to his people. Within the enclosure were

ten or twelve square pavilions. The most important of these was the Kasr al-Dahab within which was the Qa'at al-Dahab, one of the two principal throne rooms. The other was in a pavilion called the Iwan al-Kabir or Great Iwan, built by al-Aziz. This was domed and occupied the center of the enclosure. Probably the arrangement as a whole was complex and asymmetrical, as at Medina al-Zahra. In this it must have differed notably from the more symmetrical Abbasid palaces or those at Mahdiya and Ashir.

The Mosque of al-Azhar

The modern Sharia al-Azhar may mark a former west-east axis of Jawhar's enclosure. Directly south of this, near the Bab al-Barqiya gate, Jawhar began the great Mosque of al-Azhar in April of 970. The *Khutba* (Friday prayer) was first read from its *minbar* in June of 972 and a university was founded in it in 988. Salvaged shafts and capitals support pointed four-centered arches of burnt bricks, which are also used for the outer walls and much resemble those of the Mosque of Ibn Tulun. No idea at all is possible of the original appearance of the mosque's exterior, but Creswell has reconstructed the original plan (*Plate 168*). This shows a building which in its doubling and trebling of columns at points of stress resembles Ubayd Allah's first mosque at Mahdiya. There is the same strong emphasis on the *mihrab* axis, but the corner domes of al-Azhar seem not to have been present at Mahdiya. Furthermore, the aisles of al-Azhar run parallel to the *qibla* wall. The *mihrab* aisle was enriched with magnificent curvilinear stucco ornament (*Plate 169*). The ultimate origin of the fine overall pattern may be the spandrels of some of the arches of the sixth-century Hagia Sophia in Constantinople, but the more immediate influence is that of the stuccoes in Ibn Tulun's mosque. The facade of the prayer hall (*Plate 167*) results from a twelfth-century reconstruction of the *sahn* and is discussed later.

Reigns of the Caliphs al-Aziz (975–96) and al-Hakim (996–1021)

The Friday mosque now known by the name of al-Hakim was begun by al-Aziz outside the north wall of Jawhar's enclosure between the old Bab al-Futuh and the old Bab al-Nasr late in the year 990 (*Plate 172*). Al-Aziz held the first Friday prayer there in November of 991. His successor, al-Hakim, ordered the entrance facade finished in 1002/3, including the two minarets and the monumental entrance between them (*Plates 173, 175*). In late 1010 al-Hakim, rather inexplicably, ordered the minarets surrounded by two square salients, concealing them to a height equal to that of the walls of the mosque. In March of 1013, after gifts of curtains and rich furniture were made, the first Friday prayer was conducted in the refurbished building.

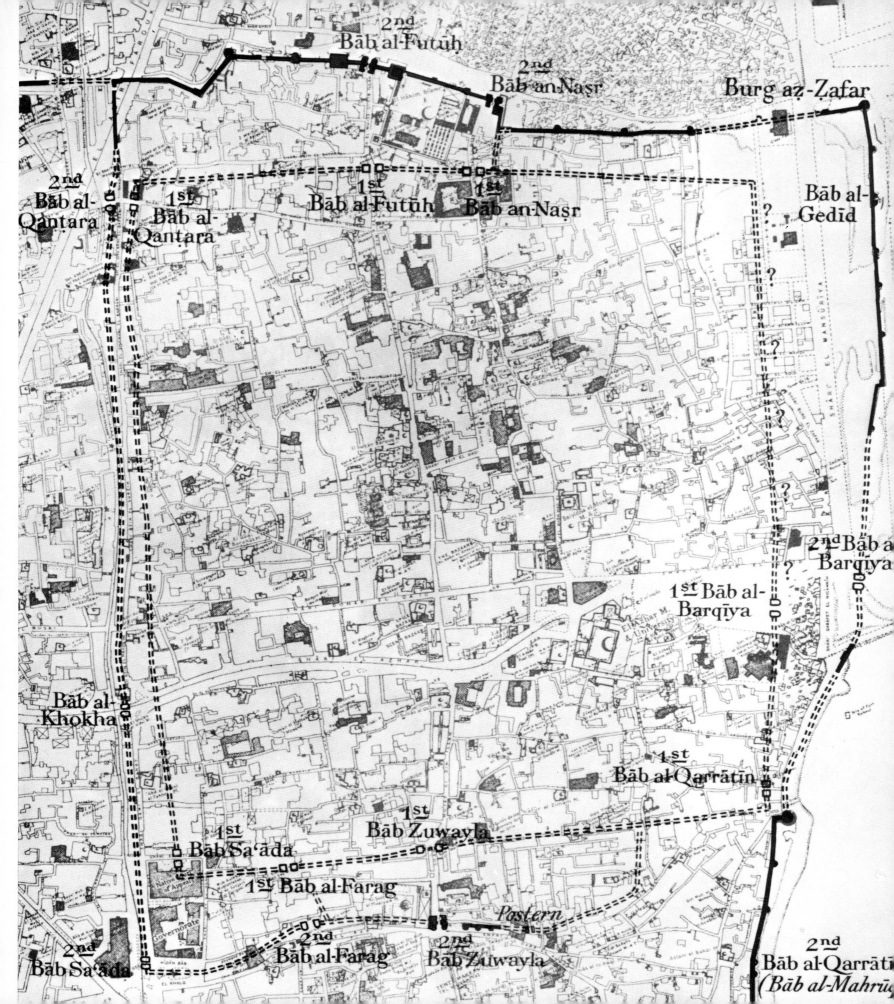

2nd
Bāb al-Futūh

2nd
Bāb an Naṣr

Burg aẓ-Ẓafar

2nd
Bāb al-
Qantara

1st
Bāb al-
Qantara

1st
Bāb al-Futūh

1st
Bāb an Naṣr

Bāb al-
Gedīd

?

?

?

?

2nd Bāb a
Barqīya

1st Bāb al-
Barqīya

?

Bāb al-
Khokha

1st
Bāb al Qarrātīn

1st
Bāb Zuwayla

1st
Bāb Saʿada

1st Bāb al-Farag

Postern

2nd
Bāb al-Farag

2nd
Bāb Zuwayla

2nd
Bāb Saʿada

2nd
Bāb al-Qarrātī
(Bāb al-Mahrū

◁ 166. *Cairo (al-Qahira), plan of the city as first enclosed in 969 by Jawhar, with additions of 1087–92 by Badr al-Gamali and of 1171 by Salah ad-Din*

167. *Cairo, Mosque of al-Azhar, facade of the prayer hall (1131–49) before the rebuilding of 1891–92*

168. *Cairo, Mosque of al-Azhar, 970–72, plan as reconstructed by Creswell*

169. *Cairo, Mosque of al-Azhar, stucco ornament on an arcade in the southwest transept*

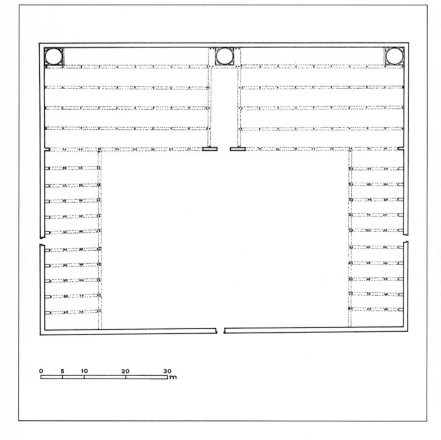

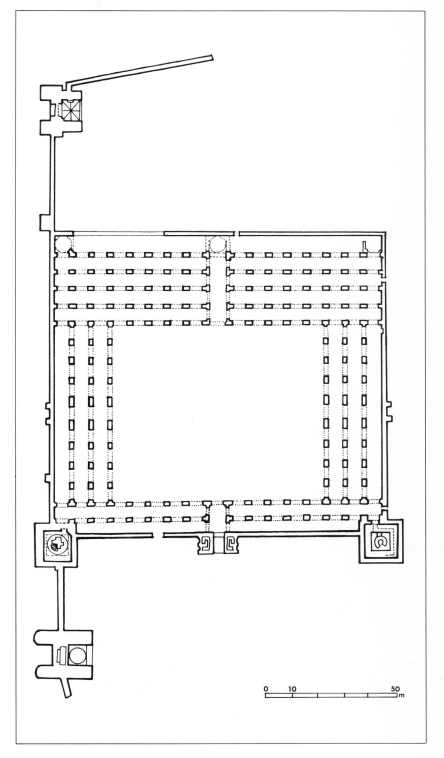

The prototype for the structure begun under al-Aziz was clearly Ibn Tulun's mosque, though here the brick piers are slenderer, while the transept or *mihrab* aisle (*Plate 176*) with its (restored) clerestory and the three domes of the *qibla* aisle (*Plate 174*) recall the Mosque of al-Azhar. The latter may also have inspired al-Hakim's facade, but this is less certain since the facade of al-Azhar no longer exists. We now, however, know much more about Ubayd Allah's mosque at Mahdiya, and al-Hakim's strange salients of 1010 approximate the square cisterns with cylindrical interiors of that structure. Though it is not known if Mahdiya's cisterns were even intended to support minarets, they now end at the height of the walls of the mosque as do al-Hakim's salients. The central portal at Mahdiya certainly provided al-Hakim's architect with his model, and even the placement of the secondary portals closer to the center than to the ends of the facade is similar. Al-Hakim's mosque originally had no less than thirteen entrances, all symmetrically arranged and three of them monumental. The two side portals provided a cross-axis at the center line of the *sahn*. The porch and the minarets of al-Hakim's facade of of 1002/3 are of superb masonry construction richly adorned with crisp and elegant ornament reminiscent of Medina al-Zahra's of a half century earlier. The frequent occurrence of the pentagram or Solomon's seal may attest to al-Hakim's known interest in black magic, though it must be remembered he was only eighteen when this work was in progress.

Reign of the Caliph al-Mustansir (1036–94)

The rapid decline of the Fatimid Caliphate became accelerated under al-Mustansir, reaching a climax in 1073 when, after years of plagues and famines, an army revolt threatened to erupt into full-scale anarchy. The Caliph then ordered Badr al-Gamali, the Armenian governor of Acre, to restore order. Badr succeeded after many executions and was rewarded with the title of Amir al-Juyushi ("army commander"), by which he is best known; he was also made vizier and chief of the Shi'ite missionary organization. After he returned from a campaign in the Sudan in 1085, Badr ordered work begun on a mosque, in which he may have intended to be buried, and new walls for Cairo.

The Mosque of al-Juyushi

The Mosque of al-Juyushi (*Plates 177, 178*) is a small *mashad* or oratory of rubble masonry and brick, situated on an exposed hillside dominating Cairo from the east and overlooking its southern approaches. It has recently been pointed out by Farid Shafe'i that the prominent minaret would hardly have been necessary in a neighbor-

173. *Cairo, Mosque of al-Hakim, reconstruction by Creswell* 175. *Cairo, Mosque of al-Hakim, monumental entrance, detail*
174. *Cairo, Mosque of al-Hakim, interior,* qibla *aisle looking northeast*

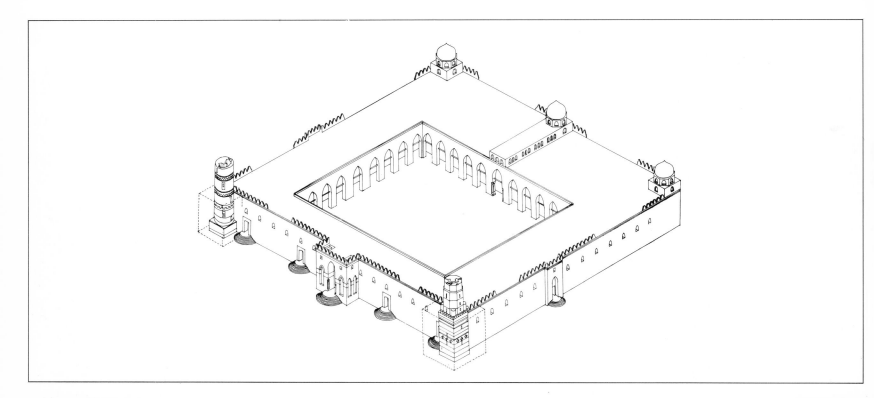

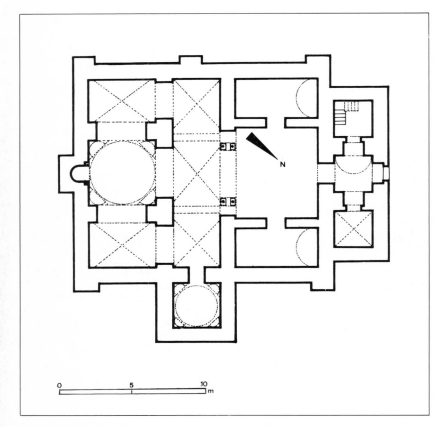

hood with very few residents to call to prayer. However, the minaret and four small domed structures on the roof, too small for kneeling in prayer, would have provided excellent observation posts for those interested in preventing civil unrest or attack from the south, both real possibilities in view of the disturbances within the Caliphate. The elegant interior, reached through a small door at the base of the minaret on axis with the *mihrab*, seems to have been arranged for residential purposes as well as for worship, since the barrel-vaulted chambers flanking the minute *sahn* have no connection with the prayer hall. Symmetry is broken only by the tomb chamber, its dome supported on the usual squinches, opening from the first bay of the prayer hall through the northeast wall. The cornice terminating the square base of the minaret is formed of large-scale *muqarnas*, the earliest extant example in Egypt. The superb carved stucco *mihrab* so closely recalls Seljuk work in Iran, though admittedly the surviving examples there are somewhat later, that one wonders if these designs and the *muqarnas* were not transmitted from Iran or even further east at the same time.

Origin of the Muqarnas
The origin of the *muqarnas* or stalactite vault (also called the honeycomb vault), an essential element in one form or another of all "classic" Islamic architecture, has never been settled. Until recently it was generally accepted that a triple squinch of the type in the famous North Dome Chamber of the Great Mosque at Isfahan was elaborated into a multiple form that gave rise to all the later decorative uses. The oldest datable example of such a squinch occurs in the tomb of Arab Ata at Tim in Transoxiana and is dated 977–78 (*Plate 230*). However, a number of concave pointed elements of stucco with flat bases were found some years ago in the excavations conducted at Nishapur by the Metropolitan Museum of Art. They may originate as early as the late eighth or early ninth century, but have never been published in their entirety. If these were indeed elements of a *muqarnas* composition, then the ornamental use of such vaulting may have preceded the structural.

The Gunbad-i-Ali at Abarquh in central Persia, dated 1056, provides the earliest example of an exterior *muqarnas* cornice (*Plate 257*). A *muqarnas* dome in stucco, obviously well beyond the experimental stage, appears for the first time in the Imam Dur at Samarra of 1085–86 (*Plate 264*). As we have seen, the *muqarnas* fragments in stucco from the Qala of the Bani Hammad cannot be securely dated, but may be as early as the late eleventh century. It seems, then, that when al-Juyushi's architect built his cornice he was probably recalling Seljuk Persian architecture either in Persia proper or in Iraq and

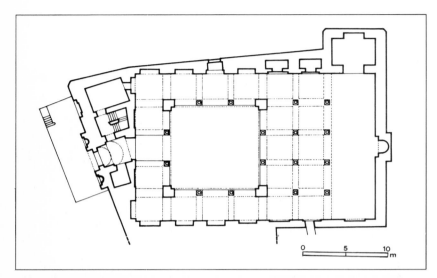

that after this date the form proceeded westward rather rapidly. It must, however, be kept in mind that new discoveries may modify this explanation at any time.

The Walls of Badr al-Gamali

Between 1087 and 1092 Badr al-Gamali extended and strengthened the defenses of Cairo. The mud brick walls of Jawhar were replaced and extended in stone to the north by a curtain between a new Bab al-Nasr (called the Bab al-Izz or Gate of Glory in the inscription, which states it was begun in May of 1087) and a new Bab al-Futuh (*Plate 179*). In the same inscription the Bab al-Futuh is called the Bab al-Iqbal or Gate of Prosperity, begun in 988. (The names of Jawhar's old gates were retained in common usage regardless of the new ones given them by Badr and al-Mustansir.) To the south the Bab Zuwayla is known to have been dated according to a now-lost inscription at 1092; east of it, a stretch of wall with two towers survives for about 505 feet.

The new extensions were executed by three Christian architects from Urfa, ancient Edessa, which had fallen to the Sunni Seljuks in 1086 and was probably much less hospitable toward Christian artisans than the currently more tolerant Shi'ite Fatimids. The style of all three gates, which introduced a standard of stone masonry into Egypt never to be surpassed, is Armenian and Syrian. The round arch is used throughout, whereas before it had appeared only in the windows of the mosques of al-Azhar and al-Hakim. The spherical pendentive in stone masonry, also Syrian, is here introduced into Egypt for the first time, as is the decorative use of the cushion voussoir. However, both had been used in the eighth century at Khirbat al-Mafjar.

FROM THE REIGN OF AL-AMIR (1101–31) TO AL-ADID (1160–71)
The Mosque of al-Aqmar

The Fatimid Caliphs of the twelfth century were, like their Sunni counterparts in Baghdad, nothing but the puppets of their military commanders. The Fatimid dream of a universal Shi'ite state had been reduced to a tenuous hold upon Egypt, soon to be broken. In 1125 al-Amir and his vizier al-Mamun al-Bataihi completed the small Mosque of al-Aqmar on the east side of the Sharia al-Muizz li-din-Illah, in the northeast quadrant of Jawhar's original enclosure. This is the first surviving Islamic example of the alignment of the principal facade with a pre-existing street while also preserving the required internal orientation of the mosque proper toward Mecca. Presumably as the city within the walls became more crowded land values rose, and this procedure became increasingly necessary. The facade—originally symmetrical, as the plan (*Plate 180*) shows—is the first in

182. *Cairo, Mosque of al-Aqmar, street facade*

183. *Cairo, Mosque of al-Salih Tala'i, begun 1160, plan*
184. *Cairo, Mosque of al-Salih Tala'i, entrance porch*

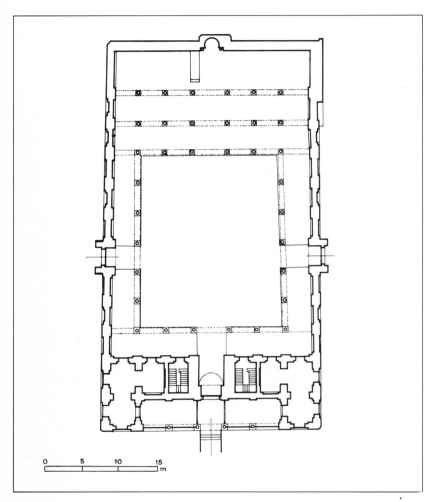

Egypt to exhibit a carefully articulated ornamental scheme (*Plate 182*). There is also a more complex and sophisticated use of *muqarnas*, here defining for the first time the square heads of the shallow niches flanking the portal (*Plate 181*). This niched portal, set into a projecting porch and reminiscent of al-Hakim's but shallower, begins to exhibit the keel-shaped arch so characteristic of later Fatimid architecture. This type of arch is fully developed in the arcades of the *sahn*. The keel arch with ribs had already been seen in brick in the Baghdad Gate of Raqqa of 772, but here the stonemasons (perhaps Armenian or Syrian) have added cushioned voussoirs.

The Sahn of al-Azhar

The Caliph al-Hafiz (1131–49) was probably the patron of a reconstruction of the *sahn* of the Mosque of al-Azhar. His work was drastically rebuilt in 1891–92, but old drawings and photographs record its original appearance. The facade of the prayer hall (*Plate 167*) now shows the keel-shaped arch throughout, including the niche heads where ribbed decorations combine with a row of *muqarnas*. These niches recall the real openings used earlier at the Mosque of Ibn Tulun to lessen the load on the arches below. The *pishtaq* over the *mihrab* aisle, with its balustered parapet recalling the railings of Khirbat al-Mafjar, conceals a dome in the first bay of the *mihrab* aisle; the dome was added in the same period. Domes in this position are found elsewhere in North Africa, whence the Fatimids may have imported the idea. The richly carved plaster of the interior (*Plate 171*) seems flatter and on a smaller scale than earlier Fatimid stucco decoration.

The Mosque of al-Salih Tala'i

When the Caliph al-Faiz (1154–60) acceded to the throne at the age of four, the women of the palace cut off their hair and sent it as a symbol of their distress to al-Salih Tala'i ibn Ruzziq, Governor of Ashmunayn in upper Egypt. He restored order for a time, but could not prevent the fall of Ascalon to the Crusaders. At Ascalon had been preserved the head of Husein, a sacred Shi'ite relic which was then transferred to Cairo. Maqrisi tells us that al-Salih built his mosque outside Badr's walls just southwest of the Bab Zuwayla to house the relic, but that the Caliph wanted it in the palace itself, where he built a *mashad* for it. According to an inscription, however, the mosque (*Plate 183*) was begun in 1160, when the head had already been in Cairo for some time. Even so the unique entrance facade, with a portico *in antis* like a Persian *talar* (*Plate 184*), might have been designed for the building's intended function as a reliquary. Although the *talar* of the tomb of the seventh and ninth *imams* at al-Kazzamain dates

185. *Cairo, Mosque of al-Salih Tala'i,* sahn

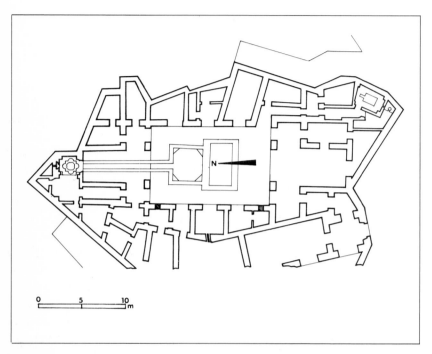

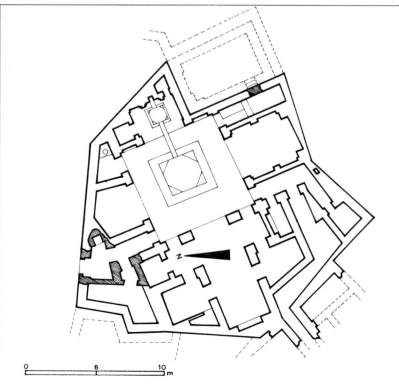

only from 1519 and that of Fatima, daughter of the seventh and sister of the eighth *imam*, at Qum is probably even later, the tradition of adding *talars* to such shrines may well have originated much earlier.

Al-Salih's mosque was freestanding on at least three sides, unlike that of al-Aqmar. It was also designed as a *mu'allaqa* or suspended mosque with vaulted shops across the front and sides. The salients flanking the keel-arched portico might have been intended for minarets, though there is no evidence for this. The northwest *riwaq* of the *sahn* opposite the sanctuary (*Plate 185*) was a later addition not provided for in the original plan, where the monumental side entrances would have occupied the center arches of the northeast and southwest *riwaqs* as they do at the Mosque of al-Hakim. The salients and the exterior facades of the northeast and southwest *riwaqs* introduce a new method of articulation that was to have a long future in Egypt. Shallow niches frame square windows in regular succession.

FATIMID HOUSES
The Houses of al-Fustat

Information on residential architecture of Fatimid times is very limited, but excavations of the suburb of al-Fustat, begun in 1912 and recently resumed, show a house type (*Plates 186, 187*) similar to the Abbasid *bayts* at Ukhaidir and Samarra and probably introduced into Egypt under the Tulunids. The typical T-shaped organization behind a tripartite facade at al-Fustat usually occupies only one end of the square or rectangular court, but in at least one instance—as at Ukhaidir—two such facades confront each other. Out of such a complex there seems to have evolved the *qa'a* or reception hall of later times. The dating of these structures is very uncertain, but most originated in the eleventh or early twelfth centuries.

The Qa'at al-Dardir

The earliest *qa'a* preserved in Cairo is the twelfth-century Qa'at al-Dardir (*Plate 188*). Here two very tall barrel-vaulted *iwans* (*Plate 189*) face each other north and south of a sunken square, the *durka*, whose south and east walls are articulated by wall arches in the shape of the barrel vaults over tall keel-arched niches. Above the wall arches are three windows, once part of a clerestory of twelve which may have supported a wooden dome. The lower walls are of ashlar masonry, but the vaults of the *iwans* with their curious triangular squinches are of brick. The squinches recall the Fatimid restoration (1035) of the Mosque of al-Aqsa at Jerusalem, but the keel-arched niches suggest a date not before the first half of the twelfth century. Later *qa'as* are roofed in wood throughout. The form which begins here might be an adaptation of the al-Fustat house to more crowded conditions

188. *Cairo, Qa'at al-Dardir, twelfth century, section*
189. *Cairo, Qa'at al-Dardir, iwan*

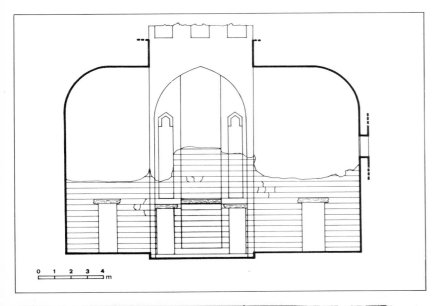

and higher land values requiring the sacrifice of the open courts and triple porticoes of the earlier houses.

Conclusion

Despite its Shi'ite orientation, the Fatimid Caliphate at Cairo seems to have been open to architectural ideas from all over Islam, including those which were Sunni. Similarly, the Fatimids' Sunni successors borrowed freely from their Shi'ite predecessors: the monumental mosque portal, like a Roman triumphal arch, seems to have been one of these. Before Mahdiya it had been used in palaces— for example, in the Umayyad bath portal at Khirbat al-Mafjar or the ninth-century palaces at Samarra. The Fatimids gave it the same bold projection for the Mosque of al-Hakim or used it in low relief as at al-Aqmar. Their Ayyubid and Mamluk successors were to do the same. Badr al-Gamali's masons probably brought the idea of the *muqarnas* from the East as early as 1085. In Egypt the motif in both stone and later in brick and wood was to have a long career. It was probably transmitted to Ifriqiya in the late eleventh century despite the religious separation that already existed between the two countries. In the twelfth century the articulation of exterior wall surfaces by means of shallow arched niches was developed; this was to have a profound effect upon later Egyptian architecture. It was also under the Fatimids that the *qa'a* evolved as the principal reception hall of both the *selamlik* and the *harem* of Cairo's richest houses.

THE AYYUBIDS (1169–1252)

Al-Malik al-Nasir I or Salah ad-Din (1169–93), the Saladin of the Crusades, was of Kurdish origin, but of a family that had become strongly Turkicized by association with the Zengids of Mosul and Aleppo under whom Ayyub, the progenitor of the dynasty, had served in 1138. Ayyub's brother, Shirkuh, gained military control of Egypt but soon died, transferring power to his nephew Salah ad-Din in 1169. In 1171, on the death of the last Fatimid, Salah ad-Din restored the name of the Sunni Caliph of Baghdad to the Friday prayer and Egypt returned with surprisingly little friction to orthodoxy. Salah ad-Din rebuilt the east and west walls of the original Fatimid city of Cairo and in 1176 began the citadel there (*Plate 190*), much altered since his time. He also introduced the *madrasa* as a religious school for the propagation of Sunni doctrine and the training of officials. The first such school had probably been founded by the Ghaznavids, but the most famous *madrasas* were those founded by the great Seljuk vizier Nizam al-Mulk (d. 1092). Salah ad-Din's *madrasa* has not survived, but those of his successors give some idea of what it was like.

The Madrasa of Sultan Salih

Few monuments of Salah ad-Din's immediate successors survive, but the last Ayyubid, Sultan Salih Negm ad-Din (1240–49), despite his brief reign, was a great builder. The now vanished remains of a palace in his citadel on Rhoda Island will be discussed later. His *madrasa* of 1241–1243/44 on the east side of the Fatimid Bayn al-Kasrayn, today the Suq al-Nahassin, was the first in Egypt to be dedicated to all four branches of Sunni law. It consisted of two complexes divided by a narrow street, the Haret al-Salihiya, from which both were originally entered (*Plate 191*). The Malikite and Shafeyite *iwans* stood to the north adjacent to the later tomb. Enough survives to show that the *sahn* between them was lined north and south with arcades and had three tiers of rooms for students. South of the Haret al-Salihiya stood the *iwans* of the Hanafites and the Hanbalites, now almost totally destroyed. The origins of the *madrasa* plan outside of Egypt is more fully discussed in Chapter XI, but if the better preserved half of this *madrasa* is examined it is apparent that local domestic architecture of the type found in the houses at al-Fustat or the Qa'at al-Dardir is here merely enlarged. Since it is well known that private houses often served as *madrasas*, we need not look beyond Egypt for the source of this type.

The facade on the Suq al-Nahassin (*Plate 192*), if the screen of later structures were removed, would be one of the grandest urban monuments in Islam (*Plate 193*). Eight bays survive to the right of the

190.   *Cairo, Citadel of Salah ad-Din, 1176 and later*

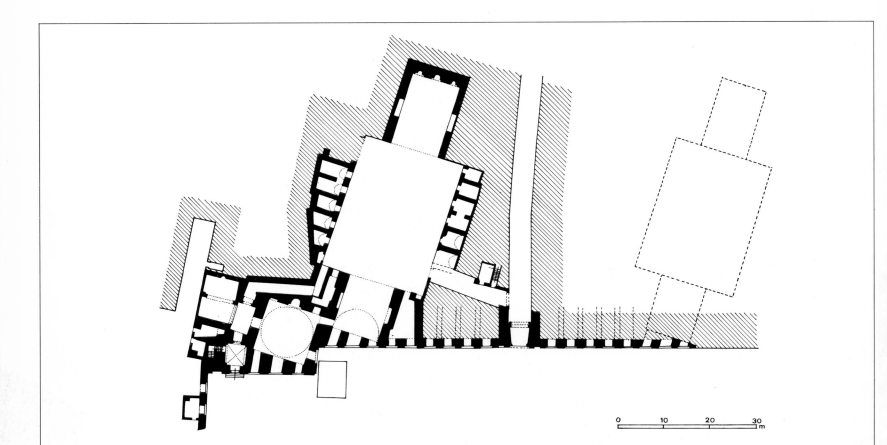

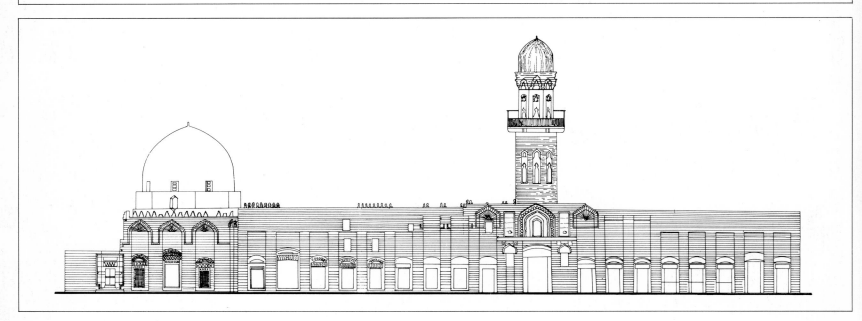

194. *Cairo, Madrasa of Salih Negm ad-Din, detail of the portal*
195. *Cairo, Tomb of Salih Negm ad-Din, 1249–50, interior, detail of*
muqarnas *in the dome* ▷

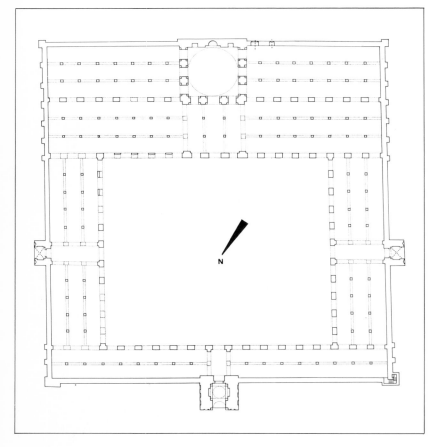

minaret which straddles the Haret al-Salihiya, and there are nine to its left plus five more for the tomb. The articulation by tall shallow niches after the manner of the Mosque of al-Salih Tala'i builds to a climax at the elaborate portal (*Plate 194*), recalling that of the Mosque of al-Aqmar but much larger. The second and third niches to the left of the portal have been restored with keel-shaped niches. Creswell believes this to be incorrect: his own solution (*Plate 192*) would be more in keeping with the evident desire to emphasize the central portal. The minaret consists of a square base with triple windows supporting an octagonal pavilion above which a fluted "pepper pot" dome rises from a rich *muqarnas* cornice. The architect has here elaborated and refined forms already in current use under the Fatimids. The Ayyubids may have imported Syrian stonemasons, as the elaborate joggled voussoirs attest, but not Syrian designers.

The tomb was begun by Sultan Salih's widow, Shajarat al-Dur, after his death in battle with the Franks late in the year 1249; Salih was buried there a year later. The square stone base, articulated by four keel-headed niches and capped by stepped crenellations, supports a brick dome rising from three tiered *muqarnas* squinches, also of brick and the earliest of their type in Egypt (*Plate 195*). The large *mihrab* is lined with contemporary marble paneling, also the earliest surviving in Egypt. Both the paneling and the new use for the *muqarnas* are probably Syrian imports.

THE BAHRI MAMLUKS (1250–1390)

The slave troops of Sultan Salih had been quartered in his fortress at Rhoda, from which this dynasty took its name (meaning pool or sea). Family succession confirmed by a majority vote generally prevailed among them, but was forbidden by their successors—the Burjis. The Bahri Mamluks fell heir not only to Egypt but to Syria, and their works show an increasing influence from that quarter as well as from Iraq after the Mongols took Baghdad in 1258.

The Great Mosque of Sultan Baybars

The first great Bahri Sultan was Baybars al-Bunduqdari (1260–77). He almost completed the expulsion of the Crusaders, saved Egypt from the Mongols, and established a somewhat questionable Abbasid Caliphate in Cairo which his successors used until 1516 to give legitimacy to their reigns. In that city Baybars ordered built a large congregational mosque north of the walls of Salah ad-Din early in the year 1267. In March of the following year Jaffa fell to the Egyptians and Baybars had wood for the *maqsura* and marble for the *mihrab* sent to Cairo from that city. The mosque was dedicated in 1269. The plan (*Plate 196*), a square of about 1,076 feet, is based in part on that of

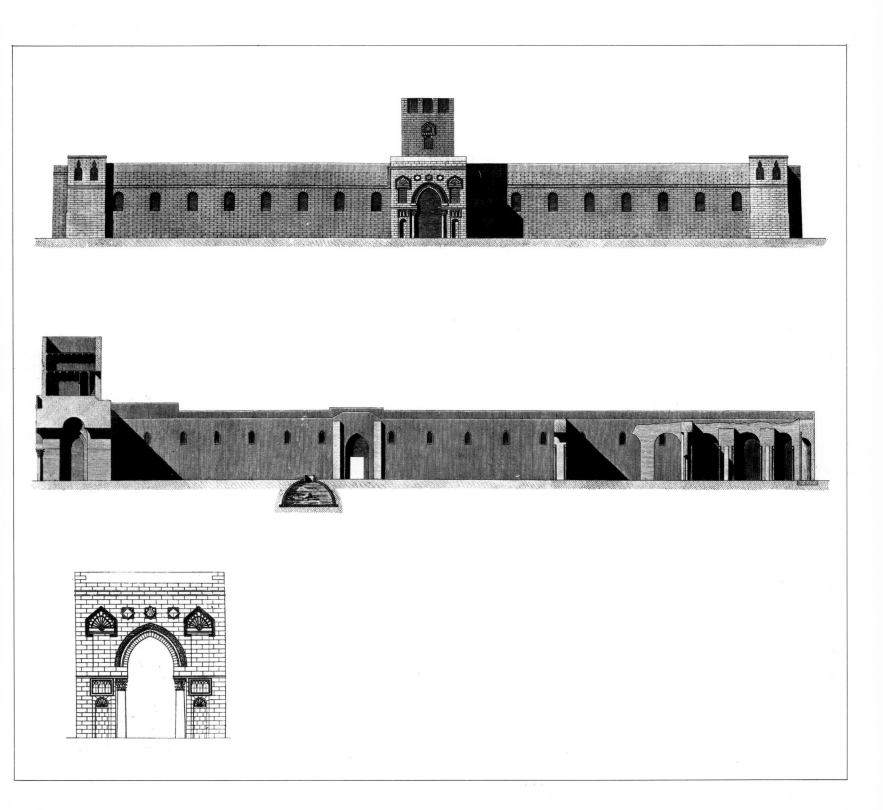

198. *Cairo, Great Mosque of Baybars, northwest portal*
199. *Cairo, Great Mosque of Baybars, northwest portal, detail*
200. *Cairo, Great Mosque of Baybars, east corner of the prayer hall*

201. *Cairo, Great Mosque of Baybars, southwest side*

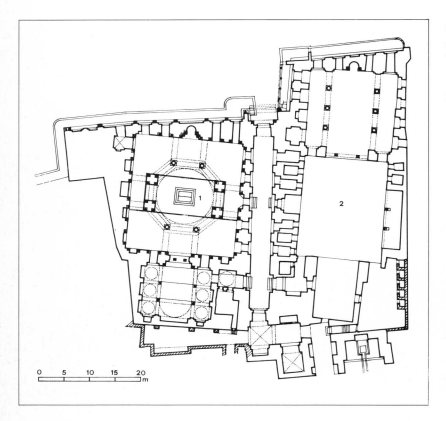

0   5   10   15   20
                  m

al-Hakim. The boldly projecting portal of the northwest facade (*Plates 197–199*), flanked by corner towers, once supported a square-based minaret in the manner of Sultan Salih's *madrasa*. The less prominent northeast and southwest portals form an axis exactly bisecting the *sahn*. The buttresses at the sides of the building correspond, though not quite accurately, to the arcades within and, with their slanting tops, show Crusader influences (*Plate 201*). Although the general arrangement of all the portals follows that of the mosques of al-Aqmar or Sultan Salih, the presence of cushioned voussoirs, stone pendentives, and the intricate marble inlay within the northwest portal all recall Syrian examples.

Until recently—when an almost complete reconstruction was begun—the interior had been totally gutted except for the piers of the *maqsura*. However, vestiges of piers, column bases, and the springing of vanished arches (*Plate 200*) permit us a glimpse of some of its original elements. From each portal the *sahn* was entered through a high-ceilinged "transept." The *maqsura* was approached through a triple "transept" with a higher center aisle, almost a basilical hall. The *maqsura* proper, about 167 square feet, was doubtless domed with the wood from Jaffa. The tripartite form of its supports goes back to the dome of Malik Shah at Isfahan, but Creswell suggests that the more immediate inspiration was the mosque built by the Artukids at Mayyafariqin (Silvan) in 1152–57.

The Tomb and Madrasa of Sultan Qala'un

Al-Mansur Sayf al-Din Qala'un (1280–90) of Kipchak Turkish origin, a slave purchased by Sultan Salih and freed in 1247, was a veteran of many campaigns in Palestine and Syria against the Franks, Armenians, and Mongols. His magnificent tomb and equally beautiful *madrasa*—together with a *muristan* or hospital, now almost entirely destroyed—were all built within the remarkably brief period between December of 1283 when land was purchased and the middle of 1285 when the *madrasa* was finished. Like the two halves of Sultan Salih's *madrasa*, Qala'un's is separated from his tomb by a great corridor from which both open and which continues on to the *muristan* (*Plate 202*). The tomb is preceded by a small court, almost an atrium, in which rises a superb carved stucco facade (*Plate 203*). Within the nearly square chamber four pink granite columns and four square piers rise to support eight arches (*Plate 204*) which lead to the octagonal-windowed drum of the dome (*Plate 205*). The wooden *muqarnas* squinches are original and suggest that the dome, now replaced, was also of wood. The whole seems a deliberate reference to the Dome of the Rock in Jerusalem, where in 1281 Qala'un had ordered a *ribat* built. The interior crowded with supports, the complex divisions into

204. *Cairo, Tomb of Sultan Qala'un, interior*
205. *Cairo, Tomb of Sultan Qala'un, interior, drum of the dome* ▷

arches, the blue and gold coffered ceilings around the central octagon, and the beautiful *mushrabiyya* screen around the cenotaph (added by al-Nasir in 1303) add up to an almost overpowering effect of richness within a small space. The *mihrab*, set in a marble-paneled dado under a frieze of carved and gilded wood (*Plate 207*), has a round-headed horseshoe arch and is of similar form in its plan. Miniature blind arcading, probably Syrian, is used here for the first time in Egypt.

The round-headed horseshoe arch is used frequently in the complex of Qala'un. It appears in the *mihrab* of the *madrasa*, in a number of windows including those of the two square stories of the minaret, and at the entrance to the great corridor on the Suq al-Nahassin. Although the Marinids of North Africa had on occasion revived this form, it was nowhere common after the fall of the Cordoban Caliphate. Perhaps along with the recall of the Dome of the Rock this was a deliberate and conscious archaism.

The *madrasa* has been much damaged. In addition to the two principal *iwans*, it must originally have had two much smaller ones (hardly more than niches) on a cross-axis, of which the survivor serves as a door to the great corridor. The *qibla iwan* is unique in that it has the form of a tripartite basilica (*Plates 206, 208*) with a clerestory (restored) over the higher "nave," whose original wooden roof was probably flat. The "nave arcades" are decked with bands of carved plaster interlacing around oculi just as they are in the tomb, while the *qibla* wall is almost as richly carved as the latter's facade. Basilical throne halls are frequent in Umayyad and Abbasid architecture, and the later but now-lost Kasr al-Ablaq in the Citadel took this form. Again there is an apparent archaism.

The facades of Qala'un's tomb and *madrasa* facing those of Sultan Salih across the Suq al-Nahassin are quite unlike them. Qala'un's tomb facade is articulated by sharply defined niches capped by pointed two-centered arches which shelter two light windows with oculi above. The niches rise like an enormously stilted arcade from salvaged columns set flush with the wall (*Plate 209*). All this recalls, as Creswell has noted, the Sicilian palaces of the Norman kings—in turn related to the secular architecture of North Africa. It is quite possible that the Western Palace of the Fatimids (built in the last quarter of the tenth century and rebuilt in 1058), which Qala'un's complex replaced, would have looked very much like the twelfth-century Norman structures. If so, it represents another deliberate antiquarianism.

These curious archaisms need an explanation. Three earlier styles or monuments seem to be invoked: the Dome of the Rock, the major Palestinian shrine; the glories of the Cordoban Caliphate; and Fatimid palace architecture. At this moment the power of Egypt

◁ 208. *Cairo, Madrasa of Sultan Qala'un, qibla iwan, interior*

209. *Cairo, Tomb of Sultan Qala'un, facade and minaret overlooking the Suq al-Nahassin*
210. *Cairo, Tomb and Madrasa of Sultan Hasan, 1356–59, plan*

was reaching its apex. The Abbasid Caliphate was reestablished in Cairo in 1261, Mecca and Medina were under Mamluk control, their rule reaching west into Lybia, eastward into Anatolia, and south to Nubia. The Mamluks were unquestionably the most powerful contemporary champions of orthodox Islam against Mongols, Franks, and Armenian Christians. Qala'un's revivals may, therefore, have been a deliberate recall of forms associated with powerful Islamic regimes of the past even if one of them had been Shi'ite. The same antiquarian interests seem occasionally to have been held by Qala'un's immediate successors. In 1291 his son Khalilo brought the portal of the church of St. John from Acre to Cairo, where it was later (sometime between 1295 and 1303–4) reassembled as the portal of the tomb and *madrasa* of another son, al-Nasir. Meanwhile a usurper, Lajin, had the spiral minaret of Ibn Tulun's mosque rebuilt between 1296–99 employing distinctively Cordoban details. After 1304 such revivals seem to have lost their appeal, and later Mamluk architecture again took up the line of development initiated by Sultan Salih, last of the Ayyubids.

The Tomb and Madrasa of Sultan Hasan

Sultan Hasan al-Nasir, last of Qala'un's line to rule in Egypt, succeeded to the throne in 1347 at age eleven, was deposed in favor of a brother in 1351, and returned in 1354 to reign until his murder in 1361. His great tomb-*madrasa* complex, the most remarkable monument of all Egyptian Islamic architecture, was begun in 1356, perhaps by a Syrian architect, and was substantially complete by 1359. In February of 1361 the right minaret over the vast entrance portal (*Plate 212*) collapsed. Its reconstruction and that of its companion on the left were then abandoned. Of the other two minarets flanking the projecting tomb chamber (*Plate 211*), that to the left is original; the one on the right fell in 1660 and was replaced on a reduced scale, though the slenderer support below it suggests this pair was never intended to match. The dome of the tomb fell in 1661. The original, probably of wood, was described by the Italian traveler Pietro della Valle (1586–1652), who saw it in 1617, as of markedly onion shape—like the present dome over the *shadrivan* in the *sahn*. The marble encrustation of the tomb chamber was finished one or two years after the Sultan's death.

The intricate plan (*Plate 210*) provides a separate and distinct *madrasa* complex for the four rites. Each, entered individually from the *sahn*, has its own modest court and vaulted *iwan*. This may explain the planned four minarets, unique for an Egyptian building. These complexes cluster around the four immense *iwans* opening from the *sahn*. Accessible mainly from the *sahn*, the east and west

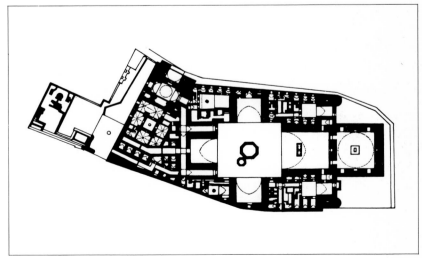

iwans were much smaller than the other two. Given the widespread use of the four-*iwan* plan for all types of buildings in Islam, the considerable literature on its application to *madrasas* seems superfluous. Since the plan existed long before the *madrasa*—let alone the four-rite *madrasa*—was invented, it would seem inevitable that the two should be combined occasionally.

Second only to the *sahn* in visual impact is the enormous portal (*Plate 212*), in its cliff-like solemnity an awe-inspiring sight even without the paired minarets originally planned. The deep niche allows for a fluted half dome supported by multiple tiers of *muqarnas*. Since the upper portion of the frame remains unfinished, how the minarets would have been adjusted to the enormous *muqarnas* cornice (which runs all the way around the building, crowned by fleur-de-lis crenellations) remains uncertain. Spiral fluted quarter columns frame the portal and accent its height, as is frequent in brick and tile buildings of Ilkhanid Persia. Paired minarets surmounting portals are of Persian origin—going back at least to the additions of the early twelfth century at the Masjid-i-Jami at Isfahan and to the thirteenth century in Anatolia—but the pattern for this one is probably Ilkhanid, perhaps the portal at Yazd (after 1324 and before 1365). The origin of the *muqarnas*-vaulted portal poses the third problem presented by this structure. Such portals appear for the first time in stucco and brick in Damascus at Nur al-Din's *muristan* of 1154, though the rest of the structure is of stone. Before the end of the twelfth century the motif had been translated into stone at the Shadbakht *madrasa* in Aleppo. In Egypt the earliest *muqarnas* portal, now destroyed, was the one in stone at the Zahiriya *madrasa* of Baybars of 1262–63. Hence Hasan's portal seems to be the reworking of an old and well-known Syrian type, augmented by a more recent Persian inspiration.

Islamic architecture acquired in the early twelfth century if not in the later eleventh that total integration of inscriptions and decoration which remained in the future one of its most important stylistic elements. Far too few studies have yet been made of the content of the inscriptions in relation to the parts of the building to which they were applied. One such study of the inscriptions of Sultan Hasan's *madrasa* has recently been made by Erica Cruikshank Dodd. In the great portal Surah XXIV, verses 36 and 37, of the Koran is quoted, equating the niche itself with a *mihrab* lighted by a lamp which is the Word of God. This quotation often appears in a *mihrab* proper or is symbolized, as on the facade of the Mosque of al-Aqmar of 1125, by the image of a lamp. It is probably not the first time that the *muqarnas* ornament is itself associated with light. The *mihrab* quotes verse 139 from Surah II, which refers to the Light of Heaven and not to that in the *mihrab* alone. Miss Dodd suggests that the portal's ref-

◁ *212. Cairo, Tomb and Madrasa of Sultan Hasan, portal*

213. Cairo, Tomb and Madrasa of Sultan Qayt Bay, 1472–74, plan
214. Cairo, Tomb and Madrasa of Sultan Qayt Bay, exterior from the northeast

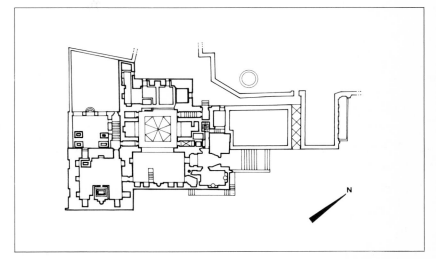

erence to the light of the *mihrab* prepared the believer for the *mihrab* inscription, which describes the mosque as the *mihrab* of the world. Much the same feeling is evoked by the huge images of the Christ Pantocrator in the apses of Cefalù and Monreale, inscribed "I am the Light of the World." Within each of the four great *iwans* an ornamented Kufic inscription in stucco quotes verses 1 to 6 of Surah XXVIII, the so-called Victory Surah with its descriptions of Paradise. In addition, over each of the six doors of the *sahn* verses 21 and 22 of Surah IX and 45 and 46 of Surah XV all refer specifically to the pavilions, fountains, and gardens of Paradise. Just as the portal's Surah referring to the lamp replaces the actual image of a lamp, so here the descriptions of Paradise replace the images of Paradise seen in the Umayyad mosque at Damascus. Ultimately Miss Dodd equates the inscription around the walls of the tomb itself (verse 256 of Surah II) with a royal symbolic image equivalent to the Christ Pantocrator in the dome of Christian churches, but also with the crowns and other royal jewels of the mosaics encircling the ambulatory of the Dome of the Rock. Here in its maturity Islam has achieved a synthesis between the sentiment expressed in the inscriptions and the architectural program which deserves more study elsewhere.

THE BURJI MAMLUKS (1382–1517)
The Tomb and Madrasa of Sultan Qayt Bay

The Burji Mamluk Sultans, named after the citadel in which Qala'un had quartered his guards, succeeded each other entirely through election and/or murder, yet the prosperity of Egypt and its provinces continued uninterrupted almost to the Turkish conquest. Between 1472 and 1474 Sultan Qayt Bay (1468–96) had built a tomb and *madrasa* in total contrast to the majesty of Sultan Hasan's foundation. Qayt Bay's architect stressed a subtle disposition of asymmetrically composed elements into a balanced whole. A virtue is made of the necessity of fitting a multipurpose building into an already crowded quarter, in contrast to the decision of Hasan's architect to screen off most of the asymmetry dictated by his site.

A four-*iwan madrasa* with cells for students, a tomb, a *sabil* or public drinking fountain, and above the *sabil* a loggia for a *kuttab* or elementary school are all expressed as interlocking rectilinear shapes (*Plate 213*). While maintaining a certain independence, all these elements are given unity by the exquisite minaret and the tall pointed dome of the tomb, dematerialized through its richly carved surface (*Plate 214*). The *sahn* with its four striped arches (*Plates 215, 216*), two stilted and two slightly horseshoe-shaped, is a compendium of Egyptian decorative styles including the keel-shaped *muqarnas*-lined niches of the Fatimids. The sanctuary and the space opposite form inde-

215. Cairo, Madrasa of Sultan Qayt Bay, sahn
216. Cairo, Madrasa of Sultan Qayt Bay, roof of the sahn (restored)

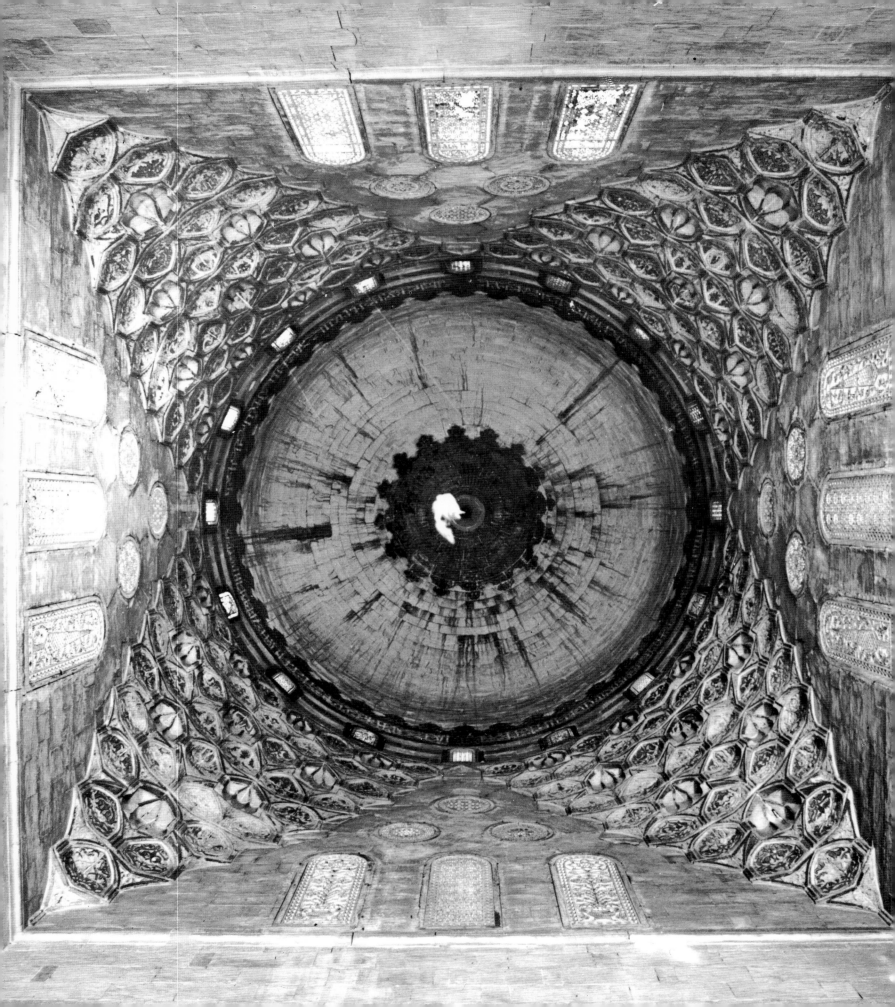

pendent chambers broader than the *sahn*, suggesting a Syrian precedent. Since the restoration of the latter's wooden roof with its lantern the domestic character of the design is more marked. Domed *sahns* with central oculi were fairly frequent in thirteenth-century Turkish *madrasas*, but seem to have been given up by the Ottomans even before the siege of Constantinople. The rich *muqarnas* squinches supporting the stone dome over the burial chamber (*Plate 217*) lead up to a zone of tiny windows, producing the effect of similar small openings in twelfth-century Syrian *muqarnas* vaults of stuccoed brick.

DOMESTIC ARCHITECTURE OF THE AYYUBIDS AND MAMLUKS
The Palace of Sultan Salih on Rhoda Island

Only the plan and the elevation of one interior doorway were recorded of the now-destroyed palace of Sultan Salih which he ordered built next to the nilometer in 1241. These were published in E.F. Jomard's *Description de l'Egypte, état moderne* in 1809. The portal shows clear evidence of the use of Crusader captives in its construction, as attested by contemporary historians. The plan, however, owes nothing to Europe: it is a later stage in the development of the *qa'a* (*Plate 218*). The grandiose cruciform structure seems to have projected two large *iwans*, perhaps groin-vaulted, north and south of an almost square central chamber whose roof, probably of wood, was supported by arches rising from four clusters of three columns each. The central square was probably finished off by a clerestory covered by a domed lantern also of wood. Three short passages and a stairwell flank the *iwans*, and two shallow niches east and west of the central square make the structure basically cruciform. There would almost certainly have been a fountain in the center.

Although the Qa'at al-Dardir and certain of the early houses at al-Fustat are the ultimate ancestors of this building, a recently found *qa'a* from an Artukid palace at Diyarbekir (without the columns, however) is otherwise similar. Oktay Aslanapa suggests that this building with a fountain richly decorated in glass mosaic and colored marble and built in the early thirteenth century (before 1222) was inspired by those of Nur al-Din Zengi in Damascus. It is not impossible, given the fairly close contacts between the Artukids and the Ayyubids, that the influence was from Cairo.

The Kasr al-Ablaq in the Citadel

Until it was wrecked by the explosion of a powder magazine in 1824 and its ruins soon after covered by the Mosque of Muhammad Ali, the splendid remains of Sultan al-Nasir's Kasr al-Ablaq of 1313–15 were often described by European travelers. The term *ablaq* refers to the use of alternate yellow and black or white and black masonry,

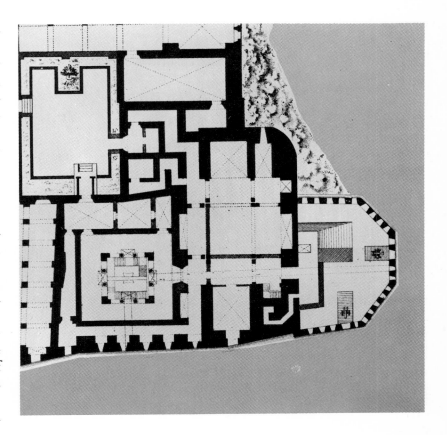

219. *Cairo, Kasr al-Ablaq on the Citadel, 1313–15,* iwan, *plan*
220. *Cairo, Kasr al-Ablaq on the Citadel,* qa'a

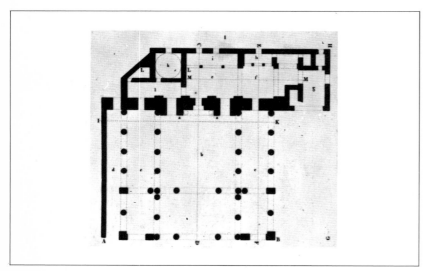

and there seems little doubt that al-Nasir not only named but modeled his palace after the likewise destroyed Kasr al-Ablaq of Sultan Baybars at Damascus (1266–67). The building was a complex association of structures in one part of which was a great *qa'a* (*Plate 220*), recorded by the Viscount Valentia in 1814, not unlike that of Sultan Salih at Rhoda. Another complex is recorded in the *Description de l'Égypte* (*Plate 219*). This was a vast columned porch or *iwan* whose western facade seems to have rested on or near a substructure of five immense corbels of nine tiers, each visible in *Plate 190* just below the mosque of Muhammad Ali. This porch, open to the north and west, was screened by a structurally independent wall to the east. To the south was a heavy wall with a niche on axis before which, according to the literary evidence, stood the throne beneath a vast wooden dome (part of whose *muqarnas* squinch appears in *Plate 221*). Although the squarish proportions of the porch and its use of columns clustered in threes recall the palace of Sultan Salih, the open west and north facades and the independence of the eastern one suggest a Persian *talar*. The elevated position portends the later Ali Kapu at Isfahan. Probably the inspiration for both should be sought in Persian Seljuk palaces from which Baybars' Kasr al-Ablaq in Damascus, a city more open than Cairo to Persian influence, would have served as intermediary.

The House of Gamal al-Din al-Zahabi

By the time Gamal al-Din built a house for himself near the Mosque of al-Azhar in 1637 Egypt had known more than a hundred years of Ottoman Turkish rule, but there is nothing Turkish in the style of its construction. Domestic architecture in the Turkish manner appears not to have been introduced into Egypt until the nineteenth century, and then in a form strongly influenced by a taste for things European. Gamal al-Din's house provides a model of all the features of a luxurious Mamluk residence unchanged since at least the fourteenth century if not before. Adapted to an irregular site, the ground floor (*Plate 223*) provided space for several shops in time-honored Mediterranean fashion. Otherwise there were only two entrances, each with its *dirka* or offset passage. One of these led into the *hosh* or interior court and the other into the *mandara* or public reception hall, articulated after the manner of a *qa'a*. From the *hosh* (*Plate 222*) a *muqarnas*-enriched portal leads to the principal residential floor (*Plate 224*). Here was the *maqad* or open porch, consisting of two arches, but in the grander houses of sometimes as many as five. Again one is reminded of the Persian *talar* and these private porches may well be the equivalents of the vast *iwan* of al-Nasir's palace. Adjacent to the *maqad* was the *khazna* or private reception hall with a projecting

221. *Cairo, Kasr al-Ablaq on the Citadel,* iwan, *interior looking toward the northwest*

222. *Cairo, House of Gamal al–Din al–Zahabi, 1637,* hosh *and* maqad   224. *Cairo, House of Gamal al–Din al–Zahabi, first floor, plan*

223. *Cairo, House of Gamal al–Din al–Zahabi, ground floor, plan*

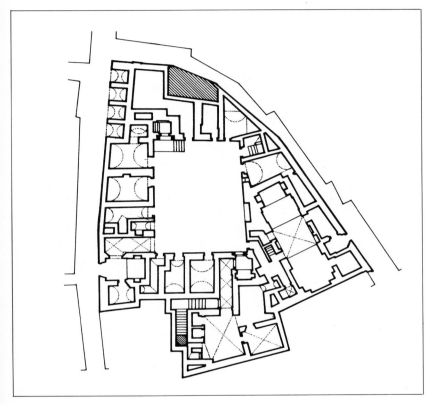

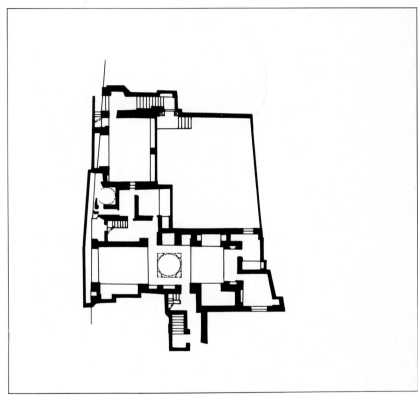

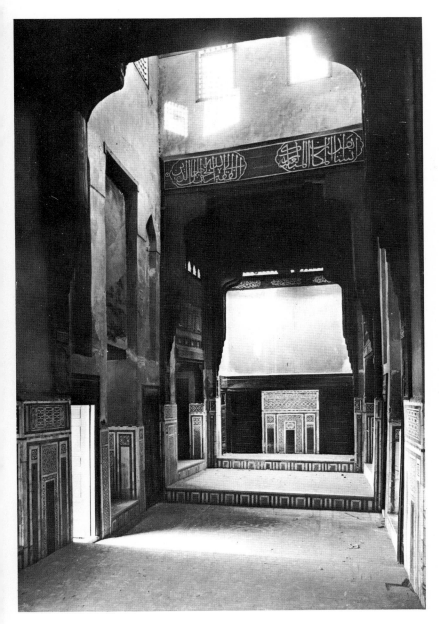

225. *Cairo, House of Gamal al-Din al-Zahabi, clerestory and dome over the* durka

226. *Cairo, House of Gamal al-Din al-Zahabi,* qa'a

mushrabiyya balcony from which the woman of the house could observe activities in the *hosh* and *maqad*. Beyond this was the *qa'a* for more intimate family gatherings with its *iwans* roofed in painted wooden beams and its lower walls richly encrusted in marble (*Plate 226*). Over the sunken *durqa* rose a windowed clerestory covered with a wooden domed lantern (*Plate 225*).

Conclusion

The Ayyubid and Mamluk periods in Egypt continued a style already being defined under the Fatimids. With the removal of the religious barrier of a Shi'ite Caliphate, Cairo was more than ever open in the late twelfth and thirteenth centuries to inspiration from Turkey and Iran via Syria. This process was enormously accelerated after the fall of Baghdad when artisans and scholars of all types sought refuge there from the Mongols. To a somewhat lesser degree the same situation repeated itself with the conquests of Timur (Tamerlane) in the early fifteenth century. Nevertheless, indigenous tradition was strong enough to impose a local style upon the imports. In late Mamluk times a reduction in the scale of ornament in relation to the structures it adorned is apparent, equivalent to what took place in North Africa and Spain in the fourteenth and fifteenth centuries and accompanied by a certain preciousness. However, it was not until after the Ottoman conquest, and then only very slowly, that another style was adopted.

If one were to sum up what makes Egyptian Islamic architecture unique between the Fatimid and the Ottoman conquests it might be said that in relation to that of North Africa and Spain it is virile and expansive. There is no evidence that either the Marinids or the Nasrids could have conceived a palace on the scale of al-Nasir's on the Citadel or that the Egyptians would have cared for the introspective refinements of the Alhambra. The contrast with the glazed polychrome architecture of Timurid Iran is one of materials as well as of intent. It is true that some of the shimmering translucency of the Iranian dome was achieved by the later Mamluk practice of carving the surfaces of stone domes in relief, but the means were altogether different and the effect remained linear, clear, and somewhat harsh. In fact the relation between Seljuk Turkish stone ornament of the thirteenth century and contemporary Ayyubid and Mamluk work is much like that between the rather lean and spare intricacies of so-called Isabelline Spanish Gothic and the richer and more plastic extravagance of the Portuguese Manueline style.

227. *Bukhara, Tomb of Ismail the Samanid, late ninth–first half of tenth century, plan of the ground floor; plan of the upper gallery; section*
228. *Bukhara, Tomb of Ismail the Samanid, exterior*

The Samanids arose from a family of *dihkans* or landed aristocracy of pre-Muslim times near Balkh in present-day Afghanistan and by 875 had assumed the governorship of the whole of Transoxiana. They protected their province and, therefore, the whole of Iran from Turkish inroads, at the same time profiting from the trade in Turkish slaves. By 900 Ismail (892–907) was made governor of Khorassan and in his capital, Bukhara, there was taking place a literary renaissance of the Persian language. By the mid-tenth century revolts against Samanid rule began and by 1005 their power had passed to the Ghaznavids and others.

The Ghaznavids descended from Turkish slave commanders who had served as governors for the Samanids. Their capital, Ghazna, in Afghanistan, became nominally independent in 977. Under the famous Mahmud (998–1030) their empire extended from Khorassan to the Ganges. Although the Ghaznavids were Turks, their culture was entirely Persian. In the eleventh century Khorassan and Khwarazm were lost to the Seljuks. Finally in 1186, with the fall of Lahore to the Ghurids, the line became extinct.

The pre-Seljuk history of Persian Islamic architecture must largely be reconstructed from literary sources and scant archaeological remains. Except for the mosque at Damghan, already discussed, no mosque even partially intact survives from this period. This is particularly unfortunate because during this time two new types probably evolved. Four types seem to have been already current in contemporary Persia: the so-called Arab type of Samarra, exemplified by the first mosque at Isfahan, and the open pavilion on a quincunx plan either alone as at Balkh in the Masjid-i-Tarikh or perhaps standing within the *sahn* of an Arab-type mosque as at Nishapur or Shiraz—both imported from the West; the other two, probably of local origin, were the domed pavilion open on at least three sides (a Sassanian fire temple adapted to Islamic ritual) and the mosque with an *iwan* opening on some form of an enclosure, like the now much rebuilt mosque of 975 at Niriz in southern Persia. Ultimately, all four types were to be combined to form the typical Persian great mosque of the Seljuk and all later periods.

The Tomb of Ismail the Samanid

We are better informed about tombs, as several survive more or less intact. The earliest is that of Ismail at Bukhara (*Plates 227, 228*). Since Ismail had given land for the tomb of his father, the building might have been begun as early as 900 or even shortly before. The complex contained several tombs, and an inscription in wood—once over the eastern entrance—names Ahmad ibn Ismail who died in 943. The structure is a square pavilion open on all four sides, with no trace of a provision for doors. Because early Muslim doctrine opposed the architectural adornment of tombs, Creswell supposes that early examples like the Qubbat al-Sulaybiyah at Samarra and Ismail's observed the prohibition by omitting the means to close them off from the outside in any direction. The pattern for such an open structure was familiar in local tradition, the Chahr Tak or fire temple pavilion where the sacred fire was displayed to the people. These might be simple four-arched structures supporting a single dome on squinches, but they might also have an ambulatory with smaller domes at the corners, and the four facades crowned by a blind arcade. At Bukhara the crowning arcade corresponding to the ambulatory is functional (*Plate 228*), even to its connection with the corner domelets, if only to admit a diffused light to the interior. Such borrowing of an earlier cult form, particularly from a cult which rejected burial, seems strange, but it should be remembered that domed spaces opening on all four sides also appear in Sassanian palaces such as that at Sarvistan and therefore already had royal as well as religious connotations.

The particular beauty of the tomb of Ismail consists in its exploitation, both inside and out, of the decorative possibilities of its tawny golden brick, only occasionally aided by a discreet use of carved terracotta. This is doubly surprising in view of the extensive use in other buildings of the Samanid period and before in Nishapur and Afrasiyab (Samarkand) of carved stucco in designs similar to those of early Samarra. Although baked brick is used decoratively for the Baghdad Gate of Raqqa of 775 and later in the Great Mosque at Samarra, no scheme so rich or so imaginative is recorded anywhere else as early as this. It must certainly have been the work of brick masons from Transoxiana, who were to be employed a century later by the Seljuks for their masterpieces in this material.

The Tomb of Arab Ata at Tim

This recently discovered tomb in the mountains above the Zerafshan Valley is, according to local tradition, the burial place of an early Arab conqueror or *ghazi*, but it has not yet been possible to associate it either with that historical personage or with the ruins of the city that arose near the tomb. The badly damaged inscription, not yet completely published, bears the date of 977–78. The building and much of its ornament is of brick, but considerably augmented by carved terracotta for the inscription and by inserts of stucco. Stucco is also used for pointing between the courses of brick, producing a much softer effect (*Plate 229*) than that of the tomb of Ismail. Like the tomb of Ismail, however, Arab Ata's uses columnar corners, but they are polygonal. The plan is quite unlike that of the older tomb. The single monumental entrance under a triple blind arcade is re-

231. *Gurgan, Gunbad-i-Qabus, begun 1006/7, plan*
232. *Gurgan, Gunbad-i-Qabus, detail of entrance and inscription*

233. *Gurgan, Gunbad-i-Qabus* ▷

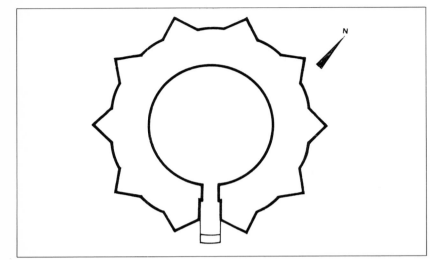

cessed into a shallow *iwan* within a tall *pishtaq*. The tomb chamber, lighted only through the portal, supports its dome with the earliest known example of the tripartite squinch (*Plate 230*) which may have been ancestor to the *muqarnas*. There appears to have been no *mihrab*, although the tomb and its cenotaph are correctly oriented toward Mecca. Not only is the triple squinch extremely sophisticated and mature, but the classic combination of shallow *iwan* and domed chamber behind it so characteristic of later Islamic architecture of all types is here achieved with a balance and elegance of proportion far removed from the still somewhat archaic tomb at Bukhara.

The Gunbad-i-Qabus at Gurgan

Gurgan, near the shore of the Caspian north of the Elburz Mountains, was always the scene of great contention between rival powers long before the establishment of Islam. Its tenth- and eleventh-century Ziyarid rulers, threatened to the south by the Shi'ite Buyyids and by the Sunni Samanids and Ghaznavids to the east, sat upon uneasy thrones. The Ziyarids were finally forced to accept Ghaznavid suzerainty and the last members of the dynasty, having evaded the Seljuks, were overthrown about 1090 by the Ismalis of the Elburz Mountains.

Shams al-Ma'ali Qabus (978–81 and 988–1012), despite his long exile, was the most vigorous and enlightened of the Ziyarids, making his court a center for the arts. According to its inscription, he ordered work begun on his tomb (called a *kasr* or castle) in 1006/7 on an artificial hill, perhaps originally fortified, north of the now-ruined city. From a circular base (*Plate 231*) about 56 feet in diameter rise ten buttresses planned by rotating a square five times within the circle. They clasp an inner cylinder about 48 feet in diameter which surrounds a circular chamber about 31 feet at its base. This chamber rises without a break the full height of the tower to end in a dome with an eastern window. The outer walls (*Plate 233*), slightly battered, ascend to a cornice, into which the buttresses sink, supporting a slender cone of specially curved bricks. The total height is 167 feet, about three times the diameter of the base, but solid brick foundations (there is no crypt) extend down another 33 feet through the man-made hill, giving the structure its astonishing command of the landscape. An early literary source claims that the body of Qabus, in a glass coffin, was suspended by chains from the dome, presumably where it would have caught the light of dawn through the east window. Although nomad tents usually opened east for the same purpose, the explanation (often made for Turkish tomb towers of similar type) that they are based on a traditional Turkish *yurt* or portable tent with a conical roof must be viewed with some reservation.

The only ornament consists of the two identical inscriptions once

234. *Lashkari Bazar, early eleventh century, plan of the principal monuments*
   a) *North Palace b) Dovecote c) Pavilion d) Main Palace and adjoining building*
   e) *South Palace (or Great Palace) f) Mosque g) South Gate (Bazar Gate)*
   h) *Bazaar*
235. *Lashkari Bazar, plan of the mosque*
236. *Lashkari Bazar, plan of the south palace*

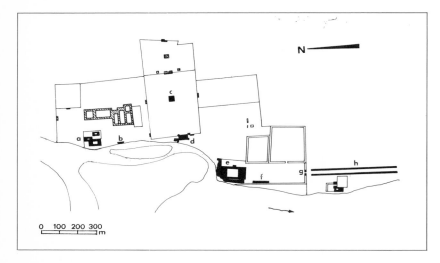

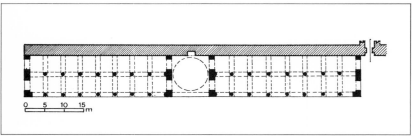

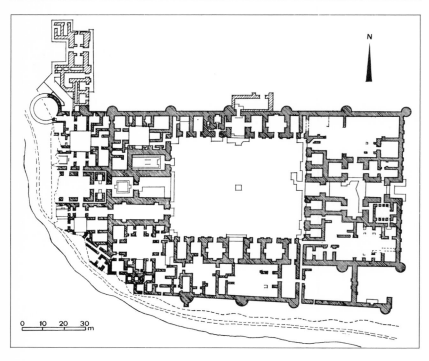

heavily coated with stucco, one just above the entrance (*Plate 232*) and the other just beneath the cornice; a simple lozenge pattern in stucco in the soffits of the entrance arch; and crude two-tiered *muqarnas* squinches, once stucco-covered, flanking the inner portal. Given the presence of the stucco one cannot speak here of "pure" brick decoration, but the vigorous geometry of the design constitutes its basic element. This is the first great masterpiece of Persian Islamic architecture.

The Palace of Lashkari Bazar at Bust
The great palace complex of Lashkari Bazar (*Plate 234*), formerly Lashkargah (the Barracks), near Bust, stretches for three or four miles along the west bank of the river Hilmend at its junction with the Argandab and was explored by Daniel Schlumberger beginning in 1948. To the south a broad avenue is lined with the stalls of the bazaar itself. Then through a monumental gate a court is reached along whose south side was the Friday mosque of baked brick; its two aisles supported on decorated columns were parallel to the *qibla* and joined at the *mihrab* by a domed chamber. The whole, open on three sides, was 282 feet long and 34 deep (*Plate 235*). The court seems to have served as its *sahn*. The south palace, its facade aligned with the monumental portal, closed the north end of the court. Further north were two more palace complexes and a series of walled courts and gardens.

The south palace (*Plate 236*), probably built during the lifetime of Mahmud of Ghazna, shows evidence of considerable rebuilding both before and after the Ghurids sacked and burned it in 1149. Its final destruction was at the hands of the Mongols in 1221, after which the site was deserted. The walls are of adobe reinforced with timbers and baked brick on stone foundations, and the decoration was of polychromed terracotta and stucco. Frescoes of the sultan's armed guard were in the throne room as well. The original nucleus, still partly recognizable, formed a rectangle about 253 by 430 feet and was probably rigidly symmetrical. A monumental south entrance led to a cruciform hall of honor, probably domed, from which, through an *iwan*, one entered a court of about 167 by 207 feet. This had east and west *iwans* and, to the north, a larger *iwan* leading to a square throne room, probably once domed. Flanking this were two cruciform apartments. Later, perhaps in the reign of Mas'ud I (1030–41) who is said to have been an accomplished architect, a passage was opened west of the throne complex which led to a northern extension directly over the Hilmend where two more cruciform apartments flanked an *iwan* open toward the river. Fountains and water channels abounded throughout the building.

The obvious inspiration for all of this came from the Abbasid palaces of Baghdad and Samarra, but the prevalence of cruciform plans points to Khorassan where, particularly near Merv, domestic architecture had exhibited every variation on this theme since pre-Muslim times.

The Buildings at Ghazna

Of Mahmud's capital almost nothing survives but his tomb (which has been totally rebuilt), but the stone panels of his cenotaph show that the pointed lobate arch was a popular Ghaznavid device in his time. The minaret, once believed his, was in 1953 shown to have been built by Bahram Shah and thus later than the much more elaborate tower of Mas'ud III (1099–1115; *Plate 238*). The surviving base, richly encrusted with carved terracotta and brick panels in geometric patterns, is unfinished toward the bottom; this would suggest that work stopped at his death. Both minarets have lower sections in the form of eight-pointed stars which once supported richly ornamented cylindrical superstructures, now fallen (*Plate 237*). Though both must have served as minarets, neither seems to have been attached to another structure. They should therefore probably be interpreted as towers commemorating a victory, a custom the Ghaznavids may well have learned from their Hindu subjects. The minaret of the Kalayan Mosque at Bukhara by the Qarakhanid Arslan Shah (1127; *Plate 248*) and the Ghurid minarets of Jam and Delhi, all independent structures, should probably be interpreted in the same manner.

Mas'ud's palace at Ghazna (*Plate 239*), destroyed by the Ghurids in 1150, was excavated by the Italians under Bombaci and Scerrato beginning in 1957. An inscribed *mihrab* bears Mas'ud's name and the date of 1112. The general layout is quite similar to that of Lashkari Bazar, but the ornament in marble, terracotta, and stucco is much richer. The four-*iwan* court is surrounded by buttresses which probably supported arched niches. They are sheathed in carved marble panels depicting three lobed arches filled with palmettes and scrolls on which are perched animals and birds. Along the top runs a Kufic inscription in Persian (*Plate 240*). Above this more scrolls and inscriptions appear in polychrome terracotta and stucco. The inscription carried by the marble panels (of which 44 out of 510 are *in situ*, painted blue on a bright red ground) originally covered 820 feet. In the poetic scheme of Firdausi's *Shah Namah*, it was a eulogy of the Ghaznavid Dynasty and, judging by the fragments remaining, a eulogy also of the palace itself. This is one of the earliest surviving examples of such a secular inscription lauding both a building and its patron. Arabic inscriptions in Messina and Palermo in praise of buildings erected by Roger II and his successors (1130–89) are similar. They may have provided the inspiration for the Alhambra inscriptions already men-

238. *Ghazna, Minaret of Mas'ud III*
239. *Ghazna, Palace of Mas'ud III, 1099–1113, plan*
    1) court 2) throne hall 3) court 4) prayer hall 5) vestibule 6) bazaar
240. *Ghazna, Palace of Mas'ud III, west side of the court, detail*

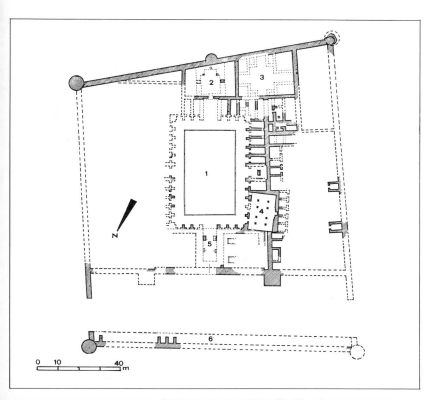

tioned. It may be that such secular inscriptions had become common in the world of Islam by the eleventh century, spreading both west and east, but the actual monuments by which such a development could have been traced have been lost.

Conclusion

So few monuments survive from this period that conclusions are difficult to draw. For the mosque we can only say that the ingredients of the later classical Persian mosque were all being experimented with, but their definitive fusion had not yet emerged. Tomb types were already multiplying: the centrally planned polygon with a conical roof, destined for a long development, had already received a monumental treatment; the minaret, which may have originated in Persia as a simple cylinder, had been elaborated into the star form so influential later in India. The Abbasid palace type of Samarra had traveled eastward and acquired new cruciform emphasis. However, the most important development seems to have been the new emphasis on brick structure and decoration, soon to be carried to new heights by the Seljuks.

The Seljuks, originally a military family of the Kiniq clan of the Oguz Turks in the steppes north of the Caspian and Aral Seas, became converted to Islam in the late tenth century. They entered Transoxiana as auxiliary troops for various warring powers and their strength rapidly increased. Having taken Khorassan from the Ghaznavids in 1038, Tughril (1038–63) proclaimed himself Sultan at Nishapur. He declared Sunni Orthodoxy a state policy and, in 1055, achieved his aim of rescuing the Abbasid Caliph from Buyyid Shi'ite tutelage. Although the Seljuks had long been exposed to Persian culture, it is significant that Tughril had to speak to the Caliph through an interpreter. In 1071 the Byzantines were defeated at Manzikert, opening the way to Anatolia—which eventually became an independent Seljuk state. Late in the reign of Malik Shah (1072–92) the Qarakhanid power was broken in Transoxiana. At the same time Fatimid influence in Syria was blocked and trustworthy governors installed. Despite the vast extent of its possessions and the intellectual renaissance it fostered under Nizam al-Mulk (1020–92) and the theologian al-Ghazzali (1038–1111), the Seljuk state nowhere outlasted the twelfth century. This was mainly due to the traditional tribal custom of dividing the sultan's patrimony among multiple heirs whose frequent quarrels embroiled the country in civil wars and created opportunities for aggressive neighbors to intervene.

As mentioned in the previous chapter, very few monuments have escaped intact the enormous destruction of the Mongol invasions of the thirteenth century or the slightly less devastating forays of Timur in the fourteenth. Since the surviving monuments preclude drawing conclusions from a chronological ordering, they are treated typologically instead: mosques, *robats* or *caravanserais* (to which discussion belongs what little we know of *madrasas*), and, finally, tombs.

THE MOSQUE

The Great Mosque of Isfahan

Isfahan was occupied in 1051 and, under Alp Arslan (1063–72), it became the capital of the empire. The heart of the Seljuk city was arranged around a square at the entrance façade of the existing Great Mosque or Masjid-i-Jami of the late ninth or early tenth century. This square was bordered on the northeast by the Masjid-i-Ali, of which only the somewhat later minaret survives, situated to the southeast of the palace (now vanished without a trace) and on the northwest by a bazaar.

The original form of the Great Mosque, still traceable in the present plan (*Plate 241*), was of the Arab type in baked brick with cylindrical piers supporting a flat wooden roof. Probably in the tenth century a *maqsura* was built of massive clustered cylindrical piers,

241. *Isfahan, Masjid-i-Jami, plan of the Abbasid mosque, ninth and tenth century*

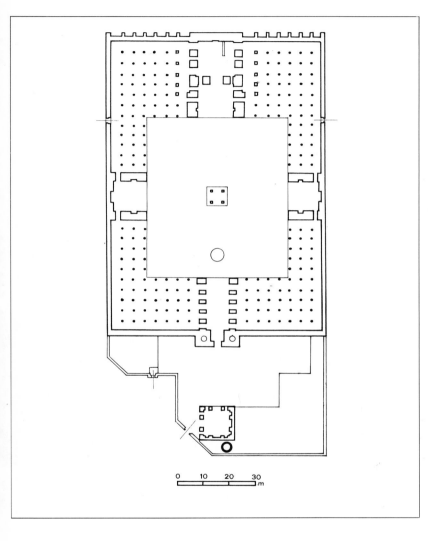

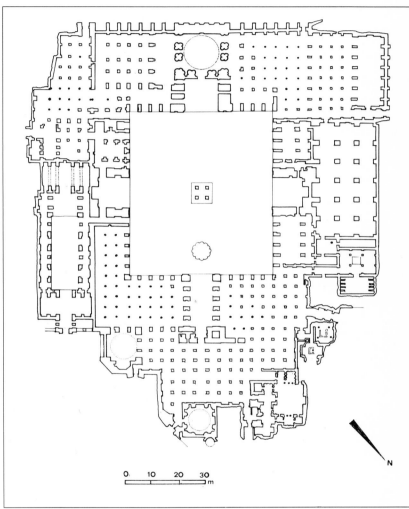

244. *Isfahan, Masjid-i-Jami, section and plan of the North Dome Chamber*
245. *Isfahan, Masjid-i-Jami, sahn* ▷
246. *Isfahan, Masjid-i-Jami, North Dome Chamber, interior* ▷
247. *Isfahan, Masjid-i-Jami, North Dome Chamber, dome* ▷

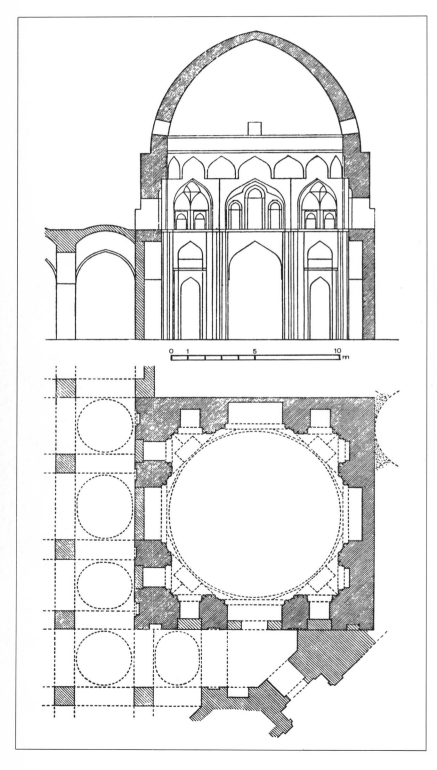

whose surviving stucco ornament is in the style of Samarra. How it was originally covered is unknown, but between 1072 and 1075 a great brick dome 49 feet in diameter was raised on the old supports by the order of Nizam al-Mulk under the direction of the architect Abul Fath, son of Mahmud the Treasurer. Here the triple squinch of the tomb of Arab Ata at Tim is again employed.

The next addition was that of the North Dome Chamber, in which brick architecture attained a perfection seldom equaled and never surpassed (*Plates 244, 246, 247*). It was built in 1088–89 for Terkan Khatun, the wife of Malik Shah and daughter of the Qarakhanid Sultan Tamghach Khan. It is on the *mihrab* axis, but some distance north of the entrance facade, and was once freestanding though always closed on the north and west sides. It might have been a private oratory for Terkan Khatun, a women's mosque, a fountain house, or a library.

The earlier south dome has traces of applied stucco ornament, though the brick was surely never entirely covered; in the North Dome Chamber, however, the brick alone generates the ornament, carved stucco appearing only as "plugs" between the vertical joints. Since here the architect was not required to adapt his work to existing supports, he achieved a structural consonance and a hierarchy of ordered parts not again approached until the High Gothic of thirteenth-century France.

The next additions to the original mosque, probably made in the early twelfth century (*Plate 242*), were the four *iwans* and the north portal flanked by paired minarets, producing, perhaps for the first time, the typical Persian four-*iwan* mosque of which the earliest dated example now known is that of Zaware of 1135/36. The roof, still of wood, was destroyed in a fire of 1121/22. Perhaps the first brick vaults were erected on the old supports at this time. Of the innumerable later additions, extensions, and reconstructions (*Plate 243*), we need only be concerned here with the curious attempt in or around 1447 to imitate a type of two-storied mosque-*madrasa*, current since the fourteenth century. The double arcades (*Plate 245*) conceal the early one-storied structure preserved inside.

Minarets

The earliest Persian minarets seem to have been square, at least in their lower stories. By the early eleventh century elaborately decorated, tapering brick shafts came to be the preferred type. One at Saveh is dated 1010 and that at Damghan 1026–29. The very elegant tapering minaret of the twelfth-century Masjid-i-Ali is an excellent example; decorated only by the sober geometry of its brick, it has two projecting balconies for the *muezzin*. The much more massive but more sharply tapered Kalayan Minaret at Bukhara (*Plate 248*), built in 1127 by the Qarakhanid Arslan Shah (1102–29), represents a Turkistan variant of the western Seljuk form.

The "Mosquée Kiosque"

The Seljuks also favored another type of mosque, called by André Goddard the *mosquée kiosque*. These, in emulation of the Sassanian fire temple, stood open on three sides, usually through triple portals like the pavilion type of the Bib Mardun at Toledo. They were, however, domed and without interior supports. Presumably they stood in some form of enclosure which might include a minaret, but all the surviving examples are now incorporated in much later structures.

The mosque at Gulpaygan, built by the Khajar Dynasty in the nineteenth century, incorporates a *mosquée kiosque* erected in 1105–18 under the patronage of Abu Shuja Muhammad, a son of Malik Shah (*Plate 249*). Here the arches are four-centered and the elements of the squinch have multiplied into decorative *muqarnas* (*Plate 250*).

In Qazvin a *mosquée kiosque* of the late eleventh or the early twelfth century was incorporated under the Khajars into a *madrasa* called the Haydariya (*Plate 251*). The ornament is very rich: *muqarnas* niches frame the smaller side portals; a superb stucco frieze of florid Kufic script forms a band below the vaults; narrow bands of inscription, also in stucco, frame the squinches and wall arches which supported the now fallen dome. The *mihrab* is perhaps the richest surviving example of Seljuk stucco work, notable for the three-dimensional character of its extravagant arabesques (*Plate 252*).

THE CARAVANSERAI

Caravanserais are often called *robats* or *ribats* in Persia, but they seem here to have little of the religious character of such buildings at Sussa in Ifriqiya. They appear to have been founded by the Seljuks and their predecessors primarily to encourage trade by protecting caravans, but they also served as royal post houses.

The Robat-i-Malik

This work, on the Bukhara-Samarkand road, was built in 1078–79 under the patronage of the Qarakhanid Sultan Nasr (1068–80), who had married the daughter of the Seljuk Sultan Alp Arslan. The burnt brick structure formed a square of 926 feet; it was buttressed by corner towers and had two stories of vaulted chambers surrounding a central court. The outer walls were articulated by groups of semi-circular and quarter-round buttresses sunk into them and crowned by pointed arches. This device is frequent in the fortress-manor houses

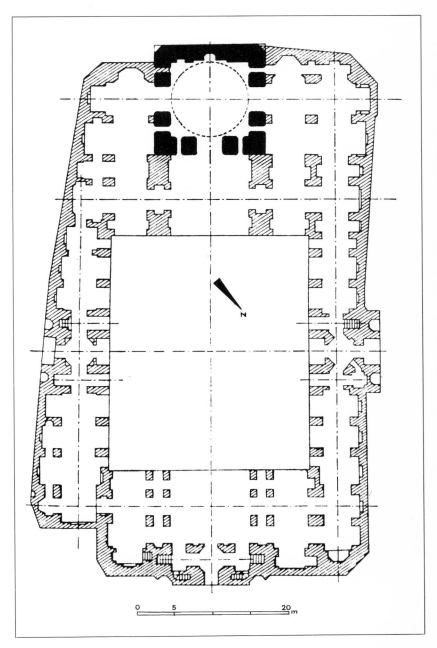

of pre-Islamic Merv and is used again in the early twelfth-century Maghak-i-Attari Mosque in Bukhara (also Qarakhanid).

The badly damaged inscription on the lone portal is in Persian verse and compares the building to Paradise. It may have been a precedent for Mas'ud's inscription in his palace at Ghazna. The interlaced star patterns in boldly projecting brick moldings are among the earliest and best examples of a kind of ornament which will constantly recur from North Africa to India.

The Robat Sharaf

This *caravanserai* on the Nishapur-Merv road was probably built in 1114–15, but was extensively redecorated in 1154–55. The later date is associated with an inscription in the furthest *iwan* to the rear of the building, which names the Seljuk Sultan Sanjar (1118–57) and his wife Terkan bint al-Kaghan, daughter of the Qarakhanid ruler Arslan Shah. The couple were imprisoned by the Oguz Turks after an uprising between 1153 and 1156 during which time the new and more elaborate stucco ornament was added, probably because the couple lived in the *robat*. From the beginning the building may have been intended as a royal post house, and the similarities between its plan (*Plate 253*) and that of the Palace of Lashkari Bazar are striking indeed. Both have semicylindrical corner towers, monumental projecting entrances, are bilaterally symmetrical with four *iwan* courts, and terminate in pairs of cruciform apartments flanking an *iwan* which leads to a domed chamber. The latter appears four more times, foretelling the much more complex works of the Timurids, while the double court (*Plate 254*)—the southern area perhaps for retainers—anticipates the thirteenth-century royal *hans* or *caravanserais* of Seljuk Anatolia.

THE MADRASA

Of this most important type hardly anything survives in Persia from the Seljuk period. The first *madrasas* seem to have been built by the Ghaznavids, but no information is available as to their form. The first Seljuk *madrasa* was founded shortly before 1046 at Nishapur by the Sultan Tughril. The institution soon became an important instrument of the state for combatting Shi'ite influence, spreading Sunni doctrine, and training state officials. The great vizier Nizam al-Mulk was an enthusiastic builder of *madrasas*, but of his many foundations the ruins of only two have been identified: that at Khargird of 1087 and another at Rayy. Both have been investigated, but the results are equivocal. They had *iwans*, although precisely how many and their placement are uncertain. In view, however, of the prevalence of the cruciform plan for palaces and *caravanserais* and of the general principle of interchangeability of so much Islamic planning, it is more

251. *Qazvin, Haydariya Madrasa, late eleventh–early twelfth century, plan*
252. *Qazvin, Haydariya Madrasa,* mihrab
253. *Nishapur–Merv road, Robat Sharaf, 1114–15, plan*
254. *Nishapur–Merv road, Robat Sharaf, general view* ▷

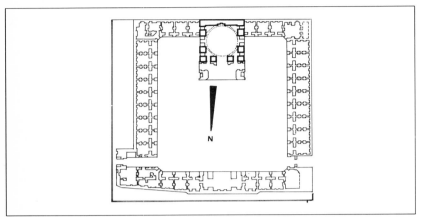

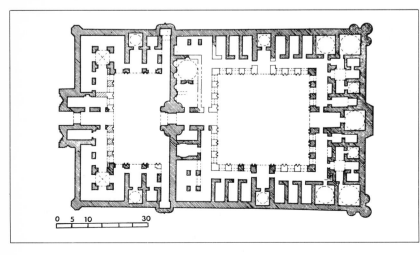

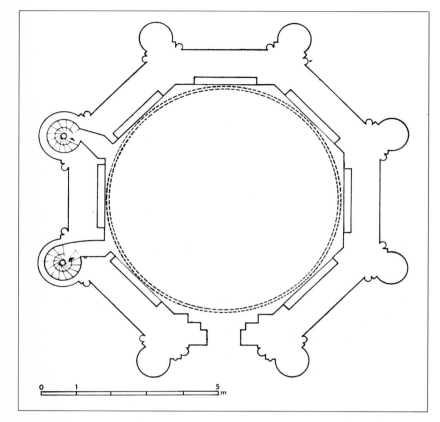

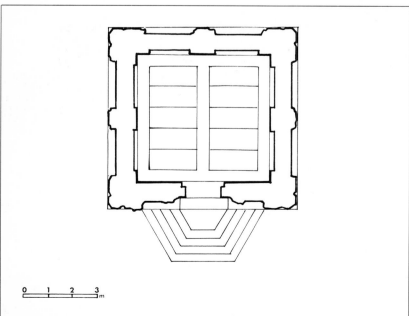

likely than not that some of them had four *iwan* courts and domed chambers behind the *iwans*.

TOMBS

The Gunbad-i-Ali at Abarquh

This octagonal tomb tower, of rubble masonry rather than the usual brick (*Plate 257*), was built in 1056 for Hazarasp ibn Nasr, descendant of a local dynasty, by his son. The bold three-tiered *muqarnas* cornice, also of rubble, once probably supported a pyramidal roof. The lack of articulation except for the cornice and the inscription below it gives the building a more archaic look than that of the many octagonal towers built during Seljuk times.

The Tomb Towers of Kharraqan

These two recently discovered octagonal brick tomb towers in western Persia show how the brick tradition of the tomb of Ismail the Samanid was maintained and refined under the Seljuks. The earlier one (1067–68; *Plate 255*) was built by the architect Muhammad ibn Makki of Zinjan, and the latter (1093) by either his brother or his son. Both tombs are articulated by blind arcades of four centered and stilted arches between semicircular buttresses, some concealing stairs. The brickwork is exceedingly intricate and enormously varied in its patterns, accented, as at Bukhara, by the deeply recessed bonding and no stucco fillers at all except as a background for the bands of inscription. Both have double domes, and in the earlier tower this feature occurs for the first time in a dated monument. The principle of the double dome had, however, long been known in Islam—at least for wooden domes—and the dome under a pyramid, which employs a similar principle, at least since the time of the Gunbad-i-Qabus.

The Tomb of Tughril

This tomb at Rayy, near Teheran, is dated 1139–40 on the basis of an inscription, now in the University of Michigan, claimed on good authority to belong to it. Multiple prismatic flanges (*Plate 258*) relate the design to that of the Gunbad-i-Qabus, but the tiers of *muqarnas* effecting the transition from a stellate shaft to a circular cornice are reminiscent of the arches linking the sunken semicircular buttresses of the Robat-i-Malik. Indeed, the Jar Kurgan minaret of the late eleventh or early twelfth century has a shaft of clustered semicircular buttresses linked by arches at the top; and similar tomb towers exist, such as that at Kishmar, which alternate prismatic and semicircular forms. Although this last probably dates from the fourteenth century, it suggests that there was an earlier tradition in Khorassan for the Qtub Minar at Delhi (c. 1200).

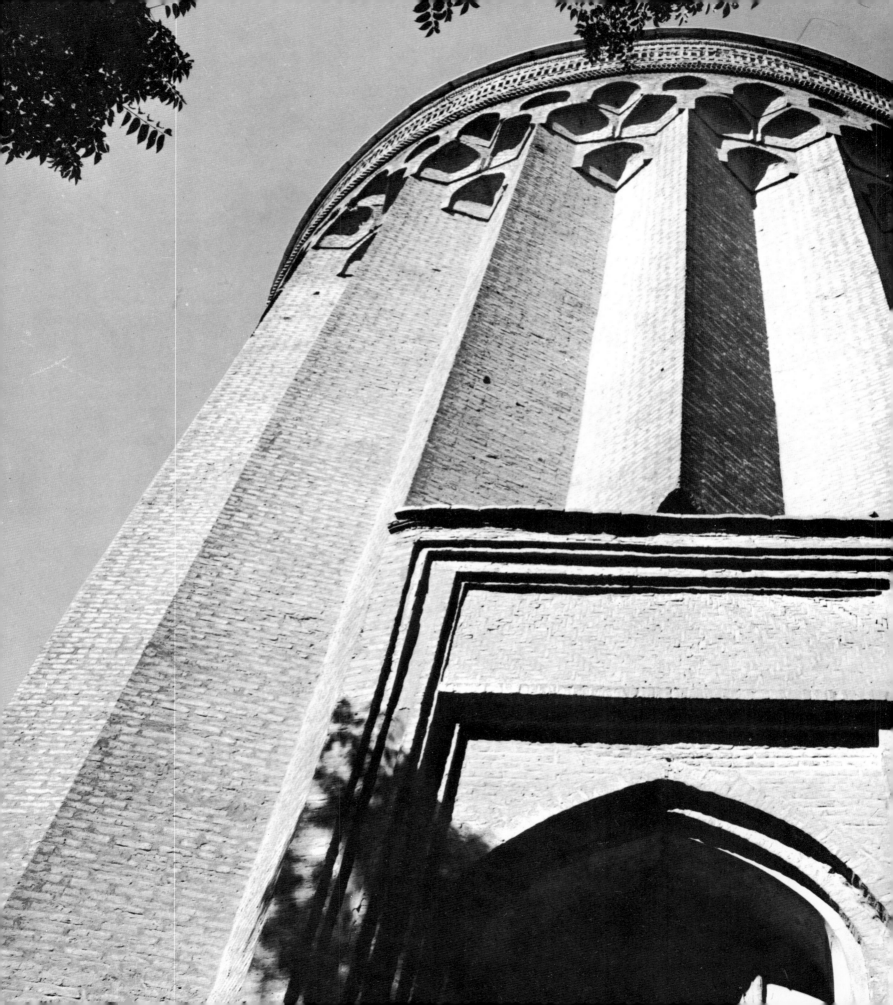

258. *Rayy, Tomb of Tughril, 1139–40*
259. *Merv, Tomb of Sultan Sanjar, 1157, plan and section*
260. *Merv, Tomb of Sultan Sanjar, exterior from the east*

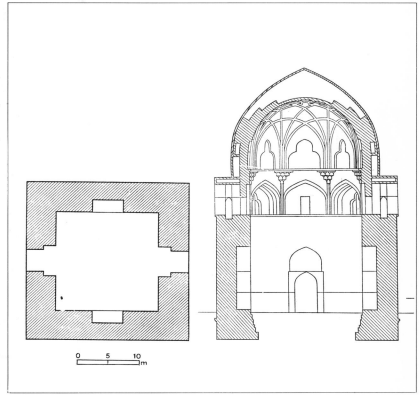

The Gunbad-i-Surkh

Like the tomb of Ismail at Bukhara, the Gunbad-i-Surkh or "red dome" at Maragha in western Persia is square and has semicircular corner buttresses as well (*Plate 256*). However, its builder, Bakr Muhammad, who completed it in 1147–48, gave it only one entrance and articulated the whole much more rigorously, with double blind arcades on the other three sides. Pyramidal shed roofs cover interior *muqarnas* squinches, effecting the transition to an octagonal windowed drum which once supported a pyramidal roof over the domed interior. Here, in contrast to Bukhara or even to Kharraqan, an architectonic discipline imbues the whole design with a strength and vigor comparable to the North Dome Chamber of the Masjid-i-Jami at Isfahan. As at Kharraqan too the joins are recessed throughout to strengthen the brick patterns through the play of shadow. Here also is one of the earliest uses of glazed brick, in this case vivid turquoise against the mat red brick ground. The principle of polychromy in Seljuk ornament is already apparent in the eleventh century, and Goddard believes the first glazed brick was employed as early as the first decade of the twelfth century to make the higher inscriptions on minarets more visible.

The Tomb of Sultan Sanjar at Merv

A square plan reappears in the monumental brick tomb begun by the architect Muhammad ibn Atsiz of Sarakhs for Sultan Sanjar, last of the great Seljuk sultans of Persia, soon after his death in 1157. The tomb is a massive unarticulated cube about 420 square feet, with an eastern entrance and a western window once closed by a grille (*Plate 260*). The cube is surmounted by a gallery of alternating wide and narrow bays which filtered light into the interior, as at Bukhara. Above the gallery another series of wide and narrow niches stood at the point where the inner dome rises from a sixteen-sided polygon. This supported the now-ruined outer dome which, according to an early thirteenth-century source, was once covered with blue tiles. Inside, the square chamber is surmounted by a dome 56 feet in diameter (*Plate 259*). Clusters of boldly projecting ribs rise from eight *muqarnas* squinches. Traces of carved stucco, some of it painted, attest to the richness of the original ornamental scheme.

When Edmond O'Donovan visited Merv in 1879 he reported that the tomb was then in the center of an enclosure about 661 square yards, with baked brick double walls and semicircular turrets. Four gates giving onto as many causeways led to the tomb. He also remarked on the absence of ruins within the enclosure, but assumed this had been Sanjar's city. It seems more likely the enclosure constituted the remains of a four-part garden or *chahr bagh*. If so, this is the earliest surviving example of a form later to be so superbly exploited in Moghul India.

The Gunbad-i-Kabud at Maragha

Although dated well past the period of undivided Seljuk rule (1196–97), this elaborate tomb shows the survival of their style in Azerbaijan. The structure is octagonal (*Plate 261*) and stands on a stone foundation containing a crypt. Each wall is treated as a *mihrab* niche under a *muqarnas*-filled arch. The flat panels below and the semicircular buttresses between are covered with an interlaced net pattern based on the pentagon. The portal, the *muqarnas* of the arches and the cornice, and all the inscriptions are heavily encrusted with glazed blue tile.

Conclusion

The Seljuk achievement in architecture remains prodigious. Thanks to structural or symbolically structural devices, they have been equaled in the articulation of interior space (less often exterior) only in thirteenth-century France. In the imaginative manipulation of brick masonry they have no equals. It is to be noted that glazed brick or tile, later to be so important in Islamic architecture, had little appeal for the Seljuks and then only late in their dynasty and favoring only a single color, turquoise blue. In stucco, however, a traditional Persian material, they excelled—the sumptuous *mihrab* ornament of the Haydariya at Qazvin providing inspiration for a host of later stone decoration throughout Seljuk Anatolia.

The classic form of the four-*iwan* mosque was developed during the Seljuk period, along with the palace-*caravanserai*. Both were to transmit their forms to the Ilkhanids and Timurids and, indeed, to have echoes far beyond Persia proper.

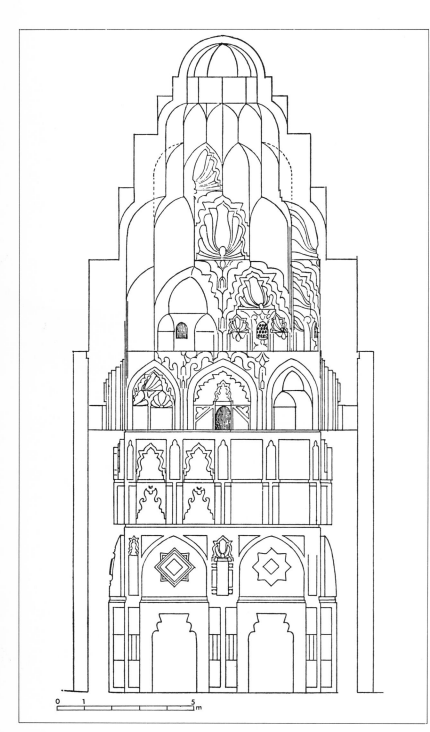

262.   *Samarra, Imam Dur, 1085–86, section*
263.   *Samarra, Imam Dur, exterior* ▷

Syria and Iraq between the Buyyid conquest of 945 and that of the Mongols in 1258 were no longer the most powerful or the richest of the Islamic states. Nevertheless, architecture of considerable importance was produced during brief periods of stability under prosperous Arab emirs, Turkish *atabegs*, or even the later Abbasid Caliphate. One of these moments of productivity occurred under the Arab Uqaylids of Mosul (c. 990–1096). They were usually Shi'ite in sympathy, but played both sides and controlled large territories in Syria and Iraq. Persian Seljuk penetration into Syria after the mid-century conquest of Baghdad was intermittent. In 1086 Malik Shah installed Aq Sonqur, a Turkish *ghulam*, as governor of Syria whose son, Zengi (1127–46), *atabeg* of Mosul and Aleppo, established a dynasty which survived in Damascus until 1181 and in Mosul and Aleppo until 1222. The wealth and security the Sunni Zengids provided encouraged an architectural renaissance that profoundly affected the Egyptian architecture of the Ayyubid and Mamluk dynasties, which succeeded to the control of Syria. In Iraq, after 1180 when Seljuk power declined, the Caliphs of Baghdad came to reassert a certain political power which gave them control of the revenues and hence the means to build again. This relative prosperity, which also nurtured a renaissance in the art of the illuminated manuscript, lasted until the final conquest and destruction of Baghdad by the Mongols in 1258. We are here concerned with the few surviving monuments of these three stable periods.

The Imam Dur at Samarra
Muslim ibn Kuraisb (1061–85) ruled from Baghdad to Aleppo at the apex of the power and culture of the Shi'ite Uqaylids. He had apparently begun or planned a *mashad* or memorial for a son of the fifth Shi'ite imam, Muhammad ibn Musa, at Samarra. When Muslim was killed in battle, he too was buried there in the shrine (completed in 1086).

Above a square brick base with projecting cylindrical corner buttresses and a single entrance rises a spectacular *muqarnas* dome from an octagonal base (*Plate 263*). It is the earliest of a series of such buildings in Iraq and western Persia continuing into the following century. The extrados, rising like an enormous artichoke from the simple base, is a rather exact expression of the interior space (*Plate 262*). The architect, Abu Shakir ibn Abi al-Faraj, signed both the exterior and the interior. He must, then, be responsible for the extraordinary but remarkably hideous interior stucco ornament (*Plate 264*). This employs recognizable Samarran motifs of two centuries before, but has lost all restraint.

The Minaret of the Great Mosque at Aleppo

This square stone minaret, the most beautiful in Syria, was begun in 1089 under the governorship of Aq Sonqur and completed under Tutush, brother of Malik Shah, who had taken Aleppo in 1194 but was killed in battle the following January. The architect was Hasan ibn Mufarraj al-Sarmani, whose *nisbah* ("epithet of origin") indicates he came from a town near Aleppo.

The tower rises in five stories (*Plate 265*) and is crowned by an open verandah above a richly carved *muqarnas* cornice of a more Turkish than Egyptian form. The precise articulation seems almost Western European and suggests the strong influence surviving antique monuments must have had on the local masons. However, the exuberant lobate arches point elsewhere, perhaps to Samarra (*Plate 266*). Ernst Herzfeld notes the probable influence of this work on the architecture of the later Crusaders since it was seen by a number of their builders only twenty years after its completion.

The Muristan Nuri in Damascus

Nur al-Din Zengi (1146–74) took Damascus in 1154 and in the same year ordered the construction of a *muristan*. The term comes from the Persian *bimaristan*, and means an infirmary where an outpatient clinic, a small hospital, and medical teaching center were combined. The institution was introduced into Syria long before the *madrasa*, the Caliph al-Walid having founded the first one in Damascus. What remains of the masonry structure, except for the great portal, has no exterior, since the building—like many of the later structures in Cairo—was entirely incorporated into an already dense urban context. The surviving court (there may originally have been another to the south) follows a symmetrical cruciform plan around a pool (*Plate 267*). The four *iwans* (one at the entrance, two of them perhaps lecture halls, and the last a place of prayer) alternate with enclosed consulting rooms. No accommodations for patients survive, but they may have been provided in a court to the south.

The monumental entrance complex begins with a shallow *iwan* (*Plate 268*) roofed by a half vault of nine tiers of *muqarnas* in stucco. They spring from blind arcading of mixtilinear arches very like those of the Imam Dur and terminate in a gored semidomelet. Around the arch a rectangular frame like an *alfiz* is formed by a band of interlace not unlike that of the Robat-i-Malik, but of stucco rather than brick. The doorway itself is, somewhat incongruously, spanned by an antique pediment, probably from an aedicule like those surviving at Baalbek. The portal leads to a square antechamber flanked by deep niches, that to the south leading to a well-equipped latrine. Over the square chamber rises an eleven-tiered *muqarnas* dome from a cavetto

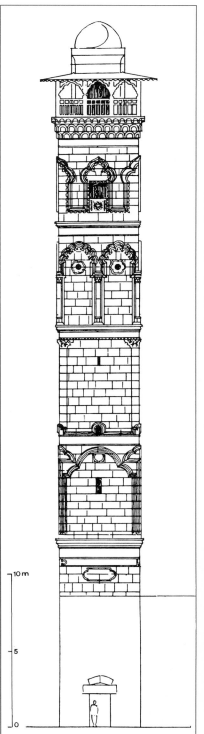

267. *Damascus, Muristan Nuri, begun 1154, plan*
268. *Damascus, Muristan Nuri, portal*

269. *Damascus, Madrasa al-Nuriya al-Kubra, begun 1172, detail of the dome* ▷

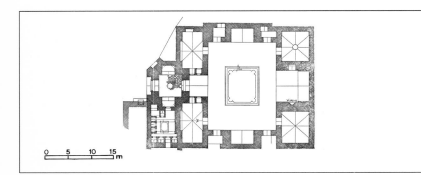

cornice very like that at Tlemcen of 1136. In addition to the four windows at the springing, numerous small openings admit a diffuse and indirect light which dissolves the solid forms. As at the Imam Dur, each *muqarnas* facet has multiple edges, increasing the seeming dissolution of the forms; however, there is not the confusion of the earlier monument. Also like the Imam Dur, the extrados of the vault here is exposed—though, at least at present, it does not appear to reflect the interior space.

The Madrasa al-Nuriya al-Kubra in Damascus

In April of 1172 Nur al-Din signed the *waqf* or document of endorsement for this building, dedicated to the teaching of both the Hanafite and the Shafeyite disciplines, though nothing in the plan (*Plate 270*) suggests any division between them. A monumental but severely plain masonry entrance leads to a groin-vaulted vestibule, south of which is the tomb chamber and to the west an *iwan* leading to the court. From the south side of the court, through a triple portal, one enters a mosque with a wooden roof. Opposite is a very large *iwan*, once probably also roofed in wood. The west *iwan* shelters a fountain whose water empties into the central tank, an arrangement at least as old as the houses at al-Fustat if not earlier, and found, by this time, all over the Islamic world. The rest of the court is occupied by two stories of students' cells, the upper reached by stairs north of the vestibule.

The tomb chamber, about 72 square feet, is covered by a stucco *muqarnas* dome of eleven tiers ascending from a cavetto cornice (*Plate 271*). Unlike the earlier dome of the Muristan Nuri which had no fixed underlying geometric framework, this one has—even to the transition to a ten- rather than eight-part gored domelet supported by as many intersecting arches. As Herzfeld remarks, an old foreign pattern imported from Iraq for the Muristan had, eighteen years later, been reworked and given logic and clarity by a Syrian architect.

The Palace in the Qala of Baghdad

The Caliph al-Nasir li din Allah (1180–1225) found a way for a time to revive some of the former economic and political power of his predecessors. This began after the extinction of the Seljuk Sultanate of Iraq with the death of Tughril in 1194 at the hands of the Khwarazm Shah, who was in turn defeated, with al-Nasir's connivance, by the Mongols. Al-Nasir even succeeded in persuading Hasan III (1210–21), Grand Master of the Assassins, to accept Sunni Orthodoxy.

Herzfeld believes the palace in the Qala to have been built by al-Nasir. All that survives is part of a squarish court built of very fine baked brick (*Plate 272*). This is surrounded by a two-story cloister

270. *Damascus, Madrasa al–Nuriya al–Kubra, plan*
271. *Damascus, Madrasa al–Nuriya al–Kubra, dome of the tomb chamber*

272. *Baghdad, Palace in the Qala, c. 1180–c. 1225, plan*
273. *Baghdad, Palace in the Qala, courtyard, detail of the portico*

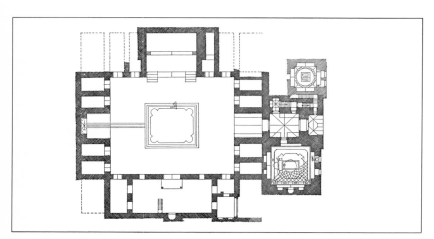

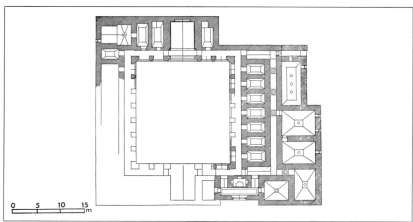

274. *Baghdad, Palace in the Qala, courtyard*
276. *Baghdad, Palace in the Qala, interior of the portico*
275. *Baghdad, Palace in the Qala,* muqarnas *vault in the portico*

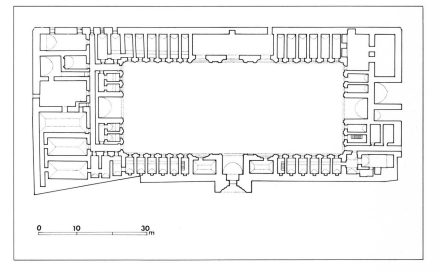

(*Plates 273, 274*) of *kundi* or deep niches vaulted with *muqarnas* whose elements are of richly carved terracotta (*Plate 275*). Narrow passages connect the niches on both floors (*Plate 276*), interrupted only by barrel-vaulted *iwans* at the east and west. All the arches are defined by boldly twisted moldings of considerable scale, a motif probably of Seljuk origin which survived in Persia through the Safavids. In the southwest corner a water gate with an elaborate baffled entrance leads into the court and other parts of the palace.

The Talisman Gate at Baghdad

This gate in the walls of Baghdad no longer exists, having been destroyed by the Ottoman Turks in 1917. Quarter-round towers of baked brick linked it to the wall and framed the stone-built gate proper, a slightly stilted three-centered arch springing from crouching lions on engaged columns. The spandrels were occupied by intricately coiled dragons whose tongues were grasped by a seated personage. As Max van Berchem interpreted these, one dragon is the Grand Master of the Assassins, Hasan III, after his conversion, and the other the Khwarazm Shah overcome by the Mongols three years after he had set up an anti-Caliph in 1220–21. The sculptor must have been trained in Seljuk Turkey, perhaps in Konya where similar coiled dragons and lions existed, though no longer *in situ*. Since Iraqi architects used primarily brick, molded terracotta, and stucco, it would seem natural in cases where stone was to be carved to have imported a specialist from an area with a tradition in this technique.

The Mustansiriya at Baghdad

The Caliph al-Mustansir (1226–41), second to the last ruler of the Baghdad line, dedicated this *madrasa* in April of 1233. In it were taught all four rites and there was also included a *Dar al-Hadith* or school of tradition and a *Dar al-Koran*. In 1823 the structure became a customs house and was drastically altered. Creswell's plan of 1959 is the first to show it freed of later additions (*Plate 279*). The building (of baked brick throughout) is immense, measuring 348 by 157 feet overall, with an interior court of 205 by 87 feet. A projecting portal on the long northeast side leads to an *iwan* on the court, flanked by two large rooms with monumental portals (*Plate 280*). Opposite is a mosque, long and narrow with a three-portal facade in the Syrian manner. The only *iwans* possible to use as lecture halls penetrate the narrow ends of the court and must have been shared by the four rites. Elsewhere double tiers of students' cells open directly onto the court below and to a cloister above (*Plate 281*). Heavy twisted moldings define the arches—like those of the palace in the Qala, though *muqarnas* decoration seems wholly absent.

280, 281. *Baghdad, Mustansiriya, courtyard*

282. *Aleppo, Madrasa al-Firdaus, 1235–36, plan*

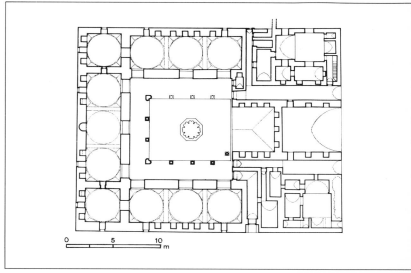

The Madrasa al-Firdaus at Aleppo

Aleppo was united with Egypt by Salah ad-Din (the famous Saladin) in 1183 and given first as an apanage to his brother al-Malik al-Adil (who between 1200 and 1218 was Sultan of Egypt and head of the Ayyubid Dynasty). In 1186 Aleppo was transferred to the rule of Saladin's son, al-Malik al-Zahir, who died in 1215/16. The *madrasa*, devoted to the Shafeyite rite, was founded by Daifa Khatun, daughter of al-Adil, widow of al-Zahir and mother of his heir al-Malik al-Aziz. The date 1235–36 inscribed over a window probably indicates its completion.

The building, of well cut masonry, is entered through a passage at the northeast corner of the court (*Plate 282*), which is surrounded on three sides by an arcade on columns and on the fourth by a vaulted *iwan*; to the south a three-domed *masjid* opens by as many portals to the cloister and two domed corner chambers. To east and west, where one would expect students' cells, there are two more triple-domed and portaled halls. The students must have been housed elsewhere, but two northern residential complexes (probably for visiting scholars) flank the large *iwan* facing outward to the north, like that toward the northwest at the Mustansiriya in Baghdad. Perhaps both served as Koranic schools, often built opening outward onto busy streets probably because of the noise emanating from them. Here is a very early example of how the dome generates spatial units as in certain Turkish Seljuk architecture, a practice later to be carried to perfection by the Ottomans.

The *mihrab* is surmounted by an interlaced pattern in colored marbles of a type which first appears in Aleppo in the late twelfth century and in the thirteenth and fourteenth centuries was carried by Syrian stone workers west to Palestine and Egypt and east to Anatolia. Herzfeld suggests that the pattern had a Sassanian origin—a combination of the lobate ornament of the great arch at Ctesiphon and the tapered archivolt at Taq-i-Bostan.

Conclusion

The divergent styles of the buildings discussed in this chapter typify the flow of ideas between one part and another of the Islamic world from the later eleventh through the thirteenth centuries. The *muqarnas* dome, probably of Khorassanian origin, was imported to Iraq, infused with a local inheritance, then traveled still further west to Morocco and was brought to Syria where it was refined. *Muqarnas* ornament had already been produced in stone in Syria in the late eleventh century; probably the idea was passed from there on to Egypt, though examples in stone were never common. Half domes of stone *muqarnas* for portal *iwans* appear first in late twelfth-century Aleppo and probably about the same time in Seljuk Anatolia. It was the type developed in Aleppo which was soon imported into Ayyubid and Mamluk Egypt.

When Syrian masons began to build for their Zengid patrons (whose ideas stemmed from Persia), the cruciform plan came into its own. As Herzfeld has remarked, the Persians had used the cruciform plan for everything at least since Parthian times, and Egypt received a new impetus from Syria in this direction. On the other hand, since an enclosed prayer hall was better suited to the Syrian climate, the *madrasa* type was established, which had reflections in Morocco. The Egyptians, with a milder climate, were more inclined toward the Persian *iwan*.

The same free flow of ideas is evident in Iraq. The high quality of the brick architecture is a continuation of Persian Seljuk practice, though the prominent use of twisted moldings for the articulation of arches may be new. At any rate, this innovation was to have a long future. When, however, a patron ordered a work in masonry, outside specialists—in this case Seljuk Turks—seem to have been called in.

Finally, well into the thirteenth century, the dome as a space definer was introduced in Aleppo probably from Anatolia, where it was long popular. We have also already noted the widespread use of the kind of inlaid marble frame found over the *mihrab* of the Madrasa al-Firdaus. All this interchange will result in a "classic" style—not necessarily uniform, but sharing so many motifs that, whether built in stone or brick, works of this period wherever they may stand bear an unmistakable imprint.

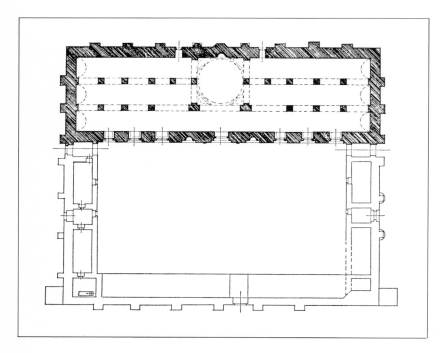

The peninsula of Anatolia is open both by sea and land to multiple influences from abroad. By land it is inseparable from northern Syria and, as the source of both the Tigris and the Euphrates, is linked with northern Iraq via Mosul. To the east and north it has connections with Persia through Azerbaijan, a frequent invasion route in both directions. Finally, near the Black Sea coast lay the powerful Christian state of Georgia, whose culture stemmed from the Baghratid state with its capital at Ani near Lake Van. Although the culture of Baghdad had exercised some influence on that of the Armenians in eastern Anatolia, Islamic architecture was unknown in the area until the late eleventh century, and few monuments survive which date before the late twelfth.

In 1071, after the crushing defeat of the Byzantines at Manzikert, the Persian Sultan Alp Arslan left his cousin Suleyman in charge of the western campaign while he turned eastward, dying the following year in pursuit of the Khwarazm Shah. In 1077/78 Malik Shah appointed Suleyman governor of the Anatolian province, whose capital was at Nicea (Iznik). When Suleyman took Antioch in 1086 he declared himself independent, but was defeated and killed in the same year by Tutush, brother of Malik Shah. In the chaos which ensued and out of the vast hordes of nomadic Turkomans who had accompanied the Seljuks into Anatolia, a number of independent emirates came into existence. The most durable of these were the Danishmends in the Sivas–Kayseri–Malatya region (1092–1178), the Saltukids of Erzurum (1092–1202), the Artukids in the Dunaysir–Mardin–Diyarbekir region (1098–1234) and, a generation later, the Mengujukids in the Erzincan–Divrig region (1118–1252). The first two were absorbed by the Seljuk Sultanate of Rum (1071–1308), the third by the Ayyubids of Egypt, and the fourth succumbed only after the Seljuks themselves had become vassals of the Mongols.

Continual dynastic crises in the Seljuk royal house and constant warfare with the Crusaders, the Danishmends, and the Artukids in the eleventh and most of the twelfth centuries left the Sultanate of Rum little time for architecture. The early development in Anatolia of the mosque, the *madrasa*, and the tomb took place in the territories of the emirates. In the early thirteenth century, however, the economic position of the Sultanate of Rum was suddenly improved when, under Keykavus I (1210/11–19), Antalya on the Mediterranean and Sinope on the Black Sea were recaptured. Kaykubad I (1219–36), his relatives, and his emirs began to found numerous sumptuous charitable foundations of all kinds, and Seljuk architecture entered what Tamara Talbot Rice has called its classic period. Under Kaykhusrav II (1236–46), after the battle of Kuzadag in 1242, the Sultans became vassals of the Mongols. Yet, since the Mongols did not devastate Anatolia as

283.   Dunaysir, Great Mosque, completed 1204, plan

they had Persia, economic prosperity and security returned after a brief period of chaos. Patronage, however, was no longer in the hands of the Sultans but of their viziers, some of them Mongol appointees, and of the great emirs whose power had considerably increased. Nowhere is there evidence that the Mongols introduced any new architectural forms into Anatolia, probably because they had none; nor was there a marked increase of influence from Persia, an architectural wasteland from 1220 to 1280. Instead, the architects of the later thirteenth century, elaborating upon what had gone before, developed an almost baroque taste for ostentation and fantasy.

Further Mongol interference occurred after an unsuccessful invasion by the Egyptians under Baybars in 1276–77. This led to an economic decline and, under the youthful Kaykhusrav III (1264–83), to the beginning of political fragmentation. Again as in the late eleventh century, Turkoman emirates independent of the Sultanate—and later of the Mongols as well—came into being. Among the more than twenty that arose the most important for the history of architecture were those of the Sarubanids of Manisa (1300–1410), the Aydinids of Seljuk near Ephesus (1313–1425) and, most important of all, the Ottomans of Iznik (the former Nicea) and Bursa (the former Brusa).

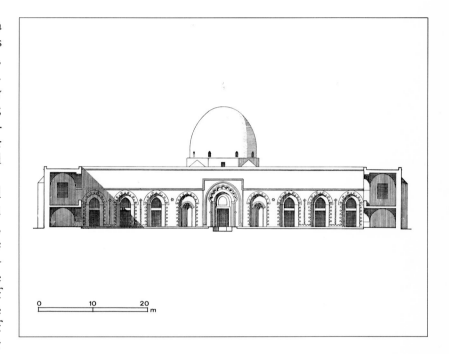

THE CONGREGATIONAL MOSQUE BEFORE THE SELJUK SULTANATE OF RUM
The first great congregational mosque to be built in Turkey—with the possible exception of the ruined structure in Ani, of which very little is known—was that founded by Malik Shah in Diyarbekir in 1091. The prayer hall is a simplified version of that in Damascus, with the same gabled roofs and transept but no dome. It is, however, separated from the *sahn* by a substantial wall with sixteen portals. The *riwaqs*, some of them reemploying antique materials, were added under Artukid domination in the twelfth century and later. In 1152–57, at Silvan, the Artukids varied the theme with a prayer hall entirely enclosed and a dome over the *mihrab* 44 feet in diameter. There seems never to have been a *sahn*, but there was a portico across the entrance facade with an exterior *mihrab* on axis with the inner one, as at Diyarbekir.

The Great Mosque of Dunaysir
The congregational mosque at Dunaysir (Kiziltepe), completed in 1204, is the masterpiece of Artukid architecture (*Plate 283*). Despite its advanced state of ruin, it is apparent that two-story *riwaqs* (as at Diyarbekir) seem once to have surrounded a rectangular *sahn* except along the high facade of the prayer hall (*Plate 284*), with its richly carved central portals flanked by exterior *mihrabs*. The three

285. *Divrig, Great Mosque and Hospital, 1228–29, plan*
286. *Divrig, Great Mosque and Hospital, longitudinal section*

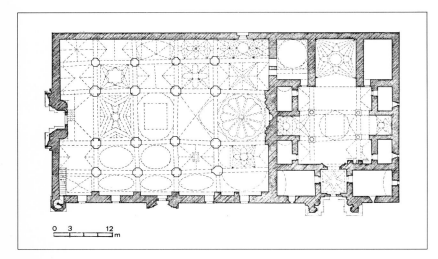

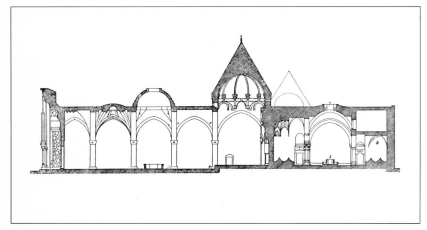

interior aisles parallel to the *qibla* are barrel-vaulted, as at Silvan; the central dome over the *mihrab*, cutting across two aisles, is about 33 feet across. The *mihrab*, flanked by columns with *muqarnas* capitals, takes the form of a shell niche set in a seven-lobed arch and is covered with deeply incised patterns of great intricacy. The model of the Great Mosque at Damascus as already modified at Diyarbekir and Silvan was certainly influential here. There are also Zengid elements in the design, but the masonry is extremely close to Armenian work, which might account for the lack of a real understanding of formal vocabulary of Islamic ornament. The sculptured borders around the portals of the prayer hall, which reappear in a more disciplined form in later Seljuk work, have been compared by some to local braided costume ornament. Others detect Crusader influences in the tympanums of the portals, but, if so, this last is so general as to be negligible.

The Great Mosque and Hospital at Divrig
The Friday mosque at Harput, an Artukid foundation of 1156–57, has a very small *sahn* (three bays long and two wide) surrounded by two aisled *riwaqs* and fronting a three-aisled prayer hall. At Kayseri the Koluk Mosque, a Danishmend foundation of the second half of the twelfth century (repaired in 1210), has reduced the *sahn* to a single bay covered by a small open dome with a pool beneath.

The form established by the Koluk Mosque was followed by Khurramshah of Ahlat, architect for the Mengujukid Ahmet Shah, when he designed the Great Mosque or Ulu Cami at Divrig (*Plate 285*). In an inscription of 1228/29 Ahmet Shah acknowledges the suzerainty of the Seljuk Sultan Kaykubad I, but this must have been no more than nominal. Malikaturan Malik, wife of Ahmet Shah, founded the adjacent hospital or *muristan* for the insane (it will be discussed later), built simultaneously by the same architect. A single five-aisled prayer hall five bays deep recalls the original *sahn* surmounted by a pierced dome over a pool in the middle bay of the *mihrab* aisle. The *mihrab* bay is marked by a ribbed dome on squinches, covered outside by a tall prismatic cone of masonry (*Plates 286, 287*) which dominates the whole building. The sixteen surviving stone vaults are of very complex form and have been compared to those of Gothic Europe, but in reality nothing so complicated had as yet been invented there. They probably owe more to Armenian prototypes or to the translation into stone of complex Persian forms in brick.

If the interior of the Divrig mosque is, though somewhat irregular, successful and impressive and that of the hospital even more so (*Plate 291*), the exterior of neither is as effective. The three major

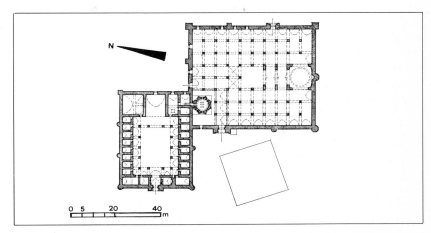

portals, of incredible complexity—one on the *mihrab* aisle to the north (*Plates 288, 290*), another to the west opening off-center into the third bay—and the vast hospital portal (*Plate 289*) bear very little relation to the walls in which they are set, or to each other. The mosque's north portal and the hospital's west portal, called "baroque" by Oktay Aslanapa, have been compared to embroidery patterns. Such patterns, although assembled less harmoniously at Divrig, also recall the extravagant stucco *mihrab* of the Haydariya *madrasa* at Qazvin. The porch of the hospital has a distinctly Gothic look with its receding archivolts, but the tympanum and the surround of the door can be matched in contemporary Armenian and Georgian architecture. A fourth portal or window to the east is in classic Seljuk style and was probably added in 1241, when the *minbar* was built by Ahmad of Tiflis.

THE SELJUK MOSQUE

The Great Mosque at Konya is so haphazardly assembled from structures of diverse periods that in only a few aspects does it yield accurate historical information. The first phase of work is dated at 1155 by the *minbar*, but only this and a *turbe* survive. The *mihrab* dome, an *iwan* north of it (now incorporated into later constructions), as well as a portal (blocked off today) on axis in the north wall were all probably finished in 1219 by an architect from Damascus. Over the north portal he installed a stone knot-patterned *alfiz* like those developed in twelfth-century Aleppo. The *iwan*-dome combination suggests, however, a more direct inheritance from Persia. The Great Mosque at Malatya of 1224 also has a brick dome over the *mihrab*, preceded by a deep *iwan* fronting a small court with a pool.

The Khwand Foundation at Kayseri

As at Konya and Malatya, the Friday mosque of the Khwand Foundation, although entirely of stone, has a domed *mihrab* bay preceded by an *iwan* opening from a small open court (*Plates 292, 293*). The *waqf* was established in the name of Mahperi Khatun, widow of Kaykubad I, and the complex completed in 1237–38 during the reign of her son Kaykhusrav II. This was one of the earliest Turkish charitable complexes or *kulliyes*; these included a Friday mosque, a *madrasa*, and a bath. It is notable that all three of the indubitably royal Seljuk great mosques have *mihrab* domes preceded by *iwans* even if their *sahns* are very small: probably the royal family was far more conscious of its Persian antecedents than were the earlier and contemporary Turkoman dynasties.

The west portal has a broad frame of restrained geometric interlace within which a four-centered arch frames a smooth tympanum

pierced abruptly by an acutely pointed *muqarnas* semidome surmounting the rectangular door recess. The whole forms an excellent example, as does Mahperi Khatun's *turbe*, discussed later, of the "classic" Seljuk style. Here the exuberance to which stucco or even carved terracotta may tempt the Persian architect is subdued and disciplined by Zengid and Armenian stone masonry traditions.

Wooden Mosques

Central Asia, particularly under the Ghaznavids, may have provided inspiration for the Seljuk mosques with flat roofs supported by columns of wood. The earliest is now known to have been built at Konya in 1258 under the Vizier Fakreddin Sahip Ata, though only the masonry portal and the *mihrab* survive. The others belong to the last third of the thirteenth century. The Friday mosque at Afyon Karahisar of 1272 has forty columns with *muqarnas* capitals arranged in nine rows perpendicular to the *qibla*. The largest of all wooden mosques is the Eshrefoglu Mosque of Suleyman Bek at Beyshehir (1297–99), with seven aisles perpendicular to the *qibla*; the aisles are formed by no less than forty-eight columns. The *mihrab* dome, encrusted with faience, rises from its own arched supports independent of the rest of the structure and has a conical exterior. An opening on the *mihrab* aisle over a pool recalls the traditional *sahn*. The Eshrefoglu family ruled by this time over an independent Beylik with its capital at Beyshehir, and their octagonal mausoleum is attached to the east side of the mosque.

Single-Unit Mosques

Small *masjids* or places of prayer without *minbars* were, in the Seljuk period, frequently roofed by a single dome and provided with a porch or vestibule. At least ten survive in Konya as independent structures, but they were also sometimes attached to *madrasas*, as at the Ince Minare Madrasa of 1260–65 (*Plate 298*). They range in date from 1213 through the end of the century. The Sirçali Masjid of brick, built in the second half of the thirteenth century, has a two-columned portico (*Plates 294, 295*) important as a prototype for later Ottoman mosques. From it the 28-foot-square prayer hall is entered through three doors. The dome is supported by pendentives of "Turkish triangles" and the *mihrab* is not—as is frequent in these buildings—on axis, but on the left wall.

THE MADRASA

The Anatolian *madrasa*, both pre-Seljuk and Seljuk, falls into two broad categories: those with open central courts of one or two stories and those whose courts are covered with a dome or vaulting. In the latter type a central opening and pool recall the open court, as in the mosques. Such buildings were by no means always used for the teaching of the law, but as hospitals, infirmaries, asylums for the insane, and even as observatories.

The earliest covered court *madrasa* was built by the Danishmend Yaghi Basan at Tokat in 1151–57. Of rough stone and without ornament, it has an asymmetrical plan with two *iwans* opening onto a square central court, which is covered by a pierced dome on squinches. At Divrig the hospital attached to the mosque (1228–29) is rigidly symmetrical and, with its arcades, very reminiscent of the open court form (*Plate 291*). Three barrel vaults with a lantern over the pool in the central bay enclose the space. The presence of three *iwans* and a vestibule at the portal recall Nur al-Din's *muristan* at Damascus.

The Mas'udiyya Madrasa (1198–1223) attached to the north arcade of the Great Mosque of Diyarbekir was built for the Artukid Sultan Sokmen II by the architect Jafar ibn Muhammad of Aleppo. It was intended for all four rites, but has only one large *iwan*. There is, nevertheless, a cross axis aligned on the north portal provided by the ordering of the two-story cloisters on three sides of the open court. One of the earliest Seljuk foundations with an open court is that of the single-storied hospital of Keykavus I at Sivas of 1217–18. This building of cut stone has a rectangular court cloistered on the long sides only with a large *iwan* facing the portal and a cross axis marked by wider arches. The Sultan died in 1219 and his brick tomb to the right of the court was probably added then. The elegant *madrasa* of the Khwand Foundation at Kayseri is more symmetrical, with rows of cells flanking a fully cloistered court and a single large *iwan* opposite the portal (*Plate 292*).

The Karatay Madrasa at Konya

This badly damaged building once had a plan very like that of the Ince Minare Madrasa (*Plate 298*), except that its portal is off axis. The *waqf* was established in 1251–52 by the Vizier Karatay, who served Keykavus II during the triumvirate dictated by the Mongols (1248–57). The portal (*Plate 296*) is of extraordinary quality. The *alfiz* of gray and white marble is in the knot design typical of Aleppo, but within the tympanum of the arch (supported by twisted colonnettes) there are six tiers of *muqarnas* forming a shallow vault above a lintel of joggled voussoirs. Syrian influence dominates, yet the design has a restraint and elegance typical of "classic" Seljuk work and the flared *muqarnas* is typically Anatolian. Inside, the court (*Plate 297*) is covered by a dome on triangular pendentives. The dome, the pendentives, and the lower walls were once entirely encrusted with a mosaic of turquoise, cobalt blue, and purple tile, much of it in relief.

294. *Konya, Sirçali Masjid, second half of thirteenth century*   296. *Konya, Karatay Madrasa, 1251–52, portal*
295. *Konya, Sirçali Masjid, plan*

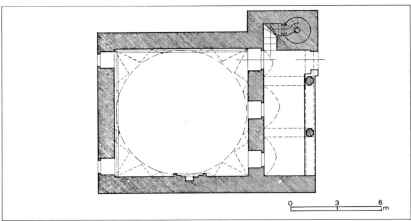

◁ 297. *Konya, Karatay Madrasa, interior*

898. *Konya, Ince Minare Madrasa, 1260–65, plan*
299. *Konya, Ince Minare Madrasa, portal and minaret*
300, 301. *Konya, Ince Minare Madrasa, details of the portal* ▷

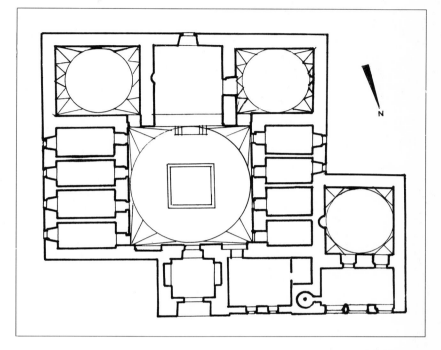

The Ince Minare Madrasa at Konya

This *madrasa* (Plate 298) was founded by the Vizier Fakreddin Sahip Ata between 1260 and 1265 and built by the architect Keluk b. Abdullah, possibly a Christian who converted to Islam. The upper portion of the slender minaret (Plate 299) which gave the *madrasa* its name has since collapsed. Of tile-encrusted fluted brick, it once had two *şerefes* or *muezzins'* balconies. Behcet Ünsal believes it may be earlier than the rest of the building and actually belong to the single-domed *masjid* to the right. The portal (Plates 299–301) has boldly entwined bands of inscription, knot designs in high relief, and very curious attached colonnettes diminishing toward their bases. Although the knots are Syrian motifs, the composition as a whole heralds a "baroque" phase in Seljuk architecture which began in Sahip Ata's mosque of 1258, built by the same architect.

The Gök Madrasa at Sivas

This twin-minaret *madrasa* (Plate 302) was begun for Fakreddin Sahip Ata in 1271 by the architect Kaluyan al-Qunawi, who in 1267–68 had also built him a *han* or *caravanserai* and a bath at Ilgin, northwest of Konya. The architect's possible Armenian origin and even his identification with Keluk b. Abdullah have been much discussed, but no conclusions can be reached though their styles are similar. The earliest surviving twin-minaret facade in Turkey is that of Fakreddin's wooden mosque in Konya (1258); the next is the Çifte Minareli Madrasa at Erzurum, followed by the Gök Madrasa and another built by the Ilkhanid Vizier Zuwaini (of which only the facade survives)—both in Sivas and dated 1271. The use of twin minarets certainly occurs earlier in Persia, where there are many Ilkhanid examples.

The Gök Madrasa is of the open-court cruciform type, whose cloisters north and south of the court were once two-storied (Plate 303). The rich blue and black tile mosaic ornament on the brick minarets and on the dome of the small *masjid* to the right of the portal give it its name of the "blue (*gök*) *madrasa*." J.M. Rogers has shown that the style is a later development of that of the unfinished Çifte Minareli Madrasa at Erzurum, often dated 1253 but probably much later. The facade's richly molded stone ornament (in high relief) derives in part from Syrian models, but the foliate palms and the plastic relief of the corner buttresses are a local development fully justifying the term "baroque" for this phase of Seljuk design. The facade is asymmetrical: a fountain left of the portal, like the one at Erzurum, does not match the mosque's portal to the right. Nevertheless, when the corner buttresses still had their (probably conical) finials rising above a rich *muqarnas* cornice—only parts of which are preserved to the left—the whole would have shown a considerable advance in exterior articulation over that at Divrig.

◁ *302. Sivas, Gök Madrasa, begun 1271, facade*

303. Sivas, Gök Madrasa, plan
304. Sultan Han near Kayseri, 1232–36, plan
305. Sultan Han near Kayseri, reconstruction

THE HAN OR CARAVANSERAI

With the conquest of Sinope and Antalya, the Seljuks were able to bring to central Anatolia a prosperity unknown there since the Antonines. The Alay Han near Aksaray, probably a royal foundation built late in the reign of Qilich Arslan II (1156–92), established a pattern for most of the later royal *hans* and those of the great emirs as well. There are few exceptions to this pattern, which was well adapted to the severe Anatolian winters. Such buildings have two distinct parts: the first is a three- or five-aisled barrel-vaulted hall of stone masonry throughout, often with a windowed lantern at the midpoint of the center aisle. This complex opens through a monumental portal on axis into an open court with one- or two-story arcades behind which are rooms with fireplaces, a bath, and quarters for the staff (which sometimes included physicians, musicians, and dancers). A *masjid* sometimes stood in the center of the court, raised up over a fountain, or it might be placed over the always monumental portal, on axis with that of the covered section. *Hans* were charitable foundations in that they were endowed to provide all travelers with three days of free lodging and other services. Nevertheless, they also existed for profit, and income from them is often mentioned in the *waqf* or articles of endowment for other institutions.

The best preserved surviving examples of the type described above are two foundations of Kaykubad I—the Sultan Han near Aksaray, begun in 1229, and the somewhat smaller Sultan Han near Kayseri (*Plates 304, 305*), whose hall was built in 1232–36 (the court was completed a few years later). The covered halls of both are very similar. A high central "nave" with a pointed barrel vault opens into aisles roofed by transverse barrel vaults. A "crossing" in the center is covered by a domed lantern on spherical pendentives (*Plate 306*). The court portal of the *han* near Aksaray (*Plate 308*) is a perfect example of "classic" Seljuk style. The rich yet disciplined geometric ornament of the broad jambs recalls Persian brick ornament, but the channeled corner columns, joggled voussoirs, and marble paneling are Syrian (*Plate 309*). The later hall portal of the *han* near Kayseri (*Plate 307*), owing less to Syria, shows a dominant interlace motif. Both make the fullest use of luminous cascades of *muqarnas*. In both *hans* the central *masjids* are the most richly ornamented parts of the buildings, that near Kayseri (*Plates 310, 311*) being the better preserved. In the latter, the portal to the north is approached by a double stair, and to east and west there are windows. The interior, once groin-vaulted like the open space below, is no more than 86 square feet. An inner stair led to the roof (probably flat), from which the *muezzin* gave the call to prayer.

In terms of decoration, the influence of Azerbaijanian brickwork

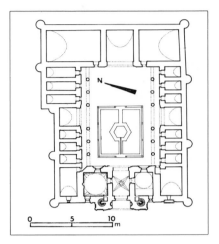
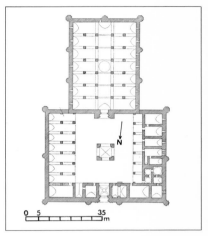

306. *Sultan Han near Kayseri, hall*
307. *Sultan Han near Kayseri, portal of the hall*
308. *Sultan Han near Aksaray, begun 1229, entrance portal*

309. *Sultan Han near Aksaray, detail of the entrance portal*

310, 311.   Sultan Han near Kayseri, masjid

312. *Kobadabad, begun 1236, plan of the site and of the palaces*
313. *Kobadabad, smaller palace, plan*

314. *Amasya, Halifet Ghazi Kumbed, 1145–46* ▷

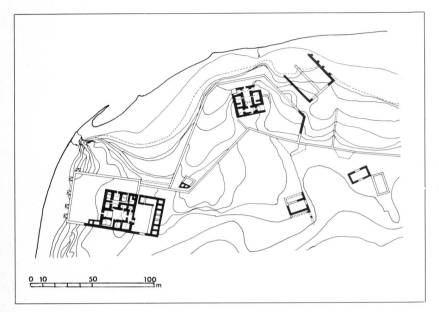

0 10   50   100
m

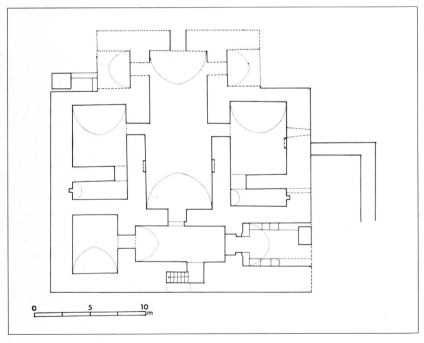

0   5   10
m

(modified by Syrian stone masonry) is apparent in these and many other thirteenth-century *hans*, though by this time the two had been assimilated into a vigorous new style. The halls also owe a great deal to Armenian religious architecture which was still a living art, in Georgia, at Ani near Lake Van and in southwestern Anatolia. Not only is the technique of facing a rubble masonry core with a beautifully cut stone skin very old in Armenia as well as Syria, but the spherical pendentives of the domes and their originally conical exteriors are closely related to the crossing lanterns of Armenian churches and monasteries, perhaps imported to Anatolia by returning stonemasons who had worked on these very buildings.

THE PALACE

Until recently very little positive information about Seljuk palaces or their settings was available. The richly ornamented *qa'a* in the early thirteenth-century Artukid palace at Diyarbekir is more closely related to Egypt and Syria and had few if any Seljuk descendants. The pavilion of Qilich Arslan II at Konya was rebuilt over one of the towers of the citadel wall and not an independent structure. It was square and had balconies set on protruding brackets of brick. Its ornament of stucco and tile was very rich and included numerous figures of men and animals. The polychrome tiles were executed in a technique like that of Persian Minai ware, not used in Turkey after 1192. In 1224–26 Ala al-Din Kaykubad I built three small pavilions near Kayseri, of which one stood on a structure of four stone arches supporting a groin vault very like the *masjids* of some of the royal *hans* and possibly their inspiration.

About ten years later the Sultan, on a journey from Kayseri to Antalya, came upon a site on the west shore of the lake of Beyshehir and ordered his vizier, Sa'd al-Din Kopek, to build him a palace there. Begun in 1236, its ruins (under excavation since 1965 by K. Otto Dorn) consist of at least sixteen rather modest constructions of masonry-faced rubble scattered irregularly along the shore (*Plate 312*). Two are residential and one is a two-berth dockyard. The larger northern palace measures about 164 by 115 feet and stands on a terrace along the lake. Judging by the fallen tiles on the terrace, there were probably pavilions of lighter construction on the roof. Inside there were two throne complexes, both with *iwans* opening from larger barrel-vaulted stone-paved halls with antechambers. The halls would doubtless have been open to the sky in regions further south. The smaller palace (*Plate 313*) is more symmetrically disposed around the same antechamber-great hall-*iwan* complex. Doors from the *iwan* give a direct view of the lake and lead also to two exterior *iwans* facing north and south. A stair from the antechamber once led to a pavilion on the roof.

For the first time rich tile dadoes are found *in situ*; these were composed of crosses, octagons, and eight-pointed stars decorated in polychrome underglaze and luster with innumerable courtly scenes and animals both fabulous and real. The themes expressed seem to have been those of power, happiness, and Paradise, as in most if not all other Islamic palaces. J. M. Rogers has suggested that these tiles, though locally made, have much in common with the northern Iraqi manufactures of Raqqa, whose ceramic tradition survived until 1259. Tiles also served as window grilles and may have framed colored glass. In a northern chamber of the larger palace, one wall is lined with at least three tiers of stucco niches whose spandrels are filled by carvings of peacocks. The motif comes ultimately from the Bulkawara Palace in Samarra, but future research will probably show it is characteristic of all "classic" Islamic architecture. Such niche walls will be much exploited in the domestic architecture of the Ottomans, the Safavids, and the Moghuls of India.

Pre-Seljuk Tombs

Tombs—called *turbes* in Turkish and also *kumbeds* as in Persian and Arabic—are nearly all centrally planned structures, usually in stone, most often octagonal (but also ten-sided or more) or square or cylindrical. A few take the form of freestanding *iwans*. Most are raised above crypts which contain the actual remains, often embalmed. Although most are freestanding in cemeteries, as in Egypt, Syria, and Persia, they may also be attached to mosques, stand within the corner chamber of *madrasas*, or even in *hans*, if those of the founders.

The tomb of a vizier of the Danishmend ruler Melek Ghazi at Amasya was built, according to tradition, in 1145–46. Called the Halifet Ghazi Kumbed, its archaic style (*Plate 314*) is in accord with the early date. The simple octagonal structure, once with a pyramidal roof, has an eastern entrance. This, with its scattered, casually organized ornament, nevertheless represents the earliest known use of a *muqarnas* demi-vault in stone over a door. At Divrig the so-called Sitte Melik Kumbed (*Plates 315, 316*) of 1196—probably built for the Mengujukid Emir Suleyman ibn Saif al-Din Shahanshah—has the simple prismatic form of the earlier monument. However, the decoration is here articulated into a unified composition of great elegance.

Seljuk Tombs

A simple prismatic form is also taken by the decagonal mausoleum built in the *sahn* of the Ala al-Din Mosque in Konya for Qilich Arslan II (before 1192). Ten-sided tomb structures may have been royal prerogatives, since one such in brick was added for Keykavus I c. 1219 to his hospital at Sivas. This tomb was built by Ahmad of

Marand, whose name appears on the remarkable entrance facade of turquoise, purple, and white glazed tile mosaic, forming a Kufic inscription on a mat ground of red brick (*Plate 317*). Nothing comparable is known from Persia at this date, and the inspiration for the Sivas tomb may perhaps be Central Asian.

The octagonal *turbe* of Mahperi Khwand Khatun in her foundation at Kayseri (1237–38) represents a further step in the monumental development of the tomb (*Plate 318*). Each face of the octagon is articulated by a blind arch with a rich decoration in the spandrels, like that on the hall portal of the Sultan Han near Kayseri founded by her husband. The corners are enriched by attached colonnettes standing on a *muqarnas* cornice marking the crypt and terminated by the projections of another cornice, which forms the colonnettes' capitals and signals the transition to the pyramidal roof.

The undated Döner Kumbed at Kayseri (*Plate 319*) was built for the Princess Shah Jihan Khatun and illustrates the "baroque" phase of Seljuk architecture. The double-headed eagles and date palms in high relief relate it to the Gök Madrasa at Sivas and to certain dated tombs at Ahlat, suggesting a year around 1275 for its construction. The twelve sides are articulated by continuous moldings forming pointed blind arches. Above these a *muqarnas* cornice marks the tent-like conical roof, carved to suggest roof plates, perhaps of lead. The whole vividly recalls the lanterns of many Armenian churches of the tenth or eleventh centuries, which certainly influenced its design. The square crypt below even displays transition zones similar to extradoses of the pendentives of a cupola above a square crossing.

THE ARCHITECTURE OF THE BEYLIKS

The period between the final collapse of the central power of the Seljuk Sultans in the last quarter of the thirteenth century and the gradual increase in the territory of the Ottomans in the early fifteenth is again marked by an increase in experimental forms sometimes based on Seljuk antecedents, but sometimes also departing radically from them. Two monuments destined to have a profound effect upon later Ottoman architecture best illustrate this process.

The Great Mosque at Manisa

In 1376 Ishaq Bek, the Sarubanid Emir, built the Friday mosque here as part of a complex which included a *madrasa* (finished two years later) and a tomb (*Plate 320*). The plan of the mosque (*Plate 321*) shows a prayer hall in the tradition of the Great Mosque at Silvan, divided from a forepart of almost equal area by seven portals. Unlike Silvan, however, the brick vaults here are supported by salvaged columns, sometimes doubled. The *mihrab* dome, 35 feet in diameter,

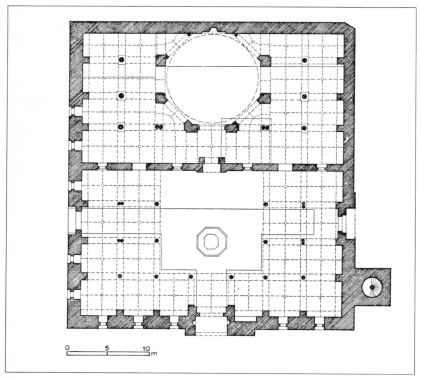

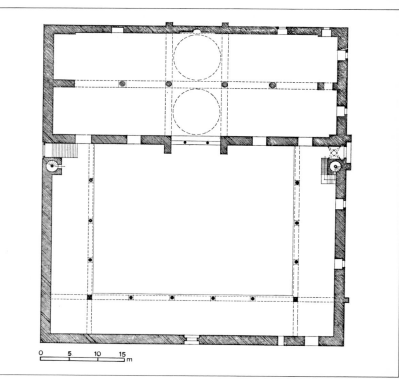

covers a square exactly as large as the open *sahn*, which also has a cross axis provided by the side portals of the forecourt. The almost square bays throughout are covered, according to Oktay Aslanapa, by "small transverse vaults resembling domes." Symmetry, axial composition, and the conscious echo of one space by another are all notably greater here than in any previous Seljuk building.

The Great Mosque of Isa Bek at Seljuk

Seljuk was the Aydinid administrative capital near ancient Ephesus on the west coast of Anatolia, south of Izmir. There the architect Ali ibn al-Dimishqi, specified as from Damascus, built a Friday mosque for the Emir Isa Bek in 1374–75. The plan (*Plate 322*) clearly echoes the Great Mosque at Damascus. The emphasized transept has a triple portal and two domes, but the rest of the prayer hall was covered by roofs supported by wooden frameworks parallel to the *qibla*. The *sahn* was surrounded on three sides by an arcade of salvaged shafts, though many of the capitals were worked with *muqarnas*. The *mihrab* was originally surmounted by an *alfiz* of knotted interlace in colored marbles, perhaps the last appearance of this Syrian motif anywhere. Paired minarets marked the symmetrically ordered entrances to the *sahn*. Because of the unstable terrain, the west or principal facade (*Plate 323*) had to be supported by vaulted understructures, perhaps used for shops. The portal, though rather compressed, is richly ornamented in polychrome marble and *muqarnas*. The two tiers of windows of both *sahn* and prayer hall are again enriched in colored marbles. In addition, that to the upper right of the portal is completely surrounded by a *muqarnas* cornice, a Seljuk inheritance to be much exploited by the early Ottomans.

The devastation brought to Persia by the Mongols has probably never been equaled anywhere, even in modern times. Whole cities disappeared and once flourishing agricultural regions were returned to desert. In 1220–21 the cities of Samarkand and Bukhara were destroyed and the Kingdom of Khwarazm fell. Then, with the death of Chingiz (Genghis) Khan in 1227, there came a respite for Persia, though Anatolia fell in 1243. In 1256 Hulagu crossed the Oxus and two years later took Baghdad. Some cities, among them Isfahan, offered no resistance and so were spared, but under Hulagu (d. 1266) and his immediate successors Persia suffered neglect, misrule, and discrimination (the early Ilkhanids were not Muslim). For these reasons almost no buildings survive from 1220 to the 1280's, though the pious must have sponsored some construction if only on a limited scale.

With the conversion of Ghazan Khan (1295–1304) to Islam, royal patronage of architecture was resumed and the great period of miniature painting for which Persia has become so famous began. Almost nothing of Ghazan's architecture survives, but we still have some of the works erected in the reign of his brother Oljeitu (1304–17). Oljeitu's son, Abu Said (1317–35), who succeeded at the age of twelve, lost control of the realm, though major monuments continued to be built in his name. When he died without an heir, the Ilkhanid regime collapsed and was replaced by local dynasties, among them the Muzaffarids of Fars in Shiraz (1314–93) and the Jalayirids in Iraq and Azerbaijan, with their capital in Baghdad (1336–1432).

Timur (Tamerlane), who claimed descent from Chingiz Khan, was born in 1335, the year of Abu Said's death, and was the son of the Chagatayid Mongols' governor of Transoxiana. By 1370 Timur reigned supreme in Samarkand. After subduing Khwarazm and Khorassan, he turned to the central Persian lands, whose cities were again partially destroyed. Timur, however, was a devout Sunni Muslim and, from the first, a builder. He conscripted craftsmen of all kinds (including architects) and sent them back to his capital, Samarkand. They came from Shiraz, Baghdad, Damascus, Aleppo, and even from the Qipchak lands as far north as Moscow. In 1398–99 Delhi was sacked and its craftsmen sent off to Samarkand. With the defeat and capture of Bayazid I at Ankara in 1402, the rising Ottoman Empire was subdued for a generation as still more craftsmen were transferred to Samarkand. Timur's son, Shah Rukh (1405–47), at first ruled only Khorassan, but later the western lands as well, the latter lost at his death. His successors followed his lead and Timur's in their lavish patronage of all the arts, which flourished in eastern Persia until the death (1506) of Husain Baikara in Herat and the Shaybanid conquest. The Safavids were, however, the direct heirs of

324.   *Sultanieh, Tomb of Oljeitu, from al-Matraki's* Description of the Stages of Sultan Suleyman's Campaign in the Two Iraqs *(1537), Library of the University of Istanbul*

325.   *Sultanieh, Tomb of Oljeitu, 1306–17* ▷

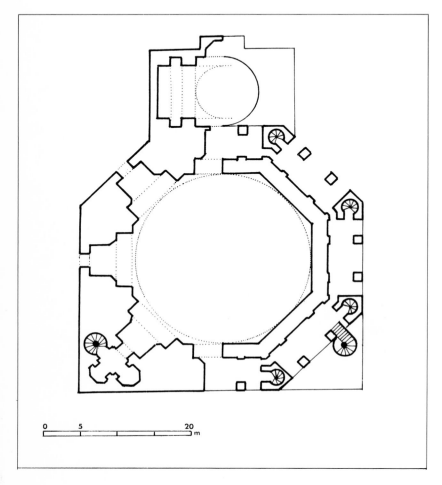

0 5 20 m

Timurid art which continued to flourish under their patronage through the early eighteenth century.

THE MONUMENTS OF OLJEITU AND ABU SAID

Oljeitu, who succeeded to the throne at the age of twenty-three, had been baptized a Christian by his mother, but later, influenced by one of his wives, became a Muslim and took the name of Muhammad Khudabanda. His vacillations between Shi'ite and Sunni Orthodoxy are hard to trace, but are important for an understanding of his principal monuments. In 1306 he ordered work begun on the town of Sultanieh near Qazvin, intended to replace Tabriz as the Ilkhanid capital—a plan already initiated by his father, Arghun, in 1270. A stone-walled citadel, an elaborate mosque, and a palace in the form of a high pavilion were soon completed, as well as whole quarters founded by the rival viziers, Rashid al-Din (d. 1318) and Taj al-Din Ali Shah. Of this splendid complex, dedicated in 1313, only Oljeitu's magnificent tomb survives.

The Tomb of Oljeitu at Sultanieh

The records state that this great octagonal structure once had iron window grilles, three doors of steel, and a steel enclosure around the cenotaph. All these have vanished, as well as the subsidiary buildings around the tomb proper, though some idea of their original appearance can be gained from the views of Sultanieh made for a sixteenth-century manuscript recounting the Ottoman Sultan Suleyman's campaign in Iraq (*Plate 324*). In 1310, when work on the building must have been well advanced, Oljeitu returned from a pilgrimage to the tombs of the Shi'ite saints Ali and Husein a confirmed Shi'ite. He planned to bring the two saints' bodies to Sultanieh for reburial in his own monument; the decorations were executed with this in mind, and a chapel was built behind the original structure (*Plate 326*) while a much more modest tomb was erected elsewhere for Oljeitu himself. The scheme fell through, and perhaps because of this Oljeitu returned to Sunni Orthodoxy. He then rededicated the building as his own tomb (probably about 1313; *Plates 325, 327*) and had much of the earlier decoration covered with a heavy coat of white plaster bearing inscriptions and floral patterns in blue paint.

The octagon has an interior diameter of about 85 feet, with walls 23 feet thick. To the north of the principal entrance the angles are filled in and to the south the mortuary chapel or oratory projects. The east, west, and north walls show traces of exterior finishes, but it is also evident that they were linked here and there to now vanished subsidiary structures. Eight tall niches penetrate the walls of the inner chamber, framing doors below and openings into a gallery above. Still

higher is another richly decorated gallery which opens only outward through triple arches. Above these runs a rich *muqarnas* cornice encrusted with turquoise and black tile mosaic. Above the cornice rise the stumps of eight slender minarets encrusted with blue tile. These surround the great dome, which is not truly double (as its fabric thins toward the summit, a cellular construction supports an outer skin of brilliant blue tile). Structurally this monument adds nothing new to Persian architecture: the techniques employed were all known to the Seljuks. Nevertheless, as Donald Wilber has noted, the relation of this building to Seljuk architecture is rather like that of the High Gothic style to its late Romanesque and Early Gothic roots, with the same striving toward verticality. The peaks of the eight original minarets, though not acting as counterweights for the vault as do Gothic pinnacles, must have effectively accented that verticality. Inside, the hollowing of the walls by tall niches and galleries approaches the linear, skeletal construction of the High Gothic style.

In comparison to pre-Mongol ceramic and stucco ornament, the tomb of Oljeitu—again without introducing new techniques—marks a considerable advance in refinement over older examples. In the first period, as a major Shi'ite shrine, the interior was sumptuously ornamented in patterns of light and dark blue glazed brick alternating with mat-surfaced brick and some carved terracotta. To the same period belong the beautifully molded and painted plaster vaults of the upper gallery, where brickwork with carved plugs is imitated. The decoration of the dome chamber in the second period (after Oljeitu's conversion) emphasized the horizontal with a dado about 13 feet high once solidly encrusted with hexagonal light blue tile, framed by engaged colonnettes of tile mosaic and bordered by underglaze-painted rectangular tiles. Above the dado all the ornament was painted. Solidly encrusted tile dadoes must have existed in Persia in pre-Mongol times, since they appear in Kobadabad in Anatolia. Probably they were more frequent in palaces, though from the fourteenth century on they are common in both religious and secular buildings.

The Mihrab of Oljeitu at Isfahan

In the Masjid-i-Jami at Isfahan there has been inserted behind the *riwaq* on the right and abutting the north wall of the western *iwan* an oratory or winter mosque. This room, five bays long and three wide, is vaulted by transverse arches supporting between them narrow barrel vaults, each with a cupola at the apex. The structure may be contemporary with the *mihrab*, dated 1310, or as late as 1447, when the portal into the *sahn* received its tiles. The *mihrab*, of exquisitely carved stucco (*Plate 328*), lacks the bold relief of earlier Seljuk stuccoes and, in the reduced scale of its traditional patterns, points toward the later Timurid style.

Cross-vaulted halls are found much earlier than the Ilkhanids, but proliferated in their dynasty and later. Transverse arches in cut stone were used in Syria at least as early as the second century A.D. At the Parthian site of Kuh-i-Khwaja they appear in rubble masonry, as they do at the Sassanian site of Iwan-i-Kharqa of about 490. In Islamic architecture they seem first to have been used at Kasr Kharanah (in Jordan) before 711. After this, few if any examples survive before the early fourteenth-century Han Ortmah in Baghdad, of fired brick (*Plate 329*). In the latter part of the same century two rectangular cross-vaulted oratories were built flanking the domed *mihrab* hall and *iwan* of the Great Mosque at Yazd. As might be expected, the form was most popular in central and southern Persia, the old Sassanian lands from which it was introduced into Timurid architecture, where it was to play an important role.

The Funerary Complex of Abd al-Samad at Natanz

This complex grew up around the tomb of Shaykh Abd al-Samad al-Isfahani, probably identical with Abdu'l Samad, a follower of the famous Sufi Shaykh Abu Said who had died in 1049. The oldest surviving structure is an octagonal pavilion mosque, probably of the Seljuk period (*Plate 330*). Perhaps this was the original tomb, or an earlier tomb occupied the site of the present one (whose *qibla* varies ten degrees from that of the octagon). The four-*iwan* congregational mosque incorporating the octagon bears the dates of 1304 and 1309 (*Plate 331*). Wall arches within the redecorated octagon and, until they were rebuilt, the arches of the second tier of the mosque had a broken outline later to have a long history, reappearing as the "Bursa arch" in early Ottoman Turkey.

The tomb, dated 1307, is a cruciform chamber within a square, which becomes an octagon at the window level and is roofed by an octagonal pyramid encrusted in blue tiles. Inside, angle colonnettes lead to a continuous stucco inscription from which rises a superb *muqarnas* vault (*Plate 333*). Ceramic grilles filter the light from the eight windows, four of them pierced through the corner squinches, as in the tombs of Ismail at Bukhara and Sanjar at Merv. The *muqarnas* in this diffused light has a subdued golden glow compared by Arthur Upham Pope to a "sunlit summer cloud."

In 1316–17 a *khanaqah* or dervish hostel was built southwest of the tomb of which only the portal has survived (*Plate 332*). The design, richly encrusted with glazed and molded tile, predominantly blue, has a strongly vertical accent. In 1964 the *muqarnas* half dome was restored. The development of such a group of structures around the

331. *Natanz, funerary complex of Shaykh Abd al-Samad, courtyard of the mosque looking southwest*

332. *Natanz, funerary complex of Shaykh Abd al-Samad, portal of the khanaqah, 1316–17*

333. *Natanz, funerary complex of Shaykh Abd al-Samad,* muqarnas *vault* ▷

334. *Tabriz, Masjid-i-Jami, c. 1310–c. 1320*, iwan
335. *Tabriz, Masjid-i-Jami, plan*

336. *Varamin, Masjid-i-Jami, 1322–26, plan*

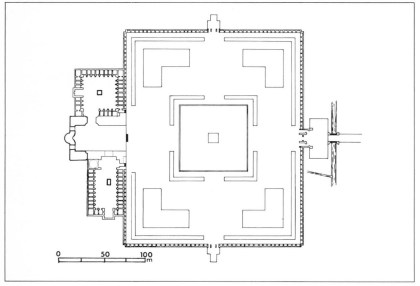

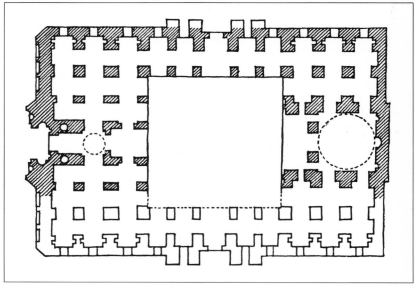

tomb of a local religious teacher began early in Islam around the tombs of the Shi'ite *imams* and that of Ali al-Rida at Mashad. With the rise of Sufism, more modest complexes like that at Natanz became numerous, especially among Sunni Muslims. Sometimes, as we will see later, all earlier structures are swept away and a wholly new, unified plan is imposed; such was not the case at Natanz, however.

The Masjid-i-Jami at Tabriz

Taj al-Din Ali Shah Jilan Tabrizi, who died in 1324, was vizier first to Oljeitu and then to Abu Said. Between c. 1310 and c. 1320 he built the Masjid-i-Jami, which consisted of a single immense *iwan* of brick (*Plate 334*). This was 99 feet wide, about 213 feet deep and, to the springing of the now-collapsed vault, about 82 feet tall. The total plan (*Plate 335*), based on literary evidence (some of it contradictory), shows an immense *sahn* with a center pool and single-aisled porticoes faced with luster tile, as the *mihrab* also may have been. A *khanaqah* for dervishes and a *madrasa* flanked the *iwan*, providing an early example of an Anatolian Turkish *kulliye* in which a charitable complex surrounds not a saint's tomb but a congregational mosque. The gigantic size of the *iwan*—compared by contemporaries to the arch at Ctesiphon, as were all such monuments—prefigures the megalomaniac spirit inherent in some of the early Timurid royal projects.

The Masjid-i-Jami at Varamin

This much ruined structure, built between 1322 and 1326 in the name of Sultan Abu Said, is notable for the absolute symmetry of its four-iwan plan (*Plate 336*). This recalls the Seljuk prototype of Zaware, except that at least those portions flanking the *mihrab* dome had two stories (*Plate 337*). A small dome behind the main portal completes the portal *iwan*, but also serves as a vestibule marking a cross-axis—an innovation with a long future. Another notable change is the subordination of all other parts of the building to the very prominent *mihrab* dome, which may have been intended to have an even taller outer shell. The dome chamber (*Plate 338*) is articulated, as is all else, by squinches filled with *muqarnas* in brick, which signal the transition from the square to the octagon; the latter in turn is converted to a sixteen-sided polygon of alternating squinches and windows.

The Tomb of Turabek Khanum at Urgench

Urgench, the ancient capital of Khwarazm and, under Ozbeg Khan of the Golden Horde (1313–41), a flourishing commercial center, lies far to the north of the Ilkhanid territories near the Oxus and not far south of the Aral Sea. Nevertheless, this remarkable tomb—built for the wife of Ozbeg's governor, Kutlu Dumur, between c. 1320 and c.

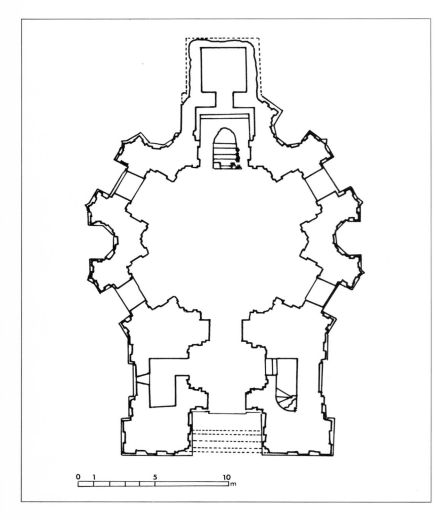

1330 and praised by Ibn Battuta, who saw it in 1333—is essentially Persian in style. The governor, certainly Turkish, followed a frequent Turkish custom already seen among the Anatolian Seljuks of building an elaborate tomb for a favored wife, a practice continued among the later Timurids and the Moghuls of India, both by inheritance Turkish.

The structure is dominated by a monumental portal with a high *pishtaq* now stripped of its original ornament. This is attached by an antechamber with a ruined *muqarnas* vault to a construction that is dodecagonal outside and hexagonal inside, which led in turn to a square chapel with another *muqarnas* vault. Later the collapsed rear wall was apparently replaced by a small-domed chamber over a crypt. Arches alternately filled with *muqarnas* and floral arabesques in polychrome tile mosaic convert the hexagonal central chamber into a dodecagon and then into a twenty-four-sided polygon by means of twelve panels with arabesques and twelve windows. From this springs the interior dome, encrusted in an elaborate net of ten- and twelve-pointed star interlaces in tile mosaic. With its symbolization of a star-filled sky, the whole is a metaphor for Paradise (which may alternatively be represented by a *muqarnas* vault). Outside, the dome was concealed by a conical roof encrusted in blue tile.

The richness of the continuous encrustation of tile mosaic and the lavish use of *muqarnas* in the portal, vestibule, and oratory all suggest that Timur may have made liberal use of Khwarazmian craftsmen, at least for his earlier works at Shahr-i-Sabz and Samarkand.

THE MONUMENTS OF THE REIGN OF TIMUR (c. 1370–1405)
The Palaces at Shahr-i-Sabz and Samarkand
Timur was born at Shahr-i-Sabz, then Kesh, where he may first have decided to establish his capital. Among the remains there is a vast ruined arch, the Akserai—of baked brick, sheathed in geometric patterns created in alternating glazed and mat-surfaced brick as well as in panels of polychrome tile mosaic. Contemporary chroniclers state that tile workers from Urgench were employed on it, and the mosaic is indeed similar to that of Turabek Khanum's mausoleum. The outer arch (*Plate 340*), flanked by cylindrical towers or minarets on polygonal bases, is over 72 feet wide and was probably 164 feet tall; the inner arch is 42 feet wide. Even as a truncated ruin, the scale is colossal. Here for the first time an arch is flanked by towers springing not from the *pishtaq* but from the ground, a practice later to become characteristic of Timurid design.

In 1404 Gonzalez de Clavijo, Spanish ambassador to the court of Timur, visited a palace at Shahr-i-Sabz, almost certainly this one, which, he said, was not yet finished though it had been under con-

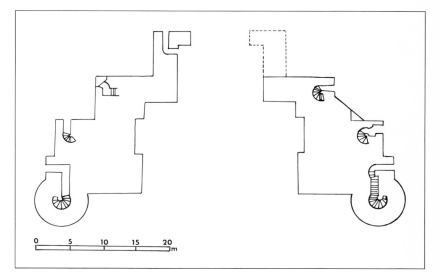

struction for twenty years. A hundred years later Babur, future Moghul emperor of India, recorded a briefer description. Neither is very specific, but they agree regarding the general layout. A monumental gate led to a corridor lined by guardrooms opening on a stone-paved court three hundred paces wide and probably square. This had a large pool in the center and was surrounded by arcades, richly ornamented and probably of two stories. At right and left were two lesser *iwans* and, on axis, a very large one, which is probably the surviving ruin and which Babur inevitably compared to the arch at Ctesiphon. Behind this was a square chamber painted in blue and gold, with a golden vault (almost certainly a dome). This was surrounded by a complex of chambers no less than six stories high, fragments of which cling to the rear of the existing ruin. Clavijo adds that beyond this unit were other more private chambers opening onto a spacious enclosure with trees, fountains, and pools. Both descriptions suggest that the palace had a plan rather like that of the Ghaznavid Lashkari Bazar, with a cruciform forecourt devoted to official business and more private residential quarters beyond.

The palaces in Samarkand ascribed to Timur by Clavijo and Babur seem to have been very different. Clavijo was received in a succession of gardens in September of 1404. He describes them often as walled, with corner towers and monumental gates. Inside were shade and fruit trees, and water channels; on a central platform, often surrounded by water, were cruciform pavilions of great magnificence. Only one building, the Chehel Situn ("forty pillars") in the Bagh-i-Maydan, is more completely described by Babur. This was square, with corner towers, and had two-story facades carried on carved stone columns. Four portals appear to have led to a great central hall, perhaps domed. The building's radial symmetry would suggest that the garden too had a central setting—in short, that this was a *chahr bagh*. As Clavijo describes such garden pavilions, they were used for feasting on a grand scale. They are close equivalents to the enchanting "tent palaces" at the *ordo* or campsite of Timur, also visited by Clavijo. Here the enclosures, gates, and central chambers with their embroidered silks and brocades often imitated architectural forms. A Persian tradition of enclosed gardens and garden pavilions going back as far as the Achaemenids seems to have been revitalized at this time by a new influx of nomads.

The Shrine of Ahmad Yasavi in Turkestan City

The famous Sufi Shaykh Ahmad Yasavi died in Yasi (now Turkestan City) in 1166. His successors, usually bearing the title of Ata, have continued his teachings there down to the present day. These teachings, closely related to pre-Islamic Turkish Shamanism, ultimately

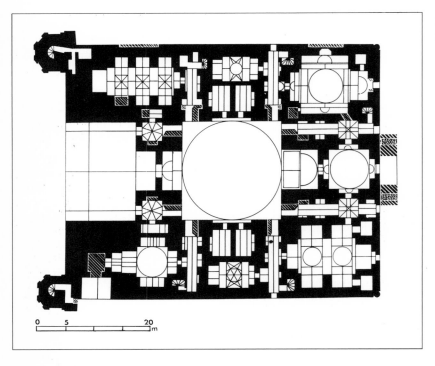

0   5   20
                           m

formed the basis of the Sufi mysticism of the Anatolian dervishes (particularly of the Bektashi sect), and links between Yasi and Anatolia appear to have been maintained. The present shrine complex, which probably replaces an earlier one, was built between 1394–95 and 1397, but seems never to have been entirely finished. The architects, according to Lisa Golombek, were Khwajah Hassan Shirazi and Shams Abd Allah Shirazi. The plan (*Plate 341*) is unusual. A monumental facade with an *iwan* nearly 59 feet wide is flanked by the stumps of cylindrical minarets on polygonal bases. The whole facade, apparently unfinished and intended to have been even taller, leads through a lesser *iwan* into a domed chamber about 194 square feet, off which open access passages and four cells. On axis through another *iwan* is the domed tomb chamber with a monumental northwest entrance. This and the tall outer dome might have been added in the fifteenth century. The position of the tomb chamber recalls the tombs of Oljeitu and Turabek Khanum, but the overall organization is very like that of a covered Anatolian *madrasa* and one wonders if this building or its predecessor had been projected by a follower of Shaykh Ahmad returning from Anatolia. The central space, without a *mihrab*, could only have served as an assembly hall. The west corner chamber must have been the mosque and the rest, with its typically central Persian complex transverse vaulting, was used as library and *khanaqah*. The intricate configurations of the plan and the interlocking recessions of each chamber create a pattern beautiful in itself, though not yet rigidly symmetrical.

The Bibi Khanum Mosque in Samarkand

On September 29, 1404, the Spanish ambassador Clavijo was received by Timur in a house near one of the city gates. In its chapel was buried the mother of Timur's wife: this must have been the *madrasa* founded by Bibi Khanum, of which her tomb survives opposite the portal of the mosque. Clavijo says Timur had gone there to supervise the rebuilding of the portal of his great Friday mosque, whose first design had not been tall enough. This mosque, popularly called that of Bibi Khanum, is now generally accepted as that which Timur had begun in 1399. Babur says the building was of stone and a contemporary chronicler says that two hundred stonecutters were brought from Azerbaijan (probably Baku), Fars, and India to work there. The 480 stone columns were each 10 1/2 feet tall; some of these, of gray marble or granite, still lie among the ruins. They and the elaborate marble dado (about 10 feet high) around the massive baked brick walls explain Babur's error.

The colossal portal (*Plate 344*), about 59 feet wide and perhaps once 108 or more tall, was flanked by minarets and projected from a

342. *Samarkand, Bibi Khanum Mosque, 1399–1404, detail of portal*

343. *Samarkand, Bibi Khanum Mosque, plan*

344. *Samarkand, Bibi Khanum Mosque, general view*

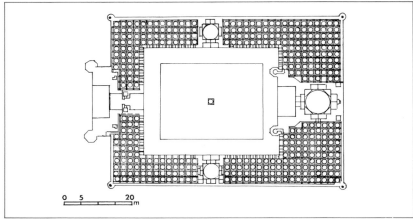

345. *Samarkand, Gur-i-Amir, 1404, plan*

346. *Samarkand, Gur-i-Amir, view from the east*

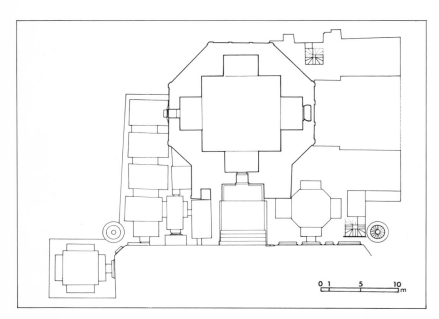

rich tile-encrusted facade flanked by two more corner minarets (*Plate 343*). Within a second niche once stood an inner portal of marble, very like a door in the palace of the Shirvan Shahs at Baku and probably the work of Azerbaijanian craftsmen. Within, a vast cruciform *sahn* of about 197 by 295 feet leads to the *qibla iwan* (*Plate 342*), projecting like the portal and flanked by tapering polygonal minarets. The dome chamber beyond—only about 151 square feet, though nearly 108 feet tall—seems an anti-climax after the splendid orchestration and gorgeous color of the colossal exterior. There three tall blue outer domes, two gigantic *iwans*, and no less than eight tall minarets are theatrically arranged in an overwhelmingly powerful display.

The Gur-i-Amir in Samarkand

Muhammad Sultan, Timur's favorite grandson, died in Turkey of wounds received at the battle of Ankara in July of 1402. Timur ordered the Gur-i-Amir built as his tomb, along with what Clavijo calls a house and a mosque. The "house" was probably a *madrasa* or a *khanaqah* perhaps already founded by Muhammad Sultan before his death. Timur did not return to Samarkand until the spring of 1404. At that time, Clavijo reports, he found the tomb too low and ordered the entire structure rebuilt. This was accomplished in ten days by the architect Muhammad ibn Mahmud of Isfahan. On October 30, 1404, Clavijo was summoned by Timur to a feast in the *madrasa* to celebrate the completion of the rebuilt tomb. The structure we see today must therefore, allowing for the Oriental love of the miraculous, have been completed by that date. When Timur himself died in January of 1405 he was buried there, as were most of his male descendants. Ulugh Beg, son of Shah Rukh and governor of Samarkand for his father, completed a *madrasa* in 1434, the rear facade of whose court linked the tomb to its flanking minarets (*Plate 345*).

An octagon 29 feet across contains a cruciform chamber whose arms project from a square of about 15 feet; below this is a likewise cruciform crypt once contained entirely within the square and now entered from outside the east wall. The principal entrance to the upper chamber was from the north through a deep *iwan*; it was flanked by minarets, but the nature of their original relationship to tomb and portal is obscured by the additions of Ulugh Beg. The original building must have been almost if not entirely freestanding (*Plate 346*). The exterior walls of the octagon, where they are visible, rise to the spring of the squinches, which support both the inner and outer domes and are encrusted with a bold diagonal pattern of glazed and mat-surfaced bricks. A similar pattern in spirals adorns the minarets. With almost no transition, the drum with its enormous Kufic inscription rises above the octagon and supports the vast blue ribbed outer dome springing from a *muqarnas* cornice in tile mosaic to a total exterior height of about 108 feet.

A north-south section of the interior, published in 1905, reveals the extraordinary elaboration of its ornament, which has been obscured for the last few years by heavy scaffolding. Here the pointed inner dome rises 74 feet above the inner square, a proportion much more vertical than that of the *mihrab* chamber of the Bibi Khanum Mosque. A dado of hexagonal alabaster panels imitating tile is crowned with *muqarnas* and then with an inscription band in greenish jasper. Above this, much of the ornament is painted in blue and gold on pressed and molded paper—a technique (of Central Asian if not ultimately Chinese origin) also used to cover the *muqarnas* vaults of the four niches (*Plate 347*). Above the inner dome, flanges of brick resting on its lower courses reinforce the swelling form of the outer dome with the aid of wooden braces.

With the Gur-i-Amir the first stage of Timurid architecture closes. It was a period of extreme ostentation, slight intellectual content and, in most structures, of an almost megalomaniac demand for size and splendor. The Ilkhanid trend toward verticality is still evident in Timur's own taste, but this was combined with massive, vividly polychromed walls and the orchestration of forms into a decidedly theatrical totality.

THE MONUMENTS OF THE REIGN OF SHAH RUKH (1405–47)

Shah Rukh, never his father's favorite, was of a totally different temperament than Timur. A scholar and enlightened patron of the arts, he brought peace to the empire—though it was soon reduced to its eastern half, which he ruled from Herat. His wife, Gawhar Shad (d. 1457), was a great builder in her own right, as was his son Ulugh Beg (d. 1449). Baysunghur Mirza (d. 1433), a younger son, became one of the greatest patrons of the manuscript painters of the period. Poets, astronomers, and philosophers as well as architects clustered about the courts at Samarkand and Herat, and the period of Shah Rukh's reign has been called a true golden age.

The Mosque of Gawhar Shad at Mashad

Ali al-Rida, an eighth-generation descendant of Muhammad in the Alid line had been named as his successor by the Caliph al-Ma'mun, but was poisoned at Tus in 818. His tomb at Mashad, where he rests with the Caliph Harun al-Rashid (d. 809), soon became a great Shi'ite pilgrimage center. The first buildings of the huge complex there were begun in the tenth century, and it has been growing ever since (*Plate 348*).

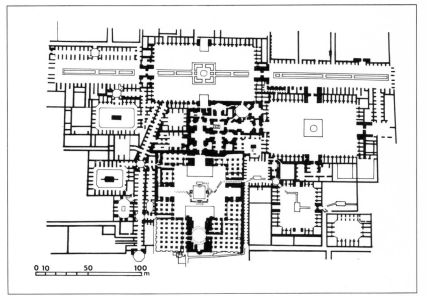

349. *Mashad, Great Mosque of Gawhar Shad*, qibla iwan   351. *Samarkand, Madrasa of Ulugh Beg, facade*
350. *Samarkand, Madrasa of Ulugh Beg, 1417–20, plan*

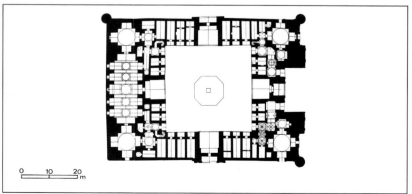

Although the Timurids were Sunni and the Shi'ite shrine at Mashad was within their dominions, Harun himself had been orthodox. The Great Mosque added by Gawhar Shad to the complex in 1405–1417/18 possesses hardly any exterior walls and no entrance facade, since it is contiguous with the tomb complex proper, to which Gavam al-Din of Shiraz (d. 1438), the architect, also added the Dar al-Siyadah and the cross-vaulted Dar al-Huffaz (both since totally redecorated). The mosque is a classic four-*iwan* cruciform structure around a court about 538 square feet (*Plate 348*). The *qibla iwan* (*Plate 349*), flanked by cylindrical minarets rising from the ground level, is doubly recessed—as is the portal of the Bibi Khanum Mosque, but unlike the latter's, the *sahn* is surrounded by a standard two-story Persian arcade beautifully articulated with broad bands of inscription and interlacing. The geometric ornament of glazed and mat-surfaced brick, the arabesques in polychrome tile mosaic, and the smooth monochromatic blue of the dome (relieved only by sparse yellow tendrils) achieve a maturity and sureness unknown in earlier monuments. There is a moderate return to the use of alternately glazed and mat-surfaced relief tiles, principally as margins between the areas of mosaic. Molded relief tiles, usually glazed, are common on the fourteenth-century tombs in the Shah-i-Zindeh Cemetery at Samarkand but rare later. Everywhere at Mashad there is evidence of the work of a consummate architect who never lost control of his design to the decorators. Truly he was, as contemporaries claimed, one of the noblest ornaments of the court of Shah Rukh.

The Madrasa of Ulugh Beg at Samarkand

In 1417 three major monuments were begun at Samarkand and Herat. At the former city, Ulugh Beg commissioned a *madrasa* fronting the Registan, a great open square later surrounded on two more sides by Shaybanid foundations. The plan (*Plate 350*), though now showing some variation in detail, was once probably totally symmetrical. An immense *iwan* in a facade flanked by two of four intended corner minarets (*Plate 351*) gives access to a cruciform court 355 feet square surrounded by two tiers of students' cells. In its corners passages lead to four cruciform domed chambers, which may have been intended for tombs. The axial *iwan* leads to a transverse cross-vaulted mosque, which also has access to the corner chambers.

The entrance *iwan* is edged by a continuous corkscrew molding like that of the Abbasid palace in Baghdad, but here formed of specially made curved segments decorated in polychrome glazing in a *haft aurang* or *cuerda seca* technique (*Plate 352*). Between the minarets and the *pishtaq* there probably were reeded domes on tall drums rising above the cruciform chambers. These survive in the matching facade

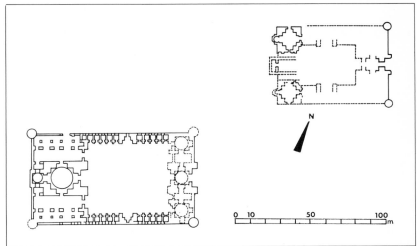

267

of the Shir Dor *madrasa*, built opposite Ulugh Beg's in 1619–36.

The Musalla and Madrasa of Gawhar Shad at Herat

The two monuments begun at Herat on or about 1417 can be attributed with some certainty to Gavam al-Din who, we know, rejoined the court there at about that time. Both were foundations of Gawhar Shad: a *madrasa* completed in 1432 and a *musalla* left incomplete, probably at the death of the architect in 1438. The ruins of the *musalla*, except for a single minaret, were destroyed in 1885; of the *madrasa* there survive only the left-hand minaret of the entrance facade and a domed chamber at the right rear corner (*Plate 355*) where, according to a tradition at least as old as the time of Babur, Gawhar Shad was buried in 1457. Recently that tradition has been questioned by G.A. Pugachenkova, who points out that the Timurid dynasty always employed separate tombs for male and female members of the family. Since we know Baysunghur Mirza was buried here in 1433, Gawhar Shad probably had another resting place. The plans of both buildings can be hypothetically reconstructed through descriptions and a drawing made before 1885, which shows the facade of the *madrasa* and part of the *musalla* behind it (*Plate 353*).

The surviving minaret of the *musalla* (*Plate 354*) shows that the art of tile mosaic had, since Mashad, made considerable advances in intricacy of design and subtlety of colors. Deep blue, azure, and purple predominate; the panels and bands are divided not by relief tile but by white marble moldings.

The tomb chamber from Gawhar Shad's *madrasa* (*Plate 356*) was one of a pair along the *qibla* wall. The remaining wall fragments show it once belonged to a larger complex. The plan is based on a square of 102 feet, with rectangular niches as at the Gur-i-Amir. However, the four original entrances of the almost freestanding Gur-i-Amir precluded a *mihrab*, while here a pentagonal "bay window" forming a kind of oratory indicates the direction of Mecca. With the shallow inner vault we part company entirely with the style of the earlier mausoleum. Each niche has a cross vault with a domelet like those arranged in series in so many Timurid structures, but the central square is reduced by intersecting arches supporting a low dome. Numerous shallow squinches begin as fan or conch-like elements and descend in cascades of shallow *muqarnas* to die away in the lower walls, the whole executed in polychrome plaster. Hidden above the inner ceiling is an intermediary structural dome which supports the ribbed and tiled outer dome, a more refined version of the Gur-i-Amir (*Plate 355*). Another innovation is the extensive use around the base of square tiles in *haft aurang* technique bearing floral motifs in shades of blue and white.

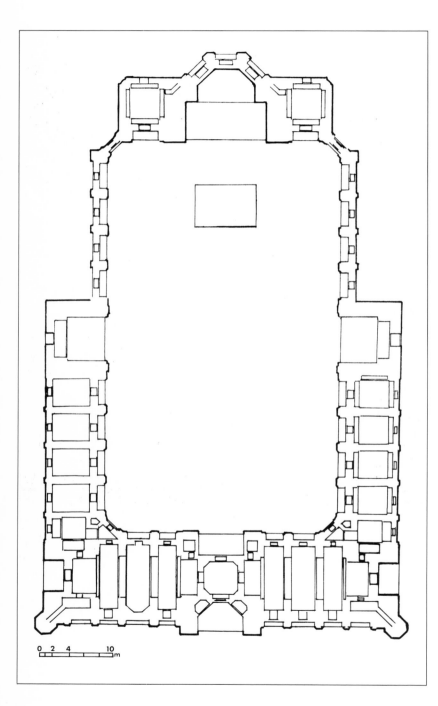

The Shrine of Abdallah Ansari at Gazur Gah

Among the rare monographs on individual Timurid monuments is Lisa Golombek's excellent study of the shrine of this Sufi Shaykh who died in 1089 at Gazur Gah near Herat. Built in 1425 under the patronage of Shah Rukh, it is a *hazira* or funerary enclosure (*Plate 357*) oriented upon the tomb, which is backed by a tall *iwan* with a polygonal niche. Its *pishtaq* has an arcaded terminal element flanked by *guldastahs* or small open pavilions, the whole a model for much later Moghul architecture in India. The *hazira* is a very old form of tomb enclosure, preferred among the pious to the domed mausoleum. The tomb proper commands the space thanks to the *iwan* whose gorgeous ornament, here employing a rare peach color in the tiles, contains symbols of Paradise. Since the *iwan* faces east and not the *qibla*, it can have no other function than to honor the tomb.

Whether or not Gavam al-Din had anything directly to do with the design is unknown, but it is certainly a work of his school. This is apparent in the entrance complex (*Plate 358*), where a pentagonal *iwan* penetrates a wall flanked by the polygonal bases of what were probably meant as minarets. Behind the portal is a vestibule or *dargah* where a strong cross-axis is established by a rectangular mosque to the left and a matching meeting hall to the right. Both have tile dadoes and are cross vaulted with elaborate *muqarnas* fan squinches in pure white. The court beyond is cruciform, about 90 by 52 feet, and has chamfered corners, one of their earliest appearances.

The Ghiyathiya Madrasa at Khargird

This beautiful building was, according to an inscription, begun by Gavam al-Din of Shiraz (therefore before 1438) and completed by Ghiyath al-Din of Shiraz, who was perhaps his son, either in 1444 or 1445. The patron was Shah Rukh, one of whose titles, Ghiyath al-hakk wa'l-dunya wal'-din ("Savior of the truth, the world, and the religion"), gave the *madrasa* its name—not, as some suppose, that of its second architect. A trustee also mentioned was the vizier Pir Ahmad from Khwafi near Khargird. We can assume Gavam al-Din was responsible for the plan (*Plate 359*), which is bilaterally symmetrical with chambers hollowed out into the mass of the brickwork in interlocking pattern. The entrance facade (*Plate 360*) lacks the megalomaniac scale and spirit of the previous reign, but far surpasses the earlier monuments in the logic of its articulation and exquisite finish. A stronger vertical emphasis was probably originally created by corner minarets on polygonal bases and perhaps by tall reeded domes over each of the principal chambers. These, like the mosque and assembly hall at Gazur Gah, flank the *dargah* or vestibule, and, as in the earlier building, have side entrances from exterior *iwans*. On axis,

359. *Khargird, Ghiyathiya Madrasa, shortly before 1438–1444/45, plan*

360. *Khargird, Ghiyathiya Madrasa, entrance facade*

361. *Khargird, Ghiyathiya Madrasa, dome chamber to the left of the entrance* ▷

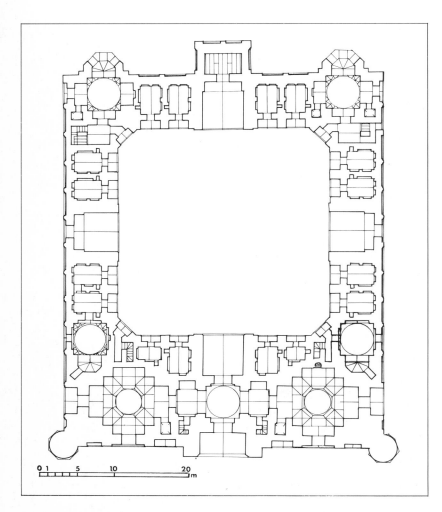

the *dargah* leads to a cruciform court with chamfered corners 306 square feet surrounded by double tiers of students' cells. Toward the *qibla* the structure terminates in two lesser domed chambers with projecting "bay windows" like Gawhar Shad's *madrasa* at Herat.

The *darshane* or assembly hall to the left of the vestibule (*Plate 361*) is vaulted over a 75-foot square in a manner very like that of Gawhar Shad's *madrasa* save that the shallow dome of the latter is replaced by a windowed octagonal drum opening into a space between the inner structure and an outer one corresponding to the hidden intermediary dome at Herat. Had this been covered by a third dome with a windowed drum, as may have been intended, the correspondence between the two projects would have been complete except for the diffused light which would have entered the chamber probably through plaster grilles (now vanished). The interlaced arches of the earlier monument are here reduced to thin ribs and well on their way to becoming the "net" squinches so frequent in later Timurid, Safavid, and Moghul monuments. Again, as is frequent in Islam, a once structural device has engendered a decorative one.

LATER TIMURID MONUMENTS
The Shrine of Khwaja Abu Nasr Parsa at Balkh

This curious structure dedicated to the famous Timurid Sufi Shaykh who died in 1460 or 1461 would appear at first glance to be a tomb, yet it is usually called a mosque and by the local people a *madrasa*, while the historian Khwand Amir called it a *takyah* or dervish monastery. This confusion in nomenclature leads Golombek to identify it as a *hazira*. She notes that the burial occupies a platform before the vast *iwan* of the northwest portal, further emphasized by the surviving stumps of a pair of cylindrical minarets (*Plate 362*). A blue reeded dome about 89 feet high must once have been concealed by the enormous *pishtaq* flanked by corkscrew moldings. Based on a study of earlier photographs, the *pishtaq* was probably crowned by an arcade, as at Gazur Gah.

The plan shows a four-portaled structure, hence not a mosque, with a square inner chamber converted to an octagon by simple squinches and then to a sixteen-sided polygon in which eight latticed windows alternate with eight *muqarnas*-filled niche heads. Above this, rising from a *muqarnas* cornice, is an inner dome of twenty-four flutes—suggesting that it is the interior of the reeded outer dome, though it is much lower. The windows of the outer drum bear no relation to those inside, which are lower and spaced differently. Finally, the surviving tile is predominantly a cool silvery gray tone that indicates a decline in quality; around the drum, however, panels of realistic vases of flowers strike a new note to be repeated in India. The

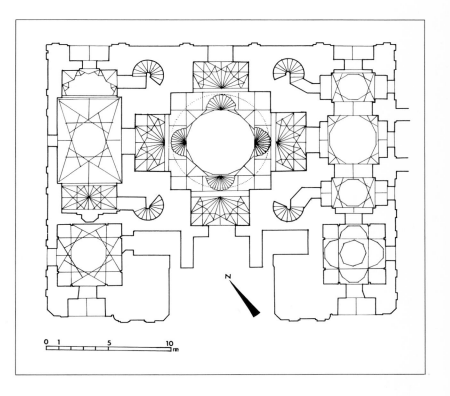

whole is a fantastic *tour-de-force* of great skill. Essentially Timurid, it nevertheless bears the seeds of many ideas exploited later by the Safavids.

The Ishrat Khaneh at Samarkand

The Ishrat Khaneh may have been begun as early as 1460 by Habibah Sultan Begum, eldest wife of Abu Said (1451–69), as the tomb of a daughter who died young. It was probably substantially complete by 1464, when a *waqf* was established for its upkeep, and continued in use as a tomb for female members of the Timurid Dynasty until the Shaybanid conquest. An earthquake in 1903 almost destroyed it, but thanks to the painstaking work of G.A. Pugachenkova the building can be studied in some detail today.

At the southwest an *iwan* portal set in a very high *pishtaq* leads directly into a cruciform chamber (*Plate 363*) that opens left into a small oratory with a *mihrab* in its southwest wall and a clerestory. To the right is a *mian khaneh*, from the center of which steps lead down to a crypt directly beneath the central chamber (*Plate 364*). The vaulting everywhere is in the tradition established by Gavam al-Din, in which relatively low ceilings and shallow domes on elaborate net-vaulted squinches contrast with the exaggerated drum and bulbous exterior dome (now fallen), which no longer even serves as a source of light.

The presence of a specialized tripartite chamber from which descent was made to the crypt called a *mian khaneh* suggests that from its inception Habibah Sultan planned her foundation for multiple burials. The term in modern Persian means "middle room" and was used for the transition between the *selamlik* or men's quarters and the *harem* of a traditional Persian house. Here the obvious reference is to the transition between the world of the living and that of the dead. The attachment of such a chamber to a tomb, never a common practice in Persia, was to become usual in Moghul India. The function of the two other ground-floor chambers and of five in the second story is uncertain. They may have been intended only as temporary shelter for the funeral parties or perhaps as shelter for itinerant dervishes, since this was a charitable foundation.

The Tomb of Ulugh Beg Miranshah and Abdu Razzaq at Ghazna

With Abu Said's death in 1469 his kingdom descended to Husain Baikara (1470–1506), who ruled in Herat over the brilliant sunset of the Timurids, and to the sons of Abu Said. Among these Umar Shaykh (1469–94) ruled Ferghana, leaving it to his eleven-year-old son, Babur, future Emperor of India, and Ulugh Beg Miranshah (1469–1501) received the by then provincial kingdom of Kabul. He

was succeeded by his son, Abdu Razzaq. This unfortunate prince lost his throne in 1502; when in 1504 it was regained for the Timurids by Babur, the latter kept it for himself. Ultimately, Abdu Razzaq was assassinated (in 1513/14) and buried beside his father.

The tomb, probably projected by Ulugh Beg Miranshah shortly before his own death near that of the great Mahmud, was unfinished and remains so today. Despite its complex design (*Plate 365*), the whole structure from one projecting portal to the other is no more than 269 square feet. It is built of dark brown fired brick, with no surviving ornament, and finished inside in *coghel*, a coarse mixture of earth and straw. The well-built crypt beneath the entire structure may once have been entered from the more elaborate southeast chamber, which possibly served as a *mian khaneh* and has the same orientation as that of the Ishrat Khaneh. The building was thus intended as a dynastic tomb no matter how lowly its materials or workmanship.

The structure, despite its paucity of ornament, is historically of considerable importance as the last and most evolved example of a Timurid mausoleum and a major link between Timurid and Moghul funerary architecture. The strict radial symmetry, the four *pishtaqs*, the presence of four bases for minarets (even if never built), the central dome (perhaps intended to support a bulbous outer dome on a tall drum), and even the polygonal niches chamfered between the *pishtaqs* and the walls (*Plate 366*)—all will reappear on a far larger scale and in nobler materials in Moghul India.

Conclusion

There has probably never been a period in the history of world architecture when color and form achieved such a perfect balance of design and meaning as they did under the Timurids during the reign of Shah Rukh. Relying on predominantly Persian traditions inherited from the Seljuks and refined after a hiatus by the Ilkhanids, the Timurids carried the technique of tile-encrusted brick construction to a climax occasionally to be equaled but never surpassed by the Safavids. Despite the sad dilapidation of most of the surviving monuments, what is left is overwhelming. The true genius of Gavam al-Din and his contemporaries lay in the perfect articulation of their structures and in the exact balance between surface decoration and the surface itself. If the Madrasa of Ulugh Beg in Samarkand is compared to that of the Ghiyathiya at Khargird, this can easily be understood: in general organization they are much alike, but at Khargird the relationship of the parts to each other and to the whole is so perfect that one is reminded of those rare moments of classic perfection in Western architecture—the Parthenon or Bramante's Tempietto. The comparison can only be made in terms of form, for in the orchestration of

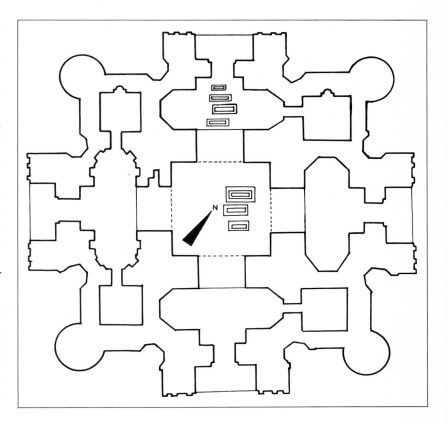

color no comparison is possible since nothing has ever been built in the West so dependent upon nor so adroit in the application of color. In the West color was applied to the forms rather than being integrated with them. Some early Timurid monuments use color in a similar fashion—for example, the exterior walls of the Shrine of Ahmad Yasavi at Turkestan City or even the Gur-i-Amir at Samarkand are covered with a bold geometry not closely related to the walls which bear it. Similar patterns are used at Khargird, but under a strict formal discipline they function in unison with the whole concept and are no longer independent.

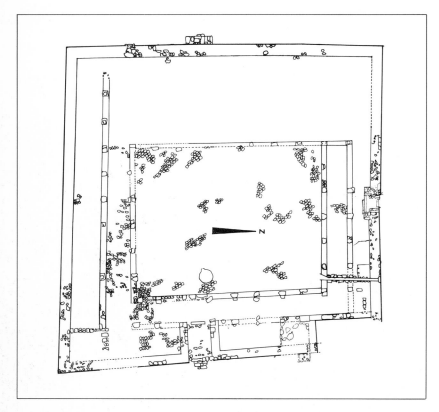

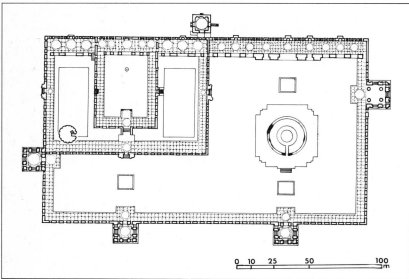

367.   *Banbhore, Congregational Mosque, probably begun c. 727, plan*
368.   *Delhi, Quwwat al-Islam, c. 1193–1316, plan*
369.   *Delhi, Quwwat al-Islam, riwaq of 1210–29* ▷

In Banbhore, about forty miles south of Karachi in Pakistan, a town once connected with the Arabian Sea by one of the many mouths of the Indus River, there have been discovered the foundations of a Friday mosque (*Plate 367*) which must have been very similar to that of Kufa, though smaller. The building was approximately 398 square feet as compared to Kufa's 1,012 feet, and its prayer hall had three aisles rather than five as at Kufa, but the *riwaqs* were two aisles deep in both buildings and both surely had flat wooden roofs (though at Kufa the columns were of stone). Neither building would appear to have had a minaret, nor is there evidence for a *mihrab* in either. If Banbhore is the famous port of Debal which fell to the Muslims in 712, this mosque—with a somewhat uncertain inscription date of 727 and a more definite one recording repairs in 907—may have been built only some forty years after that of Kufa. And if so, western India can boast an architecture as venerable as any in Islam.

No further substantial Muslim architecture survives until the conquest of India by Ghiyath al-Din Muhammad of Ghur in 1188. He ended Ghaznavid rule in Lahore (of which very few traces remain) and upon the platform of a dismantled Hindu temple in Delhi, taken in 1193, had his first Friday mosque, the Quwwat al-Islam, begun. The Ghurids, a Turkish tribe, had fallen heir in Afghanistan to the artistic tradition of the likewise Turkish Ghaznavids, but only one relatively intact Ghurid monument survives there. This is the minaret of Jam, built sometime between 1155 and 1203; its inscriptions suggest that it was a victory monument as well as a minaret. Unlike Indian minarets, its very rich ornament of glazed tile, stucco and, above all, its profusion of carved brick and the use of wooden tie beams in its structure link it to a Persian and Central Asian tradition.

Once in India, Ghurid patrons of architecture found a situation analogous to that of the Seljuks in Anatolia and Syria, namely that both regions had a local tradition of stone masonry construction. However, there was one vast difference. Armenians, Christians, and other craftsmen in Syria already practiced an architecture related through a common ancestry to that of the Muslims, as were their religions. In India Hindu architecture, like the Hindu religion, was utterly beyond Islamic experience.

Indian temples are shrines progressively excluding the laity, until at last in the *garba griha*—an enclosed chamber on the central axis of the *shikara* or ritual mountain—the idol is protectively encased. The *shikara*, preceded by one or more verandahs, may be surrounded by a temenos wall lined with cells or a colonnade, the sole element in an Indian temple equivalent to the *riwaqs* of an Islamic mosque. Only this and the tanks for ritual ablutions, praised by al-Biruni in the eleventh century, would have been familiar to a Muslim; all else

would have been not only alien, but idolatrous and repugnant. The disciplined unity of mass prayer, the firmly prescribed rites directed by laymen, not priests, toward an abstract, never depicted deity were concepts totally foreign to Hinduism.

In its structure Hindu architecture differed even more from that of Islam. By the twelfth century the Muslims were no strangers to the use of wood as a structural material, though little work in that material has survived. However, the true origins of the Islamic style lay in the vaulted brick buildings of Mesopotamia and Iran, with their encrusted ornament of stucco and carved or glazed brick. These forms had already been translated into stone in Egypt, Syria, and Turkey. The stone architecture of India, on the other hand, had never left its models of wood and thatch very far behind. Vaults and arches were unknown there or long since forgotten; the post and lintel prevailed. Columns were chamfered and bracketed in complex imitation of wooden prototypes. Roofs were corbeled and then ornamented to suggest timber construction. One element only of the repertoire of the Hindu builders may have seemed somewhat familiar to the new Muslim patrons: both styles tended, as does Gothic architecture, to use "miniature" architecture as ornament. In Islamic examples, miniature arcades in stucco relieve flat wall surfaces from the time of the Umayyads in Syria; they reappear in the Alhambra and turn up sporadically in the stone buildings of Egypt, Syria, and Turkey. The Indian building is often a very complex assemblage of smaller models of itself. In Indo-Islamic architecture, such ornament was produced almost from the beginning, first in stone relief, then in relief and intarsia and, finally, in Moghul times in intarsia alone and occasionally in tile mosaic.

QUTB AL-DIN AND THE SLAVE KINGS OF DELHI (1193–1290)
Qutb al-Din Aybak, the general and slave of Ghiyath al-Din Muhammad of Ghur (who had invaded India, capturing Delhi in 1193 and Ajmer in 1197), ruled from Delhi as governor until with the decline of Ghurid power he was enthroned as Sultan in 1206, founding the dynasty known as that of the Slave Kings (so called because most had begun as *ghulams* or military slaves either of the Ghurids or of each other, their manner of succession being very like that of the Egyptian Mamluks).

The Quwwat al-Islam at Delhi
The innermost rectangle of about 138 by 197 feet of the great congregational mosque at Delhi may have been begun as early as 1193 (*Plate 368*). It is oriented due west, the direction of the *qibla* in India. It is said that nearly all the construction material was reassembled from twenty-seven demolished Hindu temples. Two column shafts were super-

imposed to approximate the ceiling height of columned mosques elsewhere (*Plate 369*) and, needless to say, nearly every member was purged of its human and animal representations. The eastern *riwaq*, three bays deep, has (or had) a monumental entrance on axis with a corbeled dome. Five similar domes punctuated the prayer hall, which was five bays deep. Elsewhere stone beams supported a flat slab roof. For two or three years after its completion the prayer hall opened as freely into the *sahn* as did the *riwaqs*, recalling the columned temenoi of many Hindu temples. Then in 1199 a great stone screen of five pointed and slightly ogee arches was erected between prayer hall and *sahn* (*Plate 370*). The four lower arches supported a kind of clerestory and the whole recalled, if only faintly, the twelfth-century state of the Masjid-i-Jami at Isfahan or that of Herat. The arches are corbeled, clear evidence they are the work of Hindu masons following an imposed pattern. Both the screen and the Qtub Minar, begun the same year, are enriched with elaborate sculptured bands (*Plate 371*) in which *nashqi* and Kufic inscriptions recalling Ghurid work in cut brick alternate with rinceaux and draped jewelry forms of Hindu origin, though the latter are far less plastic and exuberant than their models.

The Qtub Minar at Delhi

This magnificent structure, literally the axis tower or victory tower, is destined—as its inscriptions proclaim—to spread the shadow of God to the East and to the West. Perhaps for this reason it was built some distance to the south and slightly east of the original mosque so that its shadow would be more clearly perceived. Such placement of minarets is also found at Ghazna, in the Kalan Minaret at Bukhara (1127), and the Ghurid tower at Jam—all at one time or another described as victory monuments. The battered profile and complex stellar plan recall Persian tomb towers and the lower portions of the two minarets at Ghazna. Only the first three stages, with their *muqarnas* balconies once capped by stepped crenellations, are original. They once terminated in a covered pavilion perhaps rather like that of the Kalan Minaret at Bukhara, called in India a *chatri*.

The Congregational Mosque at Ajmer

This mosque, called locally the Arhai Din Ka Jompra (from the name of the two-and-a-half-day fair held at Ajmer since pre-Islamic times), was begun some time between 1200 and 1206, and stands on a high platform about 840 square feet (*Plate 372*). The salvaged Hindu materials are better integrated than at Delhi and the proportions are slenderer. Three superimposed column shafts rather than two bring the ceiling height to 23 feet (*Plate 374*). As at Delhi, a screen, this time of seven corbeled arches, six of them lobate, conceals the prayer hall (*Plate 373*).

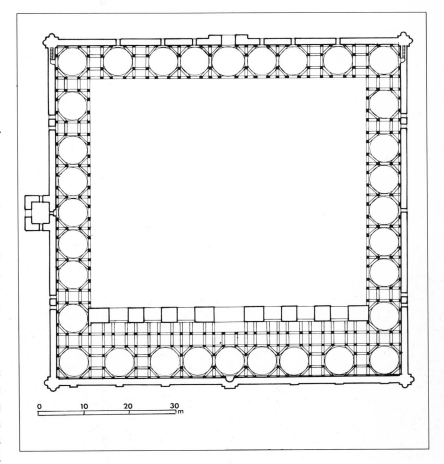

285

373. *Ajmer, Arhai Din Ka Jompra Mosque, screen, c. 1220–29*
374. *Ajmer, Arhai Din Ka Jompra Mosque, prayer hall*

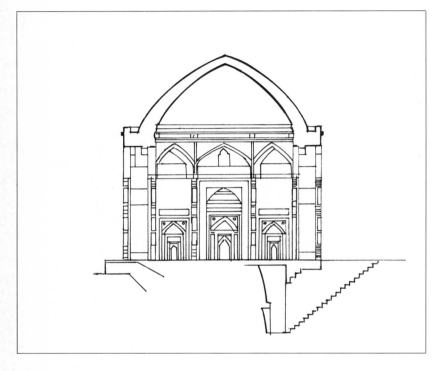

This was added to the finished building by Shams al-Din Iltutmish (1211–36) probably between 1220 and 1229 while he was engaged upon the first enlargement of the Quwwat al-Islam in Delhi (*Plate 368*). The *pishtaq* of the center arch of the Ajmer screen carries the stumps of a pair of reeded minarets, following the practice of Seljuk Persia and later Anatolia. The decorative niches in the spandrels of the arches recall the niches or actual openings in similar positions in Abbasid Iraq as well as Fatimid Egypt.

At Ajmer and Delhi the carving executed for Iltutmish contrasts sharply with the work of 1199. The exuberant ornament of Hindu inspiration is replaced by flat, almost geometric bands of small-scale repeat ornament. These alternate with beautifully cut *nashqi* and Kufic inscriptions far superior to the earlier examples. The effect is closer to the cut brick decoration of the minaret of Jam and very like the brickwork of a newly discovered Ghurid *madrasa*, the Shah-i-Mashad in Gargistan (Afghanistan), dated 1165–66.

The Tomb of Iltutmish at Delhi

In addition to the mosque, another basic form without a Hindu prototype was introduced by the Slave King Dynasty. This was the tomb which, since Hindus and Buddhists practice cremation, was virtually unknown. Iltutmish was responsible for the two earliest surviving monuments. The first was his own tomb behind the *qibla* wall of his addition to the Quwwat al-Islam. The square building has a portal on all sides save the *qibla*, where three *mihrabs* are inserted (*Plate 375*). Beneath it is a crypt entered from the north. The east or axial entrance to the monument is so close to the wall of the enlarged mosque that it was possibly begun earlier (it was not at all unusual in India for the ruler's tomb to have been begun during his reign). The form is that defined by Creswell as a canopy tomb, setting a precedent for nearly all later structures of this kind in India. Since the presence of the *mihrabs* implies an oratory, there must have been an outer enclosure on at least three sides of which no trace is recorded. The interior (*Plate 376*), once covered with a corbeled dome on likewise corbeled pendentives imitating pointed arches, is profusely ornamented with inscriptions, miniature arcades, and colonnettes exactly like those previously reused but here obviously made to order. This marks a further step toward the development of a truly Indo-Islamic architecture, as does the contrasting use of white marble and sandstone.

The Tomb of Sultan Ghari at Delhi

Nasr al-Din Muhammad, a son of Iltutmish, died in 1231 and is buried three miles outside the city in a tomb called that of Sultan Ghari ("Sultan of the Cave") because all that survives of the tomb proper is

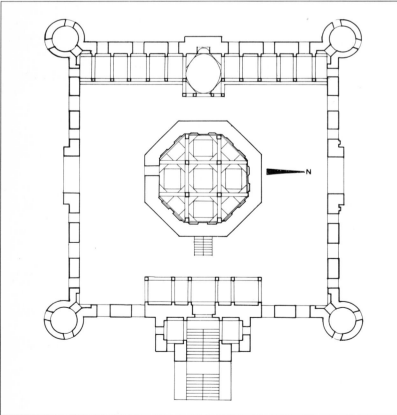

the crypt. The complex (*Plates 377–379*) consists of an arcaded enclosure of granite some 280 square feet with cylindrical corner bastions. A monumental eastern portal opens on an inner portico of white marble. In the center of the enclosure is an octagonal platform covering the crypt, which is entered from the south. On the platform there probably stood an open columned pavilion with a corbeled dome. Many later examples of such tombs survive in Delhi. The *qibla* wall has a colonnade and a central domed white marble pavilion over the *mihrab*. Wide openings in the centers of the north and south walls create a cross axis. Tombs in such symmetrical enclosures existed in Seljuk Persia at least as early as the tomb of Sanjar (1157), but none have survived intact.

The Slave King Dynasty, in its later years menaced by the Mongols (who overran the Punjab in 1241) and by Hindu revolts nearer home, produced few notable monuments. Nevertheless, one significant innovation appears at this time. When Sultan Balban (1266–87), who reigned with the title of Ghiyath al-Din, built his now much ruined tomb, his architect introduced into Islamic India for the first time the true arch with voussoirs of stone.

THE KHALJI DYNASTY OF DELHI (1290–1320)

After a series of successful raids to expand the domain of Islam in India, Ala al-Din Khalji (1296–1316) spent the booty from these conquests on a second and enormous enlargement of the Quwwat al-Islam. The vast project remained unfinished, but can be reconstructed from the existing foundations. *Riwaqs* were to enclose the older building on two sides within a rectangle of about 751 by 443 feet with four monumental domed portals. In the new northern *sahn* (on axis with a portal and the *mihrab*) is the gigantic base of a new Qtub Minar which, had it been finished in the proportions of the first, might have been about 656 feet tall. Such an edifice would have made a fitting monument for a man who described himself on his coins as "the second Alexander."

The north portal of Ala al-Din's complex, known as the Alai Darwaza (1311–16), is the only part of it completed before his dethronement (*Plate 380*). The three exterior facades are carefully articulated with richly carved inlays of white marble against red sandstone. Of the pairs of windows flanking the portals only the inner ones actually penetrate the walls through grilles of pierced stone, soon to become a favorite Indo-Islamic device. The coherence of the decorative scheme, the "spear points" lining the slightly horseshoe-shaped arches of the portals, and the much improved quality of the masonry have led a number of authors to conclude that an influx of Turkish Seljuk masons fleeing the Mongols were responsible for the work. The style would not appear to sustain this view, however:

380. *Delhi, Quwwat al-Islam, Alai Darwaza, 1311–16, facade*

381. *Delhi-Tughluqabad, Tomb of Ghiyath al-Din Tughluq, begun 1325*

382. *Delhi-Firuzabad, Kotila of Firuz Shah,* baradari, *begun 1354, plan*

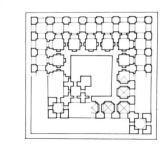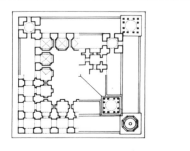

many details of the carving and the "Hindu" colonnettes suggest that the source is in fact indigenous. Nevertheless, the idea of a projecting monumental entrance reminiscent of a Roman triumphal arch applied to a Friday mosque may very well derive from Egypt where, since Fatimid times, they were fairly common and had appeared for the last time in the mosque of Baybars (1266–69).

THE TUGHLUQID DYNASTY OF DELHI (1320–1414)

The Tomb of Ghiyath al-Din at Tughluqabad

During the short reign of the founder of this dynasty, Ghiyath al-Din Tughluq (1320–25), a far more sober and restrained style than that of the Khaljis was introduced. Ghiyath al-Din had been governor of Multan in the Punjab since 1305 and must have become accustomed to the local building practice. This was in brick, with heavy and decidedly slanted walls strengthened with horizontal tie beams of wood (also used for lintels under the arches). His tomb, probably begun soon after his accidental death, is on a fortified island in an artificial lake connected by a long causeway with Tughluqabad, the new city he founded near Delhi. The tomb itself, of canopy type with three portals (*Plate 381*), draws its character from the fortifications. The outer walls slope sharply inward and are articulated by horizontal bands of white marble acting also as lintels over the doors, exactly as do the wooden beams in the style of Multan. Only the "spearhead" fringe of the arches recalls the rich ornament of the Khaljis, but the shape of the arch has been modified into the so-called Tudor or four-centered form common in Persia and Multan. The prominent dome, rising from an octagonal base and sheathed in white marble, is not yet bulbous, but approaches in its shape, material, and elaborate finial the later domes of the Moghuls.

The Works of Firuz Shah

The heavy forms and solid structures of Ghiyath al-Din Tughluq were continued by his successors. Firuz Shah (1351–88), a great builder, began a new citadel, the Kotila Firuz Shah, in 1354. Since his predecessor had nearly depopulated Delhi to build a new capital at Daulatabad far to the south, the style of Firuz made do without the fine materials and craftsmanship previously available. Nevertheless, the work done for him is innovative and soberly beautiful. In the Kotila he built what is generally called a *baradari* (*Plates 382, 383*), now almost totally ruined. Originally it consisted of a series of galleries radially symmetrical and rising in a pyramidal form around a solid core on which is mounted one of Asoka's famous stone pillars (removed from its original site near Amballa). The corners of the

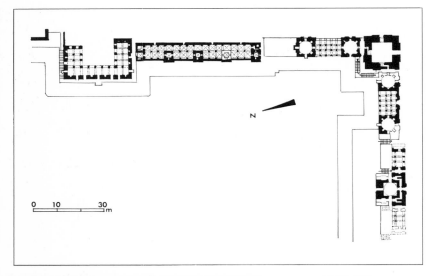

second and third stages bore *chatri* pavilions mounted on short solid towers. Circulation of both people and air at all three levels around the cool central mass of earth and stone must have been very free. Like the later Panch Mahal at Fatipur Sikri, the building would have provided an excellent retreat from the fierce heat of a Delhi summer, even though it may also have functioned as a minaret since it is adjacent to the now wholly ruined Friday mosque.

There have been attempts to trace the origin of the design, doubtless influenced by the presence of the pillar, to a freestanding Buddhist *vihara* or multistoried monastery. Although such buildings must still have been in use in Burma and Ceylon and have been seen by Muslim travelers, it is more likely that current Hindu palace architecture provided the inspiration. Little comparative material of an early date survives, but as Reuther suggests, it is reasonable to assume that, as they did elsewhere, the Muslim conquerors would not have hesitated to adapt local methods of coping with the climate for their dwellings. The mosque and the tomb were another matter, as they both involved spiritual needs which Hindu civilization did not recognize.

The same process is apparent in the Hauz-i-Khas complex, probably built late in the reign of Firuz Shah (*Plates 384–387*). The Hauz-i-Khas or private lake is in Tarbabad, the City of Joy. When Ibn Battuta visited it between 1334 and 1342, it was, he said, surrounded by forty domes. Firuz Shah replaced these with a complex of buildings originally completely enclosing the rectangular tank. The east and south ranges survive in part, hinging at the southeast corner upon the square canopy tomb of Firuz himself. Two-storied *tibaris* (porches or many-columned halls akin to the Achaemenid *apadana*) alternate with domed towers each with a *jharoka* or balcony projecting from its second story. Each level of the *tibaris* and all of the *jharokas* had *chajjas* or inclined eave boards in stone. All these elements can be traced back to the very beginnings of Hindu architecture. Even the plan, alternately closed and open, seems to have Hindu precedent, being comparable to the lower story of Man Singh's palace in Gwalior, admittedly a much later structure (1486–1518). The only Muslim innovations are the tomb itself, the arcuate lower stories of the *tibaris*, and the cloister and groin vaults throughout. Percy Brown interprets the complex as a *madrasa* rather than a palace, as Reuther sees it. The presence of the tomb and of *mihrabs* along the westward-oriented walls supports Brown's conclusions. Nevertheless, because Islamic architecture everywhere tends to give similar plans multiple uses, it seems safe to use the *baradari* in the Kotila and the Hauz-i-Khas complex as the earliest substantially surviving examples of the Islamic palace in its Indian form.

THE BAHMANID SULTANATE AT GULBARGA (1347–1527)

The Delhi Sultanate was soon to lose its preeminence, which it never completely regained after the sack of the city by Timur in 1398. Even before this, powerful local rulers had already declared their independence. The Bahmanid Sultanate established its capital in the southern Deccan at Gulbarga, where under the second member of the line, Muhammad I (1358–75), a Friday mosque was built in 1367 (*Plates 388–390*). The design departs radically from previous Indian structures in that the *sahn* is covered with a grid of multiple domes while the *riwaqs* form an enclosing U-shaped corridor. To solve the problem of lighting the previously solid outer walls, except on the *qibla* wall, became open arcades. It is probable that these arcades all originally opened at ground level into a *ziyadah* as in the Samarra mosques and that of Ibn Tulun in Cairo. Without such outer enclosures the required isolation from a busy commercial quarter would have been impossible. The multiple domes and the curious squinches in a cubical version of the *muqarnas* suggest the influence of early Ottoman Turkish architecture.

THE SHARQI SULTANS AT JAUNPUR (1394–1479)

Jaunpur, near Benares, was founded by Firuz Shah in 1359, but became independent some thirty-five years later. Many buildings there attest to the continuation of the Tughluqid style. Among the most characteristic is the Friday mosque of Husayn Shah (1458–79) of c. 1470 (*Plates 391, 392*). Three monumental domed portals give access to the *sahn*, establishing a strong cross axis; they recall those added to the Quwwat al-Islam by Ala al-Din Khalji. The building, however, achieves its greatest distinction in the facade of the prayer hall, where the center arch has become a vast screen surrounding a shallow *iwan* with the pronounced Tughluqid batter, almost like an ancient Egyptian pylon. The focal point of the *qibla* is thus most emphatically emphasized for the thousands praying in the *sahn*, while the high dome over the *mihrab* chamber behind is completely concealed.

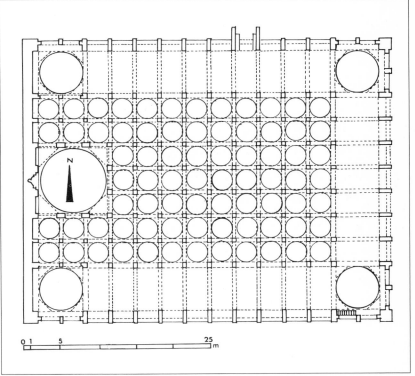

THE SULTANATE OF GUJERAT (1391–1583)

Hindu Gujerat in western India was annexed to the Delhi Sultanate in 1298, but did not formally declare its independence until 1407. This rich and commercially active province fell definitively to the Moghuls in 1583. In 1411 Ahmedabad became the capital, but when Mahmud I Begra (1458–1511) captured the Hindu city of Champanir he renamed it Muhammadabad and transferred the capital there. The Jami Masjid or Friday mosque of Champanir, begun in

390. *Gulbarga, Jami Masjid, interior, a riwaq*
391. *Jaunpur, Jami Masjid, c. 1470, plan*
392. *Jaunpur, Jami Masjid, facade of the prayer hall*

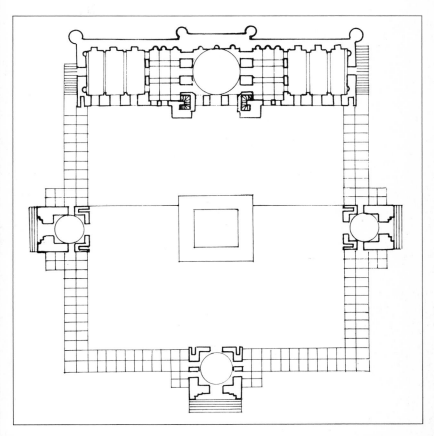

393. *Champanir, Jami Masjid, 1485–1523, exterior*
394. *Champanir, Jami Masjid, axonometric section*

395. *Champanir, Jami Masjid, facade of the prayer hall* ▷
396. *Champanir, Jami Masjid, south minaret, detail* ▷
397. *Champanir, Jami Masjid, interior, dome* ▷

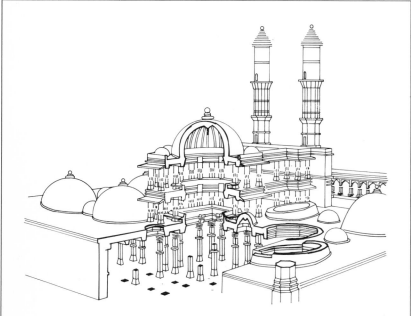

1485, was financed from the booty of his conquests (*Plates 393–396*). Its immediate predecessor was the Jami Masjid of Ahmedabad of 1423, but ultimately it is in the tradition of the Arhai Din Ka Jompra at Ajmer. Twin minarets flank the high central arch of the prayer hall facade as at Ajmer, but they rise from the paving of the *sahn*—a Timurid innovation inherited via Ahmedabad. The upper portions were restored in 1819, but the bases are original and wholly Hindu in inspiration. The triple *shikaras* of the Shiva temple at Somnathpur (1263–68) in the same region could have served as models. Rising behind the facade screen is a triple-tiered trabeate construction terminating in a single large dome surrounded by smaller domes. This solves the problem of illumination in the very deep prayer hall (*Plate 397*), which is also lighted through windows under sheltering *jharokas* in the side and *qibla* walls. The construction is exceedingly close to that of the Jain Chaumukh Temple at Ranpur of 1419–68. The lower tier of this construction, supported by elaborate brackets, is visible from the *sahn*, where the bases of the minarets (like *shikaras*) and the *jharokas* closely resemble a Jain temple. Here in an area of great commercial prosperity adjacent to still flourishing Hindu kingdoms, the specifically Indian elements of Indo-Islamic architecture have, on the eve of the Moghul conquest, become extremely prominent.

THE LODI (1451–1526) AND SURI (1540–55) DYNASTIES

After the Sayyid Dynasty had ruled Delhi on behalf of Timur and Shah Rukh, they were replaced by the Lodis (of Afghan origin) who restored much of the prestige of the Delhi Sultanate until their defeat by Babur in 1526. However, in architectural terms, a truly Moghul style was not to emerge until the defeat of the usurping Suris (another Afghan dynasty) and the return of Humayun to India in 1555.

The Baradari of Sikander Lodi at Agra

In 1495 Nizam Khan Sikander Lodi II (1498–1517) built a *baradari* at Sikandra, near Agra. The present building is a single story and about 387 square feet. *Chatris* rise over the corners and there are similar pavilions over the four portals. A low platform in the center of the flat roof may have formed the plinth for a second story in the manner of Firuz Shah's earlier *baradari*. The radially symmetrical structure, wholly open, probably had a private core in the central *chahr bagh*, as in the palace of Timur at Samarkand. There may have been some Moghul redecoration when Maryam al-Zamani, the mother of Jahangir, was buried in the *baradari* in 1623, but little structural change took place. Except for the *chatris*, the construction

398. *Agra-Sikandra*, baradari *of Iskander Lodi, 1495, section and plan*
399. *Delhi, Tomb of Isa Khan Niyazi, 1545–47, plan*

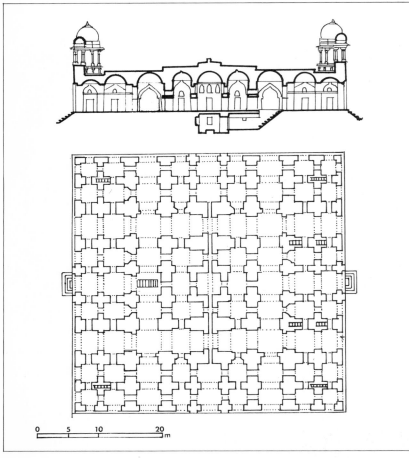

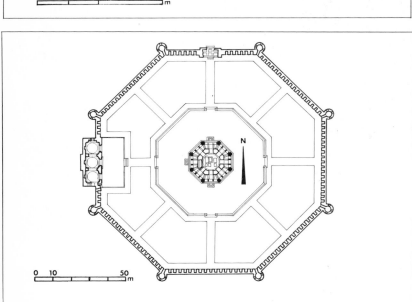

is entirely arcuate and vaulted, emphasizing as do all the Lodi buildings the Islamic rather than the Indian aspects of the Indo-Islamic style.

The Tomb of Isa Khan Niyazi at Delhi

Two of the Sayyid rulers, as well as Sikander Lodi, nearly all the Suris, and many members of their courts favored a very distinctive tomb type. This was a domed octagon communicating with a likewise octagonal ambulatory or porch, the whole set within an enclosure, either square or also octagonal. According to Percy Brown, the earliest monument of this type was built in Delhi for the Khan-i-Jahan Tilangari, an official of Firuz Shah, who died in 1368 or 1369, and the last was that of the unfortunate Adham Khan, executed by order of Akbar in 1561.

The most developed example of the type is the tomb of Isa Khan Niyazi, one of the generals of Sher Shah Sur (1540–45), built in 1545–47 in Delhi near the future site of the tomb of Humayun (*Plates 399–401*). The tomb proper is a domed octagon with portals in seven sides, the eighth (to the west) closed off by a *mihrab*. The porch ambulatory has battered projections at the corners reminiscent of the Tughluqid style of the first of the series and is surmounted by eight *chatris*. The whole rises from a broad plinth set in an octagonal enclosure about 394 feet in diameter, lined with cells like those of a Hindu temple and with projecting circular towers at the corners. A monumental entrance gives access to the enclosure from the north, but there was probably another from the south. The western side is occupied by a triple-arched prayer hall with its central dome flanked by *chatris*.

Octagonal tombs are frequent in Islam since at least the eleventh century, but octagonal canopy tombs with ambulatories are very rare indeed. It seems unlikely that the Qubbat al-Sulaybiyah in Samarra of 862 would have been known in fourteenth-century Delhi, and the first Ottoman tombs with surrounding porches date from no earlier than the sixteenth century. If the ambulatories had a function, they may have sheltered persons who wished to circumambulate the tombs as a ritual. Circumambulation is common in Islam as a gesture of respect ever since the practice began at the Kaaba. The Dome of the Rock in Jerusalem, not unlike the Indian structures, was certainly used in this fashion. The Emperor Babur records in his diary that he performed such circumambulations, usually seven times clockwise, around the tombs of certain venerated holy men. Can it be possible that the families of the deceased within the privacy of the enclosures came to practice such a rite even though their ancestors may not all have been particularly holy?

Conclusion

We have seen Islamic architecture introduced and taking root in India under conditions differing widely from those of the rest of Islam and in the midst of a continuing and vigorous alien culture. The style brought to India had, of course, had its birth under very similar conditions in Syria, Mesopotamia, and Iran, but long before the twelfth century the styles which had given it birth had ceased to exist. Christian architects in Islam with very few exceptions had long since begun to work in the style of their rulers. This was never true in India, where independent Hindu rulers kept their own culture alive. For their palaces they began to borrow many Islamic ideas but, as will be evident when Moghul architecture is treated, the Muslims repeatedly borrowed just as much from the Hindus. Despite the fact that the term Indo-Islamic has been frequently used in this chapter, the "style" to which it refers is neither consistent nor unified but a variable depending partially on the program yet more on the tastes of the patrons. Their choice was between relatively pure forms brought from Central Asia and Persia and local forms either entirely Hindu in origin or revivals of prior Indo-Islamic amalgams.

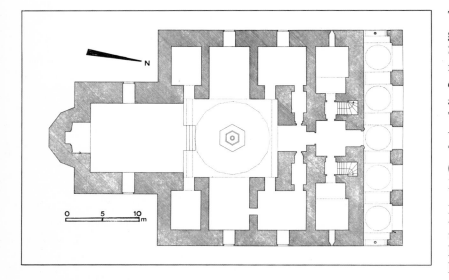

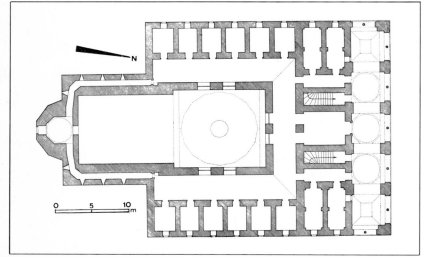

402. *Çekirge, Mosque-Madrasa of Murad I, 1366–85, plan of the
ground floor*

403. *Çekirge, Mosque-Madrasa of Murad I, plan of the first floor*

404. *Çekirge, Mosque-Madrasa of Murad I, exterior from the northeast* ▷

The ancestors of the Ottomans were one of the many Turkoman groups who entered Anatolia during the Seljuk Sultanate. After the Sultanate came under Mongol control, they established themselves not in the relatively safe east or south but in Bithynia, directly adjacent to the still threatening Byzantine Empire. In this way they became and remained *ghazis* or holy warriors and could recruit from fresh Turkoman groups from the east. In this way they maintained their vigor and acquired a military tradition which aided their expansion. The Ottoman Dynasty took its name from its founder, Osman I (1281–1324). His successor, Orhan (1324–60), captured Prusa, now Bursa, in 1326 and made it his capital. Murad I (1360–89) took Adrianople, now Edirne, in 1366, thus establishing a capital on European soil. Bayazid I (1389–1402) acquired the title of Sultan from the Abbasid Caliph in Cairo in 1394, establishing the tradition which later enabled the Ottomans to rule as autocrats over a unified country; however, his defeat by Timur at Ankara temporarily freed a number of conquered provinces and threw the budding empire into a period of confusion. Under Mehmet II (1444–46 and 1451–81), who conquered Constantinople in 1453 and soon made it the capital, the tempo of expansion was resumed. Selim I (1512–20) took Egypt and the holy places of Arabia in 1517, also making inroads into Persian territory. The reign of Suleyman II Kanuni, called by Europeans the Magnificent (1520–66), marks the culmination of Ottoman culture and architecture. Suleyman took Hungary in 1526. Even though by 1683 the Turks were at the gates of Vienna, their power was already on the wane. World War I finally broke up the Empire, already a mere shadow of its former self. The Sultanate was abolished in 1922 and the Caliphate in 1924.

THE EARLY OTTOMAN EMPIRE

The earliest royal mosques were of two types, both with Seljuk precedent. The first was the single-domed chamber with or without a portico. The Hajji Özbek mosque at Iznik (Nicea) of 1333 with the *mihrab* on the wall to the right of the entrance is of this type, as is the Ala al-Din Bey Mosque in Bursa, founded in 1326 by the younger brother of Orhan. The domes usually rested on squinches composed of fans of "Turkish triangles" like those of their Seljuk prototypes at Konya. The form was revived for some of the great royal foundations of the fifteenth and sixteenth centuries. Aptullah Kuran has labeled the second type, based ultimately upon the Seljuk *madrasa* with a closed court, the axial and the cross-axial *iwan* mosque. The earliest was built by Orhan outside the walls of Iznik soon after 1334. Its plan, recovered through excavation, consisted of a five-part portico leading to a domed central chamber which on axis opened

through an arch to a raised *iwan*, the mosque proper. Two flanking chambers, probably barrel vaulted, opened into both the porch and the domed chamber. In 1339 Orhan began a similar mosque at Bursa. Here the basic plan is like that at Iznik, except that a domed antechamber precedes the central space while the flanking rooms are double, the larger ones opening like *iwans* into the central chamber—hence the term cross-axial *iwan* mosque. The axial *iwan* is again raised three steps, and doubtless it was only here that the worshipers went barefoot. The rest of the building was a *zawiya* or dervish *tekke*, with the side *iwans* serving as *tabhanes* or lecture halls and the smaller rooms providing shelter for pilgrims. All the sultans to the end of the dynasty were members of one or another of the dervish orders, but the relation to these somewhat heterodox groups was much more powerful in the earlier period. Later, with the growth of an imperial bureaucracy, the *Ulema* and the Shaykh al-Islam assumed ascendancy, though never wholly at dervish expense.

The Mosque-Madrasa of Murad I

In 1366 Sultan Murad I began at Çekirge (a western suburb of Bursa) a *kulliye* or charitable complex in the vicinity of a palace, now lost. It consisted of, in addition to his mosque-*madrasa*, the rebuilt Eski Kaplica, a thermal bath of Byzantine origin, his *turbe* (now totally reconstructed), a large *imaret* or soup kitchen, and a *mekteb* or Koranic school, as well as a handsome latrine presumably for students of the *madrasa*. Perhaps, because the settings are all hilly, this—like all the other royal *kulliyes* in Bursa—is loosely and informally grouped.

Murad's mosque-*madrasa*, completed by 1385, if not before, is a *zawiya* mosque of the cross-axial form (*Plate 402*), with four chambers, two of them having *ocaks* or fireplaces clearly intended to shelter visiting dervishes. Under the central dome, once open, stands a fountain for ritual ablutions before the raised mosque section, whose parapet has niches for the deposit of slippers—a clear indication that only the barrel-vaulted *iwan* was considered a mosque. Reached from the lower vestibule, the upper level (*Plate 403*) is devoted to a twelve-celled Orthodox *madrasa*, perhaps included as a recognition of the growing power of the *Ulema*. A *darshane* or lecture hall opens onto the upper porch, and a corridor wrapped around the central square hall into which it opens through arched windows corresponds exactly to the earlier porticoed *madrasa* form (*Plate 403*). A unique feature is the octagonal domed chamber over the *mihrab*, which Godfrey Goodwin thinks might have been a royal lodge.

The portico (*Plate 404*) reflects in its two stories the dual function of the building. In its biforia, alternate courses of stone and brick and blind arcaded cornices so strongly suggest late Byzantine design that

a tradition has arisen that the architect was a Greek or even an Italian. Goodwin compares the porch to the portico added in 1313–14 to Hagia Sophia at Ochrid, taken by the Turks in 1385. The minaret is here as elsewhere in these early buildings an obvious afterthought with no organic relation to the rest of the design (*Plate 404*). It is possible that if these foundations had minarets at all they were separate, freestanding structures long since destroyed by the frequent earthquakes in that region.

The Kulliye of Yildirim Bayazid I at Bursa

Yildirim or "Lightning" Bayazid I, so named because of the speed with which he maneuvered his troops, ruled from Adrianople, but founded his *kulliye* in Bursa in 1390 or 1391; it was substantially finished by 1395. The mosque, a *turbe*, a very handsome *madrasa*, baths, and the remains of a small *saray* or palace still stand within an irregular walled enclosure (*Plate 405*). In plan and scale the mosque is essentially like that of Murad I, but is of cut stone masonry throughout with some use of marble. Dervish pilgrims were housed here with magnificence: the south walls of all four chambers flanking the side *iwans* surround their *ocaks* with tiers of multilobed niches decorated with flowers and once polychromed, like those recently found at Kubadabad and characteristic of so much later Turkish domestic design. Goodwin believes they were used for holding water pipes, vases, and even turbans—but not for books, which, too precious for exposure, were stored in chests. The superb porch of stone and marble (*Plate 406*), the first major Ottoman portico, displays the broken arch which also appears within. The form has Seljuk precedent, but was also used in Persia, at Natanz and elsewhere. Here it somehow suggests there was a wooden prototype, perhaps borrowed from palace architecture.

The *madrasa* is typical of later Ottoman structures, with its high-domed *riwaqs* in the vestibule supported on columns and large square *darshane*. Flues for the *ocaks* within the students' rooms vary the skyline, but the *darshane* which opens as an *iwan* must have been extremely cold in winter. Perhaps then classes were held in the closed chambers flanking the portal. The ruined Dar al-Shifa or teaching hospital mentioned in a *waqf* document of 1400 follows an almost identical plan.

The Congregational Mosque at Bursa

Bayazid's victory at Nicopolis probably supplied the booty which paid for the Ulu Cami or Friday mosque begun in late 1396 or early 1397 at Bursa. Completion was rapid, as the *minbar* is dated 1399–1400. The outer walls and twelve piers of limestone support twenty brick

405. *Bursa, Kulliye of Yildirim Bayazid I, 1390/91–95, site plan*
406. *Bursa, Mosque of Yildirim Bayazid I, porch*

407. *Bursa, Ulu Cami, 1396–1400, plan*
408. *Bursa, Ulu Cami, interior, prayer hall*

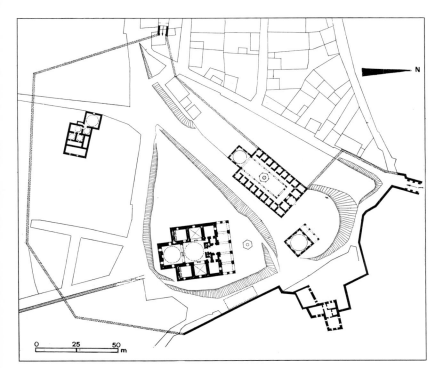

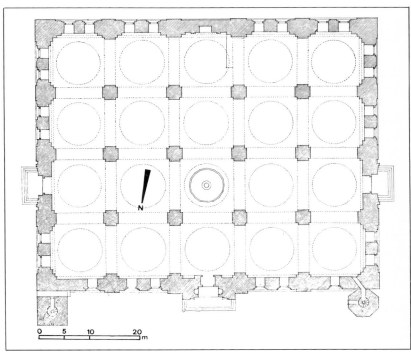

409. *Bursa, Yeşil Cami, 1412–13, 1419–20, section*
410. *Bursa, Yeşil Cami, plan*

411. *Bursa, Yeşil Cami, west chamber of the tribune (the* ocak, *here a door, has since been restored)* ▷
412. *Bursa, Yeşil Cami, north wall of the covered* sahn, *with royal tribunes* ▷
413. *Bursa, Yeşil Cami, prayer hall looking toward the* mihrab ▷

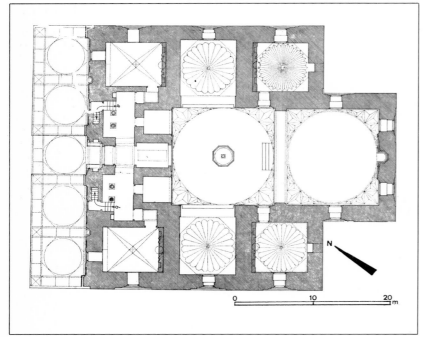

domes—all about 30 feet in diameter, on windowed drums (*Plate 407*). Those of the *mihrab* aisle are higher; the highest of all, with an oculus, rises over the central ablution fountain. Double tiers of windows along non-bearing walls give ample light to an interior which manages considerable grandeur despite the dreadful modern paint (*Plate 408*). Two minarets flank the north facade: that to the west (on an octagonal base) may be early; the other was probably built in 1413–21, but neither is well integrated. This is strange, since the rest of the structure is so much clearer and more logical than any of its Seljuk prototypes. This and the smaller and later mosque at Edirne mark almost the last appearance of this form of multiunit mosque. In the future the congregational mosque changed considerably.

The Yeşil Cami Complex at Bursa
The Yeşil Cami or Green Mosque at Bursa, so called because its domes were once covered with green tiles, was begun for Mehmet I (1403–21) in 1412/13 when the civil strife caused by Timur's victory at Ankara was nearing its end. Hajji Ivaz, son of Ahi Bayazid, is said in the portal inscription to have established the proportions of the building and therefore must have been responsible for the overall design. He could not, however, have closely supervised its construction, complete by 1419/20 except for the never added portico, as he was also vizier and governor of Bursa. The wonderful tile ornament of modeled and *cuerda seca* tiles in blue, green, brilliant yellow, and purple in the mosque and *turbe* was not completed until 1424. The decoration in general was probably under the direction of Ali ibn Ilyas of Bursa, called Nakkas ("Designer"). The royal box is signed in Persian by Mehmet the Mad, and the *mihrab* bears to the right a statement that it is "the work of the masters of Tabriz." In the equivalent place to the left appear verses of Saadi referring to tyranny and injustice. It is possible, since the Kara Koyunlu or Black Sheep Turkomans who took Tabriz from the Timurids in 1406 were Shi'ite and the craftsmen probably Sunnis, that this was the tyranny in question.

In plan the mosque is an elaboration of that of Bayazid (*Plate 410*), although here the sanctuary as well as the east and west *iwans* and the south pilgrims' rooms is domed. All four of these subsidiary chambers have *ocaks* set in niched walls, as do the two small chambers flanking the imperial tribune (*Plate 411*). Two royal boxes, richly tiled, flank the portal on the north wall of the covered *sahn*, while the Sultan's tribune opens above it as though the shrunken north *iwan* of a cruciform plan had been thrust into the air (*Plates 409, 412*). The superb tile ornament reaches a climax in the enormous *mihrab* (*Plate 413*), executed with a splendor unknown to the Seljuks.

414. *Bursa, Yeşil Cami, north facade*
416. *Bursa, Yeşil Cami, north facade, detail of portal*
415. *Bursa, Turbe of Mehmet I, completed soon after 1421, section*

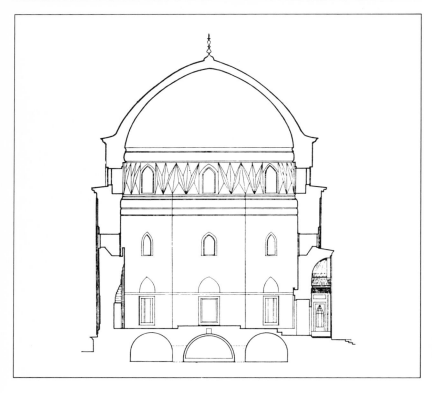

Even without its planned portico the north facade (*Plate 414*) is beautifully articulated with rich moldings and a splendid portal (*Plate 416*) entirely in marble. With its cascade of crisp *muqarnas*, the portal is essentially in the Seljuk tradition except for the intricate interlacing in the tympanum, which is pierced by the *muqarnas* semidome. There seems to have been an attempt to reproduce in relief the complex arabesques in tile mosaic which occupy similar positions in many Timurid buildings.

The Turbe of Mehmet I, completed after his death (1421) by Hajji Ivaz on the orders of Murad II, has an exterior encased in panels of blue tiles (restored in 1855) framed in stone. The octagonal shape (*Plate 415*), as Goodwin notes, breaks with earlier Bursa mausoleums and returns to a Seljuk (but also an Azerbaijanian) tradition. The *mihrab* (*Plate 417*) is on a scale similar to that of the mosque and rivals it in magnificence. Within the *muqarnas* niche is a panel of hyacinths, pinks, and roses surrounding a lamp—a reference to the well-known Surah which compares God to the illumination of a niche.

With the Yeşil Cami complex Ottoman architecture achieves its first great triumph. The harmonious repose of this extraordinary combination of crisp marble and rich tile, even unfinished and sadly battered, is unique. There may be greater accomplishments to come, but nothing like this will ever be repeated.

IMPERIAL ARCHITECTURE BEFORE SINAN
The Üç Şerefeli Cami at Edirne

Goodwin has noted that Murad II (1421–44; 1446–51) had close connections with Manisa, a major dervish center, where he hoped to retire, and he must have been familiar with the Great Mosque there (*Plate 321*). How much influence he had over the design of the Üç Şerefeli Cami, the congregational mosque he ordered built in 1438, is unknown; however, if not the Sultan, then the unknown architect must not only have seen the building at Manisa but also the Isa Bek Mosque at Seljuk (*Plate 322*). Elements from both were combined in the Edirne project, completed in 1447.

The Üç Şerefeli Cami (*Plate 418*) marks the first in the great series of imperial Ottoman mosques, culminating in the work of Koca Sinan. The 79-foot dome rising from a hexagon exceeds by far anything previously attempted either by Seljuk or Ottoman builders, and the prayer hall—though its total area is less than that of the Ulu Cami at Bursa—seems much more spacious (*Plate 421*). In a sense we begin here the search for an absolutely unimpeded interior on a larger scale than was possible with the single-domed mosque. Even so, the two-domed flanking spaces, with their own entrances from the

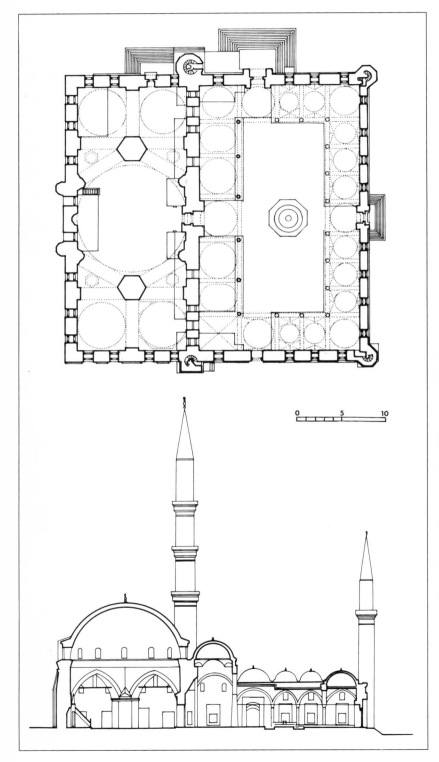

◁ *422. View of Constantinople in 1537, from al-Matraki's* Description of the Stages of Sultan Suleyman's Campaign in the Two Iraqs *(1537), Library of the University of Istanbul*

423. Istanbul, Fatih Cami, 1463–70, plan

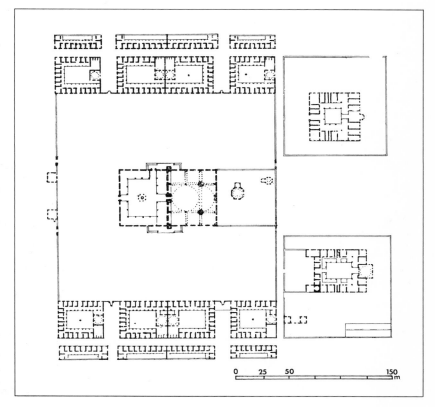

sahn, could still have served as dervish *tabhanes*. The prayer hall has a seven-bay domical portico like the royal mosques at Bursa, but to this is appended a lower set of *riwaqs* forming a *sahn* reminiscent of the Isa Bek Mosque (*Plate 420*).

The balcony of a minaret is called a *şerefes* in Turkish, hence the name Üç Şerefeli or "with three balconies" (from those of the tallest of the four minarets, whose height of 220 feet was not to be surpassed for a century; *Plate 419*). Two minarets had come to be the mark of the sovereign's own foundations, though all were probably afterthoughts at Bursa. Here the four towers, while deliberately varied in finish and height, were nevertheless well integrated into the design and planned from the beginning. Their multiplication may be based on Timurid precedent.

The Fatih Cami (Mosque of Mehmet II) at Istanbul

Mehmet II, also known as Fatih the Conqueror, who had come to the throne at thirteen but had been deposed briefly by his father, took Constantinople (Istanbul since 1934) in 1453, fulfilling the eight-hundred-year-old dream of Islam. The impoverished and half-ruined city did not immediately become the capital, though this must have been intended from the beginning. The appearance of the old walled city before its final transformation under the architect Sinan and his successors is preserved in the famous manuscript of 1537 produced by Matraki for Suleyman the Magnificent (*Plate 422*). The Eski Saray or Old Palace, a square enclosure in the center of the city, was begun by Mehmet II in 1454. Perhaps as early as 1459 but certainly by 1464–65, when Mehmet wintered in the city, work on the Yeni Saray or New Palace (also called Top Kapu Saray or Cannon Gate Palace) was underway. This is the walled enclosure in the upper left of the manuscript considerably distorted by Matraki but accurate in most of its details. The Bab-i-Humayun or Imperial Gate just to the left of Hagia Sophia—dated 1478 and shown with its now demolished upper pavilion—probably marks the outer limits of Mehmet's palace, but there have been many additions since. Mehmet also provided for the defense of his new capital by adding five towers to the Byzantine Golden Gate (lower right), forming the castle of Yedi Kule or seven towers, shown in the manuscript with their original conical roofs. Plans for Mehmet's congregational mosque, the prominent structure just below the Eski Saray, may have been drawn in 1459, but work began only in early 1463 and ended in 1470.

The prayer hall of the Fatih Cami collapsed in the earthquake of 1766 and was rebuilt on the old foundations in a very different form. The original design was by an architect named Sinan (not, of course, the famous sixteenth-century master), who is referred to as a "freed

man" and hence was not born a Muslim. The mosque's first form is preserved in Matraki's illumination and in a drawing of 1559 by Rorich. The dome, 85 feet wide, exceeded anything previously attempted. The plan of the Üç Şerefeli is here expanded toward the *qibla* by a semidome flanked by two lesser domes (*Plate 423*). The original north portal of the *sahn* is severely rectilinear, the *muqarnas* vault pierced through a rectangular tympanum without the usual arch. It is imbued, as Goodwin says, with an almost puritan geometry in comparison to that of the Yeşil Cami.

The *sahn* (*Plate 424*), undamaged in the earthquake, is a place of spacious calm with tall cypresses and broad arches on antique shafts —a calm untroubled even by the convoluted eighteenth-century roof of the *shadrivan*. A distinction is maintained between the portico of the prayer hall and the *riwaqs*, but the composition is better integrated than that of Üç Şerefeli. The portal of the original prayer hall, incorporated into the new structure (*Plate 425*), uses a broken and stilted arch within a severe rectangular frame. The tympanum is pierced by a rich cascade of *muqarnas*. Again restraint and severity dominate.

The vast, rigidly symmetrical outer court—with multidomed *madrasas*, dervish hostels, and other charitable foundations—is imperial in scale and Roman in the immensity of the vaulted foundations required to bring its base to a single level. Nothing could provide a greater contrast to the informality of the *kulliyes* of Bursa. Here the order is symbolic of the order and unity the Ottoman Empire was bringing to Anatolia and the Balkans. Only in the vast caliphal palaces of Samarra has such control been applied to so large a project. Here too the order, since this was a university as well as an imperial mosque and burial place, has implications beyond that of autocratic rule alone.

The Çinli Kiosk at Istanbul

This building, completed in 1472 and called the Tiled Pavilion, stands within the outer walls of Top Kapu Saray but appears to have been omitted from Matraki's view. The only element of Mehmet's original complex to have survived relatively intact, it exhibits a strong influence from Timurid Persia. The tall stone columns of the principal facade are an eighteenth-century reconstruction whose vaults cut arbitrarily into the wall behind them (*Plate 426*). The original porch was very probably of wood, *in antis* between the projecting wall ends, and consisted of six columns supporting a flat roof—in other words, a typical Persian *talar*, though nothing so early survives there. The rectilinear tile mosaics and the floral arabesques in the spandrels are all more typically Timurid than those of the Yeşil Cami. The plan too (*Plate 427*) is wholly Persian. A central cruciform

426. *Istanbul, Top Kapu Saray, Çinli Kiosk, completed 1472, main facade*

428. *Istanbul, Top Kapu Saray, Cinli Kiosk, central chamber*

427. *Istanbul, Top Kapu Saray, Çinli Kiosk, plan*

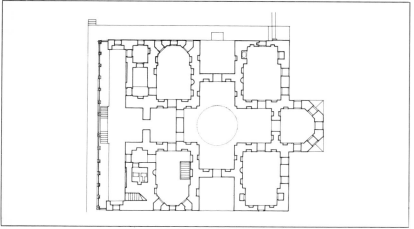

chamber (*Plate 428*) with a high windowed dome on *muqarnas* squinches gives access to open *iwans* right and left and to five reception rooms; the room on axis projects over the steep rear slope in a pentagonal "bay window" like that of the *madrasa* at Khargird. The intricate net or shield vaults recall those of the Ishrat Khaneh at Samarkand and must once have been as richly painted. The tile wainscoting throughout, consisting of hexagons and equilateral triangles with traces of gilding, recalls the sumptuous interiors with glimpses of gardens beyond of so many contemporary Persian miniatures.

The portal inscription, in Persian verse, reads as follows:

This pavilion which is as lofty as the heavens was so constructed that its great height would seem to stretch a hand up to the Gemini themselves. Its most worthless part would adorn the most precious item in Saturn's crown. Its emerald cupola sparkles like the heavens and is honored with inscriptions from the stars. Its floor of turquoise with its varied flowers . . . reminds one of the eternal vineyards of paradise.*

We find here that the central dome was once tiled in green like the domes of the Yeşil Cami in Bursa. Also as at Bursa these have since been replaced by lead sheets. Authorities differ as to when lead became normal as a covering for Ottoman vaults, but it seems probable that the Ottomans did not generally adopt this Byzantine practice until after the reign of Mehmet II. The inscription is also revealing in its use of zodiacal terms, its references to starry skies, and its association of flowers with a metaphor for Paradise. All this parallels what is found in the Alhambra inscriptions.

The Kulliye of Bayazid II at Edirne

Bayazid II (1481–1512), like his grandfather Murad II, was much attached to the dervish orders, more so than his father, Mehmet II. The *tabhane* annexes to his square single-domed mosque at Edirne (*Plates 429, 430*) confirm this. They are cruciform, with a vented dome over a four-*iwan* court and domed corner chambers. In this they resemble the Çinli Kiosk. To judge by Matraki's miniature, the now destroyed Eyub Mosque (1458) on the Golden Horn may have had similar *tabhanes*. The Edirne *kulliye* was perhaps built by Heyruddin, who may already have succeeded Ilyas Beq (d. 1486), the assistant of Mehmet II's Sinan and court architect since 1471.

The prayer hall (*Plate 431*), covered by a single dome on true

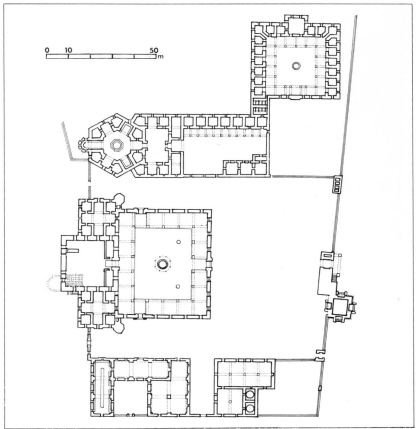

*Assuman Kilsuk, "Turkish Tiles and Ceramics," *Apollo*, July 1970, pp. 58–61.

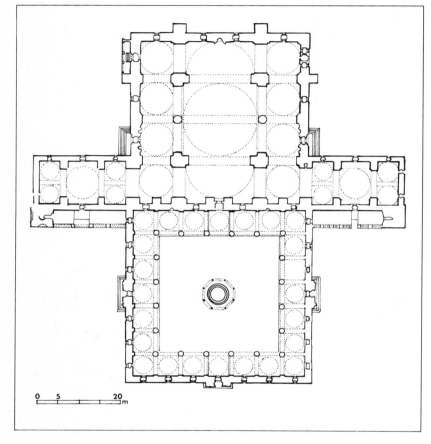

0   5   20
m

pendentives, is in its spare simplicity and despite the ugly later painting the archetypal Ottoman domed unit, the basis of all later architectural composition. The prayer hall *tabhane* unit is repeated in the Mosque of Selim I (1512–20) at Istanbul, completed two years after his death by Suleyman, but the later dome is 10 feet greater in diameter.

The Dar al-Shifa, or teaching hospital, devoted to the treatment of the mentally ill, and the U-shaped *madrasa* west of the mosque are less formally ordered than the annexes to the Fatih Cami, though much more so than the Bursa complexes. The unique hexagonal plan of the main chamber of the hospital (*Plate 432*), with its pentagonal apse recalling that of the Çinli Kiosk, was specified in the *waqf* document as the site where concerts were to be given for the patients.

The Mosque of Bayazid II at Istanbul

Bayazid's congregational mosque (*Plate 434*) appears just above the Eski Saray in Matraki's illustration. It might have been designed as early as 1491 and, if so, Heyruddin could have participated; this is unlikely, however, since, according to the inscription, actual construction took place between 1501 and 1506. Here the *tabhanes* of the Edirne complex are joined to the prayer hall in such a way as to lose their original function if, indeed, they were ever so used. The plan (*Plate 433*) adds another half dome to the scheme of the Fatih Cami to form a more balanced composition, obviously inspired by Hagia Sophia. The interior (*Plate 435*) is, however, quite different, there being little division between the space of the "nave" and that of the "aisles."

THE WORKS OF SINAN

Koca Sinan (c. 1490/91–1588), the greatest of all Ottoman architects and worthy rival of his near contemporary Michelangelo, was born, possibly of Greek, but certainly of non-Muslim, parents in Karaman. He was one of the most distinguished products of the *devşirme*, the custom of recruiting the brightest non-Muslim youths of the Empire for training and service in the corps of janissaries. After conversion to Islam, the recruit who showed the most promise had an almost unlimited future and could attain the highest offices of state, though remaining always a slave of the Sultan. Sinan was probably enrolled in 1512. Where he learned the architectural profession is unknown, but he had joined the household cavalry by 1526, the probable date at which he first came to Sultan Suleyman's attention. He then served in Austria, in the Baghdad campaign, and on the expeditions to Corfu and Puglia in 1537. The following year he was appointed Architect of the Abode of Felicity. For fifty years thereafter he

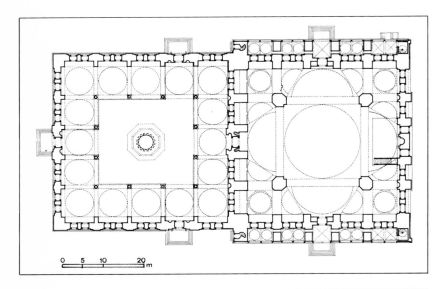

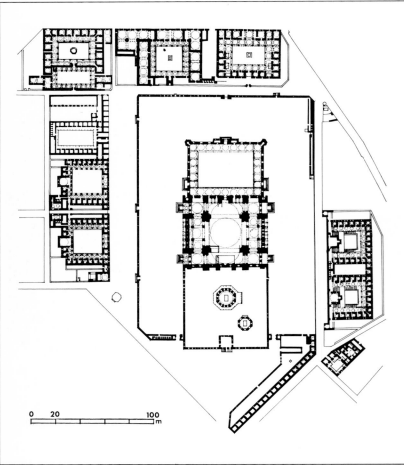

designed and often supervised the building of a vast number and infinite variety of structures, many still extant, of which only a handful may be touched upon here.

The Şehzade Cami at Istanbul

The death of Prince Mehmet, Suleyman's heir, in 1543 brought Sinan his first major commission, for the Şehzade Cami (*Plate 436*). Here the addition of lateral semidomes to the plan of Bayazid II's mosque froze the interior space into a stable composition allowing the maximum clarity and accessibility to the *mihrab* and *minbar* by the congregation. The solution was not a new one: the mosque at Dimoteka in Greece (1421) had a centralized nine-part plan and that of Fatih Pasha at Diyarbekir (c. 1520–22), very likely seen by Sinan, had four half domes and smaller domelets in the corners. The proportional balance of Sinan's building was, however, unprecedented. Here inner and outer space are firmly and precisely articulated for the first time. Nevertheless, Sinan called this the work of his apprenticeship.

The Kulliye of Suleyman at Istanbul

Sinan acknowledged this great complex (*Plate 437*) as the first work of his maturity. Commissioned in 1550 when Suleyman finally abandoned the Eski Saray as a residence and gave up half its gardens to accommodate it, the complex took seven years to complete. The land, on the city's sixth hill, slopes sharply toward the Golden Horn, and necessitated vast stone-vaulted foundations that were Roman in scale. Goodwin informs us that the masons' accounts were kept in Armenian, perhaps the origin of most, if not all, the craftsmen. As in the Fatih Cami, the prayer hall of the mosque stands between a tomb enclosure to the south and a *sahn* to the north. Unlike it, however, this central unit is separated from the surrounding *madrasas* and other charitable foundations by a windowed wall like the *ziyada* of an Abbasid mosque, but lower and more open. Seen from the Golden Horn, the mosque achieves a monumentality surpassing anything previously built. Any structure on such a site would be imposing, but a comparison with the Mosque of Bayazid II whose plan is similar reveals the essence of the transformation Sinan effected upon Turkish architecture (*Plates 328, 438*). The earlier monument is an assemblage of forms relatively opaque in their expression of interior space, let alone structure. Sinan, as in the best of French Gothic architecture, has created an exterior which corresponds exactly to the interior spatial divisions and to the structural functions of the assemblage of buttresses, arches, vaults, and counterweights needed to create them. The lessons he learned from Hagia Sophia are abundantly clear in the great east and west tympanums, but even

439. *Istanbul, Suleymaniye, prayer hall*
440. *Istanbul, Suleymaniye, prayer hall, dome* ▷

441. *Edirne, Selimiye, 1569–74, view from the west*
442. *Edirne, Kulliye of Selim II, plan*
443. *Edirne, Selimiye, prayer hall* ▷
444. *Istanbul, Ahmediye (Blue Mosque), view from the east, 1609–17* ▷

without its later accretions Hagia Sophia never expressed on the outside the much greater complexity of its interior divisions with equal clarity.

As in Bayazid's mosque, Sinan here eliminates the galleries of his model and creates a serene and spacious interior more complex than Bayazid's or the Şehzade Cami, but far better orchestrated than either (*Plates 439, 440*). Exact dimensions are hard to find and authorities differ, but in essence Suleymaniye's dome ends 174 feet above the floor and is 87 feet wide according to both Goodwin and Aslanapa. Hence the central space is a cube surmounted by a hemisphere in a proportion of two to three. Furthermore, the total interior area is a square of close to 1,873 feet divided into sixteen units, of which four form the central square. All the supports project back from this square, enlivening the subordinated spaces with more two-to-three relationships. The scheme is that of the Şehzade Cami, based on a 62-foot dome in a 409-foot square but only 121 feet high. In the Şehzade Sinan used the east and west portals to emphasize a cross axis but, wisely at the Suleymaniye, the wide spans of the center arches supporting the east and west tympanums and the larger domes beyond form this axis, leaving the four portals to enter the corner domes as vestibules—thus using spaces otherwise not logical parts of the whole.

The Selimiye at Edirne

Sinan called this mosque, begun when he was eighty years old, his masterpiece. Selim II (1569–74) ordered it built in 1569 from the spoils of the conquest of Cyprus on a hill near Edirne, where it dominated the European gateway to the Ottoman Empire with its crown of minarets more than 230 feet tall (*Plate 441*). Here they are drawn close to the corners of the prayer hall, emphasizing the radial symmetry of the pyramidal composition culminating in the windowed dome 102 1/2 feet in diameter. Eight cupola-topped counterweights rise above the piers, braced by as many flying buttresses. Within (*Plate 443*), the luminous space is serene, logical, and totally free of obstruction. The Kulliye (*Plate 442*) was originally symmetrical, comprising only the two structures behind the prayer hall. In the 1580s Davut Aga, Sinan's pupil and successor as court architect, built the covered bazaar as a source of revenue for the foundation.

THE IMPERIAL MOSQUE AFTER SINAN
The Ahmediye (Blue Mosque) at Istanbul

When Davut Aga succeeded Sinan in 1587, the greatest days of Ottoman architecture and, indeed, those of the Empire itself were drawing to a close. After designing the Yeni Cami for Safiye, mother of Mehmet III, Davut was executed for heresy in 1599. The building,

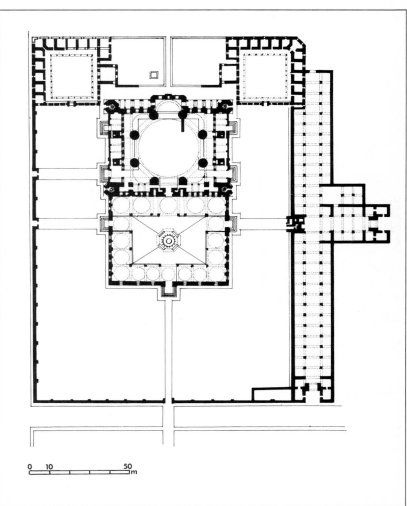

0   10   50
                m

finished only in 1663, is a not too sensitive imitation of Sinan's Şehzade. The office of court architect was conferred after Davut's death upon Dalgiç Ahmet Aga, who was succeeded in 1606 by Mehmet Aga. Mehmet, born a Christian in Europe about 1540, went to Constantinople in 1563. There he became known for his craftsmanship in mother-of-pearl, but he also had a position in Sinan's office, of which he took charge during the master's absences.

In 1609 Mehmet began a congregational mosque south of the At Meidan, the ancient hippodrome, for the Sultan Ahmet I (1603–17). Shortly before work began, the Empire had suffered a disastrous defeat and perhaps the pleasure-loving and rather scandalous Ahmet, only nineteen years old at the time, wished to placate God. The *Ulema*, however, strongly protested the funding of a Friday mosque from the state treasury rather than from the spoils of a campaign. Goodwin suggests this may be the origin of the legend that the six minarets were blasphemous, since they exceeded the number at Mecca (actually, the mosque at Mecca then had seven).

Despite the immense popularity of the Ahmediye, commonly called the Blue Mosque, the design is successful only from certain angles (*Plate 444*) in which the pyramidal effect of the Şehzade Cami is accented by corner minarets like those of the Selimiye at Edirne. The lower minarets on the north facade of the *sahn*, in the manner of the Suleymaniye, reduce rather than heighten the tension. The proportions of the prayer hall (*Plate 445*) closely follow those of the Şehzade, but Mehmet's timidity is evident in the immense cylindrical piers whose scale, far greater than needed, dwarfs all else. The harsh blue stenciled ornament, probably not original, also clashes badly with the lavish interior use of tile, still of high quality.

Neither of these mosques can live up to their predecessors and, although often charming, the later royal foundations too—with their Baroque ornament derived from the France of Louis XV—provide no further major architectural successes. On the other hand, eighteenth-century Ottoman domestic architecture provides much that is still vigorous and interesting.

THE PALACE AND THE KIOSK

Turkish domestic architecture may employ brick and stone, but many of its most characteristic forms arise out of wood construction. This was a traditional building material in the forested parts of Anatolia and readily available in Istanbul through the Black Sea ports. Multiple, double-tiered windows with only the lower sash movable were probably first executed in wood, as may have been the charming walls of painted niches often surrounding *ocaks*, although earlier surviving examples are in stucco. As is so frequent in the history of architec-

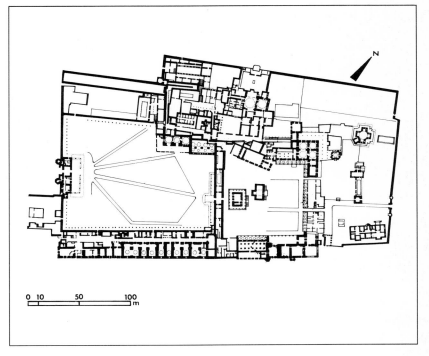

0 10   50   100
                   m

339

448. *Istanbul, Top Kapu Saray, Bab-i-Saadet (Gate of Felicity)*
449. *Istanbul, Top Kapu Saray, Arz Odasi (Throne Room), 1585*

ture, the plan tends to evolve more slowly than the elevation. Hence one observes in Ottoman domestic architecture well into the nineteenth century an abundance of cruciform rooms and emphasized cross axes, whether in palaces, kiosks, or simple farmhouses.

Top Kapu Saray at Istanbul

Matraki's view of this palace is distorted to fit his format, although the Bab-i-Humayun or Imperial Gate (*Plate 446*) is clearly indicated (without its later marble paneling, but with its superstructure). We can also see the walls of Mehmet II's original enclosure, and past the Bab-i-Humayun the first court with the Top Kapu or Cannon Gate leading to the second court. From the latter, with its tower of the Diwan, the Grand Vizier, observed occasionally by the Sultan, held audience. The third court, entered from the second by the Bab-i-Saadet or Gate of Felicity, also appears in Matraki's illustration, though distorted; its blue color suggests it then enclosed a large pond. The plans of the second and third courts (*Plate 447*) in general follow the pattern set out by Mehmet II, but lack the strong towers surviving in Matraki's view. As in his mosque, here too Mehmet needed extensive vaulted foundations to extend the level surface of the acropolis of the ancient city.

The Bab-i-Saadet (*Plate 448*), rebuilt in the eighteenth century, served, perhaps even from Mehmet II's time, an important ceremonial function. Here the Sultan was enthroned upon his succession and here he presided over the celebration of Bayram, the holiday at the end of the holy month of Ramazan. The gate received its name from the Dar-i-Saadet or Abode of Felicity, the private residence contained by the third court. Just beyond the gate was the Arz Odasi or Throne Room (*Plate 449*), built by Davut Aga in 1585; its magnificent porch surrounds a very restricted interior. To the right, a suite of four vaulted chambers with a corner loggia is the Fatih Kiosk built for Mehmet II about 1468. In the far left corner, four domed chambers—perhaps of Mehmet II's period, though redecorated—shelter the relics of the Prophet, brought here by Selim I in 1517.

Northwest of the reliquary chambers is the *selamlik*, which borders the *harem* first established here in 1550. The best room in it is the superb bed chamber of Murad III (1574–95) built in 1578 by Sinan after a disastrous fire. This splendid chamber (*Plate 450*) has stone-framed niches with mixtilinear arches lined and backed with superb Iznik underglaze tiles, a high gilded bronze *ocak*, and a painted dome (*Plate 451*) now restored to its original form. Blocked windows suggest that this room may once have been virtually freestanding like a kiosk.

We know that there were kiosks in the vicinity of the fourth

court as early as the time of Mehmet II, one of which he used as a throne room; none survive, however. The famous Baghdad Kiosk at the west end of the fourth court was built for Murad IV (1623–40) by Hasan Aga, perhaps then imperial architect, to celebrate the reconquest of Baghdad in 1639. The structure consists of a domed octagon within a cross surrounded by broad arcades (*Plate 452*). Within, a vast bronze-hooded *ocak* dominates the central chamber whose four arms are set with inlaid niches and shuttered cupboards of mother-of-pearl below windows of colored glass set in stucco (*Plate 453*). The inscription in white on blue between upper and lower windows consists of Surah II, verse 256, the so-called throne verse, which might suggest the chamber's original use as a throne room. The fine blue and white floral panels around the lower walls and the poly-chrome tiles in niches may be of mid-sixteenth-century date or copies, and reveal the failing artistic powers of the time. Nevertheless, the contemporary tiles of the upper walls and pendentives are still good and the dome, of golden star-like arabesques on a red ground, is original though in poor condition.

The Kasri of Aynali Kavak

Later kiosks built for royalty or for the nobility on the Golden Horn and along the Bosporus augmented the basic plan of the Baghdad Kiosk with the diversified apartments and service areas demanded by an increasingly Europeanized aristocracy. Such is the Kiosk or Kasri of Aynali Kavak at Hasköy on the Golden Horn, built for Selim III (1789–1807) in 1791 (*Plate 454*). Here the *piano nobile*, of wood over a ground floor of stone, has a domed salon which replaces one of the *iwans* or *sofas* of the Baghdad Kiosk's plan with an open portico. It lacks an *ocak*, since this was a summer residence only. The plan tends toward symmetry and axiality even when intercommunication is indirect. One might even suggest that the evolution of modern architecture through Frank Lloyd Wright owes something to houses of this type (the multiple windows and hovering eaves also strike a Wrightian note). The dining room is Turkish only in conception. The ornament is entirely Rococo, a style which persisted in Istanbul well into the third quarter of the nineteenth century.

Conclusion

Ottoman architecture began in an atmosphere of heterodoxy. *Ghazis* (defenders of the faith) abounded and the dervish orders, closely as-sociated with the early sultans, were extremely influential. The early architecture was a composite of Seljuk survivals (the Ulu Cami at Bursa, the *iwan* mosques) and Persian imports (the wonderful tiles of the Yeşil Cami at Bursa and the Çinli Kiosk in Istanbul). The multiple-

domed unit as a structural device and layered brick and stone masonry, both typically Ottoman, had a Byzantine origin but were already being used in a most un-Byzantine manner. With the conquest of Constantinople and Ottoman expansion into a major empire, dervish influence lessened and that of the orthodox *Ulema* headed by the Shaykh al-Islam increased. The great imperial Friday mosques adapted a standard form which soon lost all evidence of the dervish accommodations previously provided. They became the centers of vast *kulliyes* dominated by multiple *madrasas*, veritable universities of which the detached dervish *tabhane* was now only one element among many. Logic and order prevailed and coincided with the rise of Turkey's greatest architect, Koca Sinan, who applied them to the mosque proper, the exterior of which came so sensitively to reflect both the form of the inner space and the structural supporting system as to rival the best thirteenth-century French Gothic architecture. At this time—the whole of the sixteenth century and the early part of the seventeenth—the Ottoman style formed a new synthesis of what it had inherited, but accepted nothing more from other Islamic or European styles. Only in its decline was Ottoman architecture affected by Western Europe, and even then in elevation and decoration rather than in plan.

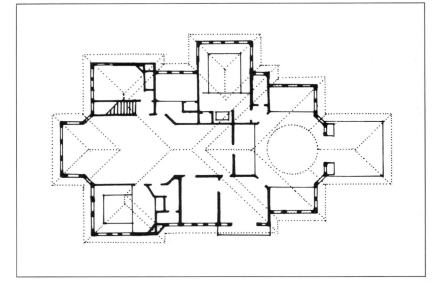

The Safavids were perhaps Persia's first truly national dynasty, yet they were probably of Kurdish origin and, at least in their early years, Turkish-speaking. The family descended from Shaykh Safi-al-Din (d. 1334), who had established a Sufi order at Ardabil in Azerbaijan. Though later Safavid histories deny it, he was very probably Sunni. Only in the fifteenth century was the order firmly Shi'ite and the founder of the dynasty, Shah Ismail (1501–24), adopted a wholly fictitious genealogy claiming descent from the Prophet through an Alid line. The early rulers were principally engaged in the defense of Persia against the Ottomans from the northwest and the Shaybanid Uzbeks from the northeast. Tabriz, the original capital, was abandoned for the safer Qazvin, while Baghdad was lost to the Ottomans and frontier towns such as Herat and Mashad frequently changed hands.

Although early Safavid architecture already shows the development toward a continuous skin of colored tile based on Timurid forms, the monuments are fragmentary and much rebuilt. Only with the removal of the capital to Isfahan under Shah Abbas I (1588–1629) can a true Safavid architecture be recognized. Such was not the case for the other arts: textiles, metalwork, ceramics, and, above all, painting flourished earlier, particularly in the first half of the reign of Shah Tahmasp (1524–76). The art of building revived under Shah Abbas had Timurid antecedents in about the same way Ottoman architecture was based on Seljuk forms. Again as with the Ottomans, contemporary influences from outside Persia were wholly rejected until, as in Turkey, European forms were introduced in the later eighteenth and nineteenth centuries.

THE BUILDINGS OF SHAH ABBAS I

Shah Abbas I celebrated Nauruz, the Persian New Year, in Isfahan in 1598 and then decided to transform the area of gardens and fields between the old walled town and the Zayandeh River into a new capital. The Isfahan of Shah Abbas, while certainly not the first planned city in Islam, is one of the very few of which enough remains or is recorded to make a nearly complete reconstruction of its general features possible (*Plate 455*). The design was not wholly new, as it adjusted itself to a number of preexisting features. The great Meidan-i-Shah, today about 1,709 by 525 feet, was probably in existence as early as 1504–5 when Shah Ismail laid out to the west of it the garden called Naqsh-i-Jahan or Picture of the World, reproducing the name of one of Timur's gardens at Samarkand. In 1509–10 the Meidan was widened. Shah Tahmasp is said to have resided frequently in a Timurid palace, probably on the site of the Ali Kapu, which may still contain parts of it. Here he may well have entertained the exiled

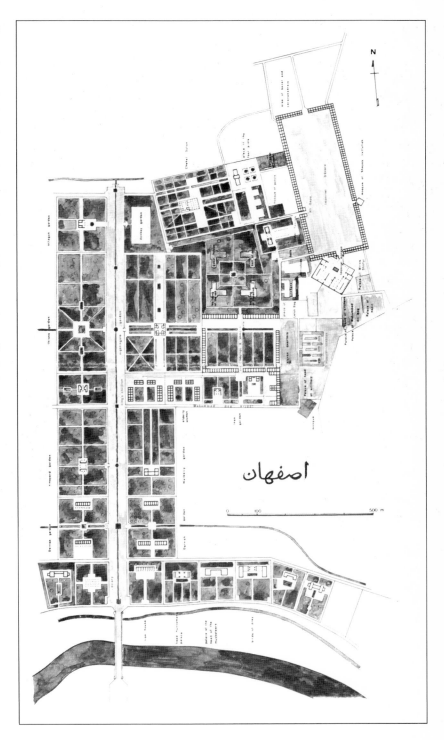

455.   *Isfahan, the suburb of Shah Abbas I, begun 1598, plan*

345

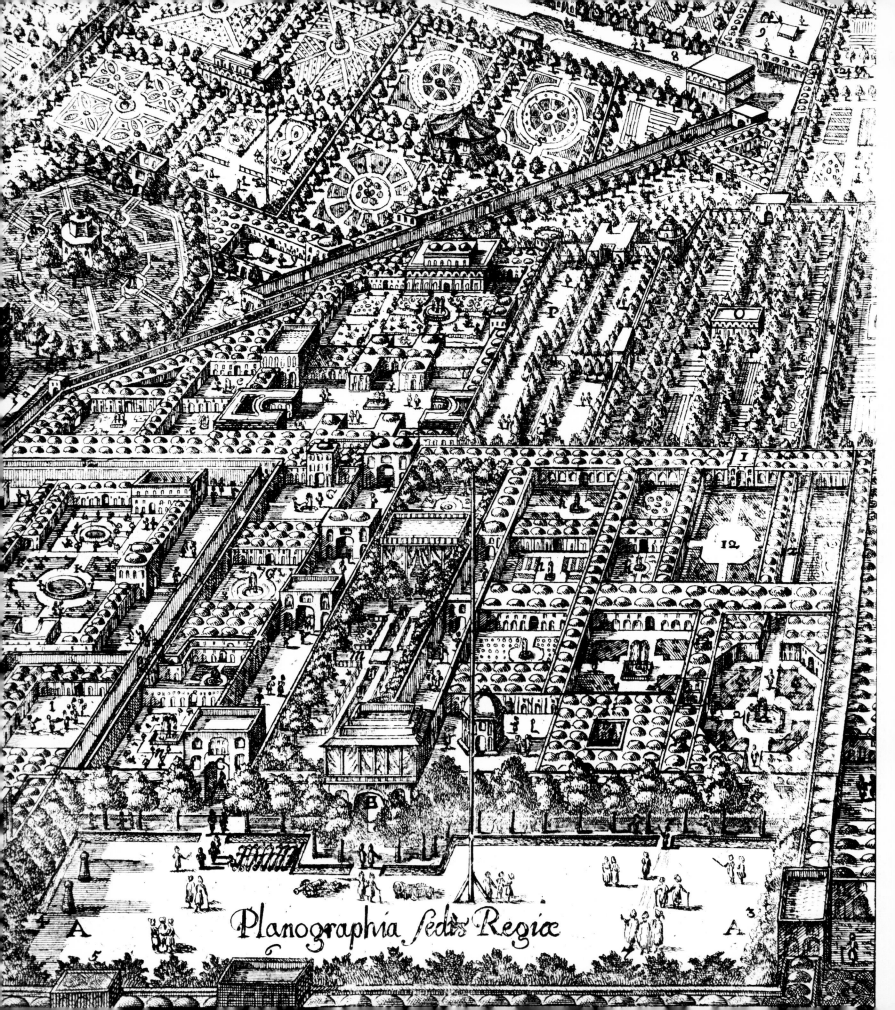

Planographia sedis Regiæ

◁ 456. *Isfahan, view of the palace complex west of the Meidan-i-Shah (from a print of 1712)*

457. *Isfahan, Ali Kapu, longitudinal section*
458. *Isfahan, Ali Kapu, the* talar
459. *Isfahan, Ali Kapu, music room* ▷

Moghul emperor, Humayun. Shah Abbas rebuilt the Meidan, providing it on all four sides with a covered bazaar lined with stalls and with another row of stalls facing the square. Rows of trees and a water channel, since filled in, separated these from the central open space used for temporary markets, polo games, public executions, and other spectacles. The orientation of the Meidan determined that of the palace area west of it in Ismail's garden. At the south end of the Meidan arose the great Friday mosque, the Masjid-i-Shah, whose monumental entrance, finished in 1616, faces (on axis) another entrance leading to a great complex of bazaars, baths, and *caravanserais* comprising the commercial quarter of the new suburb.

For the central axis of his new city, Shah Abbas departed from the direction of the Meidan and placed his promenade, the Chahr Bagh, named for the four gardens purchased for the right-of-way, almost due north-south. This led by the shortest route to the river, which was spanned by a bridge built about 1600 by a favorite general, Allahaverdi Khan. Past the river the Chahr Bagh continued south, ending at the Hazar Jerib of about 1650, a vast garden nearly a mile square which rose in twelve terraces. (The distance from the beginning of the Chahr Bagh just west of the palace enclosure to its termination at the portal of the Hazar Jerib is about equal to that between the east front of the Louvre and the Arc de Triomphe in Paris.)

The Palace Complex at Isfahan

A print of 1712 (*Plate 456*) gives a fairly accurate though not exact view of the palace area west of the Meidan-i-Shah. The Meidan is shown with its plane trees and canal bordered to the west by two monumental gates. The surviving gate on the right is the Ali Kapu, with its *talar* draped in awnings. From the gates, walled alleys, in part open and in part covered by domes perhaps serving as bazaars, both link and divide various enclosures. Just to the right of the Ali Kapu appears a small centrally planned *masjid* for the use of the palace, then isolated in a court but now engulfed by later structures. In the upper right of the print appears the Chehel Situn with its garden and to the upper left the Hasht Behisht within the Garden of the Nightingales. Above, at a contrasting angle, is the beginning of the Chahr Bagh with its canal and fountains.

The Ali Kapu

The Ali Kapu or High Gate was much more than the main entrance to the palace. A very tall structure of three principal and two intermediate stories, it served as the major reception pavilion, the *selamlik* of the palace, and is said to have been the favorite abode of Shah

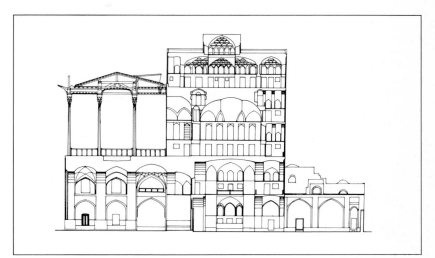

Abbas. The raised *talar* with its *iwan* facing the Meidan served as a summer throne room, banqueting hall, and reviewing stand. Although the results of structural examination have not yet been fully published, the plan suggests that Shah Abbas enlarged an originally cruciform pavilion with *iwans* and square corner rooms. This nucleus, which may have been Timurid, probably stood in the middle of a square *chahr bagh* since obliterated, in part by the widening of the Meidan in 1509–10. The Safavid additions consisted of a platform to the east for the *talar* (*Plates 457, 459*), which also permitted a passage for the covered bazaar encircling the entire Meidan. To the west two wings bordered an open passage into the palace. The central core, widened on both sides, was extended upward to include a vast rectangular reception hall or winter throne room at the level of the *talar* and above that, at the level of the *talar's* roof, a cruciform music room with a square central clerestory (*Plate 459*).

Ornament throughout was sumptuous. Against the tan brick, tiled spandrels emphasized the clear articulation of the exterior windows and *iwans*. All the double windows, according to Pietro della Valle, who saw the Ali Kapu in 1617, were closed by stucco grilles set partly with colored glass. The *talar* was painted and gilded; its intarsia ceiling, encrusted with precious metals, is supported by slender wooden columns with *muqarnas* capitals. The west wall is articulated with shallow niches, in some of which are the remains of European-style paintings of elaborately costumed Westerners. This incongruous note, confined here and at the Chehel Situn to sheltered exteriors, has not affected any element of the architectural design or interior ornament, all of which is wholly Islamic and Persian.

Unlike the imaginary interiors so frequently illustrated in Timurid and Safavid illuminated manuscripts, there seems to have been little if any use of tile dadoes inside this building. Instead exquisitely painted plaster appears everywhere, sometimes in a lacquer-like relief. Patterns range from abstract arabesques to naturalistic combinations of birds and flowering trees. The repertoire is very similar to that used for brocades and knotted carpets of the period. In the music room the upper walls and vaults, of elaborately lacquered stucco and wood, are niched for the reception of porcelain vessels, probably Chinese as well as Persian, each opening adapted to a specific shape. This is an extraordinary variation (also found at Ardabil) of the ancient Islamic device of the niched wall mentioned so often before.

The Chehel Situn
West of the Ali Kapu, the Chehel Situn still stands within its original garden (*Plate 460*). Recent research by ISMEO (Istituto Italiano per il Medio ed Estremo Oriente) suggests that Shah Abbas may have laid out the garden as early as 1590 but built only the western portion of the edifice, which consists of *iwans* facing east and west flanked by small chambers in two stories and leading to the great triple-domed reception hall of about 79 by 36 feet. Rising the full height of the building, its vaulting, between heavy transverse arches, recalls the system adapted by the Ilkhanids and the Timurids. There may already have been *talars in antis* north and south of this block. According to a recently found inscription, Shah Abbas II (1642–67) added the two-story blocks behind the great eastern *talar* and the porch itself in 1647 (*Plate 461*). A fire during the reign of Shah Sultan Husain (1694–1729) severely damaged the building and another inscription records his repairs of 1706. At one time the entire east wall behind the *talar* was encrusted with mirrors, perhaps in the Qajar period; today only the east *iwan* of the original structure preserves these.

The name Chehel Situn ("forty columns"), poetically interpreted as alluding to the reflection in the pool of the twenty-columned east *talar*, may simply refer to many columns and not to a specific number (*chehel* in Persian can mean "forty," but also "many"). At least one pavilion at Samarkand was so named, and the term was also used in India.

No other building in Isfahan so strikingly illustrates the Persian love of bringing interior and exterior space into harmonious union by the use of water. There was a fountain in the east *iwan* before the throne and another in the east *talar*, fed by the lion bases of its adjacent columns (*Plate 462*). Pascal Coste's plan, showing the garden in 1840, records another reflecting pool west of the pavilion, linked to the eastern pool by a broad moat crossed north and south only by bridges on axis with the *talar*. Inside this perimeter was another canal (much narrower and punctuated by fountains) which, though altered, survives. In Coste's day the principal entrance was to the east on axis, but the view of 1712 shows a monumental entrance pavilion to the west. The present southern gate is modern.

The decorative scheme of Shah Abbas I's structure survives in part within the north and south *talars*. There, in the shallow niches, are found paintings in a European style (they are framed in wholly Persian arabesques, however). The painting of the vaults of the great hall and its adjoining chambers is also early. In the latter, recently cleaned wall paintings show on a large scale the style of the court miniaturist, Riza Abbasi (1575–1634), who probably designed them if he did not actually paint them. Although persons in Western dress appear, the European style of the exterior paintings is absent. Despite the fact that they record events of the reign of Shah Abbas, the enormous murals in the great hall, themselves restored more than once, probably date at the earliest from the restoration conducted under Shah Sultan

460. *Isfahan, Chehel Situn, begun 1590(?), plan*

461. *Isfahan, Chehel Situn, the east* talar
462. *Isfahan, Chehel Situn, interior of the east* talar (*nineteenth-century print*)

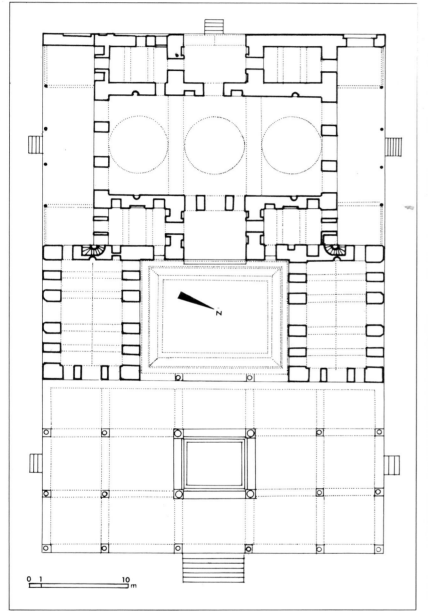

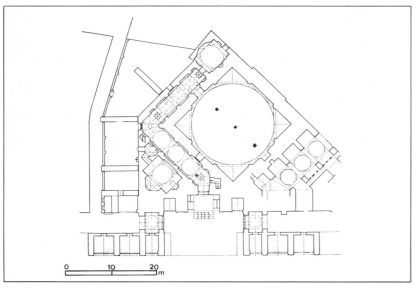

0   10   20
m

Husain, since several windows were filled in to provide space for them. The custom, however, of recording history on the walls and vaults of such royal pavilions is an early one. Timur ordered such works for at least one of his palaces in Samarkand, and Babur saw paintings recording the exploits of Abu Said (1459–69) in a pavilion at Herat, though the building itself was earlier. According to an anonymous Italian traveler, he was shown murals depicting the wars of the White Sheep ruler, Uzun Hassan (1453–78), in the dome of a pavilion at Tabriz.

What part ceramic played in the ornament of the Chehel Situn is uncertain, though, as at the Ali Kapu, the spandrels of the arches of the west facade are picked out in tile mosaic against the exposed buff brick. A number of large *cuerda seca* or *haft aurang* tile panels survive, one in the Victoria and Albert Museum in London, others in the Metropolitan Museum of Art in New York, and fragments elsewhere —all of which traditionally are said to come from the Chehel Situn. Their figural subjects are identical in style and content to the paintings in the manner of the aforementioned Riza Abbasi, but they are much more mechanical, even repeating the same figure in various colors. They might have comprised dadoes in the main pavilion or come from one of the destroyed gate houses.

THE MOSQUES AT ISFAHAN
The Mosque of Shaykh Lutfullah

According to an inscription, the portal on the Meidan opposite the Ali Kapu received its tile mosaic (*Plate 463*) in 1602–3, suggesting that the construction probably begun soon after 1598 was already well advanced. An inscription near the *mihrab* names the architect Muhammad Riza ibn Ustad Husain of Isfahan and is dated 1618. Soon after 1937 the tile revetment surrounding the *iwan*-portal was renewed, but it at least respects the articulation of the original. The mosque was once called the Masjid-i-Sadr or the Masjid-i-Fath Allah, but is now known by the name of Shaykh Lutfullah, the father-in-law of Shah Abbas. It was reserved for the private worship of the Shah, which may explain the absence of a minaret and the unusual plan (*Plate 464*).

The *iwan*-portal, with a superb *muqarnas* semidome in mosaic, is approached from a court which opens into the continuous corridor surrounding the Meidan. From the portal another corridor leads around to a principal portal on axis with the *qibla* orientation, quite other than that of the Meidan. Through this and under a balcony, probably reserved for the Shah, one enters the breathtaking 205-square-foot prayer hall, the ultimate refinement of the Seljuk *mosquée kiosque*. This is articulated by eight arches defined by bold corkscrew

◁ *466. Isfahan, Mosque of Shaykh Lutfullah, dome*

467. Isfahan, Masjid-i-Shah, portal overlooking the Meidan, 1611–16
468. Isfahan, Masjid-i-Shah, detail of portal, with minarets

moldings in turquoise, within which are inscription bands in white on cobalt blue. Four simple squinches rise from floor level (*Plate 465*), and from the octagon thus produced rises the magnificent single-shell dome on its windowed drum. The dado and the side wall panels are of painted tiles, but the corner squinches are of brilliant mosaic quatre-foil patterns. The dome centers upon a colossal golden star from which descend lozenge-shaped fields outlined in mat-surfaced buff bricks, a welcome relief after so much color. The light is filtered through double grilles of glazed arabesques, predominantly blue, which diffuse and color it at the same time (*Plate 466*).

Painted tiles were too fragile for the exteriors of domes and so were never used for this purpose. Instead narrow enameled bricks 2 to 3 1/3 inches thick were combined with molded and glazed ter-racotta elements to form vast arabesques, here in blue and white over a *café-au-lait* ground. Both here and in the blue dome of the Masjid-i-Shah the surface is in effect dematerialized; it is as insubstantial as a soap bubble and as changeable as the surface of the sea. In the Mosque of Shaykh Lutfullah polychromy achieves what stone relief in Mamluk Egypt or ribbing in the Timurid period was intended to do.

The Masjid-i-Shah

In the spring of 1611 Shah Abbas I began his new congregational mosque under the direction of the architect Ustad (Master) Abu'l Qasim. The latter is said to have absented himself for two years when the walls were about to receive the vaults to allow the building to settle onto its foundations. This occurred during the lifetime of Shah Abbas, but the mosque seems not to have been entirely completed until 1638.

The portal on the Meidan (*Plate 467*)—completed, according to its inscription, in 1616—faces north and is usually in shadow, but since it is entirely encrusted in brilliant tile mosaic it gleams with a predominantly blue light of remarkable intensity. It is deeply recessed to allow free passage for the tunnel around the Meidan. A domed vestibule and double passage beyond effect the necessary reorientation toward the southwest (*Plate 469*).

The plan, as Arthur Upham Pope has said, culminates nearly a thousand years of evolution of the four-*iwan* mosque, the immediate predecessor being that of Gawhar Shad at Mashad. In the refinement of the relationships of its truly enormous parts (the outer portal alone is 90 feet tall), the Masjid-i-Shah far surpasses its model. The rhythm with which the great voids of portal and *iwans* culminate in the vast double-domed sanctuary is apparent in Coste's fine sections, even if in detail they may be somewhat unreliable (*Plate 470*). The vast halls of the Gawhar Shad mosque flanking the sanctuary are here replaced by

469. *Isfahan, Masjid-i-Shah, 1611–38, plan*
470. *Isfahan, Masjid-i-Shah, section*
471. *Isfahan, Masjid-i-Shah, southeastern "winter mosque," interior* ▷

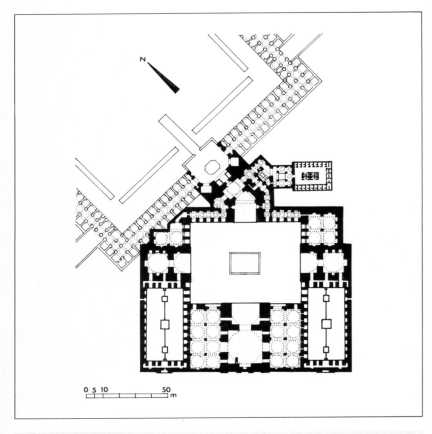

0 5 10   50 m

472. *Mashad (vicinity), Tomb of Khwaja Rabi, 1617–22, plan*

473. *Mashad (vicinity), Tomb of Khwaja Rabi, exterior*

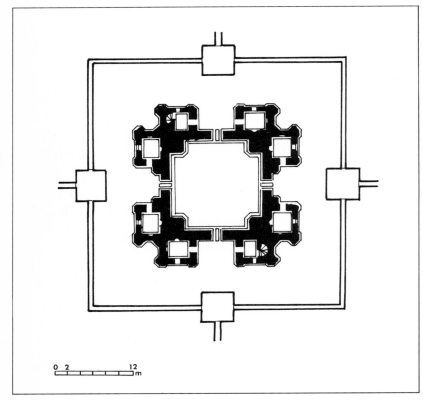

two rectangular chambers united with the sanctuary by generous openings whose domical vaults rest upon arches of great width springing from stone piers (*Plate 471*). These correspond to the cross-vaulted chambers flanking the sanctuary at Yazd and served as winter mosques. No doubt the congregation in the summer gathered more often in the spacious *sahn*, where the covered chambers are expressed by single high arches breaking the rhythm of the two-story *riwaqs*; the prayer hall facade thus repeats the tripartite motif Islam seems to have inherited from the Romans via the Sassanians. Left and right of the closed halls are open garden courts with pools and fountains surrounded by one-story arcades. They probably served for religious instruction, but could hardly have been true colleges since there is no provision for students' quarters.

Above a continuous marble dado every visible square inch of this amazing building is encrusted in square painted tiles. They are not as brilliant as the mosaic tile of the Meidan portal, but they still surround the visitor in an aura of misty blue. If the goal of Islamic architectural ornament is the dissolution of the solid mass, it reaches perfection here.

The Tomb of Khwaja Rabi near Mashad

Unlike their Sunni Orthodox predecessors, the Safavid shahs did not build royal tombs. They were buried instead at Ardabil, the family seat, or in the great Shi'ite shrines at Qum or Mashad. On occasion they ordered the rebuilding of the shrines of prominent religious figures. One such was Khwaja Rabi, one of the earliest Shi'ite saints, who had been a companion of Ali. In 1617 Shah Abbas I ordered his tomb in a garden north of Mashad rebuilt; the work was finished in 1622.

The structure is surrounded by a water channel and by fountains, thus resembling a palace pavilion. The plan (*Plate 472*) is that of a domed cruciform chamber buttressed at the corners by two stories of small square rooms and open niches which do not communicate with the interior (*Plate 473*). Four deep *iwans* lead into the central chamber, of which at least one is subdivided by a bridge-like structure (perhaps to permit passage between the upper chambers). Above the main block, rather abruptly, the once slightly bulbous dome rises on a high blind drum. Inside (*Plate 474*), the richly tiled and painted chamber, lighted only by windows above the portals, rises up through a complex system of twelve squinches and net vaults to the low inner dome.

The design, in general, is a continuation of Timurid tradition, perhaps stronger in this northeastern city than in Isfahan. Pope suggested that this building type, a variant of the Hasht Behisht discussed next, influenced the architect of the Taj Mahal, but it is much

474. *Mashad (vicinity), Tomb of Khwaja Rabi, interior view of the dome*

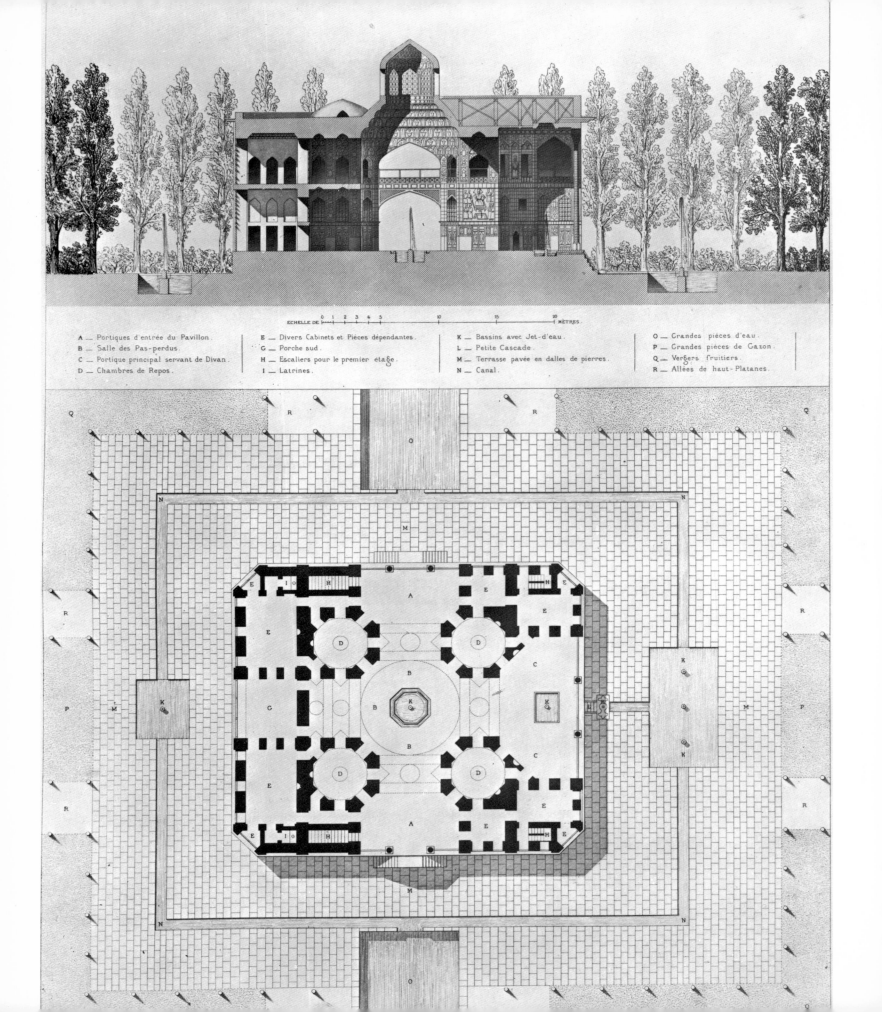

A — Portiques d'entrée du Pavillon.
B — Salle des Pas-perdus.
C — Portique principal servant de Divan.
D — Chambres de Repos.

E — Divers Cabinets et Pièces dépendantes.
G — Porche sud.
H — Escaliers pour le premier étage.
I — Latrines.

K — Bassins avec Jet-d'eau.
L — Petite Cascade.
M — Terrasse pavée en dalles de pierres.
N — Canal.

O — Grandes pièces d'eau.
P — Grandes pièces de Gazon.
Q — Vergers fruitiers.
R — Allées de haut-Platanes.

ECHELLE DE | 0 1 2 3 4 5 | 10 | 15 | 20 | MÈTRES.

more probable that the Indian monument draws directly upon a Timurid tradition and is only paralleled here.

LATER SAFAVID ARCHITECTURE

The Pavilion of the Hasht Behisht at Isfahan

In 1669–70, during the reign of Shah Suleiman (1666–94), the garden house called the Hasht Behisht or Eight Paradises was incorporated into the Bagh-i-Bulbul or Garden of the Nightingales, which had been laid out under Shah Abbas along the east side of the Chahr Bagh just south of the royal palaces. When Pascal Coste recorded the building in 1840 it was almost intact, but since then it has been sadly mutilated. It is presently under restoration, but Coste's views give a better idea of it than do any presently available photographs.

In plan (*Plate 475*) the Hasht Behisht is almost radially symmetrical and the inner core, perhaps once freestanding, is perfectly so. This consists of four octagonal chambers surmounted by four more (the Eight Paradises) surrounding a domed octagon with a lantern ascending to the full height of the building. On the south, east, and west, bridges connect the upper chambers. Beyond the inner core, on all four sides, square or rectangular chambers and stairs deepen the east, north, and west *iwans* as well as the original south *iwan*, now closed. The three remaining *iwans* have flat roofs supported by pairs of wooden columns which once had *muqarnas* capitals. The unencumbered north arch once commanded the longest axis of the now vanished garden, punctuated by pools and terminating in a monumental entrance. In Coste's time a slanting watershed in a form called a *selsebil* led down to the garden from the north *iwan*, but there were no stairs. As at the Chehel Situn, a narrow water channel dotted with fountains surrounded the building, draining into rectangular reflecting pools east and west. Nothing of these waterworks survives today. Coste's view of the central chamber looking northeast (*Plate 476*) shows that changes had already occurred with the insertion of a large painting of the court of Fatih-Ali-Shah (1797–1834) on the north pier of the eastern arch. Only the large *muqarnas* of the dome retains its original lacquer ornament in gold, red, and blue and the lantern its mirror mosaic, seen by Chardin and hence securely dating from the seventeenth century.

Since the form termed *hasht behisht* is of considerable importance in later Islamic architecture, its origins are of interest. We have already mentioned the pavilion of Uzun Hassan, built after 1468 in Tabriz and visited about 1507 by the anonymous Italian who called it an Asti Bisti, obviously a corruption of *hasht behisht*. His description is unclear, but the building in its essential layout must have been a grander version of the Isfahan structure. Babur was entertained

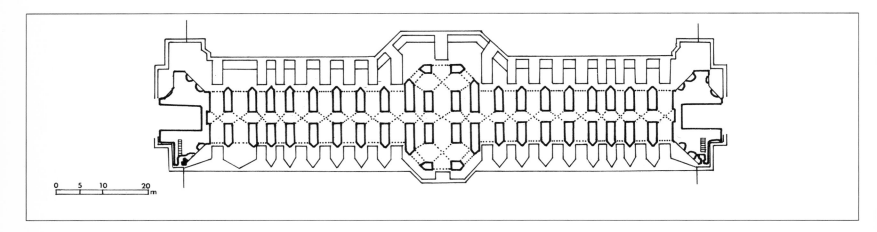

in a similar structure at Herat which he called the Tareb Khana or House of Joy; it had been built by Babur Mirza, presumably Abul Qazim Babur (1452–57) who briefly ruled Herat. After his conquest of India, Babur ordered a *hasht behisht* built of wood. The form, which reached its most monumental expression in the imperial Moghul tombs, seems clearly to have been of Timurid origin, from which both Safavids and Moghuls inherited it. It is probably much earlier than the Timurids, but only excavation may someday reveal this.

The Pol-i-Khaju at Isfahan

Works of an engineering rather than an architectural significance have seldom been treated in this volume, but the bridges of Isfahan are of such importance as civic architecture that it is essential they be discussed. The Pol-i-Khaju, downstream or east of that of Allahaverdi Khan, was ordered built by Shah Abbas II in 1650 to replace an earlier span of which no trace remains. It was once linked to the new civic center by a lane beginning at the southeast corner of the Meidan, part of it a covered bazaar. Like the earlier bridge, separate and very narrow pedestrian ways border the wider central passage at street level. Their arches are hardly above head height, probably to discourage use by equestrians. From them the view of the river in both directions can be enjoyed through wide barrel-vaulted niches (*Plate 477*). On both sides pentagonal structures at mid-stream are pierced with alternately polygonal and square *iwans*. Unlike Allahaverdi Khan's bridge, the Pol-i-Khaju was also a dam and from the stepped buttresses of the downstream side (*Plate 478*), a favorite summer promenade after dark, access is gained to a vaulted gallery. Cooled by the flow beneath, it was certainly then as now a welcome relief from the noonday heat. Since the columned streets of the eastern Roman colonies there can hardly have been built anywhere a structure designed with such concern for public comfort.

Islamic pietism, whether Shi'ite or Sunni, encourages the provision of such public services, as did Christian piety in medieval Europe. In Islam these were always built at the instigation of an individual donor for his personal salvation. It is quite possible Shah Abbas II was well aware that the experience provided by the bridge—particularly in its lower gallery, was a quasi-religious one, in which the Koranic joys of Paradise, with pavilions beneath which rivers flow, were prefigured on earth.

Conclusion

The relatively brief period in which Safavid architecture flourished contributed little that was new to Persian Islamic architecture, but it is of importance for two reasons. At this time the *mosquée kiosque* and the four-*iwan* mosque achieved their final refinement, after which no new ideas appeared and a decline in the execution of the old soon became apparent. Secondly, only from this period do palace pavilions such as the Ali Kapu, the Chehel Situn, and the Hasht Behisht survive in fair condition. Used with circumspection, these afford a valuable insight into the vanished splendors of Timurid, Ilkhanid, and even perhaps Seljuk palaces and gardens, of which only imperfect descriptions remain.

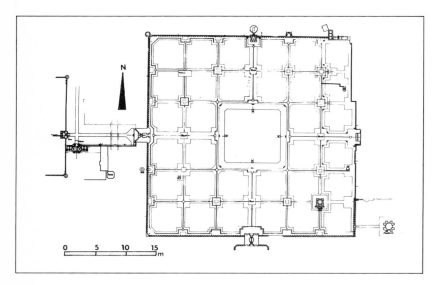

ARCHITECTURE UNDER BABUR AND HUMAYUN

Zahir al-Din Babur (1526–30), the first Moghul emperor, was a fifth-generation descendant of Timur on his father's side and, more remotely, of Chingiz Khan on his mother's. He was thus by descent and training a Chagatai Turk, in which dialect he wrote his famous diary; however, like most Timurids, he was also well acquainted with Persian traditions. After 1494, when he fell heir to the small principality of Ferghana, Babur's first ambition was to restore the Timurid Empire by regaining Samarkand from the Uzbeks. Three times, the last in 1512, he took the city but could not hold it. Only then did he turn to India, whose conquest he began from his capital at Kabul. The battle of Panipat (1526) was followed by that of Kanwa, in which the Hindu Rajputs were defeated and the foundations of the empire established.

The few years left to Babur gave him time neither for organizing the new empire nor for patronizing architecture, though his diary shows he took an unusual interest in the latter. Only the Rambagh in Agra, close to the east bank of the Jumna River, survives of the many gardens he commanded built. Its form, much rebuilt, is that of a Persian *chahr bagh*. Babur's diary also mentions a residence, built probably of wood and referred to by him as a *hasht behisht* (a form explained in the previous chapter which he may have introduced to India).

Nasir al-Din Humayun (1530–40 and 1555–56), Babur's unfortunate son, was able neither to hold nor to administer the lands his father had won, and no monuments survive of the decade before his exile. We do, however, have literary evidence for a curious floating palace built on the Jumna in 1532. Khondamir, the poet, describes four barges each with a *chahr taq* or two-story pavilion arranged in such a way as to leave between them an octagonal reservoir. He then says "from the connection of these four rooms the eight heavens were formed." It seems we have here another *hasht behisht*. In 1533, in a meeting held at the Fortress of Gwalior, Humayun made plans for his new capital at Delhi—to be called Dinpanah. At this site his tomb was later to rise. During his exile, Humayun visited Shah Tahmasp in Qazvin and Isfahan and also spent some time in Tabriz and Herat, where he is known to have taken as much interest as Babur in palaces, mosques, and tombs. Humayun finally returned to Delhi after the collapse of the Suri usurpation in 1555, only to die in an accidental fall the following year.

The Tomb of Humayun at Delhi

The tomb of Humayun was begun in 1560–61 by his widow, Sahibah Begum, his companion in exile, and so belongs to the following reign,

479. *Delhi, Tomb of Humayun, begun 1560/61, plan*
480. *Delhi, Tomb of Humayun, section*

but Akbar, only sixteen when it was begun, is unlikely, as he did in so many later buildings, to have had much influence in its design. The architect is said by Percy Brown to have been a certain Mirak Mirza Ghiyas. Babur's diary records a Mirek Mir Ghiyas at work for him on buildings in Agra and Dhulpur in 1529. If this is the same man, he might also have served Humayun on the floating Hasht Behisht and on plans for Dinpanah. Even if the later architect is the son of the earlier, it implies training in India and a Timurid rather than Safavid background.

The tomb proper stands in a great *chahr bagh* (*Plate 479*) about 437 square yards. Each major square is divided by means of canals and fountains into nine lesser squares. The tomb occupies a niched plinth about 990 square feet, deeply penetrated by rows of vaulted chambers so dark they could only have served as crypts. The structure itself, about 592 square feet, equals in area one of the minor squares of the garden. The principal gate of the enclosure lies to the west, leaving no provision for a mosque. On axis with the gate and across an interior stairway one sees the cenotaph building, entered through a vast *iwan*. An equally monumental southern entrance leads directly to the crypt through a tunnel in the plinth (*Plate 480*); or the platform may be ascended, in which case the visitor enters not an *iwan* but a tripartite two-storied hall—a *mian saray*—though it has no direct access to the crypt (*Plate 481*).

The cenotaph building is formed by the fusion of four two-storied octagonal pavilions or *chahr taqs*, exactly as Khondamir described, which here surround a likewise octagonal cenotaph chamber of two stories with a low inner dome under a high bulbous outer dome, almost certainly of corbeled construction. Broad corridors link the *mian saray* with the three *iwans*, allowing circumambulation. Humayun was destined to receive the honors due a saint, and the belief in divine kingship adapted by the later Moghuls was not far off. In fact, the form of a *hasht behisht*, implying that the deceased now dwelled in Paradise, reinforces this conclusion.

In its severely simple marble and sandstone casing, almost wholly without sculpture, as in the *chatris* with their bracketed supports, Humayun's tomb follows the tradition of the Lodi and Suri dynasties. The eight large and sixteen smaller spires—almost like miniature minarets, accenting the angles of each facade—have smaller antecedents in the mosque of Sher Shah Sur in his citadel, the Purana Qila, and in the tomb and mosque of Isa Khan. Their only equivalent in Persia might be the eight minarets of the tomb of Oljeitu at Sultanieh.

THE REIGN OF AKBAR

Jalal al-Din Akbar (1556–1605) began his long reign at the age of

twelve. The first buildings erected under his auspices were at Agra, where the Delhi Gate of the Fortress survives (1564–66); the outer bastion, flanked by heavy octagonal towers, makes extensive use of arcuate forms for articulation and for the *iwans* above. These are all enclosed in richly carved moldings continued on the inner gate, which revives motifs of the Khalji Dynasty and uses much marble. There are *jharokas* and *chatris*, but Islamic motifs dominate. Apparently the young Akbar was willing to spend more on this project than on his father's tomb, but he was influenced by the style of the latter.

The Palace-Fortress of Akbar at Ajmer

Akbar came early under the influence of the teachings of the great Sufi Shaykh, Muin al-Din Chisti, who taught at Ajmer and is buried there. Muin al-Din's tolerance for (and even interest in) Hinduism must have appealed to Akbar, whose visits to Ajmer became so frequent that in 1570–72 he built a small palace-fortress there.

The rectangular court of about 230 by 180 feet has octagonal corner towers about 75 feet in diameter (*Plate 483*). The plan, though its details recall the fortifications of the 1560s at Agra, is remarkably like the Château of Chambord of 1519–47 or the now vanished Nonsuch begun for Henry VIII in 1538. As contacts with Europeans were nonexistent until the 1580s, however, there seems no way in which plans could have been transmitted. A double gate with an inner court is the sole entrance. Although *jharokas* and *chatris* provide a Hindu element, the general feeling is arcuate. The window of appearances surmounting the portal suggests a *diwan-i-am* or public audience hall, and it is indeed known that Akbar held such audiences here. Numerous chambers for a sizeable retinue surround the court. In the center is a *baradari* (*Plate 482*) with two-story corner rooms, four-columned *iwans*, and a central audience hall. The building is trabeate and bracketed, but the organization is like that of a *hasht behisht*.

Fatipur Sikri

Akbar's devotion to Muin al-Din's teachings predisposed him to tolerance of Hinduism; to this was added the influence of his Rajput wives, given freedom to follow their own customs. By degrees he moved further and further from Sunni Orthodoxy. In 1579, from the *minbar* of Fatipur, Akbar declared himself infallible in matters of religion and three years later, scandalizing the *Ulema*, he proclaimed a new religion, the Din Illahi, a blend of ideas from Islam, Hinduism, the Jain faith, Zoroastrianism, and even Christianity, with a considerable emphasis on sun worship. He himself was to be God's vice-regent on earth and the sole exponent of His will. Possibly Akbar

482. *Ajmer, Palace-Fortress of Akbar, 1570–72, baradari*
483. *Ajmer, Palace-Fortress of Akbar, plan*

484. *Fatipur Sikri, palace, 1570–c. 1580, plan*

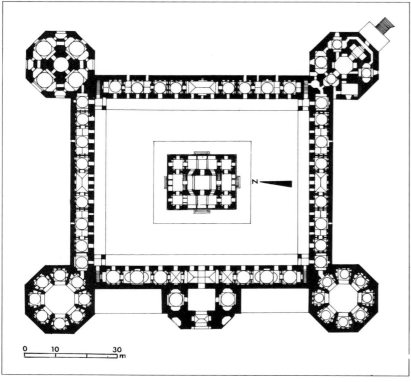

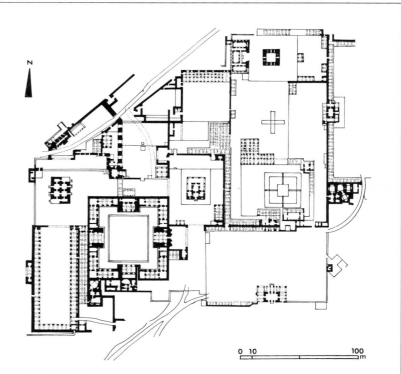

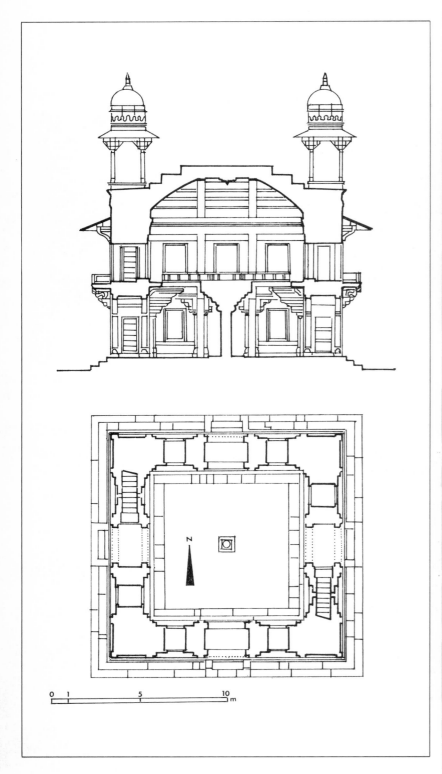

had begun to think of himself as a *cakravartin* or world ruler in the traditional Indian sense. Benjamin Rowland says of this idea that it embodied "the ancient Babylonian and also Vedic concept of the Lord of the four quarters, designated in early Indian texts as *cakravartin*, whom the celestial wheel (the sun) guides to dominion over all regions."

It is against this background that the astonishing buildings of Akbar should be assessed. Sikri, about 26 miles west of Agra, was the abode of a venerated mystic, Salim Chisti, who in 1568 had predicted the birth of a son to Akbar. In August of the next year Maryam al-Zamani, his Rajput wife, gave birth at Sikri to Prince Salim, later the Emperor Jahangir. Akbar then vowed to build a city there, renamed Fatipur Sikri after the victory over Gujerat in 1573. The site is a sandstone ridge running northeast-southwest, bounded on the north by an artificial lake now drained. Indeed, it was probably the inadequate water supply which forced the abandonment of Fatipur for Lahore in the early 1580s. Because of the necessary orientation of the mosque (Akbar never abandoned the *qibla* despite his heresies) most of the buildings are sited diagonally with respect to the ridge (*Plate 484*). The visitor entered from the northeast through the Agra Gate and then through the Naubat Khana where, were he important, his arrival would be announced by drums and trumpets. This was an ancient Turkish custom practiced by the Safavids and Ottomans as well as the Timurids. Once welcomed he might enter from the east the great court of the Diwan-i-Am or public audience hall.

The Diwan-i-Am is a severely simple trabeate structure of red sandstone with a five-bayed pavilion projecting from the west range like a royal loge. Few persons other than the emperor could have had much shade, but awnings may have been used (a miniature shows that they were at Lahore before Shah Jehan added the columned hall there). A small door behind the loge led to the Mahal-i-Khas or private palace (*Plate 486*). This complex centers around a square pool with four bridges leading to an island in the center, immediately north of the *khwabqah* or private apartments of the Emperor. Akbar, seated on the island, would have presided over a quadripartite, radially symmetrical space even in the relative relaxation of his private abode.

In the Diwan-i-Khas or private audience hall (*Plate 485*) the Emperor's central position was even more pronounced. A square, radially symmetrical pavilion contains a central column terminating in a great burst of the curvilinear brackets favored in Gujerat (*Plate 487*). This supports a circular platform with railings of *jali* or pierced stone screens. Four bridges connect this with the four corners of the room, where they meet a surrounding passage continuous with an

491. *Agra, Jahangiri Mahal (Red Palace), east facade*
492. *Agra, Jahangiri Mahal (Red Palace), east facade, detail*

exterior balcony supported on more brackets (*Plate 488*). Akbar probably entered the building from the west (on axis with his study), ascended the stair to his left, and crossed the northwest bridge to the throne. There he must have reposed, very much "the Lord of the four quarters." The suggestion that this structure is the Ibadat Khana or the hall in which the religious discussions resulting in the Din Illahi took place is no longer accepted. Nevertheless, the remarkable arrangement certainly reflects Akbar's conception of himself in relation to the new religion and to the empire.

West of the Emperor's private apartments lies the *zenana* or harem. Within it Jodh Bhai's palace, built for another Rajput queen, with its open *tibaris* and closed domed chambers recalls the Hauz-i-Khas of Firuz Shah, but it is cross axial and the four projecting pavilions recall classic four-*iwan* courts. The Panch Mahal (*Plate 489*) at the northeast corner of the harem enclosure is a five-storied *baradari*. From its terraces, once enclosed by *jali* screens, the ladies would have had the best view possible of all the activities of the palace.

Craftsmen from Gujerat as well as Malwa were certainly available after 1573 and, particularly in the *zenana* area, the buildings show a very strong, if not dominant, Hindu influence. However, the abundant low-relief sculptured ornament has a more diverse origin: Islamic geometric motifs dominate the *jali* screens, while the floral motifs and vine scrolls recall the brocades and carpets imported from Safavid Persia.

The Jahangiri Mahal at Agra

If the Jahangiri Mahal or Red Palace in the Fort at Agra was built as a residence for Prince Salim it could hardly have been begun much before he was sixteen, in 1585. The imposing west facade (*Plate 490*) recalls the Palace at Ajmer, but the entrance is deeply recessed, constituting a true *iwan*; the corner towers with their *chatris* are no longer used for military purposes. The long bracketed gallery, once probably entirely enclosed in *jali* screens, must have served the ladies of the harem, whose apartments are behind it, as a promenade. Here and on the east facade overlooking the Jumna (*Plate 491*), the contrast between white marble and red sandstone is once again exploited. The ornament is very rich and intricate, with motifs derived from the style of the Khalji Dynasty (*Plate 492*) and the earlier Delhi Gate at Agra.

The principal court (*Plate 493*) and the two great halls flanking it return to the pure Gujerat forms of Fatipur Sikri, entirely abandoning marble inlay. Opulently curved and intricately turned brackets seem very close to their Hindu wooden prototypes. A close examina-

373

493. *Agra, Jahangiri Mahal (Red Palace), central court*
494. *Agra, Jahangiri Mahal (Red Palace), plan*
495. *Sikandra, Tomb of Akbar, c. 1605–c. 1615, south facade*

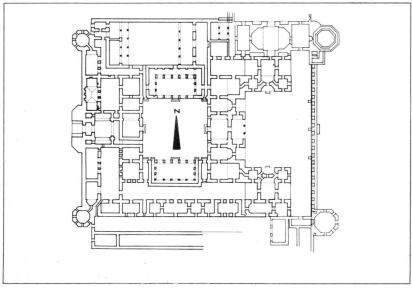

tion of the structure might show that the west and east facades are indeed later in date than most of the interior.

The plan (*Plate 494*) shows several reconstructions but was once probably bilaterally symmetrical. If the north half once echoed the surviving south half there would then have existed an isolated central core surrounded by service areas, as at Ukhaidir. Furthermore, the two pavilions flanking the eastern court recall similar *iwan* pavilions at Lashkari Bazar, where they overlooked the Helwan River. Apparently—despite the strong Hindu influence and adjustments to a very different climate—a very old tradition of Islamic palace architecture has here been revived.

THE REIGN OF JAHANGIR

Prince Salim came to the throne as Nur al-Din Jahangir (1605–27), his first task being the completion of his father's tomb. The Din Illahi did not survive Akbar and, although Jahangir could hardly have been called pious or orthodox, the authority of the *Ulema* was no longer threatened.

The Tomb of Akbar at Sikandra

It is impossible to say how much influence, if any, Akbar's own taste had upon the design of his tomb in the ancient city of Iskander Lodi, near Agra. Jahangir tells us that on first visiting the site in 1608 (construction had begun three or four years before) he found that "the masons had made it one story after their own manner." He ordered much demolished and rebuilt at that time. According to an inscription on the south (and only) gate of the 837-square-yard *chahr bagh*, that structure was completed by 1613. At the corners rise four white marble minarets, the first to be used for an imperial tomb in India (*Plate 496*) and probably there by order of Jahangir. The gate bears many inscriptions in Persian, written by Abdul Haq, son of Qazim Shirazi, who was later to design many for the Taj Mahal. Among them is the following:

Hail, blessed space happier than the garden
 of paradise!
Hail, lofty building higher than the divine throne!
A paradise, the garden of which has thousands
 of Rizwans as its servants,
The garden of which has thousands of paradises
 for its land.
The pen of the mason of the divine decree
 has written on its court:

497. *Gwalior, Tomb of Shaykh Muhammad Ghaus, 1563–64 or later*

498. *Sikandra, Tomb of Akbar, plan*

499. *Agra, Tomb of the Ittimad al-Daula, 1622–28, plan*

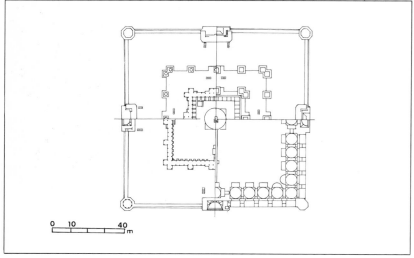

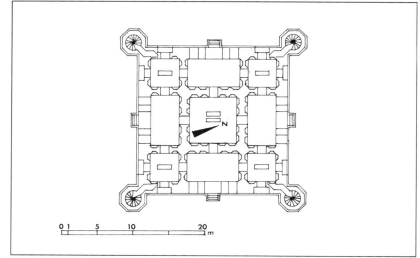

These are the gardens of Eden, enter them
  to live forever.*

There could be no clearer indication that the garden and the tomb
were metaphors for Paradise.

The plinth of the tomb proper, about 1,109 square feet, seems
modeled after the nearby *baradari* of Iskander Lodi, although it is
much larger. It has the same octagonal corner *chatris* and the same
pavilions over the four portals. The next three tiers are of trabeate
construction and suggest the *baradari* of Firuz Shah at Delhi or the
Panch Mahal at Fatipur Sikri (*Plate 495*). Finally, the uppermost
marble-screened terrace is reminiscent of the tomb of the sainted
Shaykh Muhammad Ghaus of Gwalior, dating from 1563–64 or
somewhat later (*Plate 497*). The Gwalior tomb has a dome, and it is
unlikely that Akbar's cenotaph would have been unprotected. There
is an upper crypt (*Plate 498*) just beneath the final terrace which,
although only about 22 feet high, has a cenotaph and a south entrance.
Its sixteen heavy piers suggest that it supported, or was intended to
support, a nine-part structure of the *hasht behisht* type. One of the
thirty-six distichs in praise of Akbar surrounding the uppermost
cenotaph reads (Smith, *op. cit.*, p. 31.):

Before he was a king of the seven climes;
He has now subjugated the eight paradises.

A new type of ornament is introduced in the *pishtaqs* of the
plinth and the south gate. Here the red sandstone is almost obscured
by inlays in what amounts to a *pietra dura* technique of white, gray,
and black marble. The patterns are nearly all rectilinear interlaces of
great variety, but on the gate there are broad bands of a rather
stylized floral motif on a very large scale, perhaps an innovation of
Jahangir.

The Tomb of the Ittimad al-Daula at Agra

At his accession Jahangir had promoted to high rank an official of
Akbar's, Mirza Ghiyas Beg—better known by his title of the Ittimad
al-Daula or Minister of Finance. He was a Persian who had come
to India with a son, Asaf Khan, and a daughter, Mihr al-Nisa, born
in Kandahar during the journey. In 1611, after the death of her first
husband, Jahangir made Mihr al-Nisa his empress, under the name
Nur Jahan, Light of the World. She was a woman of intelligence,
artistic taste, and ruthless ambition. She not only arranged the

*Edmund W. Smith, *Akbar's Tomb, Sikandrah, Near Agra, described and illustrated.*
Archaeological Survey of India, New Imperial Series XXXV (Allahabad, 1909), pp.
34–35.

502. *Shadera, Tomb, garden, and caravanserai of Jahangir,* 1627–34,
    plan
503. *Shadera, Tomb of Jahangir, section*

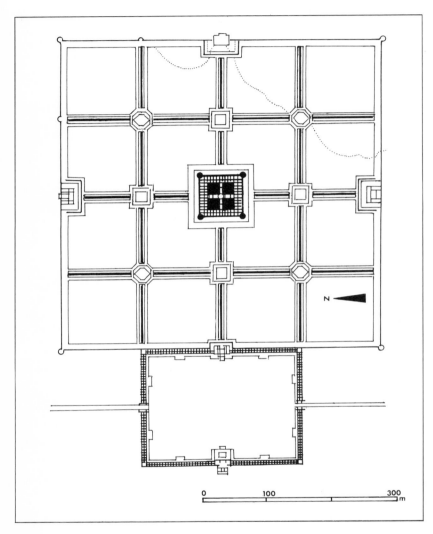

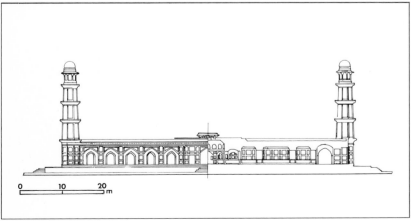

marriage of a daughter by her first husband to Prince Shahriyar, but also (in 1612) that of her niece, Arjuman Banu Begum, daughter of Asaf Khan, to Prince Khuram, later Shah Jehan.

Mirza Ghiyas Beg died in 1622. The tomb built under Nur Jahan's direction and finished by 1628 is the first structure in India in which white marble is substituted for red sandstone as the background for a new kind of polychrome *pietra dura* inlay (*Plate 500*). It stands in a *chahr bagh* bounded on the east by the Jumna River and entered from the west by a gate (*Plate 501*) which—like the enclosure walls, a guest house on the Jumna, and the plinth of the tomb proper—is of red sandstone inlaid in colored marbles. The curvilinear arabesques of the spandrels and a new motif of simulated niches filled with vessels of various shapes, some containing flowers, indicate a new influence from Persia or possibly Central Asia. Perhaps these vases and jars are containers of the wine and honey promised true believers in Paradise.

The tomb proper, which shines like a pearl in its red sandstone setting, takes the form of a nine-part *baradari* or *hasht behisht* (*Plate 499*). For the first time the *chatris* at the corners of the plinth of the tomb are raised on octagonal bases to form modest minarets.

The Tomb of Jahangir at Shadera
Jahangir's own tomb near Lahore is in a garden originally laid out during his lifetime for Nur Jahan; it is bounded on the east by the Ravi River, which has eroded away one corner. The enclosure, about 500 square yards, is entered only from the west after passing through a rectangular *caravanserai* with a mosque opposite (*Plate 502*). The garden is divided into sixteen squares, as Akbar's would have been, and the outer plinth of the tomb proper corresponds to one of them without the paths and water channels. The tomb was probably built under the direction of Nur Jahan between 1627 and 1634. The cloistered platform in red sandstone recalls that of Akbar (*Plate 503*), except that tall white marble minarets arise at the corners. Inside, four identical corridors link the crypt to the portals—a symmetry perhaps inspired by the *baradari* of Iskander Lodi, where Jahangir's mother had been buried in 1623. Once a white marble pavilion stood on the platform over the cenotaph, probably very like that of the tomb of the Ittimad al-Daula at Agra.

THE REIGN OF SHAH JEHAN
Shihab al-Din Shah Jehan (1628–58), born Prince Khuram in 1592 at Lahore, seems to have been a more conventional Muslim than his grandfather or his father, though never so fanatical as his son Aurangzeb was to become. Despite a well-earned reputation for ruthlessness and cruelty, his redeeming feature was his great love for his wife,

504. *Agra, Taj Mahal, 1631–48, plan of the mausoleum, garden, and* caravanserai

506. *Agra, Taj Mahal, mausoleum, plan and section*

505. *Agra, Taj Mahal, view across the Jumna River*

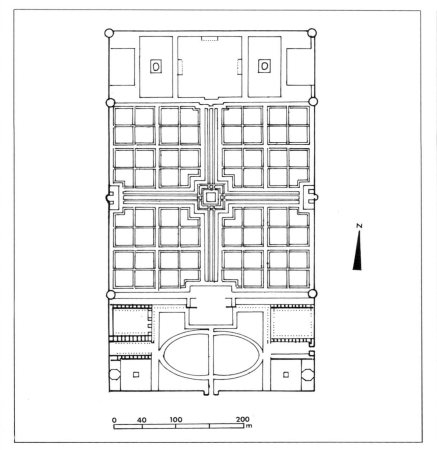

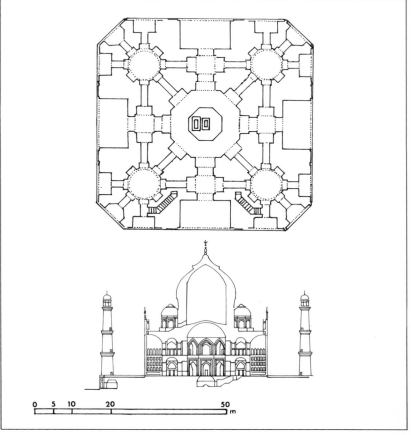

Arjuman Banu Begum, later given the title Mumtaz Mahal or Light of the Palace. On her death in 1631, he began his greatest work and one of the most famous buildings of all time in her honor—the Taj Mahal.

The Taj Mahal at Agra

Certain prior interests of the Emperor probably affected the design. In 1607 (as Prince Khuram) he was in Kabul, where he gave directions for new buildings in the garden where Babur is buried. One of these may be the graceful marble mosque with its cusped arches so like his later works. In 1619–20 he was again involved with architecture when he directed the laying out of gardens in Kashmir for his father. These took the form of *chahr baghs* not unlike that of the Taj Mahal. Shah Jehan also had a lively interest in his Timurid ancestry. He is known to have made a lavish donation to the maintenance of the Gur-i-Amir. Numerous portraits of Timur date from his reign, and one of the titles he assumed was Sahib-i-Qiran, Lord of the Happy Union (between Jupiter and Venus), a title held by Timur. The erection of such a lavish monument in honor of a woman is in itself a Turkish or Central Asian custom rather than Persian or Indian.

The Taj Mahal or crown of the palace, another title of Mumtaz Mahal, stands outside the north boundary of a *chahr bagh* about 359 square yards (*Plate 504*). From the Jumna the tomb and its platform rise in snowy white contrast to the red sandstone retaining wall on the river and to two matching triple-domed structures—to the east a guest house and to the west a mosque (*Plate 505*), a contrast first established by the tomb of the Ittimad al-Daula. The whole project was to have been linked by a bridge over the river to a matching tomb in black marble for Shah Jehan himself. This explains why the Taj and its *chahr bagh* are separated. Unlike those of his three predecessors, which could have served as *caravanserais*, the plinth of Shah Jehan's structure is solid, but a *caravanserai*, caretakers' residences, and even a bazaar are provided outside the south portal.

The incomparable central building is in massing and articulation a refinement in every detail of the tomb of Humayun. In plan the earlier tomb had a *mian saray* to the south that was perhaps only symbolic, but this interfered with the radial symmetry. The architect of the Taj worked the *mian saray* into the total design (*Plate 506*) in such a way as to preserve the symmetry. Furthermore, the true *mian saray* behind the south facade (*Plate 507*) has stairs giving access to the crypt and lies at the end of the most important axis along the length of the garden. In elevation the four *chahr taqs* of the tomb of Humayun are brought into a more logical relationship to the dome and the *pishtaqs*, while the *chatris* (pulled in toward the dome, though still directly over the "eight paradises" below) enhance the effect of an ascending pyramid.

The great corbeled double dome swelling sharply outward from its tall drum is the closest approximation in India to that of the Gur-i-Amir, and one can forgive the vast empty space inside because of the matchless exterior proportions. Such bulbous domes are said to be Persian, but in Bijapur in 1615 much more bulbous domes than that of the Taj were built; none appeared so bulbous in Persia until the eighteenth century. R.A. Jairazbhay in his exhaustive article on the Taj compares it to the famous and semilegendary castle of Khawarnak, traditionally said to have been built for Bahram Gur (421–38) by the Lakhmid Prince Numan Imru'l. The poet Nizami says of this palace that it was "wrapped in the veil of concord with the air," that its dome was "polished like a mirror . . . a sun within and moon without," and that it took on three colors in the course of the day— blue, yellow, and white. The translucent marble of the Taj, left largely undecorated, gives it the very qualities attributed by Nizami to Khawarnak. As generations of visitors attest, the Taj is blue at dawn, white at noon, and the yellow of the sky at sunset.

In contrast to that of the tomb of the Ittimad al-Daula, the *pietra dura* throughout the Taj is very restrained. It is confined to slender, abstract polychrome arabesques in the spandrels of arches and long Koranic inscriptions in black marble forming bands around the *pishtaqs* and all the arches. Within the *iwans* the vaults are carved in low relief in the form of crystalline net vaults or shallow *muqarnas* forms.

One important element of decoration has not as yet been given the attention it deserves. A continuous dado runs both inside the building and out, with flowering plants carved in low relief. The same plants, complete to the mounds of earth from which they spring, surround the cenotaphs in *pietra dura*; outside, the surrounding structures have similar dadoes in red sandstone. In a recent article it has been suggested by R. Skelton that the motif of a complete plant first appears in a manuscript of Jahangir of c. 1620, very probably following engravings from European herbals of the early seventeenth century. Such dadoes appear first at the Taj and later in Shah Jehan's works in the forts at Agra and Delhi. Since the Islamic Paradise is a garden, what could be a more appropriate symbol than to have the tomb, in itself a Paradise, rise from a flowering field? This must have been a quite conscious innovation most likely due to Shah Jehan himself. Part of a Persian verse on the Taj written by Shah Jehan confirms the interpretation of these friezes:

Like the garden of heaven a brilliant spot,
Full of fragrance like paradise fraught with ambergris.

507. *Agra, Taj Mahal, south facade*

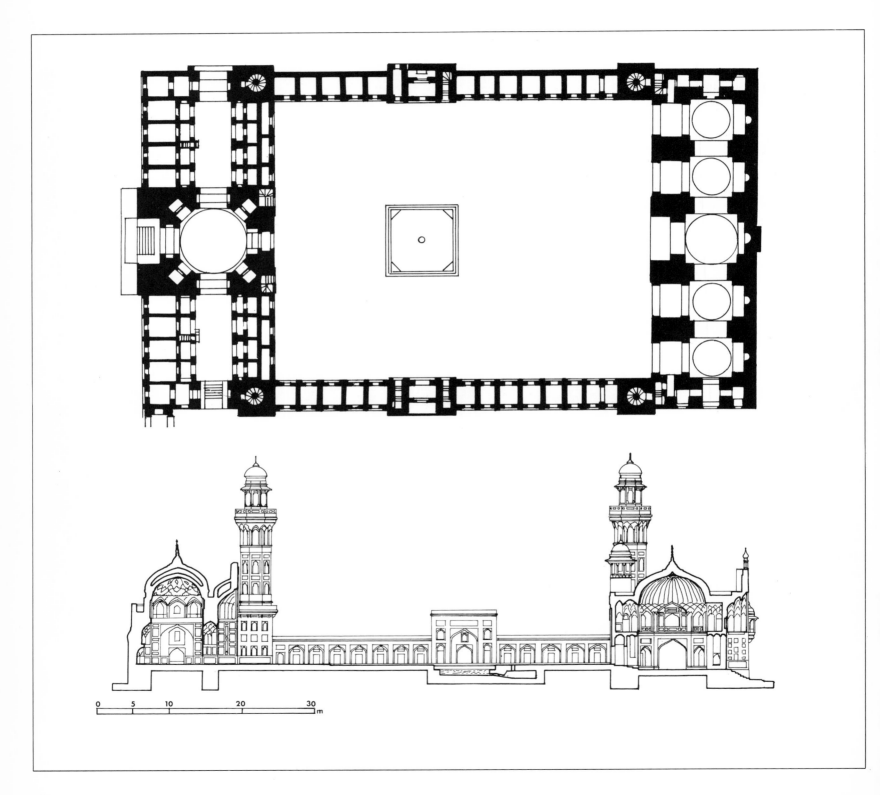

0   5   10   20   30
                            m

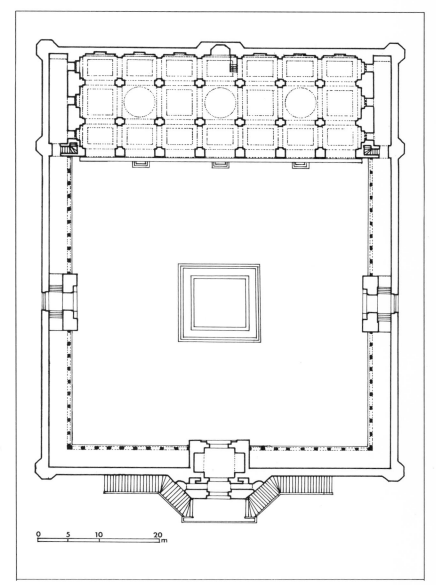

In the breadth of its court perfumes from the nose-gay
   of sweet-heart rise . . .*

The identity of the architect of the Taj Mahal is too complex for lengthy treatment here. A persistent legend of seventeenth-century origin claiming the honor for a European is now generally rejected. Three candidates, all of whom were employed on the project, seem the most credible. The first is Ustad (Master) Ahmad, whose family came from Herat. He was given the title Nadir al-Asar, and was a mathematician as well as an architect. His son, Lutfullah, also a mathematician, claimed in 1655/56 that his father had designed the Taj Mahal as well as the Fort and the Friday mosque at Delhi. The second candidate is Mir Abdul Karim, given the title Ma'mur Khan, who had worked for Jahangir at Mandu and was working on Shah Jehan's additions to the Fort at Lahore when he was called to Agra in 1631 (he died there in 1648). The third possibility is Mulla Murshid Shirazi, given the title Mukarrimat Khan, who later worked on the Delhi palaces. Probably the credit for the conception of the monument and even the general design should go to Shah Jehan himself, but he must have had expert advice.

The Mosque of Wazir Khan at Lahore
The Moghul Friday mosque with its triple-domed prayer hall, paired minarets, single-aisled *riwaqs*, and axial monumental portals differed little, save in size, from the type already established in India by earlier dynasties. This mosque at Lahore is an interesting variant of the Moghul formula both in design and material. Hakim Ali al-Din of Chiniot had served as court physician to Prince Khuram long before he ascended the throne as Shah Jehan, and it was Hakim who in 1631 had escorted the body of Mumtaz Mahal from Burhanpur, where she died, to Agra. From 1633 to 1640 he served as governor of the Punjab with his capital at Lahore, and held the title of Nawab Wazir Khan. In 1634–36 he built the mosque named for him. Unlike the buildings of his sovereign at Lahore, those of Wazir Khan employed the traditional building materials of the Punjab—brick, glazed tile, and stucco—for his new foundation. The cellular *riwaqs* suggest that the mosque functioned as a *madrasa*; east of the *sahn* provision is made for a large covered bazaar, the rental of whose stalls would have served to support professors and students (*Plate 508*).

    The four minarets relate the design to the Timurid buildings of Samarkand and Herat, all royal foundations. No rule prohibiting

*Maulvi Moin-Ud-Din Ahmad, *The Taj and Its Environments*, 2nd ed., Agra, n.d. (1907), pp. 121–22.

510. *Agra, Pearl Mosque, sahn*
511. *Delhi, Red Fort, 1638–47, restored plan*

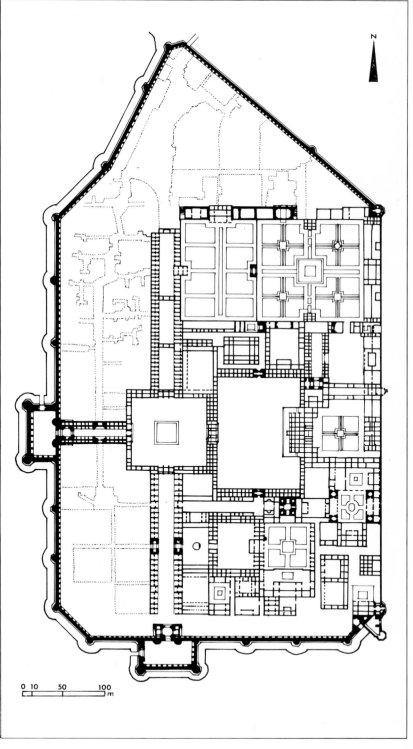

non-royal persons from building mosques with more than a single minaret seems to have operated in India.

The ornament of glazed tile mosaic is set in shallow niches paneling the walls and framed in opaque red brick with a yellow wash. Geometric patterns exist, but for the most part naturalistic bouquets in vases or freestanding plants are shown. By this time in Safavid Persia tile mosaic had almost disappeared, as had relief carving of mat-surfaced brick. Both practices existed, however, in Central Asia under the Uzbeks. As the eye ascends the tile surfaces increase at the expense of the brick until the upper parts of the minarets resemble nothing so much as immense, glistening floral bouquets.

The Pearl Mosque at Agra

The name Moti Masjid or Pearl Mosque is given to three Moghul palace-mosques at Lahore (1645), Agra (1648–55), and Delhi (1659), all of marble. Those of Lahore and Delhi are quite small, but the Agra mosque (*Plate 509*)—by far the finest—was designed for a large congregation (its *sahn* is about 517 square feet). Across the facade of the prayer hall is a long inscription which reads, in part:

> Verily it is an exalted palace of Paradise made of a
> single resplendent pearl, because, since the beginning
> of the population of this world, no mosque, pure and
> entirely of marble, has appeared as its equal, nor,
> since the creation of the universe, any place of worship,
> wholly bright and polished, has come to rival it.*

The translucent quality of the marble itself is here recognized by the builders, perhaps increasingly, as the construction of the Taj Mahal neared its end. In this case the marble is inlaid only in monochrome and that confined to the prayer-mat patterns of the floor and the inscription itself.

Within the prayer hall (*Plate 510*) and everywhere else lobate or cusped arches are used and only the increased plasticity of the "acanthus" capitals of the cruciform piers proclaim the coming "baroque" phase of Moghul architecture and its final decay. The three monumental portals suggest the classic four-*iwan* plan, but the strong distinction between the *riwaqs* and the prayer hall and the multiple *chatris* like those of Akbar's Friday mosque at Fatipur Sikri are very Indian.

*Martin Hürlimann, *Delhi Agra Fatehpur Sikri,* Atlantis Verlag, Zurich, 1964, p. 90.

The Citadel or Red Fort at Delhi

Ustad Ahmad (Nadir al-Asar), Ustad Hamid (probably not the former's brother, as has been thought), and Mulla Murshid Shirazi (Mukarrimat Khan) all began work on the new Citadel at Shah Jehanabad—the nucleus of modern Delhi—in 1638, and the Emperor took up residence there nine years later. The plan contrasts strikingly with Akbar's Fatipur Sikri. There the asymmetrical freedom reflected the tolerance of the builder for customs other than his own. Here the axial order of the vast palaces of Samarra is revived (*Plate 511*). Since enough evidence survives to reconstruct the original plan, largely the product of a single campaign, the Delhi Fort provides the best example of a Moghul palace even though Shah Jehan's works at Agra and Lahore are of higher quality. At Delhi Moghul architecture reaches its apex of magnificence, but also begins to show the "baroque" tendencies which will lead to its decline.

Volwahsen suggests that the outer walls were originally intended to form a rectangle with chamfered corners, the northern angle having been later enlarged. Within this rectangle an almost rigid symmetry prevailed. The major east-west axis began at the Lahore Gate with a bazaar leading to a square court before the Naubat Khana, where there was a juncture with a north-south axis, also lined with bazaar stalls beginning at the Delhi Gate and ending at another, perhaps never built. At the Naubat Khana the arrivals and departures of the emperors were accompanied by the music of drums and trumpets. This gate also marked the transition between the more public parts of the palace and those that were increasingly private. East of it was the vast rectangular Kila-i-Mubarik or place of welcoming, into whose east wall the Diwan-i-Am or public audience hall projects (*Plate 512*). This was a *tibari* nine bays (177 feet) wide and three bays (59 feet) deep. The supports are dodecagonal shafts with elaborate bases and "acanthus" capitals supporting four lobate arches each. The rear wall is solid and severely plain except for the *jharoka* in the center bay on a plinth with plants carved in relief, as at the Taj Mahal. Here the Emperor made a daily public appearance until Aurangzeb, increasingly reclusive, abolished the custom. Shah Jehan was the first to build *diwan-i-ams* as columned halls—at Lahore in 1631–32 and at Agra in 1636–37. His predecessors had been content with narrow porticoes overlooking large courts.

Proceeding east from the Diwan-i-Am and still on axis, two chambers connect the *jharoka* to a *chahr bagh*, east of which is the Rang Mahal, one of the private pavilions along the Jumna River. Everything north of this axis and east of the bazaar street was the *selamlik* or men's quarters. Here are found the Diwan-i-Khas or private audience hall on the bank of the Jumna and further north

512. *Delhi, Red Fort, Diwan-i-Am, west facade*
513. *Delhi, Red Fort, Diwan-i-Khas, west facade*

two gardens, the Baksh Bagh or life-giving garden and west of it the Mahtab Bagh or moonlight garden where, perhaps, only white flowers were planted. The southeast quadrant, badly preserved, seems to have been devoted to the *zenana*.

The imperial pavilions along the Jumna between the Shah Burj and the Asad Burj are in part linked by a canal, the Nahr-i-Behisht or River of Paradise. Interrupted at intervals by fountains carved in the shape of enormous lotuses, the canal flows alternately on and under the floors of the Diwan-i-Khas (*Plate 513*) and the Rang Mahal among other structures. Thus linked, these pavilions provide an exact metaphor for the Koranic Paradise, reinforced by their dadoes of flowering plants as at the Taj Mahal, but here in *pietra dura* inlays of semiprecious stones. Not only do these flowers bloom at floor level, but they also cover piers and vaults in sumptuous profusion, particularly in the Diwan-i-Khas, where the often-quoted verses of the Persian poet Jami are inscribed:

If there is a Paradise on the face of the earth,
  it is this, oh! it is this, oh! it is this!

If Shah Jehan, when he built the Red Fort at Delhi, thought he would be escaping the heat of Agra's summers he was mistaken; Delhi is worse. To capture the maximum circulation there are hardly any walls at all except in the baths. Partial privacy is afforded by the many marble screens of *jali* work which do not impede air circulation and are also used to restrict movement between one area and another. The palace today, stripped of its furnishings, is very different than was intended. Contemporary miniatures show how much use was made of awnings, both freestanding and as extensions of *chajjas* or stone eaves, to cast shade over the vast plinths on which nearly all the buildings stand. In winter equally sumptuous hangings could be rolled down over the many openings. If we add to this the magnificent rugs used out of doors as well as inside, these pavilions seem closer to the great tent cities of Timur than they now appear—as indeed do the palaces of Safavid Persia.

If there is in the Indian palaces the feeling of a nomadic camp, there is also something of the air of Peking's Forbidden City, to whose construction, it should be remembered, the Mongols under Kublai Khan had contributed. There the Wou Men Gate sheltered drums and bells to herald visitors, as did the Naubat Khana. Beyond this, on axis, were the great public audience halls, essentially open pavilions on forests of wooden columns with solid walls only to the north. Behind these, still on axis, were smaller, private audience halls and behind them the private residential areas. Up to a point the increase in political, religious, and economic power in Baghdad, India, and China led to more elaborate formal arrangements expressing the increased importance of the ruler, his family, and his courtiers; but then declining power for a time triggered even more complex and magnificent physical surroundings, as it had at Samarra. Perhaps at Delhi this point had been reached just before that decline despite the later increase in Moghul territory under Aurangzeb.

Conclusion

Moghul architecture as a manifestation of the Post-Classic Islamic style of the Ottomans and Safavids did indeed work primarily with the sources of design already available within the territories of the Empire. Even though renewed "Persian" influence seems to have entered India with Nur Mahal's buildings, careful analysis shows it to be more Central Asian than Safavid and, of course, executed in materials and techniques wholly indigenous. India is, however, unique in Islam in that two quite distinct traditions continued to flourish side by side, as in the pre-Moghul period. In the Moghul period there was a great deal more exchange of ideas and forms between the two than there had been earlier, particularly in secular matters.

Babur and Humayun, though they built very little, introduced primarily Central Asian, Timurid ideas, among them the form of the *hasht behisht*; but these were translated from brick and tile to stone by local craftsmen who transmitted the techniques and forms of the Lodis and other provincial Islamic dynasties in India which had been absorbed into the Empire. Akbar's "Indianization" of the Empire first took the form of a revival of even earlier Indo-Islamic styles—that of the Khaljis, for example, in the early years of his reign. At Fatipur Sikri only the mosque exhibits this revival, but the palace buildings, while they provide for a pattern of living still recognizably Islamic, create a setting almost wholly Hindu. During the later years of Akbar's reign this was certainly a deliberate trend. With Jahangir and his favorite Persian wife came a return to a relatively more "Islamic" style, spurred also by a gradual change to marble from the traditional sandstone and accompanied by a return to religious orthodoxy. With Shah Jehan that impetus increased, but it is significant that his principal monument, the Taj Mahal, is a reworking of an earlier Indian monument, the tomb of Humayun. Persian literary culture and language may have been dominant, but this did not imply any attempt at direct imitation of Safavid architecture. On the contrary, a Persian revival under the late Moghuls signaled a return to Timurid forms, which had previously been a part of the Indian architectural tradition.

SYNOPTIC TABLES / GLOSSARY / SELECTED BIBLIOGRAPHY
INDEX / LIST OF PLATES / PHOTOGRAPHIC CREDITS

	WESTERN ISLAM: THE MAGHRIB AND IFRIQIYA (MODERN MOROCCO, ALGERIA, AND TUNISIA)	THE MIDDLE EAST: EGYPT, ARABIA, SYRIA, MESOPOTAMIA	ANATOLIA	PERSIA, KHORASSAN, AND TRANSOXIANA (MODERN AFGHANISTAN AND RUSSIAN CENTRAL ASIA)	INDIA
622		*Hegira* (*Hijra*): flight of Muhammad from Mecca to Medina			
632		Death of Muhammad Orthodox Caliphs			
632–34		Abu Bakr			
634–44		Umar			
634–42		Arab conquest of Syria and Mesopotamia			
638		Foundation of Basra and Kufa			
642		Arab conquest of Egypt and foundation of al-Fustat			
644–56		Uthman			
647	First Arab raids in Ifriqiya				
651				Completion of the Arab conquest of Persia	
656–61		Ali Umayyad Caliphs			
661–80		Mu'awiya I			
665		Great Mosque at Basra rebuilt			
670	Foundation of Kairouan	Great Mosque and Dar al-Imara at Kufa rebuilt			
673–78			Sieges of Constantinople by Arabs		
680–83		Yazid I			
680–93		Meccan revolt			
685–92		Dome of the Rock in Jerusalem			
685–705		Abd al-Malik			
705–15		al-Walid I		Muslim raids in Transoxiana	
706–15		Great Mosque at Damascus			

	WESTERN ISLAM: THE MAGHRIB AND IFRIQIYA	THE MIDDLE EAST: EGYPT, ARABIA, SYRIA, MESOPOTAMIA	ANATOLIA	PERSIA, KHORASSAN, AND TRANSOXIANA	INDIA
709–15		Mosque of al-Aqsa in Jerusalem			
710–16	Completion of the Arab conquest of the Maghrib and the Arab–Berber conquest of Spain				
711					Muslim raids in northwestern India
714–15		Town of Anjar in Lebanon		Arab conquest of Transoxiana. Raids on Kashgar	
716			Last siege of Constantinople by Arabs		
724–43		Hisham			
727–28					Probable date of the Great Mosque at Banbhore (Debal?)
728–29		Kasr al-Khayr al-Sharki			
732	Battle of Poitiers ends the Muslim occupation of France				
739–44		Khirbat al-Mafjar			
744–50		Marwan II			
746		Palace at Mshatta begun		Abbasid movement in Khorassan begins; the Tarik Khana at Damghan	
750–89		Abbasid Caliphs (capital at Kufa)			
754–75		al-Mansur			
756	Umayyad Emirate in Cordoba				
762		Foundation of Baghdad			
764–78		Ukhaidir			
772		Foundation of Raqqah			
772–74	Great Mosque at Kairouan enlarged by Yazid ibn Hatim				
780		Reconstruction of the Mosque of al-Aqsa in Jerusalem			

	WESTERN ISLAM: THE MAGHRIB AND IFRIQIYA	THE MIDDLE EAST: EGYPT, ARABIA, SYRIA, MESOPOTAMIA	ANATOLIA	PERSIA, KHORASSAN, AND TRANSOXIANA	INDIA
785	Great Mosque at Cordoba begun				
786–809		Harun al-Rashid			
789–926	Idrissid Dynasty of Morocco				
796	Ribat at Sussa				
800	Foundation of Fez				
800–909	Aghlabid Emirate in Ifriqiya				
813–33		al-Ma'mun		Merv (the Abbasid capital, 813–17)	
827–902	Muslim occupation of Sicily				
c. 830–40				Masjid-i-Tarikh at Balkh	
833–42		al-Mu'tasim			
836	Great Mosque at Kairouan rebuilt	Foundation of Samarra: the Kasr al-Jiss and the Jausaq al-Kharqani begun			
847–61		al-Mutawakkil			
848–52		Great Mosque at Samarra			
849–59		Bulkawara Palace at Samarra			
850	Great Mosque at Sussa				
857	Mosque of Qarawiyin at Fez begun				
862–63	Great Mosque at Kairouan rebuilt with dome over *mihrab*				
868–905		Tulunid Dynasty in Egypt			
875–1005				Samanid Dynasty in Transoxiana and Khorassan	
876–79		Mosque of Ibn Tulun at Katai near al-Fustat			

	WESTERN ISLAM: THE MAGHRIB AND IFRIQIYA	THE MIDDLE EAST: EGYPT, ARABIA, SYRIA, MESOPOTAMIA	ANATOLIA	PERSIA, KHORASSAN, AND TRANSOXIANA	INDIA	
883		Samarra abandoned; Baghdad again becomes the Abbasid capital				
907				Death of Ismail the Samanid and possible date of his tomb at Bukhara		
908–32		al-Muqtadir				
909–1171	Fatimid Dynasty begins with the conquest of Ifriqiya					
912–61	Reign of Abd er-Rahman III (Emir and, in 921, Caliph of Cordoba)					
916	Foundation of Mahdiya					
921	Fatimids begin Great Mosque at Mahdiya and occupy Fez					
932–36				Beginning of the Buyyid Emirate		
935–36	Palace at Ashir					
936	Foundation of Medina al-Zahra					
941	Mosque of Medina al-Zahra					
945–1055		Buyyid domination of the Baghdad Caliphs				
953–57	Salon Rico and gardens at Medina al-Zahra					
956	Mosque of Qarawiyin at Fez enlarged and minaret added					
960				Mosque of Nayyin		
961–66	Enlargement of the Mosque at Cordoba by Hakam II					
969		Fatimid conquest of Egypt				
972		Completion of the Mosque of al-Azhar in Cairo				
972–1152	Zirid Emirate in Ifriqiya					
977–78				Tomb of Arab Ata at Tim		

	WESTERN ISLAM: THE MAGHRIB AND IFRIQIYA	THE MIDDLE EAST: EGYPT, ARABIA, SYRIA, MESOPOTAMIA	ANATOLIA	PERSIA, KHORASSAN, AND TRANSOXIANA	INDIA
986–87					Invasion by Sabuktigin of Ghazna
990–91		Mosque of al-Hakim begun in Cairo			
996–1021		Reign of al-Hakim			
998–1030				Mahmud of Ghazna Residence at Lashkari Bazar	
998–1186				Ghaznavid Dynasty	
999	Mosque of Bib Mardun at Toledo				
1002/3–13		Completion of the Mosque of al-Hakim in Cairo			
1006–7				Gunbad-i-Qabus at Gurgan	
1009		Destruction of the Holy Sepulcher in Jerusalem			
1010	Sack of Medina al-Zahra and rise of the Taifas Kingdoms in Spain				
1015–1152	Hammadid Emirate in the Maghrib; Qala of the Bani Hammad				
1026					Ghaznavids settle permanently in the Punjab
1031	Fall of the Umayyad Caliphate in Cordoba				
1036–1147	Almoravid Dynasty				
1037				Seljuk Emirs dominate Transoxiana	
1038–1157				Dynasty of the Seljuk Emirs (later Sultans)	
1041	Zirid Emirs recognize the Abbasid Caliphate			Ghaznavids defeated by the Seljuks	
1046–81	Aljaferiya Palace in Zaragoza				
1051				Isfahan falls to the Seljuks	
1052	Ifriqiya invaded by Banu Hillal				
1056				Gunbad-i-Ali at Abarquh	
1061–91	Arabs lose Sicily to the Normans				

	WESTERN ISLAM: THE MAGHRIB AND IFRIQIYA	THE MIDDLE EAST: EGYPT, ARABIA, SYRIA, MESOPOTAMIA	ANATOLIA	PERSIA, KHORASSAN, AND TRANSOXIANA	INDIA
1067–68				Tomb tower 1 at Kharraqan	
1070	Foundation of Marrakesh				
1071			Seljuk victory at Manzikert		
1073			Danishmends in eastern Anatolia		
1075–80			Dynasty of the Seljuk Sultans at Rum	Dome over the *mihrab* of the Masjid-i-Jami at Isfahan	
1077–1307				*Caravanserai* of Rabat-i-Malik on the Bukhara-Samarkand road	
1078–1117		Seljuk Dynasty in Syria			
1082	Great Mosque of Tlemcen begun				
1085–86		Imam Dur at Samarra			
1085–92		Cairo's new walls and the Mosque of al-Juyushi			
1086	Almoravids occupy Spain				
1088				North Dome Chamber of the Masjid-i-Jami at Isfahan	
1089–94		Minaret of the Great Mosque at Aleppo			
1093				Tomb tower 2 at Kharraqan	
1096	Foundation of the Great Mosque at Algiers				
1097			Nicea taken by the Crusaders		
1098–1232			Artukid Dynasty at Diyarbekir		
1099	Jerusalem falls to the Crusaders				
1099–1115				Mas'ud III of Ghazna builds Minaret and Palace	
1104–18				Dome Chamber in the Mosque at Gulpaygan	
1114–15				*Caravanserai* of Robat Sharaf	

	WESTERN ISLAM: THE MAGHRIB AND IFRIQIYA	THE MIDDLE EAST: EGYPT, ARABIA, SYRIA, MESOPOTAMIA	ANATOLIA	PERSIA, KHORASSAN, AND TRANSOXIANA	INDIA
1116–56			Sultan Mas'ud I		
1118–57				Sultan Sanjar	
1118–94		Seljuk Dynasty in Iraq			
c. 1120	Qubbat Barudiyin at Marrakesh				
1125		Mosque of al-Aqmar in Cairo completed			
1127				Kalayan Minaret at Bukhara	
1127–81		Zengid Dynasty in Syria			
1130–1269	Almohad Dynasty				
1131–49		New facades for the *sahn* of the Mosque of al-Azhar in Cairo			
1135	*Mihrab* aisle in the Mosque of al-Qarawiyin at Fez				
1136	*Mihrab* vault in the Mosque at Tlemcen				
1139–40				Tomb of Tughril Beg at Rayy	
1145–46			Halifet Ghazi Turbe at Amasya		
1146	Almohad conquest of Marrakesh				
1146–74		Reign of Nur al-Din Zengi			
1147	Almohad invasion of Spain				
1147–48				Gunbad-i-Surkh at Maragha	
1150				Ghurid sack of Ghazna and Lashkari Bazar	
1150–1215				Ghurid Dynasty in eastern Persia and later in India	
1153	First Kutubiyya Mosque in Marrakesh and Mosque at Tinmal finished				
1154		Muristan Nuri in Damascus			
1156–92			Sultan Qilich Arslan		
1156–1220				Dynasty of the Khwarazm Shahs	
1157				Tomb of Sultan Sanjar at Merv	

397

	WESTERN ISLAM: THE MAGHRIB AND IFRIQIYA	THE MIDDLE EAST: EGYPT, ARABIA, SYRIA, MESOPOTAMIA	ANATOLIA	PERSIA, KHORASSAN, AND TRANSOXIANA	INDIA
1160		Mosque of al-Salih Tala'i begun in Cairo			
1162	Second Kutubiyya Mosque at Marrakesh begun				
1162–1203				Reign of the Ghurid Sultan Ghiyath al-Din Muhammad	
1169–1260		Ayyubid Dynasty in Egypt and Syria			
1172		Madrasa al-Nuriya al-Kubra in Damascus			
1172–82	Great Mosque at Seville				
1174–93		Salah ad-Din al-Ayyubi			
1175					Ghurid Muhammad bin Sam captures Multan
1176		Citadel at Cairo begun			
1180–1225		Caliph al-Nasir at Baghdad			
1184–95	Giralda Tower at Seville				
1186					End of Ghaznavid rule
1187		Muslims recapture Jerusalem			
1191–99	Mosque of Hassan at Rabat				
1192–93					Qutb al-Din Aybak takes Delhi
1193–1316					Quwwat al-Islam at Delhi
1195	Almohad victory at Alarcos in Spain		Sitte Melik Kumbed at Divrig		
1196–97				Gunbad-i-Kabud at Maragha	
1196–1465	Marinid Dynasty				
1199					Qtub Minar in Delhi begun
1200–35					Arhai Din Ka Jompra Mosque at Ajmer
1204			Great Mosque at Dunaysir		

	WESTERN ISLAM: THE MAGHRIB AND IFRIQIYA	THE MIDDLE EAST: EGYPT, ARABIA, SYRIA, MESOPOTAMIA	ANATOLIA	PERSIA, KHORASSAN, AND TRANSOXIANA	INDIA
1206–90					Dynasty of the Muizzi or Slave Kings at Delhi
1212	Almohad defeat at Las Navas de Tolosa in Spain				
1220				Chingiz (Genghis) Khan destroys Khwarazm	
1220–22		Talisman Gate at Baghdad			
1220–36					Tomb of Iltutmish at Delhi
1227				Death of Chingiz Khan and withdrawal of the Mongols	
1228–29			Mosque and Hospital at Divrig		
1229			Sultan Han near Aksaray begun		
1230–1492	Nasrid Dynasty at Granada				
1231					Tomb of Sultan Ghari at Delhi
1232			Sultan Han near Kayseri		
1233		Mustansiriya at Baghdad completed			
1235–36		Mosque and Madrasa al-Firdaus at Aleppo			
1236	Cordoba falls to the Christians		Kobadabad palace near Beyshehir begun		
1237–38			Khwand Foundation at Kayseri		
1237–1574	Hafsid Dynasty at Tunis				
1241		Palace of Sultan Salih Negm ad-Din on Rhoda Island near Cairo			
1242–50		Madrasa and tomb of Sultan Salih in Cairo			
1243			Mongol invasions turn the Seljuk Sultans into vassals		
1248	Seville falls to the Christians				
1249–50		Mamluks take power in Egypt			
1251–52			Karatay Madrasa at Konya		

	WESTERN ISLAM: THE MAGHRIB AND IFRIQIYA	THE MIDDLE EAST: EGYPT, ARABIA, SYRIA, MESOPOTAMIA	ANATOLIA	PERSIA, KHORASSAN, AND TRANSOXIANA	INDIA
1256				Domination of the Mongol Hulagu in the north	
1258–60		Baghdad falls to the Mongols, who then enter Syria			
1260–65			Ince Minare Madrasa at Konya		
1267–69		Mosque of Baybars in Cairo			
1269	Marinids take Marrakesh				
1271			Gök Madrasa at Sivas begun		
c. 1275			Döner Kumbed at Kayseri		
1276	Fez al-Jedid founded by the Marinids				
1281–1324			Osman I		
1283–85		Madrasa and tomb of Sultan Qala'un in Cairo			
1290–1320					Khalji Dynasty at Delhi
1291		Final defeat of the Latin states in Syria			
1291–94	*Mihrab* vault in the Mosque at Taza				
1294				Ilkhanid Sultan Ghazan is converted to Islam	
1297–99			Eshrefoglu Mosque at Beyshehir		
1298–99			Osman I founds principality in Bythenia		
1298–1924			Ottoman Dynasty		
1303–36	Mosque of Mansura at Tlemcen			Complex of Shaykh Abd al-Samad at Natanz	
1304–25				Tomb of Oljeitu at Sultanieh	
1309	Gibraltar falls to the Christians				
1310–20				Masjid-i-Jami at Tabriz	
1311–16					Quwwat al-Islam, Alai Darwaza, Delhi
1313–15		Kasr al-Ablaq on the Citadel in Cairo			

	WESTERN ISLAM: THE MAGHRIB AND IFRIQIYA	THE MIDDLE EAST: EGYPT, ARABIA, SYRIA, MESOPOTAMIA	ANATOLIA	PERSIA, KHORASSAN, AND TRANSOXIANA	INDIA
1320–30				Tomb of Turabek Khanum at Urgench	
1320–1414					Tughluqid Dynasty at Delhi
1322–26				Masjid-i-Jami at Varamin	
1323–25	Attarine Madrasa at Fez				
1324–60			Orhan		
1325					Tomb of Ghiyath al-Din Tughluq at Delhi
1333–54	Hall of the Ambassadors in the Alhambra at Granada				
1336				End of the Ilkhanid Dynasty	
1350–55	Bou Inaniya Madrasa at Fez				
1354					Kotila of Firuz Shah at Delhi begun
1354–91	Court of Lions in the Alhambra at Granada				
1356–59		Madrasa and tomb of Sultan Hasan in Cairo			
1360–89			Murad I		
1366–85			Mosque-Madrasa of Murad I at Bursa		
1367					Masjid-i-Jami at Gulbarga
1370–1506				Timurid Dynasty	
1370–1405				Timur	
1374–75			Isa Bek Mosque at Seljuk		
1376–78			Ishaq Bek complex at Manisa	Ak Koyunlu in Azerbaijan	
			Ak Koyunlu in Diyarbekir		
1380–88					Hauz-i-Khas at Delhi
1380–1468		Kara Koyunlu in Iraq		Kara Koyunlu in Azerbaijan	
1384–95				Shrine of Ahmad Yasavi in Turkestan City	
1384–1404				Akserai Palace at Shahr-i-Sabz	
1389–1403			Bayazid I		
1390–95			Kulliye of Bayazid I at Bursa		
1391–1583					Sultans of Gujerat
1394–1479					Sharqi Dynasty of Jaunpur
1396–1400			Friday Mosque (Ulu Cami) at Bursa		
1398					Timurid invasion

	WESTERN ISLAM: THE MAGHRIB AND IFRIQIYA	THE MIDDLE EAST: EGYPT, ARABIA, SYRIA, MESOPOTAMIA	ANATOLIA	PERSIA, KHORASSAN, AND TRANSOXIANA	INDIA
1399–1404				Bibi Khanum Mosque at Samarkand	
1402			Timurid invasion		
1403–21			Mehmet I		
1404				Gur-i-Amir (tomb of Timur) at Samarkand	
				Mosque of Gawhar Shad	
1405–18					
1405–47				Shah Rukh	
1412–20			Yeşil Cami (Green Mosque) at Bursa		
1417–20				Madrasa of Ulugh Beg at Samarkand	
1417–32				Musalla and Madrasa of Gawhar Shad at Herat	
1420				Shrine of Shaykh Abdallah Ansari at Gazur Gah (near Herat) begun	
1421–44			Murad II (first reign)		
1438–45				Ghiyathiya Madrasa at Khargird	
1438–47			Üç Şerefeli Cami at Edirne		
1444–46			Mehmet II (first reign)		
1446–51			Murad II (second reign)		
1447–49				Ulugh Beg	
1451–69				Abu Said	
1451–81			Mehmet II (second reign)		
1453			Fall of Constantinople		
1460–61				Shrine of Khwaja Abu Nasr Parsa at Balkh	
1460–64				Ishrat Khaneh at Samarkand	
1463–70			Fatih Cami at Istanbul		
1470					Masjid-i-Jami at Jaunpur
1472			Çinli Kiosk of the Top Kapu Saray at Istanbul		
1472–74		Madrasa and tomb of Sultan Qayt Bay in Cairo			
1478			Bab-i-Humayun of the Top Kapu Saray at Istanbul		
1481–1512			Bayazid II		
1484–88			Kulliye of Bayazid II at Edirne		

	WESTERN ISLAM: THE MAGHRIB AND IFRIQIYA	THE MIDDLE EAST: EGYPT, ARABIA, SYRIA, MESOPOTAMIA	ANATOLIA	PERSIA, KHORASSAN, AND TRANSOXIANA	INDIA
1485–1523					Masjid-i-Jami at Champanir
1492	Fall of Granada to the Christians				
1495					Baradari of Iskander Lodi, near Agra
1500–98				Shaybanids in Transoxiana (capital at Bukhara)	
1501				Shortly before this date, tomb of Ulugh Beg and Abdu Razzaq at Ghazna erected	
1501–6			Mosque of Bayazid II at Istanbul		
1501–24				Ismail	
1501–1732				Safavid Dynasty	
1511–1659	Saadien Dynasty in Morocco				
1512–20			Selim I		
1517		Ottoman conquest			
1520–66			Suleyman II Kanuni		
1526–1858					Moghul Empire
1526–30					Babur
1530–40					Humayun (first reign)
1540–55					Suri Sultans of Delhi
1543–48			Şehzade Cami at Istanbul		
1545–47					Tomb of Isa Khan Niyazi at Delhi
1550–57			Kulliye of Suleyman at Istanbul		
1555–56					Humayun (second reign)
1556–1605					Akbar
1560–c. 1570					Tomb and garden of Humayun at Delhi
1563–64					Tomb of Muhammad Ghaus at Gwalior
1566–74			Selim II		
1569–74			Selimiye Mosque at Edirne		
1570–c. 1580					Fatipur Sikri
1571–72					Palace-Fortress of Akbar at Ajmer
1574–95			Murad III		

	WESTERN ISLAM: THE MAGHRIB AND IFRIQIYA	THE MIDDLE EAST: EGYPT, ARABIA, SYRIA, MESOPOTAMIA	ANATOLIA	PERSIA, KHORASSAN, AND TRANSOXIANA	INDIA
1578			Bed Chamber of Murad III in the Top Kapu Saray at Istanbul		
c. 1585					Jahangiri Mahal at Agra
1588–1629				Abbas I	
1590?				Chehel Situn at Isfahan	
1595–1603			Mehmet III		
1595–1665			Yeni Cami (New Mosque) at Istanbul		
1598				New town of Isfahan begun	
1602				Mosque of Shaykh Lut-fullah at Isfahan begun	
1603–17			Ahmet I		
1605–15					Tomb of Akbar at Sikan-dra
1605–27					Jahangir
1609–17			Ahmediye Mosque in Istanbul		
1611–38				Masjid-i-Shah at Isfahan	
1617–22				Shrine of Khwaja Rabi at Mashad	
1622–28					Tomb of the Ittimad al-Daula at Agra
1628–58					Shah Jehan
1631–48					Taj Mahal at Agra
1631–present	Filalian Dynasty in Morocco				
1634–36					Mosque of Wazir Khan at Lahore
1637		House of Gamal ad-Din al-Zahabi in Cairo			
1638–47					Red Fort at Delhi
1639			Baghdad Kiosk of the Top Kapu Saray in Istanbul		
1642–66				Abbas II	
1648–55					Pearl Mosque of the Fort at Agra
1650				Pol-i-Khaju at Isfahan	
1666–94				Suleyman I	
1669–70				Hasht Behisht at Isfahan	
1791			Aynali Kavak in Istanbul		

GLOSSARY

BADIYA = a camp or hunting lodge

BARADARI = literally, "twelve-pillared"; an open porticoed pavilion probably of pre-Islamic Indian origin

BAYT = Arabic term for dwelling; used to designate the self-contained apartments within Umayyad mansions and Abbasid palaces

CALIPH = leader of the Muslims in both a spiritual and political sense; in theory there should only be one, but in fact after the loss of power by the Abbasid caliph in the tenth century a Sunni Caliphate was established at Cordoba (925–1030) and a Shi'ite Caliphate by the Fatimids (915–1171). After the murder of the last Abbasid caliph at Baghdad in 1258 a shadow caliphate survived in Egypt until the Turkish conquest of 1517. The claim of the later Turkish sultans to the caliphate was not legitimate

CARAVANSERAI = HAN (q.v.)

CHADAR = a sloping surface, often textured, over which water is made to flow. The term comes from the Persian word for veil. See also SABIL and SHADIRVAN

CHAHR BAGH = a four-part garden divided into quadrants by water channels symbolizing the four rivers of Paradise

CHATRI = decorative pavilion in Moghul India, from the Persian word for umbrella

CHESHME = a Persian word adapted into Turkish and used to designate a fountain or SABIL

CUERDA SECA = HAFT AURANG (q.v.)

DAR = Arabic term for a dwelling arranged around a central court

DAR AL-HARB = literally, "abode of war"; the territory outside that ruled by the law of Islam

DAR AL-ISLAM = literally, "abode of peace"; the territory in which the law of Islam prevails

DARGAH = DURKA (q.v.)

DIWAN-I-AM = public audience hall

DIWAN-I-KHAS = private audience hall

DURKA or DIRKA = the square, depressed central space under a clerestory in the reception hall of a medieval Cairo house

FARADIS = a walled garden (Persian source of the term Paradise)

FUNDUK = HAN (q.v.); the term, of Greek origin, is used primarily in North Africa

FUSAYFISA = Arabic word for colored glass or stone mosaic; the term is taken from the Greek as, undoubtedly, was the technique

HAFT AURANG = tile with design executed in the *cuerda seca* technique, in which a cord burned away during the firing separates the glazes and leaves a slight depression between the colors (a much cheaper and faster substitute for ZELLIJ or tile mosaic)

HAJJ = the pilgrimage to Mecca required of all Muslims

HAMAM = a public or private bath

HAN = term for a fortified hostel along a trade route, also CARAVANSERAI and FUNDUK (q.v.)

HARAM = an area set apart; for example, the Haram al-Sharif around the Dome of the Rock in Jerusalem

HASHT BEHISHT = literally, "eight Paradises"; a radially symmetrical (usually octagonal) pavilion with a central two-storied chamber. Probably the form originated in Seljuk Persia, but it may be older

HAZIRA = an enclosure around an unroofed tomb (or tombs) with the addition of a mosque; this became a religious institution under the Timurids in the fifteenth century

HEGIRA or HIJRA = the flight of Muhammad from Mecca to Medina in 622 and the beginning of the Muslim era, reckoned in lunar years of twelve months

HOSH = inner court of an Egyptian house

IWAN = a vaulted niche or open porch sometimes framing a portal or used to emphasize the importance of something within or in front of it, probably also a Paradise symbol

JALI = perforated stone screen, the equivalent in Moghul India of a MUSHRABIYYA. The word may derive from the Arabic *jalli*, meaning transparent

JAMI = MASJID-I-JAMI (q.v.)

JHAROKA = projecting roofed balcony much used in Moghul India

KASR = a fortified dwelling, sometimes a synonym for palace

KHAN = HAN (q.v.)

KHANAQAH = a monastery, usually of a Sufi order of dervishes

KHUTBA = the Friday prayer spoken from the MINBAR. When not pronounced by the Caliph himself, his name was always mentioned

KIBLA = QIBLA (q.v.)

KIOSK = a pavilion for feasting, generally not intended for permanent occupancy (Turkish *kösk*, Arabic *kushk*). See also HASHT BEHISHT and BARADARI

KUBBA = Arabic term for a domed tomb, used throughout the Islamic world

KULLIYYA = a foundation complex consisting of a congregational mosque, one or more MADRASAS, a hospital, a HAN, and a soup kitchen. Usually associated with Ottoman Turkey (Turkish *kulliye*)

MADRASA = an endowed theological school providing student lodgings, a prayer hall, and sometimes classrooms. Perhaps invented in the tenth century by the Ghaznavids to combat Shi'ism, it was adapted for the same purpose by the Persian and Turkish Seljuks, whence it spread to Syria

MAHAL = a house or palace in Moghul India, from the Arabic term for realm, district, or place

MANAR = tower. See also MINARET

MAQAD = an open loggia, usually on the second story, overlooking the HOSH of an Egyptian house

MAQSURA = a protective barrier, usually of wood, surrounding the MINBAR and MIHRAB of a Friday mosque

MASJID = literally, "place of prostration"; a mosque

MASJID-I-JAMI = a Friday or congregational mosque. In early Islam a structure capable of accommodating the entire male population of the community for the Friday prayer when the local leader of the faithful read the KHUTBA. In large cities there came to be more than one Friday mosque as the population grew

MAYDAN or MEIDAN = open square or plaza

MEDERSE = MADRASA (q.v.)

MIAN SARAY = literally, "middle part"; in Persian the term refers to the antechamber of the harem of a house or of a tomb containing the stairway to the crypt

MIHRAB = a niche in the QIBLA wall of a mosque indicating the direction of Mecca; first installed in the early eighth-century rebuilding of the mosque at Medina and perhaps of Egyptian Christian origin

MINARET = tower from which the call to prayer is made. The term as well as the form may have been derived from a lighthouse

MINBAR = a seat or pulpit, first used in Medina by Muhammad himself, which came to be installed to the right of the MIHRAB in all Friday mosques for the reading of the KHUTBA. Its use gradually became universal in all mosques

MUQARNAS = Arabic term, derived from the Greek word for scales used in roof tiles, applied to what are called stalactite or honeycomb vaults. *Muqarnas* units have been found in ninth-century Nishapur, and so their earliest use may have been purely decorative. Spreading throughout Islam in the late eleventh century, this element became characteristic of the Classic phase of Islamic architecture

MURISTAN = Persian term for hospital

MUSALLA = an enclosure, usually unroofed, used as a place of prayer outside the walls of a city. The actual meaning is still obscure. In Persian the term signifies a burial ground or cemetery

MUSHRABIYYA = interlaced wooden screen, used wherever privacy is desired without impeding the flow of air

NAUBAT KHANA or NAGGAR KHANA = pavilion over a palace entrance where drummers announced the arrival of a person of importance

NISBA = part of an Arabic name indicating lineage or territorial connection; it is perhaps too often used to suggest the place at which an architect may have been trained

PISHTAQ = rectangular screen rising above a roofline and framing a portal or an IWAN

QA'A = the reception hall in an Egyptian house

QASR = KASR (q.v.)

QIBLA = the direction of prayer; the wall of a mosque oriented toward Mecca

RIADH = interior garden, equivalent of a CHAHR BAGH; the term is used principally in the Maghrib

RIBAT or ROBAT = a fortified enclosure used as a dwelling and place of prayer for a semireligious brotherhood of Muslims dedicated to the *Jihad* or holy war against the infidel

RIWAQ = one of the porticoes or arcades surrounding the SAHN of a mosque or a central shrine

SABIL = a public drinking fountain. See also CHADAR

SAHN = the interior central court of a mosque

SARAY = a palace

SELSEBIL = SABIL (q.v.)

SEREFE = a Turkish term for the balcony of a minaret, used by the *muezzin* for the call to prayer

SHADIRVAN = literally, "weir"; that part of a fountain over which water flows in a thin sheet. In Turkey the term refers to a fountain in the center of the SAHN of a mosque. See also CHADAR

SHI'ITES = the followers of Ali who believe in the succession of twelve or more *imams* after him and reject the legitimacy of the Umayyad and Abbasid caliphs

SUNNI = the major or Orthodox sect of Islam, which in addition to the Koran and the *Hadith* or tradition preserved by the faithful, accepted as legitimate the Umayyad and Abbasid caliphates

TABHANE = guest quarters usually reserved for wandering dervishes in Turkish royal foundations

TALAR = a columned porch (usually of wood) of pre-Islamic Persian origin. The form was much used by the Timurids and Safavids

TURBE = Turkish term for a domed tomb, equivalent to KUBBA. The form is a revival of the Classic Arabic *turba*

ULU CAMI = Turkish term for a congregational mosque

WAQF = a pious foundation, endowed perpetually and governed by a trust; used to support mosques and MADRASAS, but also fountains, public baths, hospitals, and even HANS

ZELLIJ = the term used in the Maghrib for a tile mosaic

ZIYADAH = the outer enclosure of a mosque, probably an Abbasid innovation which reappears in certain of the imperial Ottoman foundations

AHMAD, M. *The Taj and Its Environments*, 2nd ed., Agra, n.d. (1907).

ARSEVEN, C. E. *L'Art turc, depuis son origine jusqu'à nos jours*, Istanbul, 1939.

ASLANAPA, O. "Erster Bericht über die Ausgrabung des Palastes von Diyarbakir," *Mitteilungen des Deutschen Archäologischen Instituts, Istanbuler Abteilung*, XII, 1962, pp. 115–28.

———. *Turkish Art and Architecture*, New York, 1971.

BARGEBUHR, F. P. *The Alhambra: A Cycle of Studies on the Eleventh Century in Moorish Spain*, Berlin, 1968.

BEAUDOIN, E. E. "Isfahan sous les grands Chahs, XVII siècle," *Urbanisme*, II, no. 10, 1933, pp. 29 ff.

BOMBACI, A. *The Kufic Inscriptions in Persian Verses in the Court of the Royal Palace of Mas'ud III at Ghazni*, Istituto Italiano per il Medio ed Estremo Oriente, vol. V, Rome, 1966.

BOSWORTH, C. E. *The Islamic Dynasties: a Chronological and Genealogical Handbook*, Edinburgh, 1967.

BOYLE, J. A., ed. *The Saljuq and Mongol Periods* (*The Cambridge History of Iran*, vol. V), Cambridge, 1968 (section on the visual arts by O. GRABAR, pp. 626–59).

BRANDENBURG, D. *Der Taj Mahal in Agra*, Berlin, 1969.

———. *Islamische Baukunst in Ägypten*, Berlin, 1966.

BRIGGS, M. S. *Muhammadan Architecture in Egypt and Palestine*, Oxford, 1924.

BROWN, P. *Indian Architecture* (*The Islamic Period*), Bombay, 1942 (1943).

CAILLÉ, J. *La mosquée de Hassan à Rabat*, 2 vols., Paris, 1954.

CASIMIR, M., and GLATZER, B. "Sah-i Mashad, a Recently Discovered Madrasah of the Ghurid Period in Gargistan (Afghanistan)," *East and West*, n.s., XXI, 1–2, March–June, 1921.

CHAGHTAI, M. A. *Le Tadj Mahal d'Agra* (*Inde*), Brussels, 1938.

CHEHAB, M. "The Umayyad Palace at Anjar," *Ars Orientalis*, V, 1963, pp. 17–25.

CHUECA GOITIA, F. *Historia de la arquitectura española: edad antigua y edad media*, Madrid, 1965.

COSTE, P. *Monuments modernes de la Perse, mesurés, dessinés et décrits*, Paris, 1867.

CRESWELL, K. A. C. *A Short Account of Early Muslim Architecture*, Baltimore, 1958.

———. *Early Muslim Architecture*, I: *Umayyads, A.D. 622–750*; *Early Muslim Architecture*, II: *Abbasids, Umayyads of Cordova, Aghlabids, Tulunids and Samanids, A.D. 751–905*, Oxford, 1932–40 (2nd ed., 1969).

DAVIS, F. *The Palace of Topkapi in Istanbul*, New York, 1970.

DE BEYLIÉ, L. *La Kalaa des Beni Hammad, une capitale berbère de l'Afrique du Nord au XIe*, Paris, 1909.

DE CLAVIJO, R. G. *Historia del gran Tamorlan e itinerario y enarración del Viaje...*, Madrid, 1782. English ed.:

Embassy to Tamerlane, 1403–1406, translated by G. le Strange, London, 1928.

DENNY, W. B. "A Sixteenth-Century Architectural Plan of Istanbul," *Ars Orientalis*, VIII, 1970, pp. 49–63.

Description de l'Égypte, État Moderne, 2 vols., Paris, 1809–22.

DEVONSHIRE, H. C. *Rambles in Cairo*, Cairo, 1917.

DIETZ, E. *Die Kunst der islamischen Völker*, Berlin, 1917.

———. *Persien, islamische Baukunst in Churâsân*, Hagen, 1923.

———, and GLÜCK, H. *Die Kunst des Islam* (*Propyläen-Kunstgeschichte*, vol. V), Berlin, 1925.

DIMAND, M. S. *L'Arte dell'Islam*, Florence, 1972.

DODD, E. C. "The Image of the Word; Notes on the Religious Iconography of Islam," *Berytus, Archaeological Studies*, XVIII, 1969, pp. 35–79.

EGLI, E. *Sinan, der Baumeister osmanischer Glanzzeit*, Zurich-Stuttgart, 1954.

ERDMANN, K. *Das anatolische Karavansaray des 13. Jahrhunderts*, 2 vols., Berlin, 1961.

———. "Seraybauten des dreizehnten und vierzehnten Jahrhunderts in Anatolien," *Ars Orientalis*, III, 1959, pp. 77–94.

ETTINGHAUSEN, R. *From Byzantium to Sassanian Iran and the Islamic World: Three Modes of Artistic Influence*, Leiden, 1972.

Excavations at Samarra, 1936–1939 (Iraq Government Department of Antiquities), 2 vols., Baghdad, 1940.

FERGUSSON, J. *History of Indian and Eastern Architecture*, London, 1910.

FLANDIN, E., and COSTE, P. *Perse Moderne* (*Voyage en Perse*, vol. VI), Paris, 1854.

GABRIEL, A. "Le Masdjid-i-Djum'a d'Isfahan," *Ars Islamica*, II, 1935, pp. 7–44.

———. *Monuments Turcs d'Anatolie*, 2 vols., Paris, 1931–34.

———. *Une capitale turque, Brousse, Bursa* (Institut français d'Archéologie d'Istamboul), 2 vols., Paris, 1958.

———. *Voyages Archéologiques dans la Turquie Orientale avec un recueil d'inscriptions arabes de J. Sauvaget* (Institut français d'Archéologie d'Istamboul), Paris, 1940.

GARDIN, J. C. "Lashkari Bazar, une résidence royale Ghaznevide, II: Les trouvailles," in *Mémoires de la Délégation Archéologique Française en Afghanistan*, vol. XVIII, Paris, 1963.

GODDARD, A. *The Art of Iran*, New York, 1965.

GOLOMBEK, L. "Abbasid Mosque at Balkh," *Oriental Art*, XV, no. 3, 1969, pp. 173–89.

———. *The Timurid Shrine at Gazur Gah* (Royal Ontario Museum), Toronto, 1969.

GOLVIN, L. *Essai sur l'architecture religieuse musulmane*, 2 vols., Paris, 1970–71.

———. "Le Mihrab de Kairouan," *Kunst des Orients*, V, no. 2, 1968, pp. 1–38.

———. "Le Palais de Ziri à Achir (dixième siècle J. C)," *Ars Orientalis*, VI, 1966, pp. 47–76.

———. *Recherches archéologiques à la qal'a des Banū Hammâd*, Paris, 1965.

GÓMEZ MORENO, M., *El arte árabe español hasta los Almohades: Arte Mozárabe* (*Ars Hispaniae*, vol. III), Madrid, 1951.

GOODWIN, G. *A History of Ottoman Architecture*, Baltimore, 1971.

GRABAR, O. "Al-Mshatta, Baghdad and Wasit," in J. Kritzneck, R. Bayly Winder, *The World of Islam*, New York-London, 1959.

———. "The Earliest Islamic Commemorative Structures, Notes and Documents," *Ars Orientalis*, VI, 1966, pp. 7–45.

———. *The Formation of Islamic Art*, New Haven-London, 1973.

———. "The Umayyad Dome of the Rock in Jerusalem," *Ars Orientalis*, III, 1959, pp. 33–62.

———. "Three Seasons of Excavations at Qasr al-Hayr al-Sharqi," *Ars Orientalis*, VIII, 1970, pp. 65–85.

GRUBE, E. J. *The World of Islam* (*Landmarks of the World's Art*), New York-Toronto, 1967.

GURLITT, C. *Die Baukunst Konstantinopels*, 2 vols., Berlin, 1912.

HAMILTON, R. W. *Khirbat al-Mafjar; an Arabian Mansion in the Jordan Valley* (with a contribution by O. Grabar), Oxford, 1959.

———. *The Structural History of the Aqsa Mosque*, Oxford, 1949.

HARDING, G. L. *The Antiquities of Jordan*, London, 1959.

HERZFELD, E. "Damascus: Studies in Architecture–I," *Ars Islamica*, IX, 1942, pp. 1–53.

———. "Damascus: Studies in Architecture–II," *Ars Islamica*, X, 1943, pp. 13–70.

———. *Erster vorläufiger Bericht über die Ausgrabungen von Samarra*, Berlin, 1912.

———. *Geschichte der Stadt Samarra*, Hamburg-Berlin, 1948.

HILL, D., and GRABAR, O. *Islamic Architecture and its Decoration A.D. 800–1500*, Chicago, 1964.

HOAG, J. D. "The Tomb of Ulugh Beg and Abdu Razzaq at Ghazni, a Model for the Taj Mahal," *Journal of the Society of Architectural Historians*, XXVII, no. 4, December 1968, pp. 234–48.

———. *Western Islamic Architecture*, New York, 1963.

HOLOD-TRETIAK, R. "Qasr al-Hayr al-Sharqi: a Mediaeval Town in Syria," *Archaeology*, XXIII, no. 3, January 1970, pp. 221–31.

HOLT, P. M., LAMBTON, A. K. S., and LEWIS, B., eds. *The Cambridge History of Islam*, 2 vols., Cambridge, 1970.

HOMMAIRE DE HELL, X. *Voyage en Turquie et en Perse exécuté pendant les années 1846, 1847, et 1848*, 4 vols., Paris, 1853–60.

HOURANI, A. H., and STERN, S. M., eds. *The Islamic City: a Colloquium* (see in particular S. A. EIALI, "The Foundation of Baghdad"; J. LASSNER, "The Caliph's Personal Domain"; J. M. ROGERS, "Samarra, a Study in Mediaeval Tarsis Planning"), Oxford and Philadelphia, 1970.

IÑIGUEZ ALMECH, F. "La Aljafería de Zaragoza: presentación de los nuevos nallazgos," in *Primer Congreso de Estudios Árabes e Islámicas, Córdoba, 1962, Actas*, Madrid, 1964.

JAIRAZBHOY, R. A. "The Taj Mahal in the Context of East and West: a Study in the Comparative Method," *Journal of the Warburg and Courtauld Institute*, XXIV, 1961, pp. 59–88.

KAHN, F. A. *Bandhore: a Preliminary Report on the Recent Archaeological Excavations at Bandhore* (Ministry of Education, Government of Pakistan), Karachi, 1960 (updated, 1963).

KÔLSUK, A. "Turkish Tiles and Ceramics," *Apollo*, July 1970, pp. 58–61.

KÜHNEL, E. *Islamic Art and Architecture*, London, 1966.

KURAN, A. *The Mosque in Early Ottoman Architecture*, Chicago-London, 1968.

LA ROCHE, E. *Indische Baukunst*, 6 vols., Munich, 1921–22.

Les Mosquées de Samarcande, I: Gour Emir (Commission Impériale Archéologique), St. Petersburg, 1905.

LÉZINE, A. *Architecture de l'Ifrīqiya: Recherches sur les monuments aghlabides*, Paris, 1966.

———. *Deux villes d'Ifrīqiya: Sousse, Tunis; études d'archéologie, d'urbanisme, de démographie*, Paris, 1971.

———. "La Salle d'audience du palais d'Achîr," *Revue des Études Islamiques*, XXXVII, 1969, pp. 203–18.

———. *Le ribat de Sousse, suivi de notes sur le ribat de Monastir* (Direction des antiquités et arts de Tunisie: Notes et Documents, XIV), Tunis, 1956.

———. *Mahdiya: Recherches d'archéologie Islamique* (Archéologie méditerranéenne, vol. 1), Paris, 1965.

———. "Notes d'archéologie ifriqiyenne," *Revue des Études Islamiques*, XXXV, 1967, pp. 53–101.

MARÇAIS, G. *L'Architecture musulmane d'occident: Tunisie, Algérie, Maroc, Espagne, et Sicile*, Paris, 1954.

———. *L'Art musulman*, Paris, 1962.

MAYER, L. A. *Islamic Architects and their Work*, Geneva, 1956.

MEUNIÉ, J., and TERRASSE, H. *Recherches archéologiques à Marrakech*, Paris, 1952.

———, ———, and DEVERDUN, G. *Nouvelles recherches archéologiques à Marrakech*, Paris, 1957.

MONNERET DE VILLARD, U. *Introduzione allo studio dell'archeologia islamica: le origini e il periodo omayyade* (Istituto per la Collaborazione Culturale), Venice-Rome, 1966.

MOSTAFA, S. L. *Kloster und Mausoleum des Pharo Ibn Barquq in Kairo* (Diss. Aachen, 1966; Deutsches Archäologisches Institut, Kairo, Abh. Islam, Reihe 2), Glückstadt, 1968.

MUHAMMAD, A. M. "A Preliminary Report on the Excavations at Kufa During the Second Season," *Sumer*, XIX, 1963, pp. 36–65.

ÖRS, H. "The History of the Topkapi Palace," *Apollo*, July 1970, pp. 6–16.

OTTO-DORN, K., and ÖNDER, M. "Bericht über die Grabung in Kobadabad (Oktober 1965)," *Archäologischer Anzeiger*, no. 2, 1966, pp. 170–83.

———. "Bericht über die Grabung in Kobadabad 1966," *Archäologischer Anzeiger*, no. 4, 1969, pp. 438–506.

———. "Grabung im umayyadischen Ruṣāfah," *Ars Orientalis*, II, 1957, pp. 119–33.

———. *Kunst des Islam*, Baden-Baden, 1964.

PAGLIERO, R., VIALE MARIETTI, E., and VIALE, G. "Ukhaidir, an Instance of Monument Restoration," *Mesopotamia*, II, 1967, pp. 195–217.

PAVÓN, M. B. *Memoria de la excavación de la mezquita de Medinat al-Zahra* (Dirección de Bellas Artes), Madrid, 1966.

POPE, A. U. *Persian Architecture; the Triumph of Form and Color*, New York, 1965.

———, and ACKERMAN, P., eds. *A Survey of Persian Art*, vol. II, Oxford, 1939; vol. IV, Oxford, 1938.

PUGACHENKOVA, G. A. "Ishrat-khāneh and Ak-Saray, Two Timurid Mausoleums in Samarkand," *Ars Orientalis*, V, 1963, pp. 177–89.

———. *Iskutsva Turkmenistana*, Moscow, 1967.

———. "Les Monuments peu connus de l'architecture médiévale de l'Afghanistan," *Afghanistan*, XXI, 1968, pp. 17–52.

———. "Mazar Arab-Ata B. Time," *Sovietskaya Arkheologia*, no. 4, 1961, pp. 198–211.

———. *Puti razvitija arhitektury Iuzhnogo Turkmenistana*, Moscow, 1958.

———, and REMPEL, L. I. *Istoriia Iskusstv Uzbekistana*, Moscow, 1965.

REUTHER, O. *Indische Paläste und Wohnhäuser*, Berlin, 1925.

———. *Ocheïdir* (Wissenschaftliche Veröffentlichung der Deutschen Orient-Gesellschaft), Leipzig, 1912.

RIVOIRA, G. T. *Architettura musulmana; sue origini e suo sviluppo*, Milan, 1914.

ROGERS, J. M. "Recent Work on Seljuk Anatolia," *Kunst des Orients*, VI, 1969, pp. 134–69.

SCHLUMBERGER, D. "Le palais ghaznévide de Lashkari Bazar," *Syria*, XXIX, 1952, pp. 251–70.

———. "Les fouilles de Qasr el-Heir el-Gharbi (1936–1938). Rapport préliminaire," *Syria*, XX, 1939, pp. 195–238.

SEBAG, P. *The Great Mosque of Kairouan*, London-New York, 1965.

SEHERR-THOSS, S., and SEHERR-THOSS, H. *Design and Color in Islamic Architecture* (Smithsonian Institution Publications), Washington, D.C., 1968.

SHAFE'I, F. "The Mashad Al-Juyushi: Archeological Notes and Studies," in *Studies in Islamic Art and Architecture in Honour of Professor K. A. C. Creswell*, Cairo, 1965, pp. 237–52.

SMITH, E. W. *Akbar's Tomb, Sikandrah, near Agra, Described and Illustrated* (Archaeological Survey of India, New Imperial Series, XXXV), Allahabad, 1909.

SOURDEL, D., and SOURDEL, J. *La civilisation de l'Islam classique*, Paris, 1968.

SOURDEL THOMINE, J. "La mosquée et la madrasa," *Cahiers de Civilisation Médiévale*, XIII, no. 2, April-June 1970, pp. 97–115.

STRONACH, D., and CUYLER YOUNG, T., JR. "Three Octagonal Seljuk Tomb Towers from Iran," *Iran*, IV, 1966, pp. 1–20.

TALBOT RICE, D. *Islamic Art*, New York, 1965.

TALBOT RICE, T. *The Seljuks in Asia Minor*, New York, 1961.

TERRASSE, C. *Médersas du Maroc*, Paris, 1928.

TERRASSE, H. *La grande mosquée de Taza, avec une étude d'épigraphie historique de G. S. Colin*, Paris, 1943.

———. *La mosquée al-Qaraouiyin à Fès, avec une étude de G. Deverdun sur les inscriptions de la mosquée* (Archéologie méditerranéenne, vol. 3), Paris, 1968.

———. *La mosquée des Andalous à Fès*, Paris, 1942.

———. "Les influences orientales sur l'art musulman d'Espagne," *Studia Islamica*, XXVII, 1967, pp. 123–48.

TEXIER, C. *Description de l'Armenie, la Perse et la Mésopotamie*, 2 vols., Paris, 1842–52.

THIERSCH, H. *Pharaos, Antike, Islam und Occident: ein Beitrag zur Architekturgeschichte*, Berlin, 1909.

TORRES BALBÁS, L. *Arte Almohade. Arte Nazarí. Arte Mudéjar* (Ars Hispaniae, vol. IV), Madrid, 1949.

———. *Artes Almoravide y Almohade* (Artes y Artistas. Instituto Diego Velázquez de Consejo Superior de Investigaciones Científicas), Madrid, 1955.

ÜNSAL, B. *Turkish Islamic Architecture in Seljuk and Ottoman Times 1071–1923*, London, 1959.

VOGT-GÖKNIL, U. *Turquie Ottomane*, Fribourg, 1965.

VOLWAHSEN, A. *Living Architecture: Islamic Indian*, New York, 1970.

WENDELL, C. "Baghdad, Imago Mundi and Other Foundation-Lore," *International Journal of Middle East Studies*, II, April 1971, pp. 99–128.

WETZEL, F. *Islamische Grabbauten in Indien aus der Zeit der Soldatenkaiser 1320–1540*, Leipzig, 1918.

WILBER, D. N. *Persian Gardens and Garden Pavilions*, Rutland (Vermont), 1962.

———. *The Architecture of Islamic Iran; the Il-Khanid Period*, Princeton, 1955 (New York, 1969).

ZANDER, G. *Travaux de restauration de monuments historiques en Iran* (Istituto Italiano per il Medio ed Estremo Oriente), Rome, 1968.

Abarquh (Persia), Gunbad-i-Ali, 144, 204; *plate 257*
al-Abbas, 34
Abbasi, Riza, miniaturist, 350, 352
Abbasids, 10, 16, 21, 32, 34–60, 74, 136, 150, 158, 166, 169, 191, 192, 210, 267, 288, 308, 330
Abd al-Malik, caliph, 16, 18, 21, 28
Abd al-Mumin, caliph, 105, 113
Abd al-Samad, funerary complex of, *see* Natanz
Abd er-Rahman I ibn Mu'awiyah, 77, 81
Abd er-Rahman II, 81, 83
Abd er-Rahman III (al-Nasir li din Allah), 81, 83, 90, 103
Abd Allah ibn Yazd, 13
Abdallah Ansari, Shrine of, *see* Gazur Gah
Abdallah ibn al-Shaikh, sultan, 103
Abdu Razzaq, 277; Tomb of, *see* Ghazna
Abdul Haq, 374
Abdu'l Samad, 255
Abu Abd Allah al-Shi'i, 73
Abu al-Abbas, *see* al-Saffah
Abu Bakr, caliph, 13
Abu Dulaf, Mosque of, *see* Samarra
Abu Ibrahim Ahmad, 72; *see also* Kairouan, Great Mosque
Abu Inan, 119
Abu Jafar al-Mansur, *see* al-Mansur
Abu Jafar al-Muqtadir, 90, 92
Abu-l-Hasan Ali, 117
Abu Muslim, 34, 46
Abu Said, 275, 352
Abu Said, shaykh, 255
Abu Said, sultan, 250, 252, 259
Abu Said Uthman, sultan, 119
Abu Shakir ibn Abi al-Faraj, architect, 210
Abu Shuja Muhammad, 199
Abu Yaqub Yusuf I, 111
Abu Ya'qub Yusuf, 116, 117
Abu Yusuf Yaqub, 116
Abul Fath, architect, 198
Abu'l Qasim, architect, 355
Abul Qazim Babur, 363
Achaemenids, 10, 13, 261
Acre (Israel), 141; Church of St. John, 169
Adham Khan, 304
adhan, 13
al-Adid, 146
Adrianople, *see* Edirne
Afghanistan, 9, 10, 184, 280, 288
Afrasiyab (Samarkand, Soviet Union), 185
Afyon Karahisar, Friday mosque, 230
Aghlabids, 10, 64, 73, 81, 114
Agra (India), 380, 383, 386
   Delhi Gate, 366, 373

Jahangiri Mahal (Red Palace), 373–74; *plates 490–94*
Pearl Mosque (Moti Masjid), 386; *plates 509–10*
Rambagh, 364
Taj Mahal, 9, 108, 358, 361, 374, 380–83, 386, 388; *plates 504–7*
Tomb of the Ittimad al-Daula (Mirza Ghiyas Beg), 377–78, 380; *plates 499–501*
Agra-Sikandra, *see* Sikandra
Ahi Bayazid, 312
Ahlat, tombs at, 247
Ahmad (Nadir al-Asar), architect, 383, 386
Ahmad III al-Mustansir, 122
Ahmad ibn Baso, architect, 111
Ahmad ibn Ismail, 184; Tomb of, *see* Bukhara
Ahmad ibn Tulun, *see* Ibn Tulun
Ahmad of Marand, 244, 247
Ahmad of Tiflis, 229
Ahmad Yasani, Shrine of, *see* Turkestan City
Ahmedabad (India), 297; Jami Masjid, 300
Ahmediye, *see* Istanbul
Ahmet I, sultan, 339
Ahmet Shah, 224
Ajmer (India), 282; Arhai Din Ka Jompra Mosque, 285, 288, 300; *plates 372–74*; Palace-Fortress of Akbar, 366, 373; *plates 482–83*
Akbar, Jalal al-Din, 304, 366–74, 377, 386, 388; Palace-Fortress of, *see* Ajmer; Tomb of, *see* Sikandra
Aksaray (Turkey), *see* Alay Han; Sultan Han
Akserai Palace, *see* Shahr-i-Sabz
Ala al-Din Kaykubad I, *see* Kaykubad I
Ala al-Din Khalji, 290, 297
Alai Darwaza, *see* Delhi, Quwwat al-Islam
Alay Han (near Aksaray), 237
Aleppo (Syria), 122, 152, 170, 210, 213, 221, 229, 230, 250; Great Mosque, minaret, 213; *plates 265–66*; Madrasa al-Firdaus, 221; *plate 282*; Shadbakht Madrasa, 170
Alexandria, 9, 136
Alfonso X of Castile, 122
Algeciras, 117
Algeria, 9, 11, 76, 105; Qala of the Bani Hammad, 74, 76, 113, 144; *plates 78–81*
Algiers, 94; Great Mosque, 94; *plates 116–19*
Alhambra, *see* Granada
Ali, 13, 15, 16, 252, 358
Ali al-Rida, prince, 42, 265; Shrine of, *see* Mashad
Ali ben Yusuf, sultan, 98, 104
Ali de Gomara, architect, 111
Ali ibn al-Dimishqi, architect, 249
Ali ibn Ilyas of Bursa ("Nakkas"), 312
Ali Kapu, *see* Isfahan
Aljaferiya Palace, *see* Zaragoza
Allahaverdi Khan, general, 347; bridge of, *see* Isfahan

Almohads, 74, 76, 93, 94, 98, 103, 104, 105–14, 116, 117, 119, 134
Almoravids, 10, 72, 76, 92, 93, 94–105, 108, 113, 114, 116, 134
Alp Arslan, sultan, 192, 199, 222
Amasya (Turkey), Halifet Ghazi Kumbed, 244; *plate 314*
Amballa, 292
al-Amin, 42
Amir, Khwand, 272
al-Amir, 146
Amman (Jordan), 9, 32
Anatolia, 9, 10, 27, 169, 170, 192, 221, 222–49, 250, 254, 259, 280, 308, 323, 339
Andalusia, 122, 134
Ani (Turkey), 222, 223, 242
Anjar (near Baalbek), 27–28, 30, 32, 83; *plates 22–23*
Ankara, 250, 264, 308, 312
Antalya (Turkey), 222, 237, 242
Antioch (Turkey), 9, 222
Antonines, 237
Aphrodito papyri (Egypt), 21, 28
Apollonia, Governor's Palace, 32
Aq Sonqur, 210, 213
Arab Ata, Tomb of, *see* Tim
Arabs, 13, 27, 60, 77, 90, 210
Ardabil (Iran), 345, 350, 358
Ardashir I, 35
Arghun, 252
Arhai Din Ka Jompra Mosque, *see* Ajmer
Arjuman Banu Begum (Mumtaz Mahal), 378, 380, 383
Armenia, 146, 169, 222, 224, 229, 230, 242, 247, 280, 330
Arslan Shah, 189, 199, 201
Artukids, 162, 177, 222, 223, 224, 230, 242
Arz Odasi, *see* Istanbul, Top Kapu Saray
Asaf Khan, 377, 378
Ascalon (Israel), 148
Ashir (Algeria), 74, 113, 136; Palace of Ziri, 74, 104; *plates 76–77*
Aslanapa, Oktay, 177, 229, 249, 334
Asoka, 292
Assyrians, 10, 34–35
Attarine Madrasa, *see* Fez
Aurangzeb, 378, 386, 388
Aydinids, 223, 249
Ayyubids, 10, 11, 151, 152–58, 169, 177, 183, 210; 221, 222
Azerbaijan (Iran), 209, 222, 237, 250, 264, 317, 345
al-Aziz, caliph, 136, 141

Baalbek (Lebanon), 27, 213
Bab al-Amma Gate, *see* Samarra

Bab al-Futuh, *see* Cairo

Bab al-Nasr, *see* Cairo

Bab-i-Humayun, *see* Istanbul, Top Kapu Saray

Bab-i-Saadet, *see* Istanbul, Top Kapu Saray

Bab Zuwayla, *see* Cairo

Babur, Zahir al-Din, emperor, 261, 262, 268, 275, 277, 300, 304, 352, 361, 363, 364, 366, 380, 388

Babur Mirza (Abul Qazim Babur), 363

Babylon, 52; Ishtar Gate, 10

Badr al-Gamali (Amir al-Juyushi), 141, 146, 148, 151; *plates 166, 172*

Baghdad (Iraq), 34, 39, 42, 46, 50, 81, 146, 158, 183, 210, 222, 250, 343, 345, 388

Abbasid palaces, 35, 188–89, 267

Dar al-Khilafah, 34

circular city of al-Mansur, 32, 34, 42, 46, 72, 73, 136; *plate 31*

Han Ortmah, 255; *plate 329*

Mustansiriya, 219, 221; *plates 279–81*

Palace in the Qala, 214, 219; *plates 272–78*

Qubbat al-Khadra, 34

Talisman Gate, 219

Baghdad Kiosk, *see* Istanbul, Top Kapu Saray

Baghratids, 222

Bahmanids, 297

Bahram Gur, 380

Bahram Shah, architect, 189

Bakr Muhammad, 209

al-Bakri, 60, 64

Baku (Soviet Union), 262; palace of the Shirvan Shahs, 264

Balban, *see* Qhiyath al-Din

Balkh (Afghanistan), 34, 184; Masjid-i-Tarikh, 48, 90, 184; *plates 47–49*; Shrine of Khwaja Abu Nasr Parsa, 272, 275; *plate 362*

Banbhore (Pakistan), congregational mosque, 280; *plate 367*

Bargebuhr, Frederick P., 122, 126, 130

Basra (Iraq), 13, 15, 27, 34, 60; congregational mosque, 13, 14, 15; Dar al-Imara, 14, 15

Bayazid I, sultan, 250, 308, 310; Kulliye of, *see* Bursa; Mosque of, *see* Bursa

Bayazid II, 325; Hospital of, *see* Edirne; Kulliye of, *see* Edirne; Mosque of, *see* Edirne; Istanbul

Baybars al-Bunduqdari, sultan, 158, 170, 223; Great Mosque of, *see* Cairo; Kasr al-Ablaq, *see* Damascus

Baysunghur Mirza, 265, 268

Bedouins, 72

Bektashi sect, 262

Berbers, 60, 64, 73, 77, 90, 94, 103, 116, 122

Bethlehem, Church of the Nativity, 22

Beyliks, 247–49

Beyshehir, 242; Eshrefoglu Mosque, 230; palaces at, 242, 244

Bib Mardun Mosque, *see* Toledo

Bibi Khanum Mosque, *see* Samarkand

Bijapur (India), 380

al-Biruni, 280

Bithynia (Anatolia), 308

Blue Mosque, *see* Istanbul, Ahmediye

Bombaci, A., 189

Bou Inaniya Madrasa, *see* Fez

Bougie (Algeria), 74, 76

Brown, Percy, 294, 304, 366

Buddhism, 34, 35, 288, 294

Bukhara (Soviet Union), 56, 184, 250

Kalayan Minaret, 189, 199, 285; *plate 248*

Maghak-i-Attari Mosque, 201

Tomb of Ismail the Samanid, 184–85, 186, 204, 209, 255; *plates 227–28*

Bukhara-Samarkand road, Robat-i-Malik, 108, 199, 201, 204, 213

Bulkawara Palace, *see* Samarra

Burgos (Spain), 134

Burhanpur, 383

Burjis, 158, 173

Bursa (Prusa, Turkey), 223, 308, 310, 317, 321, 323, 328

Ala al-Din Bey Mosque, 308

Kulliye of Yildirim Bayazid I, 310; *plate 405*

Mosque of Yildirim Bayazid I, 310, 312; *plate 406*

Turbe of Mehmet I, 317; *plates 415, 417*

Ulu Cami, 310, 312, 317, 343; *plates 407–8*

Yeşil Cami, 312, 317, 323, 325, 343; *plates 409–14, 416*

Bust (Persia), 188

Buyyids, 186, 192, 210

Byzantium, 9, 10, 13, 21, 27, 30, 32, 81, 83, 84, 92, 192, 222, 308, 310, 325, 344

Cairo (al-Qahira), 11, 56, 72, 74, 136, 148, 151, 152, 169, 177, 183, 213; *plate 166*

Bab al-Futuh (Bab al-Iqbal), 136, 146; *plate 179*

Bab al-Nasr (Bab al-Izz), 136, 146

Bab Zuwayla, 136, 146, 148

Bayn al-Kasrayn (modern Suq al-Nahassin), 136, 152, 158, 166

Citadel of Salah ad-Din, 152, 158; *plates 166, 190*

Great Mosque of Baybars, 117, 158, 162, 292; *plates 196–201*

Haret al-Salihiya, 158

House of Gamal al-Din al-Zahabi, 178, 183; *plates 222–26*

Kasr al-Ablaq, 166, 177–78, 183; *plates 219–21*

Madrasa of Salih Negm ad-Din, 152, 158, 162, 166; *plates 191–94*

Madrasa of Sultan Hasan al Nasir, 169–70, 173; *plates 210–12*

Madrasa of Sultan Qala'un, 162, 166, 169; *plates 202, 206, 208*

Madrasa of Sultan Qayt Bay, 173, 177; *plates 213–16*

Mosque of al-Aqmar, 146, 148, 150, 151, 158, 162, 170; *plates 180–82*

Mosque of al-Azhar, 136, 141, 146, 148, 178; *plates 167–71*

Mosque of al-Aziz, 136, 141

Mosque of al-Hakim, 136, 141, 146, 148, 150, 151, 162; *plates 172–76*

Mosque of al-Juyushi, 141, 144; *plates 177–78*

Mosque of al-Salih Tala'i, 148, 150, 158; *plates 183–85*

Mosque of Amr, 56

Mosque of Ibn Tulun, 56, 60, 136, 141, 148, 169, 297; *plates 57–61*

Mosque of Muhammad Ali, 177, 178

Qa'at al-Dardir, 150–51, 152, 177; *plates 188–89*

Sharia al-Azhar, 136

Sharia al-Muizz li-din-Illah, 136, 146

Suq al-Nahassin, *see* Bayn al-Kasrayn

Tomb of Salih Negm ad-Din, 158, 166; *plates 191–92, 195*

Tomb of Sharif Tabatabai, 48

Tomb of Sultan Hasan al-Nasir, 169–70, 173; *plates 210–12*

Tomb of Sultan Qala'un, 162, 166, 169; *plates 202–5, 207, 209*

Tomb of Sultan Qayt Bay, 173, 177; *plates 213–14, 217*

walls of, 136, 146, 152; *plate 166*

Zahiriya of Baybars, 170

Capilla de Villaviciosa, Great Mosque of Cordoba, *see* Cordoba

caravanserais, 199, 201, 209, 237

Carolingian Empire, 9

Carthage, 13

Castillejo of Monteagudo, *see* Murcia

Cefalù, Pantocrator, 173

Çekirge (near Bursa), Mosque-Madrasa of Murad I, 310; *plates 402–4*

Chagatayids, 250

chahr bagh, see Paradise, gardens of

Chakravartin, 35

Champanir (Muhammadabad), Jami Masjid, 297, 300; *plates 393–97*

Chehel Situn, *see* Isfahan

Chingiz (Genghis) Khan, 250, 364

Chosroes, 30

Christians, 14, 18, 21, 22, 32, 77, 90, 94, 105, 116, 134, 146, 169, 173, 222, 280, 306, 363

Çinli Kiosk, *see* Istanbul, Top Kapu Saray

Citadel of Salah ad-Din, *see* Cairo

Clavijo, Gonzalez de, 260, 261, 262, 264

Companions of the Prophet, *mihrab, see* Damascus, Great Mosque

congregational mosques, *see* mosques

Constantinople, 11, 15, 22, 28, 30, 84, 177, 308, 321,

339, 344; view of, *see* al-Matraki; *see also* Istanbul

Cordoba (Spain), 9, 10, 77, 81, 90, 92, 103, 104, 108, 111, 113, 116, 119, 134, 166, 169
   Great Mosque of Abd er-Rahman I, 77, 81, 83; *plates 82–84*; enlarged by Hakam II, 83–84, 90, 92, 94, 98, 104, 111; *plates 91–97*; enlarged by al-Mansur (987), 84, 90; *plate 98*

Coste, Pascal, 350, 355, 361

Court of Lions, Alhambra, *see* Granada

Creswell, K. A. C., 13, 15, 25, 27, 28, 34, 35, 50, 52, 56, 60, 136, 158, 162, 166, 185, 219, 288

Crusaders, 148, 158, 162, 177, 213, 222, 224

Ctesiphon (Persia), 13, 30, 52, 221, 259, 261

Cyrene, Caesareum, 10

Cyprus, 334

Daifa Khatun, 221

Dalgiç Ahmet Aga, architect, 339

Damascus (Syria), 9, 13, 14, 22, 27, 28, 92, 177, 210, 213, 229, 250
   Church of St. John, 22, 25
   Great Mosque, 18, 21, 22, 25, 27, 32, 60, 84, 173, 223, 224, 249; *plates 13–17, 19–21*; Mihrab (Companions of the Prophet), 22
   Kasr al-Ablaq, 178
   Madrasa al-Nuriya al-Kubra, 214; *plates 269–71*
   Muristan Nuri, 170, 213–14, 230; *plates 267–68*
   Qubbat al-Khadra (Dar al-Imara), 14, 15, 22, 34
   Temple of Bel, 14
   Temple of Jupiter Damascenus, 22

Damghan (Iran), minaret, 198; Tarik Khana, 42, 184; *plates 40–43*

Danishmends, 222, 224

Dar al-Harb, 13, 15, 30, 64

Dar al-Islam, 13, 15, 30

Darabgird (Iran), 35

Dar al-Imara, 14; *see* Damascus; Kufa; Merv

Dar al-Khilafah, *see* Baghdad

Daulatabad (Deccan), 292

Davut Aga, architect, 334, 340

de Beylié, L., 74

decoration, *see* ornamentation

Delhi, 189, 250, 282, 294, 297, 300, 383, 386
   Citadel, *see* Red Fort
   Kotila of Firuz Shah, 292, 294, 300, 377; *plates 382–83*
   Pearl Mosque (Moti Masjid), 386
   Qtub Minar, 204, 285, 290; *plate 371*
   Quwwat al-Islam, 280, 282, 285, 288, 290, 297; *plates 368–70*; Alai Darwaza, 290, 292; *plate 380*
   Red Fort, 380, 383, 386, 388; *plates 511–13*
   Tomb of Humayun, 9, 304, 364, 366, 380, 388; *plates 479–81*
   Tomb of Iltutmish, 288; *plates 375–76*
   Tomb of Isa Khan Niyazi, 304, 366; *plates 399–401*

Tomb of Khan-i-Jahan Tilangari, 304
   Tomb of Sultan Ghari, 288, 290; *plates 377–79*

Delhi-Tarbabad, Hauz-i-Khas, 294, 373; *plates 384–87*; Tomb of Firuz Shah, 294; *plate 387*

Delhi-Tughluqabad, Tomb of Ghiyath al-Din Tughluq, 292; *plate 381*

della Valle, Pietro, 169, 350

Description of the Stages of Sultan Suleyman's Campaign in the Two Iraqs, see al-Matraki

devşirme, 328

Dimoteka (Greece), mosque, 330

Din Illahi, 366, 373, 374

Dinpanah, 364, 366

Divrig (Turkey), 222; Great Mosque (Ulu Cami), 224, 229, 230, 233; *plates 285–88, 290*; Hospital, 224, 229, 230; *plates 285–86, 289, 291*; Sitte Melik Kumbed, 244; *plates 315–16*

Diyarbekir (Turkey), 177, 222, 223, 224; Great Mosque, 223, 224, 230; Mas'udiyya Madrasa, 230; Mosque of Fatih Pasha, 330; palace, 242

Dodd, Erica Cruikshank, 170, 173

Dome of the Rock, *see* Jerusalem

Döner Kumbed, *see* Kayseri

Dorn, K. Otto, 242

Duma, 13

Dunaysir (Kiziltepe), 222; Great Mosque, 223–24; *plates 283–84*

Ecija, 116

Edirne (former Adrianople), Turkey, 308, 310
   Kulliye of Bayazid II, 325, 328; *plates 429–30*
   Kulliye of Selim II, 334; *plate 442*
   Hospital of Bayazid II, 328, *plate 432*
   Mosque of Bayazid II, 325, 328; *plate 431*
   Selimiye, 334, 339; *plates 441, 443*
   Üç Şerefeli Cami, 312, 317, 321, 323; *plates 418–21*

Egypt, 9, 10, 11, 21, 39, 50, 56, 73, 74, 76, 119, 122, 221, 223, 242, 244, 282, 292, 308; *see also* Ayyubids, Fatimids, Mamluks

Erzincan, 222

Erzurum (Turkey), 222; Çifte Minareli Madrasa, 233

Ettinghausen, Richard, 28, 30, 48

al-Faiz, caliph, 148

Fakreddin Sahip Ata, vizier, 230, 233

Fars (Iran), 250, 262

Fatih-Ali-Shah, 361

Fatih Cami, *see* Istanbul

Fatimid houses, 150–51; *plates 186–87*

Fatimids, 10, 72, 73, 74, 81, 103, 108, 136–51, 152, 158, 166, 173, 183, 192, 288, 292; caliphate, 22, 74, 141, 146

Fatipur Sikri (India), palace complex, 366, 371, 373, 386, 388; *plates 484–89*

Diwan-i-Am, 371
   Diwan-i-Khas, 371, 373; *plates 485, 487–88*
   Mahal-i-Khas, 371; *plate 486*
   Panch Mahal, 294, 373, 377; *plate 489*

Ferdinand I of Castile, 122

Ferghana (Soviet Union), 275, 364

Fez (North Africa), 9, 72, 81, 92, 103, 116, 122, 136
   Attarine Madrasa, 119, 122; *plates 150–52*
   Bou Inaniya Madrasa, 119, 122; *plates 153–56*
   Qarawiyin Mosque, 98, 103–4, 108, 119, 122; *plates 125–28*

Fez al-Jedid (New Fez), Friday mosque, 116; *plate 144*

Firdausi (*Shah Namah*), 189

Firuz Shah, 292, 294, 297, 304, 373; Kotila of, *see* Delhi; Tomb of, *see* Delhi-Tarbadabad, Hauz-i-Khas

Firuzabad (Iran), 35

Formation of Islamic Art (Grabar), 10

Franks, 169

Friday mosques, *see* mosques

al-Fustat, 13, 136; Fatimid houses, 150–51, 152, 177, 214; *plates 186–87*

Gamal al-Din al-Zahabi, House of, *see* Cairo

gardens, *see* Paradise

Gargistan (Afghanistan), Shah-i-Mashad, 288

Gate of the Chella, *see* Rabat

Gate of the Ouadiah Kasba, *see* Rabat

Gavam al-Din of Shiraz, architect, 267, 268, 270, 275, 277

Gawhar Shad, 265, 267, 268; Great Mosque of, *see* Mashad; Madrasa of, Musalla of, *see* Herat

Gazur Gah (near Herat), Shrine of Abdallah Ansari, 270, 272; *plates 357–58*

Genghis Khan, 250, 364

Georgia (Soviet Union), 222, 229, 242

Gerasa (Jordan), 9

Ghari, sultan, Tomb of, *see* Delhi

Ghazan Khan, 250

Ghaznavids, 10, 152, 184, 186–91, 192, 201, 230, 261, 280

al-Ghazzali, 192

Ghazna (Afghanistan), 184, 188, 189
   Minaret of Bahram Shah, 189, 285
   Minaret of Mas'ud III, 189, 285; *plates 237–38*
   Palace of Mas'ud III, 189, 201; *plates 239–40*
   Tomb of Abdu Razzaq, 275, 277; *plates 365–66*
   Tomb of Mahmud, 189, 277
   Tomb of Ulugh Beg Miranshah, 275, 277; *plates 365–66*

Ghiyath al-Din of Shiraz, architect, 270

Ghiyath al-Din Muhammad of Ghur, sultan, 280, 282

Ghiyath al-Din Tughluq, 292, Tomb of, *see* Delhi-Tughluqabad

Ghiyathiya Madrasa, *see* Khargird

Ghurids, 10, 184, 188, 189, 280, 282, 285, 288

Giralda Tower, *see* Seville

Goddard, André, 199, 209

Gök Madrasa, *see* Sivas

Golombek, Lisa, 48, 262, 270, 272

Goodwin, Godfrey, 310, 317, 323, 330, 334, 339

Gothic art, 198, 224, 229, 254, 282, 330

Grabar, Oleg, 10, 21, 27, 30, 34, 46, 84

Granada, 11, 116; Alhambra, 76, 122, 126, 130, 134, 183, 189, 282, 325; *plates 157–65*; Court of Lions, 103, 126, 130, 134; *plate 163*

Great Mosque, *see* Aleppo; Algiers; Damascus; Divrig; Dunaysir; Isfahan; Kairouan; Kufa; Mahdiya; Seville; Taza; Tlemcen

Great Mosque of: Abd er-Rahman I, *see* Cordoba; al-Mutawakkil, *see* Samarra; Baybars, *see* Cairo; Gawhar Shad, *see* Mashad; Isa Bek, *see* Seljuk; Ishaq Bek, *see* Manisa; Mansura, *see* Tlemcen

Greek architecture, influence of, 9, 10, 13, 21, 25, 32

Gujerat (India), 297, 371, 373

Gulbarga, 297; Jami Masjid, 297; *plates 388–90*

Gulpaygan (Iran), mosque, 199; *plates 249–50*

Gunbad-i-Ali, *see* Abarquh

Gunbad-i-Kabud, *see* Maragha

Gunbad-i-Qabus, *see* Gurgan

Gunbad-i-Surkh, *see* Maragha

Gurgan (Iran), 186, Gunbad-i-Qabus, 186, 188, 204; *plates 231–33*

Gur-i-Amir, *see* Samarkand

Gwalior (India), 364; Palace of Man Singh, 294; Tomb of Shaykh Muhammad Ghaus, 377; *plate 497*

Gypsum Palace, *see* Samarra

Habibah Sultan Begum, 275

al-Hafiz, caliph, 148

Hafsids, 11, 72, 116

Hagia Sophia, *see* Istanbul

Hajji Ivaz, 312, 317

Hakam II, 81, 84, 90; *see also* Cordoba, Great Mosque

al-Hakim, caliph, 136, 141; Mosque of, *see* Cairo

Hakim Ali al-Din of Chinoit (Nawab Wazir Khan), 383; Mosque of, *see* Lahore

Halifet Ghazi Kumbed, *see* Amasya

Hamid, architect, 386

Hamilton, Robert W., 21, 28

Hammad ibn Buluggin ibn Ziri, 74

Hammadids, 74, 113

Han Ortmah, *see* Baghdad

Hanafites, 152, 214

Hanbalites, 152

hans, 237, 242

Haram al-Sharif, *see* Jerusalem

Harith ibn Jabala, 32

Harput, Friday mosque, 224

Harun al-Rashid, caliph, 35, 42, 64, 265, 267

al-Hasan, 15, 16

Hasan III, Grand Master of the Assassins, 214, 219

Hasan Aga, architect, 343

Hasan al-Nasir, sultan, 169; Madrasa of, Tomb of, *see* Cairo

Hasan ibn Mufarraj al-Sarmani, architect, 213

Hasht Behisht, *see* Isfahan

hasht behishts, 361, 363, 366

Hauz-i-Khas, *see* Delhi-Tarbabad

Haydariya Madrasa, *see* Qazvin

Hazarasp ibn Nasr, 204

Herat (Afghanistan), 250, 265, 267, 275, 285, 345, 352, 364, 386; Madrasa of Gawhar Shad, 268, 272; *plates 355–56*; Musalla of Gawhar Shad, 268; *plates 353–54*; Tareb Khana, 363

Herculaneum, 9

Hermopolis Magna (Egypt), 9

Herzfeld, Ernst, 48, 50, 52, 213, 214, 221

Heyruddin, architect, 325, 328

Hillalians, 72, 74

Hindu architecture, Hinduism, 10, 280–306, 373, 374, 388

Hira (Iran), 39

Hisham, caliph, 28, 32, 34, 60, 77

Hisham II, caliph, 90

Hittite architecture, 10

Holy War, 117

Honorius, emperor, 32

Hospital, *see* Divrig

hospitals (*muristans*), 213, 224, 230, 310, 328

House of Gamal al-Din al-Zahabi, *see* Cairo

Hudids, 90, 122

Hulagu, 250

Humayun, Nasir al-Din, emperor, 11, 300, 347, 364, 366, 388; Tomb of, *see* Delhi

Husain Baikara, 250, 275

Husayn Shah, 297; Friday mosque of, *see* Jaunpur, Jami Masjid

Husein, 16, 148, 252

Huwaissalat (near Ishaqi Canal), 46

Ibn al-Ahmar, 122

Ibn al-Zamrak, poet, 126

Ibn al-Zubayr, caliph, 16

Ibn Battuta, 260, 294

Ibn Habbus, king, 122

Ibn Serapion, 46

Ibn Tulun, 39, 56, 60; Mosque of, *see* Cairo

Ibrahim ibn al-Aghlab, 64

Idrissids, 72

Ifriqiya, 60, 64, 72, 74, 77, 98, 151, 199

Ikshidids, 136

Ilgin (Turkey), 233

Ilkhanids, 11, 170, 209, 233, 250–78, 350, 363

Iltutmish, Tomb of, *see* Delhi

Ilyas Beq, architect, 325

Imam Dur, *see* Samarra

Ince Minare Madrasa, *see* Konya

India, 9, 10, 11, 52, 134, 272, 280–306, 350, 364, 388; *see also* Moghuls

Iran, 144, 183, 184, 282, 288, 306; *see also* Persia

Iraq, 32, 34, 46, 52, 56, 60, 77, 84, 144, 158, 210, 214–21, 222, 244, 250

Isa Bek, Great Mosque of, *see* Seljuk

Isa ibn Musa, 35

Isa Khan Niyazi, Tomb of, *see* Delhi

Isfahan, 192, 250, 345, 358, 364; suburb of Shah Abbas I, 345; *plate 455*

    Ali Kapu, 178, 345, 347, 350, 352, 363; *plates 457–59*

    Bridge of Allahaverdi Khan, 363

    Bagh-i-Bulbul, 361

    Chahr Bagh, 347, 361

    Chehel Situn, 347, 350, 352, 361, 363; *plates 460–62*

    Hasht Behisht, 347, 358, 361, 363; *plates 475–76*

    Hazar Jerib, 347

    Masjid-i-Ali, 192, 198

    Masjid-i-Jami (Great Mosque), 144, 162, 170, 184, 192, 198, 209, 285; *plates 241–47*; Mihrab of Oljeitu, 254–55; *plate 328*

    Masjid-i-Shah, 10, 347, 355, 358; *plates 467–71*

    Meidan-i-Shah, 345, 347, 350, 352, 355, 358, 363

    Mosque of Shaykh Lutfullah, 352, 355; *plates 463–66*

    Naqsh-i-Jahan, 345

    palace complex, view of, 347; *plate 456*

    Pol-i-Khaju, 363; *plates 477–78*

Ishaq Bek, Great Mosque of, *see* Manisa

Ishrat Khaneh, *see* Samarkand

Iskander Lodi, *see* Sikandra

Ismail the Samanid, 184; Tomb of, *see* Bukhara

Ismalis, 186

Istakhr (near Persepolis), 13, 15

Istanbul, 339, 343; *see also* Constantinople

    Ahmediye (Blue Mosque), 334, 339; *plates 444–45*

    Chalki Gate, 25

    Çinli Kiosk, 323, 325, 328, 343; *plates 426–28*

    Eski Saray, 321, 328, 330

    Eyub Mosque, 325

    Fatih Cami (Mosque of Mehmet II), 321, 323, 328, 330; *plates 423–25*

    Hagia Sophia, 22, 136, 321, 328, 330, 334

    Kasri of Aynali Kavak, 343; *plate 454*

    Kulliye of Suleyman, 330; *plate 437*

    Mosque of Bayazid II, 328, 330, 334; *plates 433–35*

    Mosque of Selim I, 328

    Şehzade Cami, 330, 334, 339; *plate 436*

Suleymaniye, 330, 334, 339; plates 438–40
Top Kapu Saray (Cannon Gate Palace), 321, 340, 343; plates 446–53; Arz Odasi (Throne Room), 340; plate 449; Bab-i-Humayun (Imperial Gate), 321, 340; plate 446; Bab-i-Saadet (Gate of Felicity), 340; plate 448; Baghdad Kiosk, 343; plates 452–53; bed chamber of Murad III, 340; plates 450–51
Yedi Kule, castle of, 321
Yeni Cami, 334
Yeni Saray (New Palace), 321
Ittimad al-Daula, see Mirza Ghiyas Beg
Iwan-i-Kharqa, 255
Iznik (Nicea, Turkey), 222, 223, 308, 310, 340; Hajji Özbek mosque, 308; Mosque of Orhan, 308, 310

Jafar ibn Muhammad of Aleppo, architect, 230
Jaffa, 158, 162
Jahangir, Nur al-Din, emperor, 300, 371, 373, 374–78, 380, 383, 388; Tomb of, see Shadera
Jahangiri Mahal, see Agra
Jairazbhay, R. A., 380
Jalal al-Din Akbar, see Akbar
Jalayirids, 250
Jam, 189; minaret, 280, 285, 288
Jami, poet, 388
Jami Masjid, see Champanir; Gulbarga; Jaunpur
Jar Kurgan, minaret, 204
Jaunpur (near Benares), Jami Masjid (Friday mosque of Husayn Shah), 297; plates 391–92
Jausaq al-Kharqani, see Samarra
Jawhar, general, 136, 146
Jerusalem, 9, 13
    Church of the Ascension, Mount of Olives, 18
    Dar al-Imara, 21
    Haram al-Sharif, 16, 21; plate 4
    Mosque of al-Aqsa, 21–22, 42, 64, 72, 76, 77, 150; plates 11–12
    Qubbat al-Sakhra (Dome of the Rock), 16, 18, 21, 22, 27, 28, 52, 60, 162, 166, 173, 304; plates 5–10
    Stoa of Herod, 21
    Tomb of the Virgin, 18
Jomard, E. F., 177, 178
Jordan, 9, 32
al-Juyushi, 141, 144; Mosque of, see Cairo

Kaaba, 13, 16, 304
Kabul (Tunisia), 275, 364, 380
Kairouan (Afghanistan), 9, 60, 64, 72, 73, 74, 76, 136; Great Mosque of Yazid, 60, 64, 72, 77; plate 62; Great Mosque of Ziyadat Allah, 64, 72, 73, 74, 81, 84, 103, 114; plates 68–73; Tleta Biban, 48
Kalayan Minaret, see Bukhara
Kaluyan al-Qunawi, architect, 233
Kanwa, 364

Karachi (Pakistan), 280
Karaman (Turkey), 328
Karatay, vizier, 230
Karatay Madrasa, see Konya
Kashmir, 380
Kasr al-Ablaq, see Cairo; Damascus
Kasr al-Jiss, see Samarra
Kasr Kharanah (Jordan), 255
Kasr al-Khayr al-Gharbi, 28, 32
Kasr al-Khayr al-Sharki, 27, 28, 32; plate 29
Kasr ibn Wardan, 32
Kasri of Aynali Kavak, see Istanbul
Kaykhusrav II, 222, 229
Kaykhusrav III, 223
Kaykubad I, Ala al-Din, sultan, 222, 224, 229, 237, 242
Kayseri (Turkey), 222, 242; Döner Kumbed, 247; plate 319; Khwand Foundation, 229–30; plates 292–93; Koluk Mosque, 224; Turbe of Mahperi Khwand Khatun, 247; plate 318; see also Sultan Han
Keluk b. Abdullah, architect, 233
Kerbela, 16
Kesh, see Shahr-i-Sabz
Keykavus I, sultan, 222, 230; Turbe of, see Sivas
Keykavus II, 230
Khajars, 199, 350
Khalid ibn Barmak, 34, 35
Khalil, 169
Khalji Dynasty, 11, 290, 292, 366, 388
Khan-i-Jahan Tilangari, 304
Khargird, 201; Ghiyathiya Madrasa, 270, 272, 277–78, 325; plates 359–61
Kharjite movement, 60, 64
Kharraqan (Persia), tomb tower, 204, 209; plate 255
Khawarnak, castle, 380
Khirbat al-Mafjar, 28, 30, 32, 52, 60, 74, 92, 146, 148, 151, plates 24–27
Khirbat Minyah, 28
Khondamir, poet, 364, 366
Khorassan, 34, 42, 60, 64, 184, 189, 192, 204, 221, 250
Khorsabad, 52
al-Khuld (near Baghdad), 46
Khuram, prince, see Shah Jehan
Khuraysh tribe, 13
Khurramshah of Ahlat, architect, 224
Khwafi (near Khargird), 270
Khwaja Abu Nasr Parsa, Shrine of, see Balkh
Khwaja Rabi, Tomb of, see Mashad (vicinity)
Khwajah Hassan Shirazi, architect, 262
Khwand Foundation, see Kayseri
Khwarazm, 184, 214, 219, 222, 250, 259, 260
kiosks, 339–40, 343
Kishmar, 204
Kiziltepe, see Dunaysir

Kobadabad (Anatolia), palace complex, 242, 244, 254, 310; plates 312–13
Koca Sinan, see Sinan, Koca
Konya (Turkey), 219, 230, 308; Ala al-Din Mosque, 244; Great Mosque, 229; Ince Minare Madrasa, 230, 233; plates 298–301; Karatay Madrasa, 230; plates 296–97; Pavilion of Qilich Arslan II, 242; Sirçali Masjid, 230; plates 294–95; Wooden Mosque, 230, 233
Koran, 21, 27, 32, 42, 117, 126, 170, 173, 317, 343, 363
Kotila of Firuz Shah, see Delhi-Firuzabad
Kublai Khan, 388
Kufa, 10, 13, 15, 27, 34, 35, 56, 60; Dar al-Imara, 14, 16, 32; plate 3; Great Mosque, 13, 15–16, 280; plates 1–2
Kuh-i-Khwaja, 255
Kulliye of: Bayazid II, see Edirne; Selim II, see Edirne; Suleyman, see Istanbul; Yildirim Bayazid I, see Bursa
kumbeds, 244; see also tombs
Kuran, Aptullah, 308
Kutlu Dumur, 260
Kutubiyya Mosque, see Marrakesh
Kuzadag, 222

Lahore, 184, 280, 371, 378, 383, 386; Mosque of Wazir Khan, 10, 383, 386; plate 508; Pearl Mosque (Moti Masjid), 386
Lajin, 56, 60, 169
Lakhmids, 39
Lashkari Bazar (Lashkargah), near Bust, palace complex, 188–89, 201, 261, 374; plates 234–36
Lebanon, 27
Lézine, Alexandre, 60, 64, 73
Libya, 9, 169
Lodi Dynasty, 11, 300, 304, 366, 388
Lutfullah, 383

Madrasa of: al-Firdaus, see Aleppo; Gawhar Shad, see Herat; Murad I, see Çekirge; al-Nuriya al-Kubra, see Damascus; Salih Negm ad-Din, see Cairo; Sultan Hasan, see Cairo; Sultan Qala'un, see Cairo; Qayt Bay, see Cairo; Ulugh Beg, see Samarkand
madrasas, 119, 152, 201, 221, 230
Madrid, 92
Maghrib (North Africa), 9, 28, 72, 74, 134
al-Mahdi, caliph, 22, 35, 64, 76
Mahdiya (India), 73, 74, 81, 136, 151; plate 74; Great Mosque, 72–74, 136, 141; plate 75
Mahmud, 184, 188, 189, 277
Mahmud I Begra, 297
Mahperi Khatun, 229, 230; Turbe of, see Kayseri
Malatya, 222; Great Mosque, 229
al-Malik al-Adil, sultan, 221
al-Malik al-Aziz, 221
al-Malik al-Nasir I, see Salah ad-Din

al-Malik al-Zahir, 221

Malik Shah, sultan, 25, 162, 192, 198, 199, 210, 213, 222, 223

Malikaturan Malik, 224

Malikites, 105, 152

Malwa (India), 373

Mamluks, 11, 151, 152, 158–83, 221, 282, 355

al-Ma'mun, caliph, 42, 56, 265

al-Mamun al-Bataihi, vizier, 146

Manisa, 223; Great Mosque of Ishaq Bek, 247, 249, 317; *plates 320–21*

al-Mansur, Abu Jafar, caliph, 22, 34, 35; circular city, *see* Baghdad

al-Mansur, vizier, 81, 84, 90, 116

al-Mansur Sayf al-Din Qala'un, *see* Qala'un

al-Mansuriya (near Kairouan), 136

Manzikert, 192, 222

Maqrisi, 148

Maragha (Persia), 10; Gunbad-i-Kabud, 209; *plate 261*; Gunbad-i-Surkh, 209; *plate 256*

Marçais, Georges, 94

Mardin, 222

Marinids, 11, 93, 105, 113, 116–122, 134, 166, 183

Marrakesh, 73, 94, 105, 113, 116, 136; Kutubiyya Mosque: first, 104, 108, 114; second, 108, 111; *plates 133–36*; Mosque of Ali ben Yusuf, 98, 104; Palace of Ali ben Yusuf, 104; Qubbat Barudiyin, 94, 98; *plates 120–22*

Maryam al-Zamani, 300, 371

Mashad, 345, 358; Great Mosque of Gawhar Shad, 265, 267, 268, 355; *plates 348–49*; Shrine of Ali al-Rida, 259, 265, 267; *plate 348*; Tomb of Khwaja Rabi, 358, 361; *plates 472–74*

Masjid-i-Jami, *see* Isfahan; Tabriz; Varamin

Masjid-i-Shah, *see* Isfahan

Masjid-i-Tarikh, *see* Balkh

Mas'ud I, 188

Mas'ud III, 188, 189; Minaret of, Palace of, *see* Ghazna

al-Mas'udi, historian, 39

al-Matraki, manuscript painter, *Description of the Stages of Sultan Suleyman's Campaign in the Two Iraqs: Tomb of Oljeitu, Sultanieh*, 252; *plate 324*; *View of Constantinople*, 321, 323, 325, 328, 340; *plate 422*

Maximianus, 32

Mayyafariqin, *see* Silvan

Mecca, 16, 25, 84, 169, 339

Medina, 13, 84, 169; house of Muhammad, 13, 15, 60; mosque, 13, 15, 64

Medina al-Zahira, 81

Medina al-Zahra (Spain), 81, 83, 90, 136, 141; *plate 85*; mosque, 74, 83, 84; *plate 90*; palace complex, 9, 81, 126; *plate 86*; Salon Rico, 81, 83; *plates 87–89*

Mehmet I, 312; Turbe of, *see* Bursa

Mehmet II (Fatih the Conqueror), 308, 321, 323, 325, 340; Mosque of, *see* Istanbul

Mehmet III, 334

Mehmet Aga, architect, 339, 340

Mehmet the Mad, 312

Meidan-i-Shah, *see* Isfahan

Meknes (North Africa), 136

Melek Ghazi, ruler, 244

Mengujukids, 222, 224, 244

Merida, aqueduct, Roman, 77

Merv (Soviet Union), 13, 42, 189, 201; Dar al-Imara, 34, 46; Tomb of Sultan Sanjar, 209, 255, 290; *plates 259–60*

Mesopotamia, 9, 10, 282, 306

Messina, 189

Meunié, Jacques, 94

Mihr al-Nisa (Nur Jahan), 377–78

Minaret of Mas'ud III, *see* Ghazna

Mir Abdul Karim (Ma'mur Khan), architect, 383

Mirak Mirza Ghiyas, architect, 366

Mirza Ghiyas Beg, 377, 378; tomb of, *see* Agra, Tomb of the Ittimad al-Daula

Moghuls, 11, 30, 32, 134, 209, 244, 260, 261, 270, 272, 275, 277, 282, 292, 297, 300, 363, 364–88

Mongols, 11, 158, 169, 183, 188, 192, 210, 214, 222–23, 230, 250, 254, 290, 308

Monreale, Cathedral, 173

Montasir, Ribat, 60, 64

Morocco, 10, 11, 77, 94, 98, 105, 116, 119, 134, 136, 221

Mosque of: Abu Dulaf, *see* Samarra; al-Aqmar, *see* Cairo; al-Aqsa, *see* Jerusalem; al-Azhar, *see* Cairo; Bayazid I, *see* Bursa; Bayazid II, *see* Edirne, Istanbul; Bib Mardun, *see* Toledo; al-Hakim, *see* Cairo; Hassan, *see* Rabat; Ibn Tulun, *see* Cairo; al-Juyushi, *see* Cairo; Mehmet II, *see* Istanbul; Muhammad Ali, *see* Cairo; Murad I, *see* Çekirge; al-Salih Tala'i, *see* Cairo; Shaykh Lutfullah, *see* Isfahan; Wazir Khan, *see* Lahore

mosques, 10, 13, 25, 32, 42, 60, 64, 73, 76, 94, 114, 116, 117, 146, 184, 191, 198, 199, 209, 229–30, 294, 308, 312, 344, 355, 386

Mosul (Iraq), 152, 210, 222

Mshatta, palace complex, 16, 32, 35, 39, 48, 83, 90; *plates 28, 30*

Mu'awiyah I, 14, 15, 16, 22, 34

Mudejars, 134

Muhammad, prophet, 9, 13, 15, 16, 34, 60, 72, 84, 265, 340

Muhammad I, 297

Muhammad I al-Ghalib (Ibn al-Ahmar), 122

Muhammad V, 126, 130

Muhammad Ali, Mosque of, *see* Cairo

Muhammad Ghaus, Tomb of, *see* Gwalior

Muhammad ibn Atsiz of Sarakhs, 209

Muhammad ibn Mahmud of Isfahan, architect, 264

Muhammad ibn Makki of Zinjan, architect, 204

Muhammad ibn Musa, imam, 210

Muhammad ibn Tumart, mahdi, 105

Muhammad Khudabanda, *see* Oljeitu

Muhammad Riza ibn Ustad Husain of Isfahan, architect, 352

Muhammad Sultan, 264

Muhammadabad, *see* Champanir

al-Muiminin, emir, 21

Muin al-Din Chisti, 366

al-Muizz (Fatimid), 72

al-Muizz (Zirid), 74, 136

Mulla Murshid Shirazi (Mukarrimat Khan), architect, 383, 386

Multan (Punjab), 292

al-Muntasir, caliph, 48, 50, 52

muqarnas, 10, 72, 76, 92, 98, 104, 111, 113, 117, 144, 146, 148, 151, 158, 170, 186, 221, 244

Murabitun, 94

Murad I, sultan, 308; Mosque-Madrasa of, *see* Çekirge

Murad II, 317, 325

Murad III, 340

Murad IV, 343

Murcia, Castillejo of Monteagudo, 104–5; *plate 129*

Muristan Nuri, *see* Damascus

muristans, *see* hospitals

Musalla of Gawhar Shad, *see* Herat

Muslim ibn Kuraisb, ruler, 210

al-Mustansir, caliph (1036–94), 141, 146

al-Mustansir, caliph (1226–41), 219

Mustansiriya, *see* Baghdad

al-Mu'tasim, 42, 46

al-Mutawakkil, caliph, 39, 50, 56; Great Mosque of, *see* Samarra

Mu'tazilism, 42

al-Mutazz, 50

al-Muwahhidun, 105

Muzaffarids, 250

al-Nasir, sultan, 166, 177, 178

Nasir al-Din Humayan, *see* Humayun

al-Nasir li din Allah, caliph, 214

al-Nasir li din Allah, *see* Abd er-Rahman III

Nasr, sultan, 199

Nasr al-Din Muhammad, 288; Tomb of, *see* Delhi, Tomb of Sultan Ghari

Nasrids, 11, 93, 122–134, 183

Natanz (Iran), 310; funerary complex of Shaykh Abd al-Samad al-Isfahani, 255, 259; *plates 330–33*

Nebuchadnezzar, 10

Neo-Babylonians, 9

Nicea, *see* Iznik

Nicopolis, 310

Niriz (Persia), mosque, 184

Nishapur (Iran), 144, 184, 185, 192, 201; Madrasa of Sultan Tughril, 201

Nishapur-Merv road, Robat Sharaf, 201; *plates 253–54*

Nizam al-Mulk, vizier, 152, 192, 198, 201
Nizam Khan Sikander Lodi II, 300, 304; Baradari of, *see* Sikandra
Nizami, poet, 380
North Africa, 9, 10, 11, 46, 60–76, 84, 94–114, 116–22, 148, 166, 183
Nubia (Egypt), 169
Numan Imru'l, 380
Nur al-Din (Nur al-Din Zengi), 170, 177, 213, 214
Nur Jahan, *see* Mihr al-Nisa
Nur Mahal, 388

Ochrid (Yugoslavia), Hagia Sophia, 310
O'Donovan, Edmond, 209
Oljeitu (Muhammad Khudabanda), 250, 252, 254; Mihrab of, *see* Isfahan, Masjid-i-Jami; Tomb of, *see* Sultanieh
Orhan, 308, 310
ornamentation, 10, 11, 18, 21, 32, 34, 39, 60, 84, 90, 92, 117, 119, 122, 134, 144, 146, 148, 170, 183, 209, 224, 242, 244, 254, 265, 267, 268, 277, 282, 355, 358, 380, 386
Orthodox Caliphate, 13, 15
Osman I, 308
Ottoman Empire, 11, 32, 177, 178, 183, 219, 221, 223, 230, 244, 247, 249, 250, 255, 297, 304, 308–44, 345, 388
Ouadiah Kasba, Gate of the, *see* Rabat
Ozbeg Khan, ruler, 259

Pakistan, 9, 280
Palace-Fortress of Akbar, *see* Ajmer
Palace in the Qala, *see* Baghdad
Palace of: Sultan Salih, *see* Rhoda Island; Ziri, *see* Ashir
palace architecture, 76, 122, 136, 151, 166, 188–89, 191, 201, 209, 242, 244, 254, 294, 310, 339–40, 363, 374, 386, 388
Palermo, 189; Cappella Palatina, 113
Palestine, 9, 221
Panch Mahal, *see* Fatipur Sikri
Panipat, 364
Paradise, gardens or symbols of, 9, 18, 27, 30, 50, 126, 134, 173, 201, 244, 260, 261, 325, 363, 377, 378, 380, 388
Pearl Mosque, *see* Agra; Delhi; Lahore
Peking, Forbidden City, 136, 388
Persia, 9, 10, 11, 13, 16, 21, 32, 34, 42, 50, 60, 84, 122, 144, 170, 178, 210, 219, 221, 222, 223, 224, 229, 233, 237, 242, 244, 280, 285, 292, 306, 308, 310, 325, 343, 345, 350, 378, 380, 388; *see also* Ghaznavids; Ilkhanids; Iran; Safavids; Samanids; Seljuks; Timurids
Piazza Armerina (Sicily), palace, 32
Pir Ahmad, vizier, 270
Poitiers, 15

Pol-i-Khaju, *see* Isfahan
Pompeii, 9
Pope, Arthur Upham, 255, 355, 358
Prophet, *see* Muhammad
Prusa, *see* Bursa
Pugachenkova, G. A., 268, 275
Punjab, 290, 292, 383

Qa'at al-Dardir, *see* Cairo
al-Qadisiyya (near Samarra), palace, 46
al-Qahira, *see* Cairo
al-Qaim, caliph, 74
Qala of the Bani Hammad, *see* Algeria
Qala'un, al-Mansur Sayf al-Din, sultan, 162, 169, 173; Madrasa of, Tomb of, *see* Cairo
Qarakhanids, 192
Qarawiyin Mosque, *see* Fez
Qasr i-Shirin, Imarat i-Khusraw, 39
al-Qatul, 46
Qayt Bay, sultan, 173; Madrasa of, Tomb of, *see* Cairo
Qazim Shirazi, 374
Qazvin, 345, 364; Haydariya Madrasa, 199, 209, 229; *plates 251–52*
Qhiyath al-Din Sultan Balban, 290
Qilich Arslan II, 237, 242, 244
Qtub Minar, *see* Delhi
Qubbat Barudiyin, *see* Marrakesh
Qubbat al-Khadra, *see* Baghdad; Damascus; Rusafa
Qubbat al-Sakhra, *see* Jerusalem
Qubbat al-Sulaybiyah, *see* Samarra
Qum (Iran), 150, 358
Qusayr Amra, 28
Qutb al-Din Aybak, 282
Quwwat al-Islam, *see* Delhi
Rabat (Ribat al-Fath, North Africa), 111, 113; Gate of the Chella, 117, 119; *plate 149*; Gate of the Ouadiah Kasba, 113; *plates 142–43*; Mosque of Hassan, 111, 113, 117; *plates 140–41*
Rajputs, 364, 366
Ramlah, cistern, 72
Ranpur (India), Chaumukh Temple, 300
Raqqa, 244; Baghdad Gate, 148, 185
Rashid al-Din, vizier, 252
Ravenna, 32, San Apollinare Nuovo, 25; Palace of Theodoric (mosaic), 25; *plate 18*
Rayy (near Teheran), 201; Tomb of Tughril, 204; *plate 258*
Red Fort, *see* Delhi
Red Palace, *see* Agra
Reuther, O., 294
Rhoda Island, Palace of Sultan Salih, 152, 158, 177, 178; *plate 218*

Ribat, *see* Sussa
Ribat al-Fath, *see* Rabat
ribats, 60, 64, 90, 199
Rice, Tamara Talbot, 222
Rio Salado, 116
Robat-i-Malik, *see* Bukhara-Samarkand road
Robat Sharaf, *see* Nishapur-Merv road
Roger II, 189
Rogers, J. M., 233, 244
Roman architecture, influence of, 9, 10, 13, 14, 18, 28, 30, 73, 77, 81, 83, 92, 119, 151, 290, 323, 330, 358, 363
Rome: Ara Pacis, 83; Basilica of Constantine, 22; Domitian's Palace, 9; Forum of Trajan, 10
Rorich, 323
Rowland, Benjamin, 371
Rum, 222, 223
Rusafa, 9, 28; Qubbat al-Khadra (Palace of Hisham), 28, 34

Sa'd al-Din Kopek, vizier, 242
Sa'di, 116
Sa'd ibn al-Waqqas, 13, 16
Safavids, 11, 219, 244, 250, 272, 277, 345–63, 380, 386, 388
al-Saffah (Abu al-Abbas), caliph, 34, 35
Safi-al-Din, shaykh, 345
Safiye, 334
Sahibah Begum, 364
Saladin, *see* Salah ad-Din
Salah ad-Din (al-Malik al-Nasir I), 152, 158, 221; Citadel of, *see* Cairo
Salih Negm ad-Din, sultan, 152, 158, 162, 169; Madrasa of, Tomb of, *see* Cairo; Palace of, *see* Rhoda Island
al-Salik Tala'i ibn Ruzziq, 148; Mosque of, *see* Cairo
Salim, prince, *see* Jahangir
Salim Chisti, mystic, 371
Saltukids, 222
Samanids, 10, 184–86
Samarkand, 42, 185, 250, 265, 345, 350, 364, 386
Bibi Khanum Mosque, 262, 264, 265, 267; *plates 342–44*
Chehel Situn, 261, 350
Gur-i-Amir, 264–65, 268, 278, 380; *plates 345–47*
Ishrat Khaneh, 275, 277, 325; *plates 363–64*
Madrasa of Ulugh Beg, 267–68, 277–78; *plates 350–52*
palaces of Timur, 260, 261, 300, 352
Shah-i-Zindeh Cemetery, 267
Shir Dor *madrasa*, 268
Samarra, 34, 42, 46, 48, 50, 52, 56, 60, 72, 74, 81, 150, 151, 184, 189, 191, 192, 213, 297, 323, 386, 388
Bab al-Amma Gate, 48; *plate 45*

Bulkawara Palace, 50, 74, 105, 244; *plates 50–51*

Great Mosque of al-Mutawakkil, 50, 52, 56, 111, 185; *plates 52–54*

Imam Dur, 144, 210, 213, 214; *plates 262–64*

Jafariya, 50

Jausaq al-Kharqani (Bayt al-Khalifa), 46, 48, 50, 83; *plates 45–46*

Kasr al-Jiss (Gypsum Palace), 46; *plate 44*

Mosque of Abu Dulaf, 50, 52, 56; *plate 55*

Palace of al-Matira, 50

Palace of Haruni, 50

Qubbat al-Sulaybiyah, 52, 185, 304; *plate 56*

San Apollinare Nuovo, *see* Ravenna

Sanjar, sultan, 201; Tomb of, *see* Merv

Sarubanids, 223

Sarvistan (Iran), palace, 185

Sassanians, 9, 13, 14, 15, 16, 21, 28, 30, 32, 34, 39, 42, 52, 60, 92, 184, 185, 199, 221, 255, 358

Saveh, minaret, 198

Sayyids, 300, 304

Scerrato, U., 189

Schlumberger, Daniel, 188

Şehzade Cami, *see* Istanbul

Selim I, 308, 340

Selim II, 334; Kulliye of, *see* Edirne

Selim III, 343

Selimiye, *see* Edirne

Seljuk (near Ephesus), 223; Great Mosque of Isa Bek, 249, 317, 321; *plates 322–23*

Seljuk: Anatolia, 10, 201, 209, 221, 260, 288; Persia, 108, 144, 178, 210, 221, 288, 290; Turkey, 183, 219, 221, 290

Seljuks, 10, 11, 117, 144, 146, 184, 185, 186, 191, 192–209, 214, 219, 221, 222, 223, 224, 229–30, 233, 237, 242, 244–47, 249, 254, 255, 259, 277, 280, 308, 310, 312, 317, 343, 345, 352, 363

Seville, 77, 105, 116, 134; Giralda Tower, 111; *plate 139*; Great Mosque, 111, 114; *plates 137–39*

Shadera (near Lahore), Tomb of Jahangir, 378; *plates 502–3*

Shafe'i, Fardi, 141

Shafeyites, 152, 214, 221

Shah Abbas I, 345, 347, 350, 352, 355, 358, 361

Shah Abbas II, 363

Shah Ismail, 345, 347

Shah Jehan, Shihab al-Din, 371, 378–88

Shah Jehanabad, Citadel at, *see* Delhi

Shah Jihan Khatun, princess, 247

Shah Namah (Firdausi), 189

Shah Rukh, 250, 264, 265, 267, 270, 277, 300

Shah Suleiman, 361

Shah Sultan Husain, 350, 352

Shah Tahmasp, 345, 364

Shahr-i-Sabz (former Kesh), Akserai Palace, 260–61; *plate 340*

Shahriyar, prince, 378

Shams Abd Allah Shirazi, architect, 262

Shams al-Din Iltutmish, 288; Tomb of, *see* Delhi

Shams al-Ma'ali Qabus, 186; Tomb of, *see* Gurgan

Sharqis, 297

Shaybanids, 250, 267, 275, 345

Shaykh Lutfullah, Mosque of, *see* Isfahan

Sher Shah Sur, 304, 366

Shihab al-Din Shah Jehan, *see* Shah Jehan

Shi'ite sect, 42, 72, 73, 81, 136, 141, 146, 148, 151, 169, 183, 186, 192, 201, 210, 252, 254, 259, 265, 267, 312, 345, 358, 363

Shiraz (Iran), 184, 250

Shirkuh, 152

Shrine of: Abdallah Ansari, *see* Gazur Gah; Ahmad Yasavi, *see* Turkestan City; Ali al-Rida, *see* Mashad; Khwaja Abu Nasr Parsa, *see* Balkh

Sicily, 32, 64, 74, 113, 166

Sidi Uqba, *see* Uqba ibn Nafi

Sijilmasa, 73

Sikandra (Iskander Lodi, near Agra), Baradari of Iskander Lodi, 300, 304, 377, 378; *plate 398*; Tomb of Akbar, 374, 377; *plates 495–96, 498*

Silvan (Mayyafariqin), 162, 223, 224; Great Mosque, 247

Sinan, architect, 321, 325

Sinan, Koca, architect, 317, 321, 328–34, 339, 340, 344

Sind, 15

Sinope, 222, 237

Sirçali Masjid, *see* Konya

Sitte Melik Kumbed, *see* Divrig

Sivas (Turkey), 222; Gök Madrasa, 233, 247; *plates 302–3*; Hospital of Keykavus I, 230; Madrasa of Zuwaini, 233; Turbe of Keykavus I, 244, 247; *plate 317*

Skelton, R., 380

Slave King Dynasty, 282, 288, 290

Sokmen II, sultan, 230

Somnathpur (India), Shiva temple, 300

Spain, 9, 10, 15, 27, 60, 74, 76, 77–93, 94–114, 119, 122–34, 183

Split, Palace of Diocletian, 25, 28

Sudan, 141

Sufism, 119, 259, 262, 345

Suleyman, 222

Suleyman II Kanuni (the Magnificent), sultan, 252, 308, 321, 328, 330; Kulliye of, *see* Istanbul

Suleyman Bek, 230

Suleyman ibn Saif al-Din Shahanshah, emir, 244

Suleymaniye, *see* Istanbul

Sultan Han (near Aksaray), 237, 242; *plates 308–9*

Sultan Han (near Kayseri), 237, 242, 247; *plates 304–7, 310–11*

Sultanieh, 252; Tomb of Oljeitu, 252, 254, 262, 366; *plates 325–27; see also* al-Matraki

Sunni sect, 42, 103, 119, 146, 151, 152, 186, 192, 201, 210, 214, 250, 252, 259, 267, 312, 345, 358, 363

Suri Dynasty, 300, 304, 364, 366

Sussa (Tunisia), Ribat, 60, 64, 90, 103, 199; *plates 63–67*

Syria, 9, 10, 11, 18, 25, 27, 56, 72, 77, 122, 146, 158, 166, 170, 177, 183, 192, 210–14, 221, 222, 230, 233, 242, 244, 249, 255, 280, 282, 306

Tabriz (Iran), 252, 312, 345, 352, 364; Masjid-i-Jami, 259; *plates 334–35*; pavilion of Uzun Hassan, 352, 361

Tagrart, *see* Tlemcen

Taifas Kingdoms, 10, 90, 104, 122

Taj al-Din Ali Shah Jilan Tabrizi, vizier, 252, 259

Taj Mahal, *see* Agra

Tamghach Khan, sultan, 198

Taq-i-Bostan, 221

Tarbabad, *see* Delhi-Tarbabad

Tarik Khana, *see* Damghan

Taza (North Africa), Great Mosque, Mihrab, 116–17; *plate 145*

Teheran, 204

Terkan bint al-Kaghan, 201

Terkan Khatun, 198

Terrasse, Henri, 94, 103, 104, 113

Thamugadi (Timgad, Algeria), 9; Palace of Trajan, 28

Tim (Transoxiana), Tomb of Arab Ata, 144, 185–86, 198; *plates 229–30*

Timgad, *see* Thamugadi

Timur (Tamerlane), 183, 192, 250, 260–61, 262, 264, 265, 297, 300, 308, 312, 345, 352, 363, 380

Timurids, 11, 183, 201, 209, 250–78, 300, 312, 317, 321, 323, 345, 350, 355, 358, 361, 363, 364, 380, 383, 388

Tinmal (North Africa), Friday mosque, 105, 108; *plates 130–32*

Tlemcen (Tagrart), 94, 105, 116, 214; Great Mosque, 94, 98, 116, 117; *plates 114–15, 123–24*; Great Mosque of Mansura, 117; *plates 146–48*

Tleta Biban, *see* Kairouan

Tojibids, 90

Tokat (Anatolia), Madrasa, 230

Toledo, 94, 134; Mosque of Bib Mardun, 48, 90, 199; *plates 99–109*

Tomb of: Abdu Razzaq, *see* Ghazna; Akbar, *see* Sikandra; Arab Ata, *see* Tim; Firuz Shah, *see* Delhi-Tarbabad, Hauz-i-Khas; Ghiyath al-Din Tughluq, *see* Delhi-Tughluqabad; Humayun, *see* Delhi; Iltutmish, *see* Delhi; Isa Khan Niyazi, *see* Delhi; Ismail the Samanid, *see* Bukhara; Ittimad al-Daula, *see* Agra; Jahangir, *see* Shadera; Khwaja Rabi, *see* Mashad; al-Muntasir, *see* Qubbat al-Sulaybiyah; Oljeitu, *see* Sultanieh; Salih Negm ad-Din, *see* Cairo; Shaykh Muhammad Ghaus, *see* Gwalior; Sultan Ghari, *see* Delhi; Sultan Hasan, *see* Cairo; Sultan Qala'un, *see*

Cairo; Sultan Qayt Bay, *see* Cairo; Sultan Sanjar, *see* Merv; Tughril, *see* Rayy; Turabek Khanum, *see* Urgench; Ulugh Beg Miranshah, *see* Ghazna
tombs, 9, 52, 117, 119, 148, 150, 185, 191, 204, 209, 244–47, 255, 259–60, 264–65, 267, 268, 272, 275, 285, 288, 290, 294, 304, 358, 363, 378, 380
Top Kapu Saray, *see* Istanbul
Transoxiana, 15, 28, 35, 48, 50, 52, 184, 185, 192, 250
Tughril, sultan, 192, 201, 214; Tomb of, *see* Rayy
Tulunids, 150
Tunis, 105
Tunisia, 9, 11, 105, 116
Tughluqabad, *see* Delhi-Tughluqabad
Tughluqids, 292, 297, 304
Turabek Khanum, Tomb of, *see* Urgench
Turbe of: Keykavus I, *see* Sivas; Mahperi Khatun, *see* Kayseri; Mehmet I, *see* Bursa
turbes, 244; *see also* tombs
Turkestan City (Yasi), Shrine of Ahmad Yasavi, 261–62, 278; *plate 341*
Turkey, 11, 50, 173, 177, 178, 183, 184, 186, 192, 199, 210, 213, 222, 223, 242, 260, 280, 282, 308, 310, 330, 339, 343, 345, 380; *see also* Anatolia; Ottomans
Tus (India), 42, 265
Tutush, 213, 222

Ubayd Allah, 73, 74
Üç Şerefeli Cami, *see* Edirne
Ukhaidir, 16, 35, 39, 42, 46, 60, 150, 374; *plates 32–39*
Ulu Cami, *see* Bursa
Ulugh Beg, 264, 265; Madrasa of, *see* Samarkand
Ulugh Beg Miranshah, 275; Tomb of, *see* Ghazna

Umar, caliph, 13, 14, 21
Umar Shaykh, 275
Umayyads, 9, 10, 15–34, 39, 60, 74, 77, 81, 92, 103, 151, 166
Umm Salama, 13
Ünsal, Behcet, 233
Uqaylids, 210
Uqba ibn Nafi (Sidi Uqba), 60, 64, 72
Urartian architecture, 10
Urfa (Edessa), 146
Urgench, 259, 260; Tomb of Turabek Khanum, 259–60, 262; *plate 339*
Uthman, caliph, 13
Uzbeks, 345, 364, 386
Uzun Hassan, ruler, 352, 361

Valentia, viscount, 178
van Berchem, Max, 219
Varamin, Masjid-i-Jami, 259; *plates 336–38*
Vienna, 308
View of Constantinople, *see* al-Matraki
Visigoths, 9, 15, 81, 90
Volubilis (North Africa), 9
Volwahsen, 386
al-Walid I, caliph, 15, 21, 22, 27–28, 64, 213
al-Walid ibn Yazid (al-Walid II), 28, 32
Wasit, 10, 56, 60
Wattasids, 116
Wazir Khan, *see* Hakim Ali al-Din
Wendell, Charles, 35

Wilber, Donald, 254
Wright, Frank Lloyd, 343

Yaghi Basan, 230
Yahya ibn Ibrahim, 94
Yaqub al-Mansur, sultan, 111, 113
Yasi, *see* Turkestan City
Yazd, 170; Great Mosque, 255, 358
Yazid, caliph, 16
Yazid ibn Hatim, 60
Yehoseph ibn Naghralla, vizier, 122
Yeşil Cami, *see* Bursa
Yildirim Bayazid I, *see* Bayazid I
Yusuf I, 126
Yusuf Buluggin, 74
Yusuf ibn Tashufin, 94, 108, 113

al-Zahir, caliph, 22
Zahir al-Din Babur, *see* Babur
Zaragoza, 90, 92, 94, 104, 113, 122, 134; Aljaferiya Palace, 90, 92, 98, 105; *plates 110–13*
Zaware (Iran), 198, 259
Zengi, 210
Zengids, 10, 152, 210, 221, 224, 230
Ziri, 74
Zirids, 72, 74, 76, 113
Ziyadat Allah I, 60, 64, 72
Ziyadh ibn Abihi, 15–16
Ziyarids, 186
Zuwaini, vizier, 233

Kufa, Great Mosque, original plan (from Creswell, 1969).   1

Kufa, Great Mosque as rebuilt by Ziyadh ibn Abihi, plan (from Creswell, 1969).   2

Kufa, Dar al-Imara, plan (from Creswell, 1969).   3

Jerusalem, Haram al-Sharif, plan (from Grabar, 1959).   4

Jerusalem, Qubbat al-Sakhra (Dome of the Rock), axonometric section.   5

Jerusalem, Qubbat al-Sakhra (Dome of the Rock), exterior.   6

Jerusalem, Qubbat al-Sakhra (Dome of the Rock), view from the Mosque of al-Aqsa.   7

Jerusalem, Qubbat al-Sakhra (Dome of the Rock), central chamber.   8

Jerusalem, Qubbat al-Sakhra (Dome of the Rock), inner ambulatory.   9

Jerusalem, Qubbat al-Sakhra (Dome of the Rock), interior view of the cupola with mosaics showing jewels.   10

Jerusalem, Mosque of al-Aqsa, reconstruction of plan (from Creswell, 1969).   11

Jerusalem, Mosque of al-Aqsa, interior.   12

Damascus, Great Mosque, sahn looking toward the western riwaq.   13

Damascus, Great Mosque, plan in the time of al-Walid (from Creswell, 1969).   14

Damascus, Great Mosque, prayer hall.   15

Damascus, Great Mosque, prayer hall.   16

Damascus, Great Mosque, entrance to prayer hall.   17

Ravenna, San Apollinare Nuovo, mosaic showing the Palace of Theodoric before 525.   18

Damascus, Great Mosque, marble window grille in west vestibule.   19

Damascus, Great Mosque, sahn, details of the mosaic decoration.   20, 21

Anjar, plan of the city (from Creswell, 1969).   22

Anjar, view of an arcaded street and the palace.   23

Khirbat al-Mafjar, general plan (from Creswell, 1969).   24

Khirbat al-Mafjar, entrance portal of the bath, reconstruction (from Hamilton, 1959).   25

Khirbat al-Mafjar, the bath, reconstruction (from Ettinghausen, 1972).   26

Khirbat al-Mafjar, mosaic floor from the diwan of the bath. Jerusalem, Archaeological Museum of Palestine.   27

Mshatta, plan of the palace (from Creswell, 1969).   28

Kasr al-Khayr al-Sharki, plan of the greater enclosure (from Grabar, 1973).   29

Mshatta, detail of the south facade of the palace. East Berlin, Staatliche Museen.   30

Baghdad, plan of al-Mansur's circular city (from Haurani-Stern, 1970).   31

Ukhaidir, plan of the palace (from Pagliero, 1967).   32

Ukhaidir, east facade of the outer enclosure.   33

Ukhaidir, detail of the outer enclosure with the main entrance.   34

Ukhaidir, Great Hall.   35

Ukhaidir, detail of the corridor.   36

Ukhaidir, Court of Honor looking north, reconstruction (from Creswell, 1940).   37

Ukhaidir, Court of Honor, south facade.   38

Ukhaidir, Court of Honor, north facade.   39

Damghan, Tarik Khana, plan of the mosque (from Creswell, 1940).   40

Damghan, Tarik Khana, the mosque seen from the sahn.   41

Damghan, Tarik Khana, prayer hall.   42

Damghan, Tarik Khana, arcade.   43

Samarra, Kasr al-Jiss (Gypsum Palace), plan (from Excavations at Samarra 1936–1939, 1940).   44

Samarra, Jausaq al-Kharqani, Bab al-Amma Gate.   45

Samarra, Jausaq al-Kharqani, plan (from Sourdel, 1968).   46

Balkh, Masjid-i-Tarikh, reconstruction plan (from Golombek, 1969).   47

Balkh, Masjid-i-Tarikh, detail of the stucco decoration.   48

Balkh, Masjid-i-Tarikh, view of the ruins.   49

Samarra, Bulkawara Palace, plan (from Creswell, 1940).   50

Samarra, Bulkawara Palace, stucco ornament in a hall.   51

Samarra, Great Mosque of al-Mutawakkil, plan (from Creswell, 1940).   52

Samarra, Great Mosque of al-Mutawakkil, aerial view.   53

Samarra, Great Mosque of al-Mutawakkil, the Malwiya (minaret).   54

Samarra, Mosque of Abu Dulaf, minaret.   55

Samarra, Qubbat al-Sulaybiyah, plan (from Creswell, 1940).   56

Cairo, Mosque of Ibn Tulun, plan (from Brandenburg, 1966).   57

Cairo, Mosque of Ibn Tulun, northeast ziyadah.   58

Cairo, Mosque of Ibn Tulun, sahn.   59

Cairo, Mosque of Ibn Tulun, interior, view of the mihrab and minbar.   60

Cairo, Mosque of Ibn Tulun, interior.   61

Kairouan, Great Mosque, modern plan (from Lézine, 1966).   62

Sussa, Ribat, plan (from Lézine, 1971).   63

Sussa, Ribat, courtyard.   64

Sussa, Ribat, wall and portal.   65

Sussa, Ribat, interior of the portal.   66

Sussa, Ribat, portal.   67

Kairouan, Great Mosque, minaret.   68

Kairouan, Great Mosque, aerial view.   69

Kairouan, Great Mosque, sahn and minaret.   70

Kairouan, Great Mosque, prayer hall.   71

Kairouan, Great Mosque, mihrab aisle.   72

Kairouan, Great Mosque, "narthex" of Abu Ibrahim Ahmad.   73

Mahdiya, restored plan of the peninsula (from Lézine, 1965).   74

Mahdiya, Great Mosque, central portal.   75

Ashir, Palace of Ziri, plan (from Golvin, 1966).   76

Ashir, Palace of Ziri, reconstruction of the south facade of the court (from Golvin, 1966).   77

Algeria, Qala of the Bani Hammad, site plan (from De Beylié, 1909).   78

Algeria, Qala of the Bani Hammad, plan of the mosque (from De Beylié, 1909).   79

Algeria, Qala of the Bani Hammad, plan of the central residential complex (from De Beylié, 1909).   80

Algeria, Qala of the Bani Hammad, southern elevation of the minaret (from De Beylié, 1909).   81

Cordoba, Great Mosque of Abd er-Rahman I, plan (from Gómez Moreno, 1951).   82

Cordoba, Great Mosque, Portal of St. Stephen.   83

Cordoba, Great Mosque, arcades of Abd er-Rahman I.   84

Medina al-Zahra, general plan (from Gómez Moreno, 1951).	85	
Medina al-Zahra, palace complex, plan (from Gómez Moreno, 1951).	86	
Medina al-Zahra, Salon Rico, exterior.	87	
Medina al-Zahra, Salon Rico, inner facade.	88	
Medina al-Zahra, Salon Rico, interior.	89	
Medina al-Zahra, mosque of 941, plan (from Pavón, 1966).	90	
Cordoba, Great Mosque as enlarged by Hakam II, plan (from Chueca, 1965).	91	
Cordoba, Great Mosque, lantern of Hakam II, supporting arches.	92	
Cordoba, Great Mosque, lantern of Hakam II.	93	
Cordoba, Great Mosque, vault of the maqsura.	94	
Cordoba, Great Mosque, vault of the mihrab.	95	
Cordoba, Great Mosque, outer facade of the mihrab.	96	
Cordoba, Great Mosque, vault above the mihrab bay.	97	
Cordoba, Great Mosque, plan as enlarged in 987 (from Gómez Moreno, 1951).	98	
Toledo, Mosque of Bib Mardun, plan and section (from Gómez Moreno, 1951).	99	
Toledo, Mosque of Bib Mardun, exterior.	100	
Toledo, Mosque of Bib Mardun, central vault.	101	
Toledo, Mosque of Bib Mardun, the eight ribbed vaults.	102–109	
Zaragoza, Aljaferiya Palace, plan (from Iñiguez Almech, 1962).	110	
Zaragoza, Aljaferiya Palace, north portico.	111	
Zaragoza, Aljaferiya Palace, oratory, vault.	112	
Zaragoza, Aljaferiya Palace, oratory, mihrab wall.	113	
Tlemcen, Great Mosque, plan (from Marçais, 1954).	114	
Tlemcen, Great Mosque, prayer hall.	115	
Algiers, Great Mosque, prayer hall.	116	
Algiers, Great Mosque, plan (from Marçais, 1954).	117	
Algiers, Great Mosque, mihrab aisle.	118	
Algiers, Great Mosque, mihrab dome.	119	
Marrakesh, Qubbat Barudiyin, exterior.	120	
Marrakesh, Qubbat Barudiyin, projection and plan of the dome (from Meunié-Terrasse, 1957).	121	
Marrakesh, Qubbat Barudiyin, vault.	122	
Tlemcen, Great Mosque, mihrab.	123	
Tlemcen, Great Mosque, vault above the mihrab bay.	124	
Fez, Qarawiyin Mosque, plan (from Terrasse, 1968).	125	
Fez, Qarawiyin Mosque, sahn and minaret of 956.	126	
Fez, Qarawiyin Mosque, vault above the first bay of the mihrab aisle.	127	
Fez, Qarawiyin Mosque, prayer hall, view from the third bay of the mihrab aisle.	128	
Murcia, Castillejo of Monteagudo, plan (from Gómez Moreno, 1951).	129	
Tinmal, Friday Mosque, plan (from Marçais, 1954).	130	
Tinmal, Friday Mosque, qibla aisle.	131	
Tinmal, Friday Mosque, mihrab.	132	
Marrakesh, second Kutubiyya Mosque, muqarnas vault.	133	
Marrakesh, second Kutubiyya Mosque, plan (from Meunié-Terrasse, 1952).	134	
Marrakesh, second Kutubiyya Mosque, prayer hall.	135	
Marrakesh, second Kutubiyya Mosque, minaret.	136	
Seville, Great Mosque, sahn.	137	
Seville, Great Mosque, reconstruction of plan (from Chueca, 1965).	138	
Seville, Great Mosque, minaret (called the Giralda Tower).	139	
Rabat, Mosque of Hassan, plan (from Caillé, 1954).	140	
Rabat, Mosque of Hassan, minaret.	141	
Rabat, Gate of the Ouadiah Kasba, plan (from Marçais, 1954).	142	
Rabat, Gate of the Ouadiah Kasba, detail.	143	
Fez al-Jedid, Friday Mosque, plan (from Marçais, 1954).	144	
Taza, Great Mosque, vault over the mihrab bay.	145	
Tlemcen, Mosque of Mansura, plan (from Marçais, 1954).	146	
Tlemcen, Mosque of Mansura, minaret.	147	
Tlemcen, Mosque of Mansura, portal at the base of the minaret.	148	
Rabat, Gate of the Chella.	149	
Fez, Attarine Madrasa, plan (from Terrasse, 1927).	150	
Fez, Attarine Madrasa, court looking west from the prayer hall.	151	
Fez, Attarine Madrasa, court, detail of a capital.	152	
Fez, Bou Inaniya Madrasa, plan (from Terrasse, 1927).	153	
Fez, Bou Inaniya Madrasa, section (from Marçais, 1954).	154	
Fez, Bou Inaniya Madrasa, prayer hall looking toward the mihrab.	155	
Fez, Bou Inaniya Madrasa, the sahn looking toward the northwest.	156	
Granada, Alhambra, plan (from Marçais, 1954).	157	
Granada, Alhambra, view of the palace from the north.	158	
Granada, Alhambra, Cuarto Dorado, south facade.	159	
Granada, Alhambra, Court of Myrtles looking north.	160	
Granada, Alhambra, Hall of the Ambassadors.	161	
Granada, Alhambra, Hall of the Ambassadors, wooden vault.	162	
Granada, Alhambra, Court of Lions.	163	
Granada, Alhambra, Hall of Justice.	164	
Granada, Alhambra, Hall of the Abencerajes, vault.	165	
Cairo (al-Qahira), plan of the city as first enclosed in 969 by Jawhar, with additions of 1087–92 by Badr al-Gamali and of 1171 by Salah ad-Din (from Creswell, 1951).	166	
Cairo, Mosque of al-Azhar, facade of the prayer hall (1131–49) before the rebuilding of 1891–92 (from Creswell, 1951).	167	
Cairo, Mosque of al-Azhar, plan as reconstructed by Creswell (from Creswell, 1951).	168	
Cairo, Mosque of al-Azhar, stucco ornament on an arcade in the southwest transept.	169	
Cairo, Mosque of al-Azhar, prayer hall, mihrab aisle.	170	
Cairo, Mosque of al-Azhar, interior, dome in the transept.	171	
Cairo, Mosque of al-Hakim, plan with the wall of Badr al-Gamali (from Creswell, 1951).	172	
Cairo, Mosque of al-Hakim, reconstruction by Creswell (from Creswell, 1951).	173	
Cairo, Mosque of al-Hakim, interior, qibla aisle looking northeast.	174	
Cairo, Mosque of al-Hakim, monumental entrance, detail.	175	

Cairo, Mosque of al-Hakim, mihrab *aisle as seen from the* sahn. 176

Cairo, Mosque of al-Juyushi, plan (from Shafe'i, 1965). 177

Cairo, Mosque of al-Juyushi, section (from Creswell, 1951). 178

Cairo, Bab al-Futuh, view from the north. 179

Cairo, Mosque of al-Aqmar, plan (from Creswell, 1951). 180

Cairo, Mosque of al-Aqmar, street facade, detail of muqarnas. 181

Cairo, Mosque of al-Aqmar, street facade. 182

Cairo, Mosque of al-Salih Tala'i, plan (from Creswell, 1951). 183

Cairo, Mosque of al-Salih Tala'i, entrance porch. 184

Cairo, Mosque of al-Salih Tala'i, sahn. 185

Al-Fustat, plans of two Fatimid houses excavated in 1912 (from Creswell, 1951). 186, 187

Cairo, Qa'at al-Dardir, section (from Creswell, 1951). 188

Cairo, Qa'at al-Dardir, iwan. 189

Cairo, Citadel of Salah ad-Din. 190

Cairo, Madrasa and Tomb of Salih Negm ad-Din, plan (from Creswell, 1951). 191

Cairo, Madrasa and Tomb of Salih Negm ad-Din, reconstruction of the west facade (from Creswell, 1959). 192

Cairo, Madrasa of Salih Negm ad-Din, facade. 193

Cairo, Madrasa of Salih Negm ad-Din, detail of the portal. 194

Cairo, Tomb of Salih Negm ad-Din, interior, detail of muqarnas in the dome. 195

Cairo, Great Mosque of Baybars, plan (from Creswell, 1959). 196

Cairo, Great Mosque of Baybars, elevation of the northwest facade; transverse section; elevation of northwest portal (from Description de l'Égypte, 1809). 197

Cairo, Great Mosque of Baybars, northwest portal. 198

Cairo, Great Mosque of Baybars, northwest portal, detail. 199

Cairo, Great Mosque of Baybars, east corner of the prayer hall. 200

Cairo, Great Mosque of Baybars, southwest side. 201

Cairo, Tomb and Madrasa of Sultan Qala'un, plan (from Creswell, 1959). 202

Cairo, Tomb of Sultan Qala'un, facade from the court. 203

Cairo, Tomb of Sultan Qala'un, interior. 204

Cairo, Tomb of Sultan Qala'un, interior, drum of the dome. 205

Cairo, Madrasa of Sultan Qala'un, qibla iwan, facade. 206

Cairo, Tomb of Sultan Qala'un, mihrab. 207

Cairo, Madrasa of Sultan Qala'un, qibla iwan, interior. 208

Cairo, Tomb of Sultan Qala'un, facade and minaret overlooking the Suq al-Nahassin. 209

Cairo, Tomb and Madrasa of Sultan Hasan, plan (from Brandenburg, 1966). 210

Cairo, Tomb and Madrasa of Sultan Hasan, exterior from the southeast. 211

Cairo, Tomb and Madrasa of Sultan Hasan, portal. 212

Cairo, Tomb and Madrasa of Sultan Qayt Bay, plan (from Brandenburg, 1966). 213

Cairo, Tomb and Madrasa of Sultan Qayt Bay, exterior from the northeast. 214

Cairo, Madrasa of Sultan Qayt Bay, sahn. 215

Cairo, Madrasa of Sultan Qayt Bay, roof of the sahn (restored). 216

Cairo, Tomb of Sultan Qayt Bay, interior of the dome. 217

Rhoda Island, Palace of Sultan Salih, plan (from Description de l'Égypte, 1809). 218

Cairo, Kasr al-Ablaq on the Citadel, iwan, plan (from Description de l'Égypte, 1809). 219

Cairo, Kasr al-Ablaq on the Citadel, qa'a (from Creswell, 1959). 220

Cairo, Kasr al-Ablaq on the Citadel, iwan, interior looking toward the northwest (from Description de l'Égypte, 1809). 221

Cairo, House of Gamal al-Din al-Zahabi, hosh and maqad. 222

Cairo, House of Gamal al-Din al-Zahabi, ground floor, plan (from Brandenburg, 1966). 223

Cairo, House of Gamal al-Din al-Zahabi, first floor, plan (from Brandenburg, 1966). 224

Cairo, House of Gamal al-Din al-Zahabi, clerestory and dome over the durka. 225

Cairo, House of Gamal al-Din al-Zahabi, qa'a. 226

Bukhara, Tomb of Ismail the Samanid, plan of the ground floor; plan of the upper gallery; section (from Pope, 1939). 227

Bukhara, Tomb of Ismail the Samanid, exterior. 228

Tim, Tomb of Arab Ata, exterior. 229

Tim, Tomb of Arab Ata, section (from Pugachenkova, 1961). 230

Gurgan, Gunbad-i-Qabus, plan (from Goddard, 1965). 231

Gurgan, Gunbad-i-Qabus, detail of entrance and inscription. 232

Gurgan, Gunbad-i-Qabus. 233

Lashkari Bazar, plan of the principal monuments (from Gardin, 1963). 234

Lashkari Bazar, plan of the mosque (from Aslanapa, 1971). 235

Lashkari Bazar, plan of the south palace (from Aslanapa, 1971). 236

Ghazna, Minaret of Ma'sud III, original state (from Fergusson, 1910). 237

Ghazna, Minaret of Ma'sud III. 238

Ghazna, Palace of Ma'sud III, plan (from Aslanapa, 1971). 239

Ghazna, Palace of Ma'sud III, west side of the court, detail. 240

Isfahan, Masjid-i-Jami, plan of the Abbasid mosque (from Gabriel, 1935). 241

Isfahan, Masjid-i-Jami, plan of the Seljuk mosque (from Gabriel, 1935). 242

Isfahan, Masjid-i-Jami, plan of the present-day mosque (from Gabriel, 1935). 243

Isfahan, Masjid-i-Jami, section and plan of the North Dome Chamber (from Gabriel, 1935). 244

Isfahan, Masjid-i-Jami, sahn. 245

Isfahan, Masjid-i-Jami, North Dome Chamber, interior. 246

Isfahan, Masjid-i-Jami, North Dome Chamber, dome. 247

Bukhara, Kalayan Minaret. 248

Gulpaygan, Mosque, plan (from Goddard, 1965). 249

Gulpaygan, Mosque, interior, dome. 250

Qazvin, Haydariya Madrasa, plan (from Pope, 1965). 251

Qazvin, Haydariya Madrasa, mihrab. 252

Nishapur-Merv road, Robat Sharaf, plan (from Aslanapa, 1971). 253

Nishapur-Merv road, Robat Sharaf, general view. 254

Kharraqan, tomb tower of 1067–68, plan (from Stronach-Cuyler, 1966). 255

Maragha, Gunbad-i-Surkh, plan (from Goddard, 1965). 256

Abarquh, Gunbad-i-Ali.	257	Sultan Han near Kayseri, plan (from Erdmann, 1961).	304
Rayy, Tomb of Tughril.	258	Sultan Han near Kayseri, reconstruction (from Gabriel, 1934).	305
Merv, Tomb of Sultan Sanjar, plan and section (from Pugachenkova, 1958).	259	Sultan Han near Kayseri, hall.	306
Merv, Tomb of Sultan Sanjar, exterior from the east.	260	Sultan Han near Kayseri, portal of the hall.	307
Maragha, Gunbad-i-Kabud.	261	Sultan Han near Aksaray, entrance portal.	308
Samarra, Imam Dur, section (from Herzfeld, 1948).	262	Sultan Han near Aksaray, detail of the entrance portal.	309
Samarra, Imam Dur, exterior.	263	Sultan Han near Kayseri, masjid.	310, 311
Samarra, Imam Dur, interior of the dome.	264	Kobadabad, plan of the site and of the palaces (from Otto-Dorn, 1966).	312
Aleppo, Great Mosque, elevation of the minaret (from Herzfeld, 1953).	265	Kobadabad, smaller palace, plan (from Otto-Dorn, 1969).	313
Aleppo, Great Mosque, minaret.	266	Amasya, Halifet Ghazi Kumbed.	314
Damascus, Muristan Nuri, plan (from Herzfeld, 1952).	267	Divrig, Sitte Melik Kumbed.	315
Damascus, Muristan Nuri, portal.	268	Divrig, Sitte Melik Kumbed, detail of the portal.	316
Damascus, Madrasa al-Nuriya al-Kubra, detail of the dome.	269	Sivas, Turbe of Keykavus I, entrance facade.	317
Damascus, Madrasa al-Nuriya al-Kubra, plan (from Herzfeld, 1952).	270	Kayseri, Turbe of Mahperi Khatun.	318
Damascus, Madrasa al-Nuriya al-Kubra, dome of the tomb chamber.	271	Kayseri, Döner Kumbed.	319
Baghdad, Palace in the Qala, plan (from Herzfeld, 1952).	272	Manisa, Great Mosque of Ishaq Bek.	320
Baghdad, Palace in the Qala, courtyard, detail of the portico.	273	Manisa, Great Mosque of Ishaq Bek, plan (from Aslanapa, 1971).	321
Baghdad, Palace in the Qala, courtyard.	274	Seljuk, Great Mosque of Isa Bek, plan (from Aslanapa, 1971).	322
Baghdad, Palace in the Qala, muqarnas vault in the portico.	275	Seljuk, Great Mosque of Isa Bek, main (west) facade.	323
Baghdad, Palace in the Qala, interior of the portico.	276	Sultanieh, Tomb of Oljeitu (from a manuscript of 1537, Library of the University of Istanbul).	324
Baghdad, Palace in the Qala, iwan.	277		
Baghdad, Palace in the Qala, decorative band.	278	Sultanieh, Tomb of Oljeitu.	325
Baghdad, Mustansiriya, plan (from Creswell, 1959).	279	Sultanieh, Tomb of Oljeitu, plan (from Pope, 1939).	326
Baghdad, Mustansiriya, courtyard.	280, 281	Sultanieh, Tomb of Oljeitu.	327
Aleppo, Madrasa al-Firdaus, plan (from Creswell, 1959).	282	Isfahan, Masjid-i-Jami, mihrab of Oljeitu.	328
Dunaysir, Great Mosque, plan (from Aslanapa, 1971).	283	Baghdad, Han Ortmah, hall.	329
Dunaysir, Great Mosque, elevation (from Gabriel, 1940).	284	Natanz, funerary complex of Shaykh Abd al-Samad, plan (from Pope, 1939).	330
Divrig, Great Mosque and Hospital, plan (from Aslanapa, 1971).	285	Natanz, funerary complex of Shaykh Abd al-Samad, courtyard of the mosque looking southwest.	331
Divrig, Great Mosque and Hospital, longitudinal section (from Gabriel, 1934).	286		
Divrig, Great Mosque, exterior.	287	Natanz, funerary complex of Shaykh Abd al-Samad, portal of the khanaqah.	332
Divrig, Great Mosque, north portal.	288	Natanz, funerary complex of Shaykh Abd al-Samad, muqarnas vault.	333
Divrig, Hospital, west portal.	289	Tabriz, Masjid-i-Jami, iwan.	334
Divrig, Great Mosque, north portal, detail of the decoration.	290	Tabriz, Masjid-i-Jami, plan (from Wilber, 1969).	335
Divrig, Hospital, interior.	291	Varamin, Masjid-i-Jami, plan (from Dimand, 1972).	336
Kayseri, Khwand Foundation, plan (from Aslanapa, 1971).	292	Varamin, Masjid-i-Jami, exterior from the north.	337
Kayseri, Khwand Foundation, restored view (from Gabriel, 1934).	293	Varamin, Masjid-i-Jami, interior, dome chamber ceiling.	338
Konya, Sirçali Masjid.	294	Urgench, Tomb of Turabek Khanum, plan (from Pugachenkova, 1967).	339
Konya, Sirçali Masjid, plan (from Aslanapa, 1971).	295	Shahr-i-Sabz, Akserai Palace, plan (from Pugachenkova, unpublished).	340
Konya, Karatay Madrasa, portal.	296	Turkestan City, Shrine of Ahmad Yasavi, plan (from Pugachenkova, 1967).	341
Konya, Karatay Madrasa, interior.	297	Samarkand, Bibi Khanum Mosque, detail of portal.	342
Konya, Ince Minare Madrasa, plan (from Arseven, 1939).	298	Samarkand, Bibi Khanum Mosque, plan (from Grube, 1959).	343
Konya, Ince Minare Madrasa, portal and minaret.	299	Samarkand, Bibi Khanum Mosque, general view.	344
Konya, Ince Minare Madrasa, details of the portal.	300, 301	Samarkand, Gur-i-Amir, plan (from Les mosquées de Samarcande, 1905).	345
Sivas, Gök Madrasa, facade.	302	Samarkand, Gur-i-Amir, view from the east.	346
Sivas, Gök Madrasa, plan (from Gabriel, 1934).	303	Samarkand, Gur-i-Amir, interior of the mausoleum.	347

Mashad, Shrine of Ali al-Rida and Great Mosque of Gawhar Shad, plan (from Pope, 1939). 348

Mashad, Great Mosque of Gawhar Shad, qibla iwan. 349

Samarkand, Madrasa of Ulugh Beg, plan (from Pugachenkova, 1963). 350

Samarkand, Madrasa of Ulugh Beg, facade. 351

Samarkand, Madrasa of Ulugh Beg, detail of the entrance iwan. 352

Herat, Musalla and Madrasa of Gawhar Shad, plans (hypothetical reconstructions) (from Pope, 1939). 353

Herat, Musalla of Gawhar Shad, minaret. 354

Herat, Madrasa of Gawhar Shad, tomb. 355

Herat, Madrasa of Gawhar Shad, tomb chamber. 356

Gazur Gah, Shrine of Abdallah Ansari, plan (from Golombek, 1969). 357

Gazur Gah, Shrine of Abdallah Ansari, entrance facade. 358

Khargird, Ghiyathiya Madrasa, plan (from Herzfeld, 1953). 359

Khargird, Ghiyathiya Madrasa, entrance facade. 360

Khargird, Ghiyathiya Madrasa, dome chamber to the left of the entrance. 361

Balkh, Shrine of Khwaja Abu Nasr Parsa, northwest facade. 362

Samarkand, Ishrat Khaneh, plan (from Pugachenkova, 1958). 363

Samarkand, Ishrat Khaneh, northeast-southwest section. 364

Ghazna, Tomb of Ulugh Beg Miranshah and Abdu Razzaq, plan (from Hoag, 1968). 365

Ghazna, Tomb of Ulugh Beg Miranshah and Abdu Razzaq. 366

Banbhore, Congregational Mosque, plan (from Kahn, 1963). 367

Delhi, Quwwat al-Islam, plan (from Volwahsen, 1970). 368

Delhi, Quwwat al-Islam, riwaq of 1210–29. 369

Delhi, Quwwat al-Islam, stone screen of 1199. 370

Delhi, Qtub Minar. 371

Ajmer, Arhai Din Ka Jompra Mosque, plan (from La Roche, 1921). 372

Ajmer, Arhai Din Ka Jompra Mosque, screen. 373

Ajmer, Arhai Din Ka Jompra Mosque, prayer hall. 374

Delhi, Tomb of Iltutmish, section (from Volwahsen, 1970). 375

Delhi, Tomb of Iltutmish, interior. 376

Delhi, Tomb of Sultan Ghari, enclosure. 377

Delhi, Tomb of Sultan Ghari, plan (from Wetzel, 1918). 378

Delhi, Tomb of Sultan Ghari, view within the enclosure. 379

Delhi, Quwwat al-Islam, Alai Darwaza, facade. 380

Delhi-Tughluqabad, Tomb of Ghiyath al-Din Tughluq. 381

Delhi-Firuzabad, Kotila of Firuz Shah, baradari, plan (from Reuther, 1925, and Volwahsen, 1970). 382

Delhi-Firuzabad, Kotila of Firuz Shah, baradari. 383

Delhi-Tarbabad, Hauz-i-Khas, plan (from Reuther, 1925). 384

Delhi-Tarbabad, Hauz-i-Khas, a tibari. 385

Delhi-Tarbabad, Hauz-i-Khas, interior of a tibari. 386

Delhi-Tarbabad, Hauz-i-Khas, Tomb of Firuz Shah. 387

Gulbarga, Jami Masjid, exterior. 388

Gulbarga, Jami Masjid, plan (from Volwahsen, 1970). 389

Gulbarga, Jami Masjid, interior, a riwaq. 390

Jaunpur, Jami Masjid, plan (from Hermann, 1909). 391

Jaunpur, Jami Masjid, facade of the prayer hall. 392

Champanir, Jami Masjid, exterior. 393

Champanir, Jami Masjid, axonometric section (from Brown, 1942). 394

Champanir, Jami Masjid, facade of the prayer hall. 395

Champanir, Jami Masjid, south minaret, detail. 396

Champanir, Jami Masjid, interior, dome. 397

Agra-Sikandra, baradari of Iskander Lodi, section and plan (from Reuther, 1925). 398

Delhi, Tomb of Isa Khan Niyazi, plan (from Wetzel, 1918). 399

Delhi, Tomb of Isa Khan Niyazi, exterior. 400

Delhi, Tomb of Isa Khan Niyazi, facade of the prayer hall. 401

Çekirge, Mosque-Madrasa of Murad I, plan of the ground floor (from Gabriel, 1958). 402

Çekirge, Mosque-Madrasa of Murad I, plan of the first floor (from Gabriel, 1958). 403

Çekirge, Mosque-Madrasa of Murad I, exterior from the northeast. 404

Bursa, Kulliye of Yildirim Bayazid I, site plan (from Gabriel, 1958). 405

Bursa, Kulliye of Yildirim Bayazid I, porch. 406

Bursa, Ulu Cami, plan (from Gabriel, 1958). 407

Bursa, Ulu Cami, interior, prayer hall. 408

Bursa, Yeşil Cami, section (from Gabriel, 1958). 409

Bursa, Yeşil Cami, plan (from Gabriel, 1958). 410

Bursa, Yeşil Cami, west chamber of the tribune. 411

Bursa, Yeşil Cami, north wall of the covered sahn, with royal tribunes. 412

Bursa, Yeşil Cami, prayer hall looking toward the mihrab. 413

Bursa, Yeşil Cami, north facade. 414

Bursa, Turbe of Mehmet I, section (from Gabriel, 1958). 415

Bursa, Yeşil Cami, north facade, detail of portal. 416

Bursa, Turbe of Mehmet I, mihrab. 417

Edirne, Üç Şerefeli Cami, plan and section (from Goodwin, 1971). 418

Edirne, Üç Şerefeli Cami, exterior. 419

Edirne, Üç Şerefeli Cami, sahn and minaret. 420

Edirne, Üç Şerefeli Cami, prayer hall. 421

View of Constantinople (from a manuscript of 1537, Library of the University of Istanbul). 422

Istanbul, Fatih Cami, plan (from Ünsal, 1959). 423

Istanbul, Fatih Cami, sahn. 424

Istanbul, Fatih Cami, north portal of the prayer hall. 425

Istanbul, Top Kapu Saray, Çinli Kiosk, main facade. 426

Istanbul, Top Kapu Saray, Çinli Kiosk, plan (from Goodwin, 1971). 427

Istanbul, Top Kapu Saray, Çinli Kiosk, central chamber. 428

Edirne, Kulliye of Bayazid II, exterior from the southwest. 429

Edirne, Kulliye of Bayazid II, plan (from Kuran, 1968). 430

Edirne, Mosque of Bayazid II, prayer hall, mihrab, and minbar. 431

Edirne, Hospital of Bayazid II, main hall. 432

Istanbul, Mosque of Bayazid II, plan (from Goodwin, 1971). 433

Istanbul, Mosque of Bayazid II, seen from the southwest. 434

Istanbul, Mosque of Bayazid II, prayer hall. 435

Istanbul, Şehzade Cami, plan (from Kuran, 1968). 436

Istanbul, Kulliye of Suleyman, plan (from Goodwin, 1971). 437

Istanbul, Suleymaniye, view from the southwest. 438

Istanbul, Suleymaniye, prayer hall. 439

Istanbul, Suleymaniye, prayer hall, dome. 440

Edirne, Selimiye, view from the west. 441

Edirne, Kulliye of Selim II, plan (from Goodwin, 1971). 442

Edirne, Selimiye, prayer hall. 443

Istanbul, Ahmediye (Blue Mosque), view from the east. 444

Istanbul, Ahmediye (Blue Mosque), prayer hall. 445

Istanbul, Top Kapu Saray, Bab-i-Humayun (Imperial Gate). 446

Istanbul, Top Kapu Saray, plan (from Goodwin, 1971). 447

Istanbul, Top Kapu Saray, Bab-i-Saadet (Gate of Felicity). 448

Istanbul, Top Kapu Saray, Arz Odasi (Throne Room). 449

Istanbul, Top Kapu Saray, bed chamber of Murad III. 450

Istanbul, Top Kapu Saray, bed chamber of Murad III, dome. 451

Istanbul, Top Kapu Saray, Baghdad Kiosk, exterior. 452

Istanbul, Top Kapu Saray, Baghdad Kiosk, dome. 453

Istanbul, Kasri of Aynali Kavak, plan (from Vogt-Göknil, 1965). 454

Isfahan, the suburb of Shah Abbas I, plan (original drawing by Donald N. Wilber). 455

Isfahan, view of the palace complex west of the Meidan-i-Shah (from a print of 1712). 456

Isfahan, Ali Kapu, longitudinal section (from Zander, 1968). 457

Isfahan, Ali Kapu, the talar. 458

Isfahan, Ali Kapu, music room. 459

Isfahan, Chehel Situn, plan (from Zander, 1968). 460

Isfahan, Chehel Situn, the east talar. 461

Isfahan, Chehel Situn, interior of the east talar (nineteenth-century print). 462

Isfahan, Mosque of Shaykh Lutfullah. 463

Isfahan, Mosque of Shaykh Lutfullah, plan (from Zander, 1968). 464

Isfahan, Mosque of Shaykh Lutfullah, prayer hall, detail. 465

Isfahan, Mosque of Shaykh Lutfullah, dome. 466

Isfahan, Masjid-i-Shah, portal overlooking the Meidan. 467

Isfahan, Masjid-i-Shah, detail of portal, with minarets. 468

Isfahan, Masjid-i-Shah, plan (from Pope, 1939). 469

Isfahan, Masjid-i-Shah, section (from Coste, 1867). 470

Isfahan, Masjid-i-Shah, southeastern "winter mosque," interior. 471

Mashad (vicinity), Tomb of Khwaja Rabi, plan (from Pope, 1939). 472

Mashad (vicinity), Tomb of Khwaja Rabi, exterior. 473

Mashad (vicinity), Tomb of Khwaja Rabi, interior view of the dome. 474

Isfahan, Hasht Behisht, section and plan (from Coste, 1867). 475

Isfahan, Hasht Behisht, central chamber (nineteenth-century print) (from Coste, 1867). 476

Isfahan, Pol-i-Khaju, plan (from Pope, 1939). 477

Isfahan, Pol-i-Khaju, facade overlooking the river. 478

Delhi, Tomb of Humayun, plan (Archaeological Survey of India). 479

Delhi, Tomb of Humayun, section (from Volwahsen, 1970). 480

Delhi, Tomb of Humayun, south facade. 481

Ajmer, Palace-Fortress of Akbar, baradari. 482

Ajmer, Palace-Fortress of Akbar, plan (from Reuther, 1925). 483

Fatipur Sikri, palace, plan (from Volwahsen, 1970). 484

Fatipur Sikri, Diwan-i-Khas, section and plan (from Volwahsen, 1970). 485

Fatipur Sikri, the private apartments looking north. 486

Fatipur Sikri, Diwan-i-Khas, interior. 487

Fatipur Sikri, Diwan-i-Khas, exterior. 488

Fatipur Sikri, Panch Mahal. 489

Agra, Jahangiri Mahal (Red Palace), west facade. 490

Agra, Jahangiri Mahal (Red Palace), east facade. 491

Agra, Jahangiri Mahal (Red Palace), east facade, detail. 492

Agra, Jahangiri Mahal (Red Palace), central court. 493

Agra, Jahangiri Mahal (Red Palace), plan (from Reuther, 1925). 494

Sikandra, Tomb of Akbar, south facade. 495

Sikandra, Tomb of Akbar, south gate. 496

Gwalior, Tomb of Shaykh Muhammad Ghaus. 497

Sikandra, Tomb of Akbar, plan (from La Roche III, 1921). 498

Agra, Tomb of the Ittimad al-Daula, plan (from Volwahsen, 1970). 499

Agra, Tomb of the Ittimad al-Daula. 500

Agra, Tomb of the Ittimad al-Daula, west gate. 501

Shadera, Tomb, garden, and caravanserai of Jahangir, plan (from La Roche III, 1921). 502

Shadera, Tomb of Jahangir, section (from La Roche III, 1921). 503

Agra, Taj Mahal, plan of the mausoleum, garden, and caravanserai (from Volwahsen, 1970). 504

Agra, Taj Mahal, view across the Jumna River. 505

Agra, Taj Mahal, mausoleum, plan and section (from Volwahsen, 1970). 506

Agra, Taj Mahal, south facade. 507

Lahore, Mosque of Wazir Khan, plan and section (from La Roche, 1921). 508

Agra, Pearl Mosque, plan (from La Roche, 1921). 509

Agra, Pearl Mosque, sahn. 510

Delhi, Red Fort, restored plan (from Reuther, 1925). 511

Delhi, Red Fort, Diwan-i-Am, west facade. 512

Delhi, Red Fort, Diwan-i-Khas, west facade. 513

PHOTOGRAPHIC CREDITS